Procreation and the Spousal Meaning of the Body

Procreation and the Spousal Meaning of the Body

A Thomistic Argument Grounded in Vatican II

Angel Perez-Lopez

☙PICKWICK *Publications* · Eugene, Oregon

PROCREATION AND THE SPOUSAL MEANING OF THE BODY
A Thomistic Argument Grounded in Vatican II

Copyright © 2017 Angel Perez-Lopez. All rights reserved. Except for brief quotations in critical publications or reviews, no part of this book may be reproduced in any manner without prior written permission from the publisher. Write: Permissions, Wipf and Stock Publishers, 199 W. 8th Ave., Suite 3, Eugene, OR 97401.

Pickwick Publications
An Imprint of Wipf and Stock Publishers
199 W. 8th Ave., Suite 3
Eugene, OR 97401

www.wipfandstock.com

PAPERBACK ISBN: 978-1-4982-9256-6
HARDCOVER ISBN: 978-1-4982-9258-0
EBOOK ISBN: 978-1-4982-9257-3

Cataloguing-in-Publication data:

Names: Perez-Lopez, Angel.

Title: Procreation and the spousal meaning of the body : a Thomistic argument grounded in Vatican II / Angel Perez-Lopez.

Description: Eugene, OR : Pickwick Publications, 2017 | Includes bibliographical references.

Identifiers: ISBN 978-1-4982-9256-6 (paperback) | ISBN 978-1-4982-9258-0 (hardcover) | ISBN 978-1-4982-9257-3 (ebook)

Subjects: LCSH: Sex—Religious aspects—Catholic Church. | Marriage—Religious aspects—Catholic Church. | Catholic Church—Doctrines.

Classification: BX1795.S48 P47 2017 (print) | BX1795.S48 P47 (ebook)

Manufactured in the U.S.A.   02/13/17

With gratitude to my parents for their Christian witness

Contents

Acknowledgments | ix

Abbreviations, References, and Technical Terminology | x

Introduction | 1

Part I: Conciliar Framework

1. Marriage and Christian Responsibility | 11
2. The Kraków Document | 30
3. Continuity between Vatican II and *Humanae Vitae* | 46
4. Anthropology of Love | 61

Part II: Spousal Meaning of the Body

5. In God's Image | 99
6. Original Experiences | 119
7. Why Spousal? | 155
8. Redemption of the Human Heart | 188
9. Fulfillment and Eschatological Anticipation | 220

Part III: Procreation

10. Conjugal Common Good | 239
11. In the Sphere of Marriage's Sacramentality | 269
12. The Inseparable Connection: In Defense of Conjugal Love | 302

Selected Bibliography | 327

Acknowledgments

This book is the conclusion of a project that began many years ago, in 1998. Yet, it was not until 2012 that I published its philosophical substratum and I announced the possibility of elaborating this present theological work. Over all these years, many more people than I can list here have contributed to it in one way or another. Nevertheless, I would like to offer a special word of gratitude to my brother, Fr. Israel Pérez López, with whom I have had the pleasure to discuss in much detail the entire contents of this book. I am grateful for his reassuring insights and for his critical reading of the original manuscript. I am also thankful to Fr. Antonio Malo for his insightful comments and for providing the endorsement. I would like to express my deep gratitude, as well, to Fr. Stephen Brock and Fr. Robert Gahl for their endorsements. To Mary Justice, I am grateful for patiently proofreading the entire book more than once. I would also like to thank some of my colleagues at Saint John Vianney Theological Seminary who read some parts of this book or discussed some of its contents with me: Fr. William Breslin, Dr. Susan Selner-Wright, Sister Esther Mary Nickel, Fr. Luis Granados, and Fr. Andreas Hoeck. During my years in Rome, Fr. Sławomir Szkredka helped with some Polish texts and questions that I had at the time. His help is still very influential in my own work and I also want to express my sincere gratitude to him. Of course, despite the assistance of all these people, none of them can be held accountable for the defects of my argument or presentation. They remain entirely my own.

Abbreviations, References, and Technical Terminology

AAS	*Acta Apostolicae Sedis.*
ACV	*Acta et Documenta Concilio Oecumenico.*
AP	Karol Wojtyła, *The Acting Person.*
CA	John Paul II, *Centesimus Annus.*
Cántico	John of the Cross, *Spiritual Canticle.*
CCC	*Catechism of the Catholic Church.*
Contra Faustum	Augustine, *Reply to Faustus the Manichean.*
DA	Karol Wojtyła, *El don del amor.*
De Civitate Dei	Augustine, *The City of God.*
De Commendatione	Thomas Aquinas, *De commendatione et partitione Sacrae Scriptura.*
De Ente.	Thomas Aquinas, *De Ente et Essentia.*
De Principis Naturae	Thomas Aquinas, *De Principis Naturae ad Fratrem Sylvestrum.*
De Malo	Thomas Aquinas, *Quaestiones disputatae de malo.*
De Moribus Ecclesiae	Augustine, *Of the Morals of the Catholic Church.*
De Potentia	Thomas Aquinas, *Quaestiones disputatae de potentia Dei.*
De Perfectione	Thomas Aquinas, *De perfectione spiritualis vitae.*
De Trinitate	Augustine, *The Trinity.*
De Veritate	Thomas Aquinas, *Quaestiones disputatae de veritate.*
De Virtutibus	Thomas Aquinas, *Quaestiones disputatae de virtutibus.*
Dichos	John of the Cross, *Sayings of Light and Love.*
DH	Vatican II, *Dignitatis Humanae.*
DS	*The Sources of Catholic Dogma.*
DV	Vatican II, *Dei Verbum.*

ABBREVIATIONS, REFERENCES, AND TECHNICAL TERMINOLOGY

DVi	John Paul II, *Dominum et Vivificantem*.
EG	Francis, *Evangelii Gaudium*.
FC	John Paul II, *Familaris Consortio*.
FR	John Paul II, *Fides et Ratio*.
GS	Vatican II, *Gaudium et Spes*.
HD	Karol Wojtyła, *El hombre y su destino*.
HV	Paul VI, *Humanae Vitae*
In de anima	Thomas Aquinas, *In Aristotelis Libros de Anima Commentarium*.
In Duo Praecepta	Thomas Aquinas, *In Duo Praecepta Caritatis et in Decem Legis Praecepta Exposition*.
In Ethic.	Thomas Aquinas, *Sententia libri Ethicorum*.
In Meta.	Thomas Aquinas, *In libros Metaphysicorum expositio*.
In Sent.	Thomas Aquinas, *Scriptum super libros Sententiarum*.
KD	Karol Wojtyła, "The Foundations of Church's Doctrine concerning the Principles of Conjugal Life."
LG	Vatican II, *Lumen Gentium*.
Llama	John of the Cross, *Living Flame of Love*.
LR	Karol Wojtyła, *Love and Responsibility*.
MD	John Paul II, *Mulieris Dignitatem*.
MH	Karol Wojtyła, *Mi visión del hombre*.
Noche	John of the Cross, *The Dark Night of the Soul*.
OC	Karol Wojtyła, *Osoba i Czyn*.
OT	Vatican II, *Optatam Totius*.
PC	Karol Wojtyła, *Person and Community*.
PL	*Patrologia Latina*.
PDV	John Paul II, *Pastores Dabo Vobis*.
Q. De anima	Thomas Aquinas, *Quaestiones disputatae de anima*.
RH	John Paul II, *Redemptor Hominis*.
RMis	John Paul II, *Redemptoris Missio*.
SC	Vatican II, *Sacro Sanctum Concilium*.
ScG	Thomas Aquinas, *Summa contra gentiles*.
SR	Karol Wojtyła, *Sources of Renewal*.
ST	Thomas Aquinas, *Summa theologiae*.

Subida	John of the Cross, *Ascent of Mount Carmel.*
Super De Trinitate	Thomas Aquinas, *Super Boethium De Trinitate.*
Super I Cor.	Thomas Aquinas, *Super Primam Epistolam ad Corinthios Lectura.*
Super II Cor.	Thomas Aquinas, *Super Secundam Epistolam ad Corinthios Lectura.*
Super Eph.	Thomas Aquinas, *Super Epistolam ad Ephesios Lectura.*
Super Ga.	Thomas Aquinas, *Super Epistolam ad Galatas Lectura.*
Super Heb.	Thomas Aquinas, *Super Epistolam ad Hebraeos Lectura.*
Super Io.	Thomas Aquinas, *Super Evangelium S. Ioannis Lectura.*
Super Matt.	Thomas Aquinas, *Super Evangelium S. Matthaei Lectura.*
Super Phil.	Thomas Aquinas, *Super Epistolam ad Philipenses Lectura.*
Super Rom.	Thomas Aquinas, *Super Epistolam ad Romanos Lectura.*
Super I Tim.	Thomas Aquinas, *Super primam Epistolam ad Timotheum Lectura*
TOB	John Paul II, *Man and Woman He Created Them.*
UD	John Paul II, *Uomo e donna lo creò.*
VS	John Paul II, *Veritatis Splendor.*

When I speak of the "theology of the body," I refer to John Paul II, *Man and Woman He Created Them*. The Italian original can be found in Giovanni Paolo II, *Uomo e donna lo creò*. Unless otherwise indicated, I will follow Waldstein's translation. I will also follow his way of citing this work. TOB stands for the theology of the body. It will be followed by two numbers: the first indicates the audience and the second the paragraph number. Hence, TOB 1:1 refers to the first paragraph of the first audience contained in *Man and Woman He Created Them*. I will only cite the page number in this work when referring to parts of the book that are not the actual audiences, parts like the index, introductory studies, etc. To be consistent with John Paul II's language, unless otherwise indicated, "man" refers both to male and female. For the most part, I have used the available English translations of Wojtyła's works. However, I have also consulted the original Polish, especially for *The Acting Person*. Whenever the English translation is altered throughout the paper, I will offer the Polish text in brackets and refer in the footnote to the Polish third critical edition of Wojtyła's work, *Osoba i Czyn*. I have always consulted the original Latin text of the magisterial documents cited throughout this book. However, unless otherwise indicated, I have followed the translations found at www.vatican.va. Similarly, I have consulted the original Latin for Thomas Aquinas's works. However, unless otherwise indicated, I have followed the translations listed in the bibliography.

Introduction

Tradition and the Theology of the Body

Dare to know (*sapere aude*).[1] With this motto, Immanuel Kant sums up the spirit of modernity. He invites people to emerge from "self-incurred tutelage."[2] He wants to stimulate courage, so as to overcome "man's inability to make use of his understanding *without direction from another*."[3] In this summation, modernity has left its own imprint on contemporary theological reflection. It has promoted *the search for originality and novelty to the detriment of the value of tradition*. As a result, there has emerged a reductionistic vision of the human person, incompatible with realism and experience. Therein, autonomy is exalted, the person has been identified with consciousness, the notions of person and nature have been opposed to each other, and our very understanding of human nature has been deprived of its true metaphysical force.

This fact is extremely important for this book, located within the discipline of special moral theology, and concerned with marriage and family life. Indeed, there are still rival versions of conjugal moral theology, some of which plunge their presuppositions in an inadequate theological and philosophical anthropology that is influenced both by modernity as summed up by Kant's motto and by that search for originality. Prey of that modern idiosyncrasy, and not valuing the great tradition in their attempt to renew moral theology according to the directives given by the Second Vatican Council,[4] they fall into serious reductionisms. If I had to pinpoint what I think is their core limitation and reductionism, it would be this—that *they do not manage to harmonize the biblical and metaphysical foundations of a christocentric moral theory, which is compatible with the natural law and is grounded on the substantial unity of man as a being created in God's image*.[5] The full meaning of this last statement will become more

1. See Kant, "What is Enlightenment?," 3.
2. Ibid.
3. Ibid.; emphasis added.
4. See OT 16.

5. See GS 22, 24; RH 10; VS 19, 29, 53. This fact has been explained with depth and clarity by Joseph Ratzinger. See Ratzinger, "Il rinnovamento della teologia morale," 41. For a Christology that overcomes the limitation pointed out, see White, *The Incarnate Lord*. For a good treatment of this question, see Melina, *Sharing in Christ's Virtues*, 115–36.

apparent to the reader as this book unfolds. However, I am convinced that this great limitation is profoundly addressed by Pope Saint John Paul II's "theology of the body."[6]

This present book attempts to aid those who are serious about the study of the theology of the body. It is directed especially to those who teach it at both an academic and at a popular level. This book offers them the necessary scholarly background to be able to faithfully present John Paul II's work, understanding it with depth, and in continuity with tradition. The goal that I intend to achieve in this book is particularly relevant, for at least three reasons. Firstly, there are scarcely any works published with such a scholarly rigor on this very topic. Secondly, there are few and far between available books in English that share my same targeted audience. And thirdly, there is a curious phenomenon amongst scholars of John Paul II's theology of the body, which connects the influence from modernity described above with those reductionisms present in some versions of moral theology.

On the one hand, critics of John Paul II's teachings consider his theology archaic and retrograde. In their opinion, the pope's work is completely consonant with Paul VI's *Humanae Vitae* (HV). And precisely for that reason, TOB constitutes for them a betrayal of the novelty and originality of the so-called "spirit of the Second Vatican Council." Some even argue that John Paul II's work is insufficient. Pointing to that need for originality and novelty to the detriment of the value of tradition, there is talk nowadays of moving from a "theology of the body" to a "theology of love," as if the pope's did not offer it already. On the other hand, most authors in favor of TOB, though not all, are more worried about underlining its originality and novelty rather than its continuity with the previous magisterium and theological tradition.[7] Yet, to

---

6. For a series of articles on the general *status quaestionis* of the interpretation of this work, see Melina, "A trent'anni dalla Grande Catechesi," 9–18; Marengo, "Il contesto storico-teologico delle catechesi," 19–20; Merecki, "Sulla ricezione della teologia del corpo in Polonia," 91–99; Granados, "The Theology of the Body in the United States," 101–25; Vives Soto, "Iluminar la verdad del amor conyugal. La teología del cuerpo en la teología de lengua española," 127–50.

7. Evidently, there are some commentators to whom I owe much in my interpretation of TOB. I would especially refer to Cafarra and Waldstein. See Cafarra, "La trasmisione della vita nella *Familiaris Consortio*," 391–99; Cafarra, "La verdad y fecundidad del don," 197–202; Cafarra, "Introduzione al terzo ciclo," in UD, 255–56; Cafarra, "Introduzione al secondo ciclo," in UD, 111–12; Waldstein, Introduction to *Man and Woman He Created Them: A Theology of the Body* by John Paul II, 1–130. For different reasons, a special mention should also be made about Petri's *Aquinas*. Apparently, the author of this last book and I have been working simultaneously on very similar projects. We both substantially agree on the fact that, to interpret TOB well, one needs "an authentic appreciation of the intersection of the thought of John Paul II and Thomas Aquinas" (ibid., 1). Nevertheless, one important difference between Petri's work and mine resides in the material and formal objects of our studies. I am specifically interested in a slightly different material object. I want to concentrate on the interrelationship between John Paul's understanding of *procreation* as the *collaboration with the Creator in the transmission and education of human life* and its relationship with the *spousal meaning of the body* as the human person's *supernatural call to charity*. Moreover, my formal object is different as well. I want to show that John Paul II's argument is *not only Thomistic but also grounded in Vatican II*. In the areas in which our works converge, at times, Petri and I reach different conclusions on important matters. However, overall, I would say that our works are complementary. They certainly head in the same direction: to inspire a "theology of the body which is illuminated by and itself illumines elements

find novelty without seeing continuity is quite difficult, if not impossible. For something cannot be accurately judged as new when what is old is not well-known.

Since the scientific developments that gave rise to the questions answered by HV constitute an indisputable novelty, the theological answer given to those questions cannot lack a certain originality. However, in my judgment, the originality of John Paul II's answer in TOB consists in his similarity to that scribe, who being a disciple of the kingdom of heaven, "brings out of his treasure what is new and what is old."[8] Against Kant's motto, I will demonstrate that John Paul II is not thinking without another's guidance. This fact explains how the theological opinion of Karol Wojtyła, (before his election to the papacy and formulated in his unpublished book *Man and Woman He Created Them*), became a magisterial teaching of the church, without this transition being a mistake in any way, shape, or form. For, in TOB, the "we" of the church's magisterium and Wojtyła's "I" are not mutually exclusive. On the contrary, his "I" was at the service of, and embedded into, that "we."[9]

In light of these considerations, I would like to apply an important precision to an oft-invoked idea formulated by George Weigel. If it is true that TOB is "one of the boldest reconfigurations of Catholic theology in centuries;"[10] that it is "a kind of theological time bomb set to go off with dramatic consequences, sometime in the third millennium of the Church,"[11] or that "it will compel a dramatic development of thinking about virtually every major theme in the Creed,"[12] if all of that is true, it is true not so much because of TOB's novelty, but rather because of its rediscovery of tradition in its pursuit to renew moral theology, according to the letter and spirit of Vatican II, and against those reductionisms previously mentioned. Indeed, TOB is very original, if we understand by "original" *that which goes back to the origins*. This book attempts to shed some light on this question. For this reason, I would like to emphasize TOB's continuity with both Vatican II, and the theology of the Common Doctor of the church, Thomas Aquinas. I have chosen to do so by analyzing two of the most structural notions contained in John Paul II's work, namely, procreation, and the spousal meaning of the body.

A Thomistic Argument Grounded in Vatican II

John Paul II has a very rich understanding of procreation as irreducible to sheer generation. Since angels do not procreate and irrational animals merely reproduce,

---

of Aquinas's thought" (ibid., 8). I will note other affinities and differences between Petri's position and mine throughout the book.

8. Matt 13:52.
9. See Benedict XIV, *John Paul II*, 6.
10. Weigel, *Witness to Hope*, 336.
11. Ibid., 343.
12. Ibid., 853.

procreation is a peculiarly human phenomenon. John Paul II conceives it as *the spouses' free collaboration with the Creator in the transmission and education of human life*. In turn, our author conceives education as the leading of the human person to the state of virtue. Moreover, this collaboration with the Creator is elevated by supernatural grace, thereby becoming, as it were, a parenting for heaven. On the other hand, John Paul II's understanding of the spousal meaning of the body is also quite rich and not easy to grasp, at first. To avoid a common error amongst beginners in the study of TOB, it is important to distinguish, from the very start, the spousal meaning of the body from the unitive meaning of the conjugal act. Although these notions are related, the first one is broader, and much more radical or *foundational*. The spousal meaning of the body captures the adequate anthropology of man created in God's image. More concretely, the spousal meaning of the body refers to *man's supernatural vocation to live in charity*. The adequate anthropology of the *imago Dei* and man's vocation therein contained cannot be reduced to the unitive meaning of the conjugal act. The spousal meaning of the human body and its anthropology constitute the theological framework in which are understood *all the states of life within the church*, including that of marriage. Hence, it is quite surprising that some may talk today about going beyond John Paul II's theology of the body in search for a novel and original "theology of love."[13] John Paul II's theology of the body *is a theology of the spousal meaning of the body; it is a theology of the human person from the viewpoint of his vocation to love!*

Obviously, the married state is only one of the possible ways of living on this earth one's vocation to charity. Nevertheless, the married state is a very important object of study for TOB. Once the sacrament of marriage has been placed within the anthropology and vocation of the spousal meaning of the body, the moral theology of procreation, or the good of the offspring (*bonum prolis*), is founded on the specific grace given by matrimony. Such a grace is contained in the good of the sacrament (*bonum sacramenti*). Evidently, the theology of grace and its healing impact on our capacity to act is key to TOB's understanding of procreation and the spousal meaning of the body. John Paul II captures that healing impact of supernatural grace with the notion of *the ethos of redemption*. The ethos of redemption stands for the way in which we can morally evaluate and act, thanks to the indwelling of the Holy Spirit within us, and all of the virtues and gifts given to us by God. Within the ethos of redemption, John Paul II wants to understand and explain the specific grace of the sacrament of matrimony as a reality accompanied by Christian responsibility. Such a responsibility is contained in the fidelity (*bonum fidei*) with which spouses are to be faithful to their marriage promises as a matter of justice, to each other, and to God as *the* Author of marriage.

Only when one understands the depth of the previous assertions is one equipped to follow John Paul II's theological justification of the inseparability between the

---

13. This surprising opinion surfaced around the recent Synods on the Family. However, it is not a new criticism. It was already posited by Curran, *The Moral Theology of John Paul II*, 167, 170.

procreative and the unitive meanings of the conjugal act, of which HV 12 speaks. As I will explain, the core of this theological justification consists in acting in conformity (*adequatio*) with the divine plan for human love within marriage. This conformity is explained by our author with an expression, whose precise meaning is often misunderstood: "[T]he rereading of the language of the body in the truth about love." I will have the opportunity to explain this notion in greater detail throughout the book. For the moment, let me only remark that in this rereading, charity has the "power" to be the form of all virtues. For this reason, the spousal meaning of the body informs the conjugal act, thereby coordinating its procreative and unitive meaning, thanks to the power of charity.

The central thesis that I will prove in this book is that this whole argument concerning the understanding of procreation and the spousal meaning of the body, as well as their interrelationship, is *a Thomistic argument grounded in Vatican II*. That TOB offers a Thomistic argument does not mean that everything explicitly taught by John Paul II is found in the same exact terms in the writings of the Angelic Doctor. It only means that Thomas Aquinas's theology and philosophy is the bedrock and foundation for John Paul's understanding of procreation and the spousal meaning of the body. In this sense, I intend to prove that John Paul's argument is Thomistic. Few commentators have endeavored in this task. Yet, it seems to me that without understanding Thomas Aquinas's foundational role, it is difficult to offer a coherent, faithful, and sober explanation of TOB. Moreover, that TOB is grounded in Vatican II is also worthy of proof. It constitutes a key with which to read TOB within the hermeneutics of continuity or "principle of integration" that Karol Wojtyła himself uses for his interpretation of Vatican II. Being above all a pastoral Council, Vatican II did not want to define new doctrine with any particular theological precision. Rather, it offered an *understandable* account of the identity and mission of the church, without rupture from the previous magisterium. Such an account would then serve as a basis for a moral renewal.[14] Wojtyła names this renewal, within continuity, *the principle of integration*. It consists in:

> an organic cohesion expressing itself simultaneously in the thought and action of the Church as a community of believers. It expresses itself, that is, in such a way that on the one hand *we can rediscover and, as it were, re-read the Magisterium of the last Council in the whole previous Magisterium of the Church, while on the other we can rediscover and re-read the whole preceding Magisterium in that of the last Council* . . . In judgments passed on the work necessary for the Council and on the Church's activity in the post-Conciliar period, undue emphasis was laid on divisions and differences between so-called *integralists* and *progressives*, while too little was said about the fact that both groups, in their responsibility towards the Church, must be unswervingly guided by the

---

14. See SR, 18.

principle and demands of its identity, and that *they must both therefore respect the principle of integration* which is a precondition of the Church's identity.[15]

Additionally, to properly understand the role of procreation in marriage, and to do so within an adequate philosophical and theological anthropology that constitutes a true renewal in the sources of tradition, is a matter of no little importance nowadays. The attempts to redefine marriage against its very essence or nature, of which we are witnesses around the globe, already constitute a sufficient reason to endeavor in this research. The debates and dialogues that the recent Synod on the Family has promoted within the Roman Catholic Church are also a living testimony of the importance of understanding the role of procreation in marriage within an adequate philosophical and theological anthropology, which constitutes a true renewal in the sources of tradition. Finally, the importance of proving that TOB's understanding of procreation and the spousal meaning of the body is not only grounded in Vatican II, but also in Aquinas's theology, will be further illustrated throughout the book by the opportunities I will have to dialogue with diverse commentators of John Paul II's TOB.

Methodology and Structure of the Argument

The methodology of study used corresponds to TOB's very nature. Since this work is now part of the magisterial teaching of the church, it will be studied within the hermeneutics of the continuity or principle of integration described by our author. I will pay special attention to show its continuity with *Casti Connubi*, Vatican II, and HV. To a certain degree, we can rediscover and reread TOB in light of these documents. On the other hand, we can reread *them* in light of TOB. Additionally, for its correct interpretation, I will use other documents from John Paul II's magisterial teaching such as *Familiaris Consortio* (FC), *Mulieris Dignitatem* (MD), *Veritatis Splendor* (VS), *Redemptor Hominis* (RH), and *Dominus et Vivificantem* (DVi). The same principle of integration applies. However, since TOB was also an unpublished manuscript by Cardinal Karol Wojtyła before his election to the papacy, I will additionally study this text in light of Wojtyła's works, especially those related to his interpretation of Vatican II, his own contribution to and interpretation of HV, LR, and his philosophical integral vision of man.[16]

In order to prove that John Paul II's understanding of procreation and the spousal meaning of the body indeed constitutes a Thomistic argument grounded in Vatican II, I will divide this book into three major parts, each of them subdivided into different chapters. By means of a historical study of Wojtyła's works pertinent to our theme, the first part will clarify the conciliar framework in which TOB was gestated.

---

15. Ibid., 40–41; emphasis added.

16. Concerning Wojtyła's philosophical anthropology, I refer the reader to a previous work of mine: Pérez López, *De la experiencia*.

INTRODUCTION

I will deal there neither with Wojtyła's interventions at Vatican II nor with his work in the redaction of GS.[17] Neither will I present all of Wojtyła's works before TOB in chronological order. Instead, having studied all these writings, I have chosen to offer a selection of works ordered *thematically* in order to clearly and succinctly show how TOB was developed based upon Wojtyła's contribution to and interpretation of HV in continuity with Vatican II.

In this manner, chapter 1 will study Wojtyła's interpretation of Vatican II as found in *Sources of Renewal* (SR). Chapter 2 will analyze his contribution to HV in the so-called Kraków Document (KD)—that is, the document that our author sent to Paul VI, opposing both the majority and the minority report of the consultative commission assembled to advise the pope on the questions that HV would resolve. This analysis will settle the right context to approach, in chapter 3, Wojtyła's interpretation of HV in continuity with Vatican II. Finally, chapter 4 will explain his philosophical integral vision of man developed in *The Acting Person* (AP), a work that was written in the context of the Council and around the controversies that gave rise to HV. Although *Love and Responsibility* (LR) belongs to the writings that contribute to HV, to avoid repetition and for the sake of clarity, I have reserved its analysis for the third part, when the notion of procreation and its primacy among the ends of marriage is to be clarified in light of the spousal meaning of the body.

Once the conciliar framework in which TOB was gestated has been exposed, I will offer two additional parts wherein the prevalent methodology will be that of textual analysis. These other two parts will study the spousal meaning of the body and procreation, respectively. In both of them, the textual analysis will clarify the true thought of John Paul II concerning the reality signified by these two notions. All of my analyses in these two parts will have a threefold methodological aim: (1) to present what is explained in TOB regarding the spousal meaning of the body and procreation; (2) to show how these two notions develop within the conciliar framework studied in the first part, and (3) to unveil that the way in which John Paul II understands procreation and the spousal meaning of the body is strongly influenced by Thomas Aquinas, and by the Thomism of St. John of the Cross.

In this way, the second part will have as its subject matter the spousal meaning of the body *as man's supernatural vocation to charity*. Again, this exact understanding of the spousal meaning of the body constitutes a significant contribution, because the

---

17. Bishop González, who participated with Wojtyła in all the meetings around GS and was an expert in tachygraphy, has published all of his notes from those meetings registering Wojtyła's interventions. See González Moralejo, *El Vaticano II en Taquigrafía*. In addition, Wojtyła's official oral or written interventions in the sessions are found in *Acta Synodalia Sacrosancti Concilii Vaticani II*. For secondary literature on Wojtyła's official interventions, see Skrzypczak, *Karol Wojtyła al Concilio Vaticano II*; Scola, "Gli interventi di Karol Wojtyła." For a study on Wojtyła's participation in GS, see Antúnez, *Karol Wojtyła y Gaudium et Spes*. For a more general study on the influence of Vatican II on the Papacy of John Paul II, see Marengo, *Giovanni Paolo II e il Concilio*. It is also interesting to consult Cándido Pozo, "Juan Pablo II y el Concilio Vaticano II."

pope does not offer a direct definition in the text. Consequently, different commentators have been confused on the precise meaning of this concept. John Paul II locates this vocation to charity within the context of his anthropology of the *imago Dei* in the orders of creation, redemption, and glory. Chapters 5, 6, 7, 8, and 9 deal with this division. In all of this second part, I will show that John Paul II's adequate anthropology of the *imago Dei* in the orders of creation, redemption, and glory is a development of GS's vision of the human person, read from the viewpoint of both LG's ecclesiology, and Wojtyła's philosophical integral vision of man. In this way, the grounding in Vatican II of John Paul II's understanding of the spousal meaning of the body will become evident. To clarify that the pope's understanding of the spousal meaning of the body is Thomistic, I will show that within his anthropology, John Paul II's understanding of the spousal meaning of the body is founded upon Thomas's theology of the *imago Dei*. Moreover, the pope's theology is also founded upon Aquinas's interpretation of the human person's last end as spiritual marriage between Christ and the members of the church. This is where the Thomism of John of the Cross will play its most important role.

In the third and last part, I will study procreation and its relationship with the spousal meaning of the body. Chapter 10 will concentrate on showing how Wojtyła, in consonance with Aquinas and the magisterium, conceives procreation as the conjugal common good that *specifies* and *perfects* the peculiar friendship that exists between husband and wife. Chapter 11 will clarify John Paul's understanding of the language of the body by placing this theological category in its proper context: a theology of the goods of marriage seen from the viewpoint of the sacramentality of matrimony. At this point, the connection between Thomism, the doctrine of Vatican II, and John Paul's teachings will be found in GS 48. Therein, within the context of the christocentric anthropology of the *imago Dei* and of charity as gift of self, the Council appeals directly to the doctrine of the goods of marriage in Augustine, Thomas Aquinas, and Pius XI's *Casti Connubi*. Chapter 12, the final chapter of the book, will explain how John Paul envisions the inseparability of the meanings of the conjugal act as a doctrine which defends the integrity of conjugal love and its due development in virtue. Here, GS 48 and 51 will be the major texts from Vatican II in play. The Thomistic foundations will be placed in Aquinas's understanding of the goods of marriage as they perfect the conjugal act.

Part I: Conciliar Framework

1

Marriage and Christian Responsibility

Moral Renewal in the Sources

Vatican II is, above all, a pastoral and an ecclesiological council. It poses one foundational question: "Church, what do you say about yourself?"[1] The answer to this question should inform *both* the *mind* and the *will* of her members. We should regain consciousness of what the church is all about, according to God's revelation. But for this knowledge to be a true enrichment in the faith, it should also have an impact on our daily lives. Faith is connected to morals. It is not foreign to an alleged autonomous morality, a *Weltethos*.[2] Faith should shape our conduct and even call us to conversion in light of Christ's Redemption.[3] Consequently, the future pope's strategy for the implementation of Vatican II will be very similar to that found in TOB. It relies heavily on the metaphysical and theological role of exemplarity.[4] It consists in *forming attitudes in the will in order to conform one's life to the divine truth* about the church. This divine truth is the exemplar for the fulfillment of the church's authentic mission.

Wojtyła calls this process of enrichment in the faith "*conciliar initiation*." He argues that, first, we should "organize the Catholic consciousness in conformity with the Council's thought."[5] Second, we should "see corresponding to it the spiritual attitudes proposed by Vatican II."[6] Christian responsibility is one of these spiritual or moral attitudes. It is within its sphere that the future pope locates the correct interpretation of Vatican II's most important section for TOB concerning marriage: GS 47–52. However, as a moral attitude, Christian responsibility includes certain elements developed throughout SR. It really "presupposes the reality of creation and redemption with which is associated the dimension of values that form the Christian *ethos* in all its

---

1. SR, 38.

2. See VS, 90.

3. See SR, 99–100; VS 4; Melina, *Sharing in Christ's Virtues*, 92–114; Cessario, *The Moral Virtues*, 22–23.

4. For a philosophical analysis of this topic, see PC, 73–94. See also Doolan, *Aquinas on the Divine Ideas*.

5. SR, 38.

6. Ibid.

fullness."[7] We are interested in laying the foundations *now* in order to show *later* the exact way in which TOB's understanding of procreation and the spousal meaning of the body is grounded in Vatican II. To do so, it is necessary to explain how the truths of creation and the Trinity, the mission of the Redeemer, and the church as God's people, relate to the attitudes of mission and testimony, participation, human identity, and Christian responsibility. This will be our objective for this entire chapter.

Creation and Trinity

The Council's intellectual formation is geared towards one goal: to awaken our awareness of Christ's Redemption as the center of God's salvific plan for mankind. The mysteries of Creation, the Trinity, and the church converge in the Redemption. In Wojtyła's thought, the reading of this theological thesis is always mediated by the christocentric anthropology of man created in God's image, especially as presented in GS.[8] This anthropology is like a "golden thread." It really unites all of the future pope's theological reflections on the church's identity and mission.[9] This same anthropology will be the main Thomistic theological axis for John Paul II's understanding of the spousal meaning of the body.

With that introductory clarification, let us proceed to understand the truths of Creation and the Trinity. The truth concerning Creation discloses the sacramental economy as a gratuitous and mysterious plan of salvation prompted by the love of the Father from all eternity.[10] Human reason must be aided here by revelation. Reason can attain a certain knowledge of God from creation.[11] Yet, without revelation, it could fathom neither the content of this hidden plan (the supernatural vocation of becoming sons in the Son, *filii in Filio*), nor its motive (gratuitous love). Thus, reason and revealed truth make one aware of the fact that the created world is "sustained by the love of its maker," that it "has been freed from the slavery to sin by Christ," with the aim of being "transformed according to God's design and brought to its fulfillment."[12] Thanks to this revelation, we can attain the proper consciousness of creation. Within such an awareness, the human person knows himself as created in God's image. He also knows his call to exercise his lordship over creation *in the Lord and in justice*, acknowledging God as the Creator to whom he must be *subordinate*.

---

7. Ibid., 293.

8. See Erhueh, *Vatican II: Image of God in Man*. Aranda also notes the fact that GS served to rediscover the christocentric anthropology around the doctrine of man's being created in image and likeness of God. See Aranda, "Ley natural e imagen de Dios."

9. See Illanes, "Antropocentrismo y teocentrismo."

10. See LG 2; SR, 45.

11. See Rom 1:20; DV 6; SR, 46.

12. GS 2; SR, 47.

Consciousness of the revealed truth about Creation leads the human person to his own interiority, to the knowledge of his own place of honor within the created cosmos as hierarchically ordered by God himself.[13] For us today, the rediscovery of this place of honor implies a reconciliation with our own natural greatness as a human person.[14] This greatness implies an anti-Kantian foundational moral implication. The human person is called to read or to discover, but *not to constitute* this intelligible order or law that comes from the Creator.[15] Whence, instead of Kantian autonomy, there is "a specific *subordination* of human knowledge and activity to that reality which lies in every created being."[16] As a result, Wojtyła continues, there is a "necessity of ordering (or rather *subordinating*) all things in truth, a necessity which applies to man and all his activity in relation to the world."[17] These anti-Kantian ideas will be foundational for the rereading of the language of the body as a way of putting into practice that *subordination* to God's truth.

The mystery of Creation meets the revelation of the Trinity as the consciousness of salvation. The church is a people brought into unity, from the unity of the Father, the Son, and the Holy Spirit.[18] This declaration concerning the nature of the church informs one's consciousness with a *faith of profession*. By means of it, one assents to the truth about the Triune God. In turn, this same declaration informs one's consciousness with a *faith of vocation*, and thereby, one discovers the truth concerning his call to salvation as participation in the intimate life of the Trinity. Furthermore, thanks to this same declaration, the believer sees himself as *member of and participant in the church's mission*. As such, one is to participate in her mission to be a sign and instrument of communion with God.[19] Thus, the revelation of the Trinity is intimately tied to the awareness of salvation as an invitation to man from God, an invitation to partake in his very knowledge and love, *through the missions of the Son and the Holy Spirit*. This participation is *the ultimate reality contained in the hidden mystery of all ages in the Father's plan*. This plan has been ultimately revealed and effected for us in Christ through the Holy Spirit. It sums up man's supernatural vocation or the spousal meaning of his body, as modeled in Christ's spousal and redeeming charity for the church.[20]

---

13. See GS 34, 36; SR, 48–49.
14. See LR, 236.
15. See GS 16.
16. SR, 50; emphasis added.
17. Ibid.; emphasis added.
18. See LG 4; SR, 64.
19. See LG 1; SR, 59.
20. See Eph 5:25.

Mission of the Redeemer

The "acme of the Church's consciousness" just presented is to be inserted within GS's christocentric anthropology of man created in the image of God.[21] The point of contact between the church's awareness of her own identity and this adequate anthropology can be found in GS 24. This passage, together with GS 22, represents the most important conciliar foundations for what John Paul II will call "the spousal meaning of the body." Within this theological anthropology, the mystery of the Trinity reveals man's vocation to perfect his being made in God's image within the *ecclesial* context of *communio*. Therein, he can partake of the missions of the Son and the Holy Spirit. In this manner, the human person finds his true self-fulfillment *in the union of truth and charity with God and neighbor*.[22] Following the traditional understanding of charity, such a communion is characterized by Wojtyła as "friendship with God."[23] We are now interested in showing how the mystery of Redemption advances these truths in two complementary ways. The first is found in GS, and the second in LG. In both of them, the anthropological vision of man created in God's image and the ecclesiological perfection of that image are developed in greater detail. The mission of the Son, as a condition for the mission of the Spirit, remains the Trinitarian key that unlocks this crucial doctrine.[24]

GS proposes a vision of the human person centered in Jesus Christ, a christocentric anthropology. Much of the process called "conciliar initiation" depends on understanding and living out the practical or moral consequences of this integral view of the human person. GS's approach to the mystery of Redemption is very experiential. It begins with man's experience of disunity or disintegration within himself as the result of original sin.[25] Then, the document concentrates on Christ as *the* image of the invisible God.[26] Borrowing heavily from Aquinas's theology, GS proposes that the human person must *conform* to Christ in order to bring to fulfillment the image of creation.[27] The incarnate Lord communicates the true meaning of being a human person to man.[28]

---

21. SR, 55.
22. This idea has clear Thomistic foundations in *ST* I, q. 93, a. 9.
23. See John 15:15; DV 2; SR, 54; *ST* II–II, q. 23, a. 1, c.
24. See John 16:7; SR, 66.
25. See GS 10; SR, 71–72, 80.
26. See Col 1:15.

27. See GS 12. This theme is taken up again in ibid., 22 and 24. These texts show how the image of creation in man—that is, the natural aptitude to know and love and to do so together with others—is perfected through the image of grace, especially in charity. Ultimately, the *similitudo* with God that renders us his friends reaches its ultimate perfection only in heaven, in the beatific vision. The obvious Thomistic source for this doctrine is found in *ST* I, q. 93, a. 4, c. For a Thomistic explanation on the meaning of conformity to God and to Christ, see Torrell, *Christ and Spirituality*, 110–25.

28. See GS 22; SR, 75–80.

Additionally, Christ's redemptive Incarnation, in mediating the mission of the Holy Spirit, confers power to the human person so that he may attain his supernatural vocation of being a son in the Son.[29] Thus, the human person finds meaning in his own existence by the sincere gift of himself, in that gift that is modeled by Christ himself in his spousal love for the church.[30] To grow in conformity with Christ means to receive from him *not only the measure* or canon for one's conduct, *but also the power and grace* to be able to do so. In this light, GS presents the mystery of Christ's Redemption and of his grace in its universal ampleness: *all men and women have been created in Christ for this supernatural vocation*. Thus, they are exhorted to collaborate with God's grace in their moral life.[31] This vocation is the kernel of the "adequate anthropology" or the "integral vision of man" that GS recalls and which Wojtyła will develop philosophically in AP and theologically in TOB.[32]

The second way, in which the future pope advances the truths found in Creation and the Trinity in light of the mission of the Redeemer, consists in inserting the previous anthropological considerations in their proper ecclesiological perspective: interpersonal communion with Christ's *tria munera*. This theological "move" manifests an acute perception of words in their meaning and etymology. The word *communio* finds its true root, not in *unio* as is commonly thought, but in the words *munis*, *munia*, and *munus*.[33] From the nominal viewpoint, "communion" denotes a sharing in another's *munus*, in another's office or mission, a sharing that in itself is a gift, a good. What effects the common union inherent in communion is that exact sharing in another's mission or office, as in a common good. Thus, the very identity and mission of the church as Christ's body and God's people is envisioned in light of her participation in the *tria munera* of Christ. Such participation in the mission or office (*munus*) of the Redeemer is, in itself, a gift and a responsibility. It is a *munus* which effects in the church a common union of persons in charity and in truth. This understanding of communion, as sharing in *munus*, will also be very important to comprehend the communion of persons that is *specific* to marriage, especially in its relationship with procreation as the conjugal common *munus* or good.

The other key *locus theologicus* that Wojtyła uses to concretely explain how we are to participate in Christ's *tria munera* is very Thomistic. The humanity of Christ, united hypostatically to the Person of the Son, is the conjoined instrument of our salvation. The sacraments, in turn, are separated instruments closely linked to Christ's

---

29. See SR, 78–79. Ratzinger's commentary on GS 22 is rather illuminating and quite in accord with Wojtyła's own view. See Ratzinger, "The Church and Man's Calling." For the importance of this section of GS in TOB, see Rodríguez Luño, "In mysterio Verbi Incarnati."

30. See Eph 5:25; GS 24.

31. See GS 37; SR, 81.

32. See GS 61; SR, 81. A similar expression is also found in HV 7.

33. See Hoeck, "Holy Communion."

humanity.³⁴ As head of the church, Christ is the cause of grace by means of the instrumental causality of his humanity.³⁵ Thus, Christ's priesthood is the summit of his mission as Redeemer, of his mediation in the mission of the Spirit, and of his being founder of the church.³⁶ For this reason, LG echoes Aquinas's theology on this very matter. It considers Christ as head of the church and explains that the sacraments (matrimony included among them) effect a real ontological conformation to the Son—that is to say, to the salvific mysteries of his life.³⁷ In this way, the church's identity and mission in the sacramental sphere is also dependent upon the mystery of Redemption. She extends and continues the latter through time as an instrument, by participating in the *tria munera* of Christ in communion with him.

The hierarchy of the church participates in Christ's *prophetic munus* by its teaching office. In turn, the laity participate in it by their testimony of faith. By virtue of this testimony, the power of the Gospel shines in family and social life.³⁸ The church participates in Christ's *priestly munus* "through the sacraments and the exercise of virtues."³⁹ All the baptized, in their moral life, exercise their prophetic mission by giving testimony with their lives to the truth. Moreover, they also actualize their priestly *munus*, when by their good actions, they cooperate with the grace of the sacraments and offer their lives to God as a living host.⁴⁰ The members of the church participate in the *kingly mission* of Christ by receiving from the Redeemer the power to live in true or perfected freedom. This is the freedom of God's children, whereby serving Christ, they reign with him.⁴¹ As a result, the moral life is the point of reunion of the participation of the believing members of the church in the *tria munera*, especially of the participation in Christ's priestly and kingly mission. Indeed, according to Wojtyła, "the reality of redemption which abides in the Church through participation in the priestly and kingly mission of the Redeemer *finds expression in Christian morality*, understood in all its fullness and in every aspect, personal and social morality, *that of marriage, the family* and professional life."⁴² This idea will also be quite important later on for TOB: the entirety of conjugal morality is rooted in one's participation in Christ's priestly and kingly *munera*.

---

34. See *ST* III, q. 62, a. 5, c.

35. See Col 1:18; Rom 12:4–5; 1 Cor 12:12; SC 5; SR, 68; *ST* III, q. 8, aa. 1–8; Espa Feced, *El Papel de la Humanidad de Cristo*.

36. See LG 5; SR, 84. Torrell, *Christ and Spirituality*, 126–58.

37. See Ga 4:19; LG 7, 11; SR, 85–87.

38. See LG 35; see also SR, 94.

39. LG 11; see also SR, 97.

40. See Rom 12:1.

41. See Rom 6:12; 8:21; LG 36; SR, 97–98; AP, 105–88.

42. SR, 99; emphasis added.

People of God

Wojtyła's next step consists in unfolding even more this ecclesiological perspective by concentrating on the church as God's people. The church is primarily a trinitarian reality. Only secondarily is it also a sociological human community.[43] The *church as the people of God* presupposes the other aspects of Vatican II's intellectual formation previously treated. It places them, even more so, within a theology of communion. In this complementary reading of GS and LG, the relationship between person and community in the church is enlightened by the christocentric anthropology of man created in God's image.[44] Wojtyła understands within this domain questions such as membership in the people of God, the proper relationship between communion and authority, and also the communion of persons within marriage as the characteristic conjugal communion in friendship between husband and wife. Neither the church nor sacramental marriage can be reduced to a sheer human community. They both are that kind of community in which there is supernatural *communio*. Consequently, one finds in the church the definitive fulfillment of her individual members *in charity*.[45]

Created in God's image, the human person has an intellectual and a social nature. Having a spiritual and immortal soul, he is apt by nature to know and to love in union with others.[46] He is to do so by participating without coercion, and by following his conscience, fulfills at the same time his obligation to search for the truth and to live up to that truth once it is found.[47] All of these things belong to the human person's image of creation. However, this image of creation is to be perfected in the order of grace, so that the human person may attain his supernatural vocation. This is accomplished by Christ's Redemption, which has made possible the effusion of the Holy Spirit. Thereby, those who accept the Son in faith and receive his Spirit are constituted into Christ's body. As a result, they are empowered to live in communion within the church, and to achieve their fulfillment in charity as gift of self.[48] These ecclesiological coordinates place the christocentric anthropology of the *imago Dei* under a very influential perspective for TOB. Therein, the exemplar for this ecclesial communion and for the communion found in marriage is the Trinity; the church is conceived as that communion that brings to fulfillment the deepest aspirations of the human heart; Christ is *the* Teacher and *the* Exemplar of the gift of self, and the Virgin Mary models for us how to be responsible in responding or answering to Christ's spousal and redemptive love. Let us examine them one by one.

---

43. See LG 4; SR, 112.
44. See ibid., 114.
45. See ibid., 120; GS 24, 32.
46. See GS 12; SR, 115.
47. See GS 17; SR, 117.
48. See GS 32; SR, 119–20.

Wojtyła adequately interprets the question of membership in God's church by appealing precisely to the Trinity as the model and exemplar of the communion of persons. The human person "resembles God not only because of the *spiritual nature* of his immortal soul but also by reason of his *social nature*, if by this we understand the fact that he cannot fully realize himself except in an act of pure self-giving."[49] Thus, the future pope teaches that the "union in truth and charity is the ultimate expression of the community of individuals. This union merits the name of communion (*communio*), which signifies more than community (*communitas*)."[50] Communion is proper to persons only. It is based on their common good, on "the good that they do to one another, giving and receiving within that mutual relationship."[51]

This theological consideration has a great impact in the theology of matrimony. This sacrament is to be placed within the eternal plan of salvation of bringing to perfection in Christ our being created in God's image, within the very life of the church. The characteristic communion of persons in marriage is to be understood in terms of sharing in their peculiar *munus* in charity, and the exemplar for this communion of persons is the trinitarian communion. However, this last affirmation raises a doubt. Is Wojtyła suggesting that within this analogy between the Trinity and the human family, the husband stands for the Father, the wife for the Son, and the children for the Holy Spirit? Were he to defend that thesis, his trinitarian theology, his theological anthropology, and his theology of marriage would be in direct opposition to that of Thomas Aquinas and Augustine.[52] If this were the case, the main thesis of this book would be unswervingly damaged. We will come back to this point later on in chapter 5.

For the moment, let us consider the second theological assertion which I outlined earlier: the church is conceived as the communion that brings to fulfillment the deepest aspirations of the human heart. This consideration sheds further light on the enrichment of faith. Those who are being fully incorporated into the church *externally* also ought to belong to her *internally* through their perseverance *in charity*.[53] This notion is key to married people in the church, who are to live their vocation within the sphere of Christian responsibility. Anyone living in the married state should "do his utmost in order that external membership should be matched by inner royalty."[54] Indeed, the church's catholicity could be viewed extensively, inasmuch as all men are called to be integrated into God's people.[55] Yet, Wojtyła concentrates on a more *intensive* understanding of catholicity or universality: the kind of union that exists and

---

49. SR, 61; emphasis added.
50. Ibid.
51. Ibid.
52. See *ST* I, q. 93, a. 6, ad 2.
53. See LG 13; GS 19; LG 14.
54. SR, 127.
55. See LG 17; SR, 134.

should exist in the church as a result of *charity*.[56] Just as the human person cannot find himself except in the sincere gift of self, the community of persons that forms the church finds itself only in the self-inherent gift of charity. In this way, there develops a communion in solidarity among the different members of Christ's body, who bring to each other their gifts in accordance with their own identity and vocation.[57] This communion takes place at different levels in the church (among local churches, states of life, different individual persons, etc.). In all of them, communion is based on a certain equality that promotes fraternity without destroying diversity. This equality consists in having the same human and Christian dignity, in sharing in the same essential task of building up Christ's body, and in being equally called to holiness and salvation. Obviously, this kind of equality is no obstacle for either diversity or for the hierarchical constitution of the church, provided authority is understood with Jesus's mind as hierarchical *diakonia*.[58]

The consciousness of the church as God's people, which results from complementing LG with GS's christocentric anthropology of man created in God's image, has another important dimension in the conciliar documents: the relationship between the historical and the eschatological character of the church. Indeed, coming from the Trinity (*ecclesia de Trinitate*), the church has a unique historical character in her continuation of the missions of the Son and the Holy Spirit.[59] Unlike other historical realities, the church's historicity is not confined to the past. Instead, the church's historicity, intimately connected with the history of salvation, integrates past, present, and future. For this reason, Vatican II is able to contemplate the church's historicity from the viewpoint of her eschatological fulfillment in three ways.[60]

First, the Council explains that *the increase of the Kingdom promotes the evolution of the world*, even if the church is in the world but is not of this world. There is an encounter between the vectors of the history and evolution of the world, and the history of salvation: God's salvific plan answers the deepest aspirations of humanity.[61] The eschatological character of redemption shows that the history of salvation always surpasses the history of the world and calls it to purification, *especially from a false notion of autonomy*.[62] Human aspirations and ends are enlightened with a divine dimension. Christ's commandment of love reorients them from the perspective of their eschatological fulfillment.[63] Thus, the church is inserted into history by communicating divine life to man, and by growing in her awareness of the need for renewal.

56. See LG 9; SR, 135.
57. See LG 13; SR, 134–35, 136–37.
58. See SR, 153.
59. See DV 2–3; LG 2.
60. See LG 9; SR, 161–62.
61. See LG 6; GS 45; SR, 177–78.
62. See GS 16 and 41; SR, 171.
63. See GS 38.

Obviously, the church does not lack anything due to her divine institution. Yet, she can deepen in her self-knowledge and improve in the ways to express her essence more perfectly in her social and visible structure.[64]

Second, contemplating the church's historicity from the viewpoint of her eschatological fulfillment, the Council explains *the ultimate fulfillment of the human person* created in God's image in terms of *conformity to Christ*. We find an important idea here to comprehend TOB's appeal to the ethos of the redemption as a way to appropriate the new law, and to conform to Christ in his ontological and moral exemplarity.[65] Indeed, the ethos of the redemption of the body results in man's final end as "the *fullness of resemblance to Christ*: a resemblance *in the Spirit* through the grace of *divine sonship*, which is to lead to the ultimate reality of bodily resemblance, to be like his glorious body."[66] Since man is at the center of the visible world, his fulfillment in conformity with Christ is also the fulfillment of the world.[67] For this reason, "the eschatological consciousness of the Church is closely united to the consciousness of creation and redemption. It embraces the world as the universal created reality, at the center of which man has been placed by God: this reality, including man, must be renewed once and for all in Christ."[68]

Third, contemplating the church's historicity from the viewpoint of her eschatological fulfillment, Vatican II explains how *holiness* is not only a mark of the church, but also *a vocation for all of her members*. Before dealing with the formation of the moral attitudes, Wojtyła concludes the intellectual formation of the believing members of the church by articulating the universal call to holiness, because holiness is "the *fundamental basis* on which the *formation* of the community of the people of God must rest."[69] All members of the church are called to holiness, each "in a unique and unrepeatable manner."[70] Coherent with the christocentric anthropology, holiness is seen as the *conformity with Christ* that perfects our being created in God's image. Therefore, exemplarity as the metaphysical and experiential foundation of the moral norm has an axial role, because for Wojtyła's moral theology, Christ is both the metaphysical exemplar and the moral or experiential *exemplum*.[71]

In this manner, we can proceed now to look more closely at the way in which Christ is *the* Teacher and *the* Exemplar of the gift of self. Wojtyła distinguishes holiness in the members of the church as something already attained by those who are in glory (the image of glory), from holiness as a vocation and aspiration for the members

---

64. See GS 40, 43–44; SR, 174–75.
65. See GS 2, 45; LG 48.
66. SR, 182; emphasis added. See Phil 3:21.
67. See SR, 187; GS 48.
68. SR, 185.
69. Ibid., 190; emphasis added.
70. Ibid.
71. See LG 40; SR, 191–92, 195.

who still are on the way towards the true homeland (the image of creation and grace). "What constitutes the *essence of sanctity* according to the Gospel, namely *charity* . . . develops with the aid of grace and reaches perfection according to the particular vocation of every Christian."[72] The model, the canon, the norm, and the exemplar for charity is Christ's spousal self-gift for the church: "Christ loved the Church and *gave himself* for her."[73] Wojtyła will make of Christ, especially in this act of charity as self-gift, the model for his integral vision of man, for his entire adequate anthropology of the spousal meaning of the body. Indeed, *conformity with this action of Christ is the fulfillment of the spousal meaning of the body in all the states of life of the Christian vocation.* Christ is the measure or norm for charity. All of the moral attitudes that we will see shortly (including that of Christian responsibility) are only different ways to explain how to enact this reality. In his self-gift for the church, Christ is for married people both the exemplary cause of grace and the visible example for moral conduct.

Finally, since charity is also a *response* from man who has been loved first by Christ in this manner, one could also find a paradigmatic *exemplum* of responsibility in the Virgin Mary.[74] She is an example of holiness to every member of the church. Wojtyła singles out her virginal gift of self to God as the Divine Bridegroom. This act of love is a model for the members of the church in their answer or responsibility to Christ's self-gift. Thus, she also plays an important role in understanding the spousal meaning of the body. Indeed, "the Church sees its own resemblance to her in motherhood and also in the virginal gift of self to God, the Bridegroom."[75] Wojtyła continues explaining that the church sees in Mary "the fulfillment of that for which it was prepared by the Bridegroom and Redeemer and towards which it is constantly led by the Holy Spirit."[76] Consequently, the future pope argues, Mary "is an example of holiness to all, and to every member of God's people—an example expressing both aspiration and fulfillment."[77] Every member of the church finds, in Mary's example of receptive response and *responsibility* to God's initiative, a spousal dimension to the vocation to holiness in charity. The Virgin Mary's example of Christian responsibility to Christ's gift of self becomes the model for how to respond to God's charity and fulfill in this manner the spousal meaning of our bodies.

Basis for Christian Responsibility

All of these truths of the faith are to have a moral impact in the lives of the members of the church. They are to form a set of moral attitudes that effect a true moral renewal

---

72. SR, 194. See LG 40; *ST* II–II, q. 184, a. 1.
73. Eph 5:25.
74. See 1 John 4:19.
75. SR, 198.
76. Ibid., 198–99.
77. Ibid., 199.

in the sources of tradition, in which one's actions can conform to that divine truth as the exemplar for the fulfillment of the church's true mission. However, Vatican II "did not treat ethical problems in a detailed and specific way as had been proposed in the first drafts of its discussion papers. Nevertheless, the whole range of problems in Christian ethics determined the basic orientation of the Council as is evident in both of the central documents of Vatican II."[78] Since the Council treated ethical matters more in a pastoral than a doctrinal manner, "*it will be the task of moral theologians to expound the doctrinal foundations of the attitudes which the Council's teaching seeks to inculcate.*"[79] Hence, one can assume that in TOB, Wojtyła undertook the theological task of expounding the doctrinal foundations of the attitudes about to be explained, especially of the attitude of Christian responsibility. In SR, he limits himself to sketching their main coordinates. His dominant premise in this sketch is that faith expresses itself in a concrete attitude unless, of course, one has only dead faith without works.[80] But living faith is an *obsequiuum* of intellect and will to the content of revelation, as self-abandonment and commitment to God in *obedience* to him.[81] Thus, it implies a set of attitudes in the will.

An attitude is an active relation that is not, properly speaking, an action but an aptness to act in a certain manner. It follows upon knowledge. Yet, in itself, a *moral attitude is not knowledge but appetition*. It refers to the taking up of an intellectual position in such a way as *to be disposed to voluntarily act in accordance with it*.[82] Wojtyła speaks about a series of moral attitudes interconnected amongst themselves, similarly to the way in which virtues form a sort of organism. Within this sort of "organism of attitudes," those of mission and testimony (or witness) are really the most foundational or radical in the order of their generation. Their content is so rich that these foundational attitudes continue to unfold in two other sets of attitudes which, in turn, take complementary views on Christian witness: the set of attitudes included in participation, and the attitudes of human identity and Christian responsibility. I will begin by analyzing the attitudes of mission and testimony. Only then will I look at the foundational attitude of participation. All of them constitute the basis, as it were, for

78. Ibid., 308.
79. Ibid.; emphasis added.
80. See Jas 2:26; SR, 204–5.
81. See DV 5.
82. "In a sense it represents what Thomist psychology would call *habitus* and even *habitus operativus*, but they are not identical" (SR, 205). Wojtyła does not explain in what way *habitus operativus* and attitudes differ because his work is extremely pastoral and he needs only to polish a bit the common use of the term attitude, without explaining when an operative habit becomes a conscious attitude, thanks to the use of the will of that same habit. This seems to be one of the differences between the two notions. Moreover, while all operative habits would qualify as attitudes, not all attitudes qualify as operative habits. Using Aristotle's categories, attitude corresponds to the broader category of disposition in which *habitus* is a species. Wojtyła is not going to explain which faculty is being perfected here by the good attitudes he is discussing. That would connect his theory of attitudes with the classical view on virtues, cardinal and theological.

the attitudes of human identity and Christian responsibility, wherein Wojtyła locates conjugal morality.

With respect to the missionary attitude, Wojtyła recalls that God reveals himself through the *mission* of the Son and that of the Holy Spirit. These missions are not only God's revelation but are also his salvific actions, wherefrom the church issued forth and continues to do so even today. Thus, *the church has an essential missionary aspect that should determine the attitude of every Christian*: "Everyone in the church is in a state of mission, as is the whole Church."[83] I am particularly interested in the way in which these words are applicable to those members of the church who are in the married state. They have a peculiar way of sharing in this missionary attitude, thanks to the graces received in the sacrament of matrimony. This peculiar way of being missionary is unfolded in the attitude of *testimony*.

Indeed, "mission understood in this sense, is so linked with bearing witness that the latter must be considered as the proper expression of mature faith."[84] To support his position, Wojtyła appeals to Acts 1:8, to Christ's promise to his disciples concerning the fruits of his redemptive mission in the mission of the Holy Spirit: "[Y]ou shall receive the power when the Holy Spirit has come upon you and *you shall be my witnesses*." Thus, Vatican II "emphasizes the fact that witness consists in *believing* and *professing* the faith, that is, *accepting God's witness to himself and responding to it with one's own*."[85] Within this attitude of martyrdom or witness, the Council speaks of a *specific ethical responsibility of Christian marriages and families*.[86] Due to the sacramentality of marriage as a sign, they are to make present *in a visible manner*, Christ's spousal charity and fruitful self-gift for the church, God's presence in the world, as well as the very nature of the church. And they are to do so by being just and faithful to their spousal love, and to their generous fruitfulness.[87]

Let us turn now to *the attitude of participation* as a concrete way of giving testimony. Participation in Christ's priesthood is the attitude whereby the human person gives himself and offers the world to God in the manner of a sacrifice that is true spiritual worship (*rationabilem obsequium*).[88] In this *priestly* attitude, one fulfills the gift of self or self-offering inherent in the obedience of faith and expressed as the ethical conclusion of the christocentric anthropology of man created in God's image, explained in GS 24. Wojtyła argues that this attitude "denotes the simplest and most complete attitude."[89] He goes on to clarify that this same attitude refers to GS 24 and it "expresses the *vocation* of the person in its existential nucleus—a vocation referred

---

83. Ibid., 207.
84. Ibid., 211.
85. Ibid., 208; emphasis added.
86. See AG 11, 12, 21.
87. See GS 48, 51.
88. See Rom 12:1; PO 2; SR, 223.
89. SR, 224.

to by *Gaudium et Spes* in the words to which we must *constantly* return."[90] Hence, the fulfillment of the attitude of participation, as it is condensed in the participation in Christ's priesthood, entails the perfecting of God's image in the human person through conformity with Christ in charity. In reality, this is exactly the fulfillment of the spousal meaning of the body. For this reason, Wojtyła audaciously claims that "the attitude which derives from sharing in the priesthood of Christ is seen as one which contains in a special way *all the richness of faith*, both as regards *content* and as regards subjective *commitment*."[91] This moral attitude "is at the very center of the teaching of Vatican II and contains in a certain manner *all that the Council wished to say about the Church, mankind and the world*."[92]

Participation in Christ's priesthood "is expressed through *participation in the sacraments*."[93] As the future pope explains, "the priesthood of Christ has realized itself through the work of redemption, so that all those who truly participate in it enjoy the fruit of that work, which is holiness. This is the purpose and effect of sharing in Christ's priesthood through the sacraments of the Church."[94] Thus, those members of the church who are married also participate in Christ's priesthood by virtue of their baptism. They bring about this participation in a fruitful manner by consciously partaking in the sacraments and leading a life of virtue. This is also the light under which the sacramentality of marriage, as it is expressed in LG 11, should be interpreted. Indeed, the sacramentality of matrimony should be seen from the viewpoint of it being a cause of grace *ex opere operato*. Simultaneously, the sacramentality of marriage enters into moral theology inasmuch as it is a sign for the *opus operantis*.[95] As I will try to show, this last affirmation reflects the position taken in TOB's explanation of the sacramentality of matrimony as a cause of grace and as a sign.

Moreover, in his prophetic *munus*, the eternal Word expressed divine truth in human language. The church as a whole participates in this prophetic *munus* inasmuch as she has received from Christ himself the power and office (obligation) to express divine truth in human language. Different members of the church are called to "speak" in different ways as prophets do, that is to say, in God's name.[96] For this reason, they are to know what is contained in God's word; they are to guard its content as the most precious patrimony, and they are to transmit it to others. Thereby, the

---

90. Ibid.; emphasis added.
91. Ibid., 225; emphasis added.
92. Ibid.; emphasis added.
93. Ibid., 237.
94. Ibid.
95. "The Council's line with regard to liturgical renewal, with its emphasis on the full and conscious participation of the faithful, serves to stress what in the theology of the sacraments is called *opus operantis*. The sacraments not only confer grace, but, in addition, the very act of celebrating them most effectively disposes the faithful to receive this grace to their profit, to worship God duly, and *to practice charity*" (ibid., 239). See SC 59.
96. See SR, 250.

participation in this *munus* confers a prophetic character to the attitude of witness described above, so that by word and deed the faithful may "speak" divine truth in human language. Considering what has been said about the role of the sacraments as sign and its implications for the moral life, it seems that the conciliar foundations for TOB's understanding of the "prophetism" and the "language of the body" are to be located right here. Married members of the church partake in the prophetic *munus* by giving testimony with their lives to the truth about human love and marriage revealed by God in our Lord Jesus Christ. Conforming (*adequatio*) their lives to that truth is the essence of what John Paul II calls the prophetism and the language of the body.

The prophetic *munus* has already touched on Christian morality. Yet, Wojtyła thinks that the moral order is properly placed by LG 36 in our participation in Christ's *munus regalis*, especially as Christ's kingship is expressed by his kenotic obedience unto death to the Father's will and his consequent exaltation in authority or power.[97] As Vatican II clearly teaches, "Christ has communicated this royal power to His disciples that they might be *constituted in royal freedom* and that by true penance and a holy life they might *conquer the reign of sin in themselves*. Further, He has shared this power so that serving Christ in their fellow men they might by humility and patience lead their brethren to that King for whom to serve is to reign."[98] This freedom is perfected by conformity with the Son, *the* Exemplar. The measure of such a conformity is made known to us by Christ's own *exemplum*. This is the freedom of the sons in the Son (*filii in Filio*), the freedom of the children of God, that same freedom of the gift, which plays a key role in TOB's understanding of the spousal meaning of the body.[99] In SR, Wojtyła interprets this royal freedom within the christocentric anthropology of man created in God's image and in conformity with Christ. Thus, the human person's "aspiration towards royal freedom through dominion over sin makes him *similar to Christ*, who was glorified and exalted for his obedience to the Father even unto death."[100] Imitation of Christ in this regard is "the royal self-dominion that is proper to human beings; by so doing he shares in the *munus regale* of Christ and helps to bring about Christ's kingdom."[101] Spouses are to attain this kind of freedom as they mature in their conjugal love, and as they collaborate with the Creator in their procreative *munus*.

True or perfected freedom, according to divine truth, is that acquired freedom which is *informed by charity*, the good use of our innate freedom that translates into service to Christ in also serving others. This service is the proper way to understand the fulfillment of man's lordship over his actions (*dominus sui actus*) in the Lord

---

97. See Phil 2: 5–8; Matt 28:18.

98. LG 36; emphasis added. See also SR, 262–63. For a very valuable philosophical analysis of these theological considerations, see Millán-Puelles, *El Valor de La Libertad*.

99. See Rom 6:12; 8:12; 1 Cor 3:23.

100. SR, 263; emphasis added.

101. Ibid.; emphasis added.

(*Dominus*), as well as man's lordship over nature. Therefore, one finds a theological confirmation of man's obligation to dominate nature neither against the laws of nature nor against the Creator, but rather in participation with him through the fulfillment of the natural law.[102] These conclusions will be very relevant for the discussion on contraception.

The analysis of the attitude of participation has deepened our understanding of mature faith expressed by mission and witness. Only by participating in Christ can the human person find the reasons for the self-abandonment and self-offering inherent in living faith. The ontological and moral dimensions of Christ's exemplarity, already present in testimony, reappear now as participation in Christ's threefold *potestas* as priest, prophet, and king.[103] This participated *potestas* by the members of the church should not be understood here just as power to govern, but rather as *munus*, as an obligation to fulfill an office or mission and the gift, grace, or power to bring it about. To participate in Christ's *potestas* means both to assume the offices and obligations assumed and fulfilled by him, and to receive as a gift from Christ himself the capacity to carry them out. In this way, we take part in the mission of the Son as it remains in the church. And we do so, thanks to the mission of the Holy Spirit.

Moreover, participation in the threefold office of Christ *makes possible and conditions* Christian testimony. Participation *makes testimony ontologically possible* by conferring grace. Furthermore, participation *conditions* testimony by delineating the attitudes for its ethical development, that is, by setting the goal to which the testimony is directed, and where it reaches perfection in the human person. Once again, Wojtyła inserts this reality into GS's christocentric anthropology of man created in God's image. By this ontological and moral participation, the Christian grows in his likeness (*similitudo*) to Christ.

Human Identity and Christian Responsibility

Participation delineates the meaning of Christian witness based on LG and Christ's *tria munera*. In turn, human identity and Christian responsibility complement this witness as found in GS and *Dignitatis Humanae* (DH). In so doing, the meaning of Christian witness continues to unfold as the harmonious encounter between the growth of the Kingdom through participation, and the evolution of the world through human identity in Christian responsibility. In this harmonious encounter, Wojtyła locates Vatican II's doctrine on conjugal morality. He emphasizes the spouses' responsibility to be witnesses of Christ's spousal and fruitful self-gift for the church. Since the

---

102. See GS 35; 43 SR, 269–271; LR, 246–47. The point just made is quite important. Proponents of contraception such as Louis Janssens, Charles Curran, or Bernard Häring "would argue that the human person has complete authority over nature and therefore the church's ban on contraception should be lifted." Petri, *Aquinas*, 5.

103. See LG 31.

attitude of participation increases the Kingdom, it must also promote the evolution of the world by being imbedded in all that is *truly human*. Thereby, it promotes human identity in solidarity and Christian responsibility. To become *fully human means to love as God loves*. For this reason, John Paul II will be able to speak in TOB about our vocation to charity as the spousal meaning of the body. The attitude of human identity already foreshadows this reasoning. Wojtyła explains that "the Christian *attains his human identity by remaining faithful to the law of charity* in the various spheres of his life and activity."[104] As a result, "the Christian's *human identity coincides with his participation* in the mystery of Christ and in his mission, and the two attitudes *merge into one*."[105]

The attitude of human identity thus understood is a clear proof that religion does not alienate man from his true humanity. Rather, based on GS's christocentric anthropology, Wojtyła argues that participation in the mission of Christ makes man's humanity *flourish*. It brings to fulfillment the meaning of our very existence: the spousal meaning of the body. Participation and human identity converge in the realm of morality, especially in the precept of charity: "[T]he attitude of human identity, inwardly permeates the attitude of participation whereby the Christian identifies himself with the mission of Christ himself."[106] Every human being has the *same* dignity of being the other's neighbor, because every human being has been created in God's image.[107] And the flourishing of that dignity in the moral life, the perfection of being created in God's image, consists precisely in the precept of charity, in loving God and other human beings, as Christ has loved us when he gave himself for the church as his spouse. This spousal meaning of our existence entails that "the precept of charity is at *the root of the whole moral order. It also contains the principle of action, thanks to which human life can become more and more human,* as the Council repeatedly puts it. This principle has a decisive effect in *forming the attitude of human identity* by which the Christian should be characterized."[108] As the future pope explains, "charity respects the person above any form of calculation or thought of profit. It does not make use of man, but serves his humanity."[109] In this way, "charity conditions the attitude of human identity and how that attitude is to be understood."[110] Consequently, conjugal love will be truly and fully human, when elevated by conjugal charity. Conjugal love will be fully human when it fulfills the spousal meaning of the body as charity coordinates and perfects all of its proper virtues.

104. SR, 309; emphasis added.
105. Ibid.; emphasis added.
106. Ibid., 273.
107. See GS 29.
108. SR, 282; emphasis added. See AA 8.
109. SR, 285; emphasis added.
110. Ibid.; emphasis added.

Conformity with Christ's love is what brings about the flourishing of what is truly human in man's aspirations, and such conformity is to participate in Christ's *tria munera*. But since the perfection of the human person always takes place acting together with others in view of the common good—that is, in the fulfillment of legal justice—the attitude of human identity also relates intimately with that of solidarity, for solidarity signifies "the correct orientation of individual liberty towards the common good."[111] This principle has important consequences for those members of the church who are married and live the attitude of human identity. Not only do they fulfill in their peculiar way the spousal meaning of their bodies or vocation to charity, they also build up or enrich the entire church as the body of Christ, especially in their solidarious and just collaboration with the Creator in the transmission and education of human life.

The attitudes of human identity and Christian responsibility also converge, inasmuch as for Christians to attain their true human identity, they must remain *faithful* to the law of charity. This same law of charity is the basic Christian *responsibility* that springs from the mysteries of Creation, Redemption, and the church as God's people. After all, Christian responsibility is one specific kind of self-determination not founded on arbitrariness, but on the *good use* of freedom being subordinated to the truth about the good. "Responsibility is closely associated with the dignity of the individual, for it expresses the self-determination . . . in which man makes *proper use of his freedom* by allowing himself to be guided by *genuine* values and a law of righteousness."[112] Thus, spouses share in Christian responsibility when they partake in Christ's royal *munus*, in that royal freedom of ruling over one's actions by serving Christ (and also, others). Thereby, they offer their own lives in a priestly sacrifice and gift of self to God. This gift becomes an eloquent prophetic testimony that also shares in Christ's being a martyr for the Truth, and in his moral authority in doing so with his *exemplum*; for unlike the Scribes and Pharisees, Jesus always preached what he himself lived.[113]

In this way, Wojtyła explains the responsibility for conjugal love as expressed in GS 47–52. Both marriage and conjugal love, by their very nature (*indole sua*), are ordered to the procreation and education of offspring. The latter is a common end and good, which contributes to the perfection (good) of the spouses themselves by making their conjugal love fully human or mature.[114] This maturation, as well as the common good of marriage, are elevated by the sacramentality of matrimony to the supernatural realm by a special conformity to Christ's spousal charity. Therein, the perfection of the spouses is also the perfection of their being in God's image. Thus, to locate the maturation of conjugal love within the sphere of Christian responsibility means to

111. Ibid., 289.
112. Ibid., 291; emphasis added. See also DH 7.
113. See John 18:37; Mark 1:27; Matt 23:3.
114. See GS 50.

insert it in the theology of the *imago Dei* and its perfection in charity and in that royal freedom, whose good use implies to offer one's life in a priestly sacrifice and gift of self to God and others, and to do so as an eloquent prophetic testimony to the truth about marriage revealed by God.

Indeed, Wojtyła's considerations of marriage within the sphere of Christian responsibility place conjugal morality within the broader context of the *imago Dei* as perfected by supernatural grace and the sacraments. Christ's Incarnation, the instrumental role of his humanity, his priesthood, his paschal mystery, and his headship in the church are the sources of the sacraments in general, and of marriage in particular. As John Paul II will say, through the Incarnation, the body has entered into theology through its main door, so to speak.[115] For this reason, in TOB, the sacramentality of marriage as a cause of grace will be in strict and intimate dependence with the body, or better yet, with the humanity of Christ assumed by the Son for us, and for our salvation.[116] Through the sacrament of marriage, Christian spouses have the gift and the *responsibility* to *participate* in Christ's sacrificial and fruitful spousal gift of self for the church. Due to the sacramentality of marriage as a sign, they are to give *testimony* by making visible this same fruitful and spousal gift. In doing so, they perfect their being created in the image and likeness of God.

Moreover, their *participation* in the *tria munera Christi* empowers them to accomplish such a mission, whereby they perfect their human identity in living out responsibly the spousal meaning of the body, according to the married state of life. In Karol Wojtyła's interpretation of Vatican II, married members of the church—who are members *internally* and not only externally—participate in the prophetic *munus* of Christ by giving testimony with their words and actions. They partake of Christ's priestly *munus* by actively participating in the sacramental life of the church and by the exercise of the virtues, making of their entire life a sacrifice in true worship (*rationabilem obsequium*). Finally, married members of the church share in Christ's kingly *munus* by embodying the true freedom of God's children in that perfected freedom inherent in the gift of self. All of these theological coordinates, found in Wojtyła's interpretation of Vatican II, are like the soil where TOB will be sown and raised. They provide the foundation for John Paul's commentary on HV, where responsibility for procreation and for the integration of conjugal love will be inseparably linked in accordance with GS 51. Thus, contraceptive intercourse will be exposed as a *violation of responsibility*, especially a violation of the inseparable responsibilities for procreation and for the fully human maturation of conjugal love into virtue.

---

115. See TOB 23:4.
116. See ibid., 103:7.

2

The Kraków Document

Against Naturalism

Karol Wojtyła was part of the special commission that advised Paul VI on birth regulation. Unable to travel to Rome, he led a group of theologians in Poland who worked on this topic from January 1966 until February 1968. They produced a document known today as the "Kraków Document" (KD).[1] This document focuses on the particular issue of contraception within the realm of conjugal morality. Yet, its main thesis descends to the kernel of the argument at the levels of fundamental moral theology, philosophical and theological anthropology, and philosophical ethics. It basically argues that supporters of contraception have misunderstood both *the philosophical and the theological dimensions of natural law*. They have adopted a *naturalistic* view, which confuses the biological order with the order of natural law. Since the minority report—opposed to contraception—did not adequately address this foundational issue, KD cautions Paul VI against this *naturalistic* view.[2]

Curiously, this same naturalistic view is quite close to Max Scheler's, an author Wojtyła knows in depth. The future pope had concluded in his monographic work on Scheler's ethics that the German phenomenologist had severely misunderstood the notion of nature.[3] The same issue reappears now in another context. As FC 32 will indicate, the understanding of the relationship between person and nature radically distinguishes those in favor of contraception from those who are against it. The disjunctive between them is extremely radical. As Styczen explains, *tertium non datur* (a third option is excluded).[4]

---

1. For a study on this document, see Smith, "The Kraków Document." See also Pieronek, "The Reception of Vatican II." Note that Wojtyła will be simultaneously working during this time on AP, a book that will initially be published in 1969. We will have to come back to this point in chapter 4.

2. See KD, 323.

3. See Wojtyła, *Max Scheler*, 190–91. For a detailed analysis of Scheler's reductive view on human nature, see my *De la experiencia*, 69–134.

4. See Styczen, "Dove Sbaglia Padre Häring," 69.

In Which Sense is Natural Law Natural?

The proponents of contraception argue that "the present-day notions of nature and of the natural law have changed in their meaning."[5] From this premise, they conclude that "the teaching of the Church recognizes this fact and therefore changes."[6] However, the real issue is not whether one's understanding of the natural character of natural law has changed. The very reality of the natural law is what is really at stake here. For this reason, KD proposes to rediscover "an accurate understanding of natural law and of *human nature, on which this law rests*. For, in fact, the proponents of contraception understand these notions in a way that significantly departs from their authentic and traditional meaning in philosophy and theology."[7]

Nature is a very complicated notion indeed. It can have many different meanings. Hence, we can understand the difficulty pointed out by Wojtyła in KD. If one were to reformulate it, one could simply ask the question: in which sense is the natural law natural? In perfect alignment with his other writings, Wojtyła argues that the natural law is natural not in a physical sense but in a "metaphysical" sense.[8] This is how Thomas Aquinas understands it as well. For this reason, in VS, John Paul II warns against a naturalistic or biologistic understanding of the natural character of natural law and points to the Angelic Doctor's teaching to clarify this foundational point of Catholic morality.[9] Without losing the main thread of our argument, and without claiming to be exhaustive, allow me to briefly explain what I mean by "natural in a metaphysical sense."

Anticipating John Paul II's clarifications in VS, KD proposes that according to traditional teaching, natural law must be understood as "an objective moral order inscribed in the *rational nature of man*."[10] This way of conceiving the natural character of the natural law includes certain implicit intellectual choices that I would like to unveil. The Latin word *natura* comes from the verb *nascor*. Thus, in a very basic sense, it means birth; it is synonymous with *nativitas*.[11] However, this nominal understanding of nature does not tell us yet in which sense the natural law is natural. In another sense, nature is also understood as the realm of subhuman beings. Thus, we often say in common language that we enjoy spending time in nature, namely, in the wild, in the mountains, etc. Obviously, this use of nature does not tell us in which sense the natural law is natural. For the natural law, according to Saint Paul, is written in the

---

5. KD, 322–23.
6. Ibid.
7. Ibid., 325; emphasis added.
8. See PC, 95–100, 181–86, 279–300.
9. See VS, 47–50. The same warning was present in LR, 56–57.
10. KD, 326; emphasis added. This understanding of natural law reappears in TOB 25:1.
11. See *ST* I, q. 29, a. 1, ad 4; III, q. 2, a. 1, c.

human heart and not in the subhuman cosmos.[12] Moreover, within a theological context, nature is also understood as that which is not supernatural.[13] This other meaning of nature, however, does not completely capture the exact way in which the natural law is natural. Yet, it certainly conveys something true about its natural character: the precepts of the natural law could be known without the aid of revelation.[14]

Coming back to the realm of philosophy, it is worth noting that Aristotle developed an entire part of philosophy dedicated to the study of nature (*physis*), the Physics. Since the generation of beings comes from an intrinsic principle, Aristotle understood nature as the intrinsic principle of movement. This "physical" understanding of nature is not the whole story about natural law either, for according to KD, the natural character of natural law refers to the specific nature of the human person as such. On the other hand, within the realm of logic, the nature of a given reality refers to its essence as its definition.[15] We are coming closer and closer to the sense in which the natural law is natural. However, although definitions are highly important, when talking about the natural character of natural law, we are not moving in the sheer realm of mental being and second intentions. We are interested in identifying the *res significata* in the realm of anthropology and ethics.

There is another sense in which the adjective natural is used, which seems to belong to that which is properly human. Now and again, the term natural is used to signify something that happens in the human person without freedom. Thus, what is *natural* is sometimes distinguished from what is *voluntary*.[16] Moreover, the term natural is also used occasionally to signify that which in the human person is common to other animals.[17] These two meanings combined seem to be at the root of the position upheld by some philosophers and theologians who were part of the majority report. But they adopted and combined these meanings of nature without preserving that which allows those meanings to maintain their proper place and equilibrium in the philosophy and theology of Thomas Aquinas: the metaphysics of the human soul and man's substantial unity.[18] Thus, the advocates of contraception upheld a reductionistic vision of the human person, wherein natural is synonymous with subpersonal and nonspiritual. Viewed in this way, the natural character of natural law would amount to the laws of nature as understood by modern sciences like biology. Rhonheimer has rightfully opposed this view: "The body and with it sexuality is not—as Karl Rahner has confusingly written—a sub-personal sphere of the human being that can be treated

---

12. See Rom 2:15.
13. See *ST* I, q. 12, a. 4, arg. 3; III, q. 13, a. 2, c.
14. See TOB 119:5.
15. See *ST* I, q. 29, a. 2, c; q. 119, a. 1, c.
16. See ibid., I–II, q. 10, a. 1, ad 1.
17. See ibid., I–II, q. 31, a. 7, c.
18. See TOB 66:6.

or manipulated like a thing; rather it is the human subject itself and an intrinsically part of the human person."[19]

KD directly rejected this position as well, which comes quite close to the one of Max Scheler. This naturalistic position is untenable when one realizes that the human person is free by nature and that the whole dynamism of the human person (sensible or spiritual) springs from his rational nature. Thus, reacting against the defective understanding of natural just described, KD explains that one needs to carefully differentiate between the moral law and "the law of nature in the sense used by natural sciences today."[20] It would be a colossal mistake to reduce the *metaphysical* notion of nature to "the laws of nature," as understood by modern physics or biology. This error evokes Kant's radical separation between the laws of nature and those of freedom (or practical reason). As is known, in Kant's division of philosophical knowledge, material rational knowledge (the one that concerns some object and is not merely occupied with what he calls the form of understanding) is divided into "either laws of nature or laws of freedom. The science of the former is called physics and that of the latter ethics. The former is also called theory of nature and the latter theory of morals."[21] In this view, the realm of nature is clearly abandoned to the empirical sciences. The metaphysical understanding of nature is basically *outlawed* from the realm of freedom and ethics.

By contrast, KD proposes a more metaphysical way of understanding human nature. In this sense, nature signifies the essence of a being in the order of its proper operation.[22] Hence, the essence of man as a *rational animal* in the order of human operation is the nature signified by the natural character of natural law. Natural law is natural *because it is rational*, because *it is a rational order*. However, although we are very close, we have not yet fully answered our question. On the one hand, it is of the utmost importance not to identify the human specific difference of rational with the faculty of reason. On the other hand, it is necessary to recognize practical reason's role in the natural law. Indeed, man's rational nature includes reason but is not only the faculty of reason. We cannot lose sight of Thomas's metaphysics of the soul. Otherwise, we will fall into a serious reductionism. Aquinas explicitly denies the identification between rational as the specific difference in man's essence, and the faculty or power of reason. For Thomas and Wojtyła, natural law is not natural only because it springs from the faculty of the intellect, in its practical orientation. Natural law is also natural inasmuch as it is "an objective moral order *inscribed* in the *rational nature of man*."[23] When Aquinas talks about such a nature, clarifying in which sense we use the adjective *rational*, he has the objector arguing that an "accident is not the

19. Rhonheimer, *Ethics of Procreation*, 36.
20. KD, 326.
21. Kant, *Foundations of the Metaphysics of Morals*, 3–4.
22. See *De Ente*, cap. 1.
23. KD, 326; emphasis added. See TOB 118:5, 119:1–2, 123:3.

principle of a substantial difference. But sensitive and rational are substantial differences; and they are taken from sense and reason, which are powers of the soul."[24] Thomas answers with the following clarification: "Rational and sensitive, as differences, are *not taken from the powers of sense and reason*, but from the sensitive and *rational soul itself*. But because substantial forms, which in themselves are unknown to us, are known by their accidents; nothing prevents us from sometimes substituting accidents for substantial differences."[25]

Thus, rational is the best adjective we have found in order to signify the perfection of man's soul, the degree of participation of man's substantial form in the good. Since we do not really know how to name this degree of perfection, we take the highest activity man can do, and we use that name to signify the perfection, not of the activity, but of his very soul. This is particularly important in light of an axial principle in Thomas's metaphysics of the human soul: the soul is man's substantial form, and is united to matter *without the mediation of any accident*. Expanding on this thesis allows Aquinas to show how rich is the role of the one substantial form in the human person. He explains that the "form that is more perfect virtually contains whatever belongs to the inferior forms; therefore, while remaining one and the same, it perfects matter according to the various degrees of perfection. For the same essential form makes man an actual being, a body, a living being, an animal, and a man. It is also evident that each genus has its own proper accidents."[26]

Hence, the one rational soul gives man his rational being (*forma dat esse*). It also confers something like its essential properties or "proper accidents," namely, the properties that immediately flow from being: being one, true, good, beautiful, etc. The same applies to our being corporeal. The rational soul makes the human person to be a body and to have all the essential properties that flow therefrom. Moreover, the same rational soul makes the human person a being capable of sensation, that is, being an animal. The one rational soul is also responsible for all the essential properties that belong to the human person as an animal. Our sensible passions, for instance, spring from our one rational soul. Thus, they are not identical to the ones of an irrational animal, which spring from their irrational soul. Ours, for example, have the *real* potency, power, or aptness to be the subject of virtue. Similarly, the rational soul is the source of our intellect and will, and of their natural inclinations.

Now, it is the one rational soul that coordinates or configures, so to speak, all of these properties and powers. The inferior properties and powers are oriented from their very origin to the superior. Indeed, the superior, being prior in the order of perfection, direct and command the inferior ones.[27] Consequently, not only the intellect in its practical exercise, but also *all of the inclinations and powers* that spring from

---

24. *ST* I, q. 77, a. 1, arg. 7.
25. Ibid., I, q. 77, a. 1, ad 7; emphasis added.
26. Ibid., I, q. 76, a. 6, ad 1. Translation altered. See also I, q. 76, a. 4, c; *ScG* IV. 81.
27. See *ST* I, q. 77, a. 4, c.

man's soul, are rational in this sense and *belong to the objective order of the natural law as such, as natural.*[28] Since they spring from the one rational soul, they have an intelligible or rational order of their own. Moreover, they have a sort of "metaphysical transparency," which allows them to disclose the ultimate foundation of their rationality in the intelligible order bestowed on them from the Creator as the Author of nature. Nevertheless, human reason plays a central role here as well, especially in natural law *as law.*[29] The latter *presupposes* for its rational order the natural inclinations which spring from the one rational soul. But it is reason that directs our natural inclinations to their due end (*debitum*) and formulates moral precepts oriented to the formation of virtues. Thus, natural law is *natural* because it arises from man's *natural* principles. This is not only Thomas Aquinas's position but also that of Karol Wojtyła.[30] Kant's position is quite close to the one upheld by the advocates of contraception, but it is very far from Aquinas's and Wojtyła's.

Indeed, the view of the proponents of contraception destroys the very possibility of conceiving the natural law as *the natural promulgation of the eternal law in the rational creature*. In other words, their position is unable to show that human reason *finds* the law as something already made and *commanded* by God.[31] The natural law is something intimated by the Creator in man's being in such a *natural* way that its binding force is experienced—above all at the level of its first principles—without the necessity of a *positive* promulgation.[32] In this way, God's command is experienced in man's conscience first and foremost as an intelligible order based on truth. It is true that reason applies this law like a tribunal to order one's actions. However, it is also true that the "tribunal of reason"—to use a very Kantian image—is like a tribunal that judges based on laws, which *that same tribunal has not made*. Otherwise, it could not be explained why something in reason judges reason itself, for to judge in this sense is something that belongs to that which is superior and not equal.[33]

In this way, natural law is the human person's participation in God's eternal law as *naturally* promulgated. Thereby, man participates in a reasonable order whose origin is found in the Creator, a reasonable order that extends to all of his faculties and natural inclinations. The human person is to adhere to such an order freely, following the first basic precept that the (true) good is to be done while the bad (or false good) is to be avoided. In following this first precept intimated in his conscience, the human

28. Of course, one needs to distinguish what the natural law as "natural" is, in itself, from how we come to know it. For the epistemology of the natural law, see Jensen, *Knowing the Natural Law*. Moreover, one could also distinguish between an active and passive participation in the eternal law in the human person. See Rhonheimer, *Practical Reason and Natural Law*, 66–70, 104.

29. See TOB 124:6.

30. See LR 35; AP, 76–80, and my analysis of this section in *De la experiencia*, 290–308.

31. For a good contrast between the different way in which Thomas and Kant conceive the act of command (*imperium*), see Westberg, *Right Practical Reason*, 180.

32. See Brock, *The Legal Character of Natural Law*, 95–132.

33. See *De Veritate*, q. 17, a. 3, ad 3; q. 17, a. 5, c.

person responsibly collaborates, in accordance with his rational nature, with the Creator. Perhaps, the following texts best sum up Wojtyła's direct opposition to Kant's view of autonomy, and the indirect dispute with the advocates of contraception. The first text comes from LR:

> Man is just towards God the Creator when he *recognizes* the order of nature and conforms to it in his actions ... Man, *by understanding the order of nature and conforming to it in his actions, participates in the thought of God,* becomes *particeps Creatoris,* has a share in the law which God bestowed on the world when He created it at the beginning of time. This participation is an end in itself ... Man, being a reasonable creature, is just towards the Creator by striving in all his activities to achieve this specifically human value, by behaving as *particeps Creatoris.* The antithesis of this belief is autonomism, which holds that man most fully asserts his value when he is *his own legislator,* when he feels himself to be the *source of all law* and all justice (Kant). This is *erroneous:* man could only be his own ultimate lawgiver if, instead of being a creature, he were his own first cause ... The value of the *created* person is most fully exhibited by participation in the thought of the Creator, by acting as *particeps Creatoris* in thought and in action.[34]

The second text I am alluding to is from an article devoted to the natural law. Wojtyła explains therein how a correct understanding of the natural law leads to an adequate anthropology, to an integral and metaphysical view of the human person, which stands in opposition to Kant's views on autonomy.

> Natural law corresponds to the person. Moreover, not only does natural law correspond to the person, but it also in a particular way establishes persons in their proper place in the whole objective order of the world ... such a conception of natural law suggests *an integral conception of the human person* ... We have seen that an affinity between the person and natural law is possible only if we accept a certain *metaphysics of the human person,* which also entails a certain subordination of the human person in relation to God, a subordination that is, after all, very honorable.[35]

Wojtyła's position is clearly Thomistic but also anti-Kantian. Instead, the position upheld by contraception's advocates, combined with some Heideggerian underpinnings, supports the view of an *autonomous* morality governed by situation ethics. Such an autonomous morality denies the very existence of intrinsically evil actions. It considers its mundane realm outside of the boundaries of the church's magisterium.[36]

---

34. LR, 246–47.

35. PC, 184–85; emphasis added.

36. For a successful refutation of these positions, see Rhonheimer, *Natural Law and Practical Reason.*

This distorted view of natural law is not only postmetaphysical but a-metaphysical. As Cardinal Ratzinger explained in commenting about John Paul II's views on natural law, within the a-metaphysical view of the proponents of contraception, the rational nature of the human person has lost its "metaphysical transparency," its capacity to disclose the intelligibility and language of the Creator.[37] This position hinders the intimate compatibility and complementarity between natural law and Christ's revelation. For it "contradicts the very foundations of the Christian view, a view that takes as its starting point precisely the language of the Creator, which is perceived in a definitive and new way in the person of Christ."[38] Thus, the anthropology and ethics inherent in the advocacy of contraception has deeply misunderstood the philosophical and the theological dimensions of natural law. Indeed, as I noted in the introduction, their view cannot manage to harmonize the biblical and metaphysical foundations of a christocentric moral theory, compatible with the natural law, and grounded on the substantial unity of man.

Unchanging Human Nature and the Church's Magisterium

The previous considerations clarify why KD speaks of the need to retrieve a more metaphysical notion of human nature, understood within man's substantial unity.[39] The next step in KD is to oppose the opinion of the proponents of contraception, according to which the church's magisterium has no competency in the autonomous realm of intra-mundane ethics. Instead, KD shows that natural law precepts have their own theological dimension as elements of "the life of faith by which man strives towards his ultimate end."[40] They are part of the church's teaching on faith and morals. They do not belong to a realm isolated and autonomous, foreign to church teaching, and abandoned to consequentionalist calculi. Hence, by denying the existence of an autonomous mundane morality, natural law precepts (including those that regulate each and every conjugal act) also fall under the authority of the magisterium, an authority not restricted to the realm of the transcendental level of the so-called "fundamental option."[41]

Moreover, against the advocates of contraception's appeal for a change of doctrine, KD explains that the church's position against contraception cannot change. Once again, the appeal is made to a metaphysical understanding of human nature as the immutable basis for the permanency of the church's teaching. KD explains that the evolution in the magisterium concerning morality constitutes a change *only with*

---

37. See Ratzinger, "Il rinnovamento della teologia morale," 41.
38. Ibid.
39. See *ST* I, q. 76, a. 1; Cafarra, "Corpore et anima unus."
40. KD, 325.
41. For a good explanation and refutation of this position, see Melina, *Sharing in Christ's Virtues*, 18–24; 92–114.

respect to objects that are mutable. But it does not imply a change with respect to objects that are fixed by their very natures. Those are *unchanging*. For instance, there may be a change of position in the magisterium on something like the charge of interest for a loan. But there can never be such a change on something concerning human nature itself. That nature is unchanging and so is the church's teaching directly based on it. And the church's teaching on contraception is based precisely on that permanent and immutable human nature. Hence, the church's teaching on contraception cannot change.

KD additionally argues the same thesis from a more theological viewpoint. The continuous teaching against contraception of popes Pius XI, Pius XII and John XXIII show that the ordinary magisterium on this topic "is close to reaching the point of full development."[42] Whence, KD argues that a future statement by Paul VI on this matter could settle the infallible character of the church's position on contraception.

An Adequate Anthropology

In light of the previous remarks, it is easy to understand why KD now explains the need to base Paul VI's future teaching regarding contraception on an adequate anthropology. Such an anthropology needs to be both philosophical and theological. From the philosophical viewpoint, this adequate anthropology needs to explain why the human being is a person *by nature*. It needs to do so by overcoming both the rupture between person and nature, and the identification between person and consciousness that reduces the human person to a sheer consciousness of diverse experiences. In short, it needs a more metaphysical or ontological view of the human person that allows for a precise understanding of the human body as such. Theologically, this adequate anthropology should expand on Vatican II's christocentric anthropology of the human person created in God's image and likeness, but it should also view it in light of the ecclesiological context of communion.

To be sure, the solution is not merely to *assert* that the human being *is a person by nature*. This truth and its implications need to be *rediscovered* anew. Thus, KD says: "Doubtless all theologians are aware of this, but not all draw therefrom the consequences that logically follow from it."[43] Indeed, influenced by Kant and Scheler, some theologians propose a radical rupture between person and nature. They fall into the pit described previously regarding the combination of two senses of nature *without* Thomas's metaphysics of the human soul, and *without* his view on man's substantial unity. Thereby, they "commit the fundamental error of viewing the human body as belonging to nature—by which they mean the realm of *subhuman* beings that humans

---

42. KD, 327.
43. Ibid., 341n46.

can manipulate as they please, as though the body were an entity inferior to and dependent on the person."[44]

Such a reductionistic view is also dependent on the Kantian and Schelerian reductions of the human person to consciousness. This position ends up making the spiritual subjectivity of the human person completely irreducible to the cosmos. It amounts to an opposition between the subjective and objective understanding of the human being, the understanding of man from the viewpoint of the philosophy of consciousness and that of being.[45] One can read in KD an implicit allusion to Scheler's reductive anthropology. Thus, it is explained that "the notion of person as understood by psychology—i.e., the purely subjective notion, in which the person is conceived *as subject or even substratum of experience*—provides an *insufficient foundation for an objective moral norm*, and leads to the danger of situation ethics. It is necessary, therefore, to begin with the *ontological concept of the person*, understood as substantial subject of conscious and free actions."[46]

Against the reductionistic view already mentioned, KD proposes to rediscover a philosophy and a theology of the human body as such, as human: "[I]t is necessary to recall that *the body is not distinct from the person*, nor subject to it; rather, with the soul it constitutes one single unique person, and it participates in the rights and dignity of the person."[47] We see at work here the principle offered by Aquinas: the one substantial form in man, his rational soul, makes him corporeal; it configures, as it were, his own body *as a human body*. For this reason, because the human body as such is not really distinct from the human person, the so-called "theology of the body" is nothing but the necessary *theological anthropology* needed to understand and explain HV.

Moreover, KD notes that it is absolutely essential to locate the human person in his proper place of honor and dignity within the created cosmos, wherein he is called to be a *partner* of the Absolute, and *not an autonomous subject*.[48] Both philosophy and theology contribute to this task by explaining man's dignity in terms of his intellectual nature and of his being created in God's image and likeness. Thus, it is at this precise moment of the argument that the christocentric anthropology of GS makes its appearance in KD.

> In order to answer the question "what is man?" the Constitution *Gaudium et Spes* refers to the book of Genesis (1:26), where it is said that man is created in the image of God. This is why the *ontological definition of the person* must take into consideration his relation to God and to the world. Man is not an

---

44. Ibid., 329n20. For a clear example of this position in Scheler's moral theory, see Scheler, "The Idols of Self-Knowledge," 62n69.

45. See Scheler, *Formalism in Ethics*, 392; PC, 209–18.

46. KD, 326; emphasis added. I have explained Scheler's reduction of the person to consciousness in my "Karol Wojtyła's Thomistic Understanding of Consciousness," 411–16.

47. KD, 353.

48. See also LR, 229; TOB 6:2.

absolute nor a supreme value, but he is a creature of God. Thus, his relation to God includes not only a creaturely dependence on God, but also *the human faculty of consciously recognizing this dependence and of collaborating responsibly with God*. This structure of the person also includes his relation to the world. Man belongs to the world, but he is distinguished from other creatures by the ability to follow with full consciousness the truth and goodness that he knows—the ability to have a moral life. *Man can read in the world the order of nature and its finality with respect to himself and his good*. Set amidst this order of things, *man can recognize the normative force based on this order*.[49]

Evoking our previous considerations concerning Wojtyła's interpretation of Vatican II, and rather than announcing what TOB will attempt to accomplish, KD proposes to rediscover an integral view of the human person created in God's image and likeness. This rediscovery will help to delineate what is the proper dominion of man over nature, that lordship in the Lord described theologically by LG 36, which from the philosophical viewpoint, recognizes in man's nature both the source and the boundaries of such lordship: "This consists, among other things, in recognizing and guarding the limits of his dominion over the world, *limits that are fixed by the very nature of the faculties that he has received from the hands of his Creator*."[50]

In Wojtyła's philosophical and theological language, unlike Kant's or Scheler's anthropology, an integral vision of man should acknowledge that what is irreducible in man to the *visible* world is adequately reducible (*re-ducere*) to the worldview of the natural law, wherein the human person has a place of honor due to his rational nature and his supernatural vocation to be a son in the Son. Thus, the cosmological or metaphysical conception of the human person is the necessary *substratum* upon which one bases a more adequate interpretation and explanation of the phenomenological data concerning man's spiritual subjectivity. In this way, a proper understanding of the relationship between person and nature, congruent with natural law, can be offered.

Christian Responsibility for Parenting

KD maintains a view of conjugal love as *subordinated* to the good of the family. Moreover, the document also appeals to the theology of marriage as contained in Vatican II's moral attitude of Christian responsibility. Thus, Wojtyła emphasizes that spouses have the conscious obligation or *responsibility* to transmit life and to raise children *in accordance with the divine plan*. Discernment is not really an option that one could responsibly forgo but rather a moral necessity: "[T]he number of children called into existence *cannot be left to chance*."[51] Instead, KD argues that the number of children called into existence must be *consciously decided* by the spouses with "an attitude of

---

49. KD, 328–29; emphasis added.
50. Ibid., 329; emphasis added.
51. Ibid., 336. See LR, 279.

faith and trust in God," together with "a serene magnanimity and willingness to undergo renunciation and sacrifice."[52]

In so doing, spouses cooperate with the Creator, for "it is necessary to emphasize the special value of a life that takes its origin from the body of the parents, but whose human personality is called into existence by the creative act of God alone."[53] Moreover, their cooperation with the Creator must be informed with the same charity that unites Christ with the church in his loving gift of self, the same charity with which the Divine Persons love each other. GS 48 explicitly explains the union of married people in terms of friendship and gift of self. Based on this idea, KD argues that treating one's spouse as a sheer *bonum utile* "is opposed to the dignity of the person and to conjugal chastity (in that one seeks sexual satisfaction in a way contrary to reason); and it is certainly not in the image of the fruitful union of Christ and the Church, nor in the image of the fully disinterested union of the divine Persons in the heart of the Trinity."[54]

Wojtyła is appealing once again to his interpretation of Vatican II explained in chapter 1, in which the christocentric anthropology of the *imago Dei* is viewed from the ecclesiology of *communio*. In KD, he draws some further implications for conjugal morality. At this point, Wojtyła rejects an unjustified premise of the majority report. They argued that even if there were an active intervention in the conjugal act to render it sterile, this marital act would still be an expression of sacrificial love and gift of self. Against the claim of the majority report according to which "*copula etiam cum interventu est oblativa*," KD argues that "to cause biological changes in the woman that make fertility impossible, which at the same time frees the man of his responsibility in the sexual act, is to do violence to the person of the woman and to transgress against justice."[55] To actively frustrate the purpose of the reproductive faculty is not only to act against a part of the human person from a biological viewpoint, but within a sound anthropology that understands in which sense the natural law is natural, to act in this manner involves, above all, to act against justice, against the rational order of the natural law, against the good of the whole human person, against the union of spouses, and against the Creator.

Contraception

KD explains the argument just enunciated in different steps. First, it clarifies how the sexual act involves not only the *vis generativa* but the whole of the person in his substantial unity. It also entails a very special union of persons based on the sexual difference and the possibility of procreation. The sexual act involves the human body

52. KD, 337.
53. Ibid., 357. The same idea is affirmed in LR, 55.
54. KD, 331.
55. KD, 341. See also LR, 228–29.

and hence, the human person. By its unitive physical gesture, which is essentially a function of the *vis generativa*, one enters into a special personal bond with another person. Such a personal bond is based on "a recognition that the other possesses a value by which one is drawn towards the common union for the sake of the ends proper to human persons."[56] We are not dealing here with just any bond of friendship between persons. We are specifically dealing with *conjugal* friendship between man and woman. For "the love that is expressed through sex, that is through the genital organs, is clearly defined in its genus by the sexuality of the body. *As a consequence of the unity of the person, who is simultaneously body and spirit, the sexuality of the body and therefore the sexuality of the person creates special requirements for the personal love that is marked by sex.*"[57]

KD explains that every sexual act between spouses, by its very rational nature, ought to be an act of *virtuous conjugal and benevolent love*. It should be an act of the reciprocal gift of self and an expression of their parental attitude. Explaining the relationship between these two meanings, KD reiterates the teaching of GS 50: the parental attitude "takes in" conjugal love, as it were, and brings about its maturation in *virtue*.[58] Moreover, KD argues that an active intervention against the *vis generativa* destroys the very nature of the conjugal act *in its personal and interpersonal dimensions*. With such active intervention, the conjugal act *cannot be a sign of virtuous and self-giving conjugal love and of the parental attitude*. Contraceptive intercourse is against rational nature and right reason; it is against the good of the person and the good of the persons involved in the conjugal act: "Active intervention in the structure of the act results in its truncation, which does violence to its value as a sign [of self-gift and parental attitude]."[59] The use of the Pill and the IUD are instances of such active interventions. If contraception were to be accepted, the "woman faces not only inequality but also sexual slavery."[60] Furthermore, KD offers an additional line of thought that is more theological in nature. It appeals to Christ's spousal and fruitful gift of self for the church as normative for conjugal love between spouses. Moreover, it argues that Vatican II "articulates precisely what is required for parental attitude" in the section of LG 11 dedicated to the sacramentality of marriage.[61] It seems that here, Wojtyła is outlining his future project in TOB. Indeed, following KD's directives, TOB offers an adequate anthropology and a sound understanding of the sacramentality of marriage in order to theologically explain HV.

KD also notes that those in favor of contraception are guilty of a *false optimism* regarding human nature. Such an optimism does not take into consideration that,

56. KD, 343.
57. Ibid.; emphasis added.
58. This same thesis also appears in LR, 30.
59. KD, 345. The argument seems to be implicitly referencing *ScG* IV. 122 and LR, 229.
60. KD, 335.
61. Ibid., 342, see n50.

even after redemption, the embers of sin "continue to smolder, and we must *always* reckon with their destructive power. It is necessary to remain on guard, especially where concupiscence and sin ally with the *sarx*, the enemy of spirit."[62] There is a need to overcome this unjustified optimism. Paradoxically, KD notes that this apparent optimism is really grounded in a theological pessimism. According to this pessimistic view, the human person as the subject of disordered tendencies would be *practically incapable* of ordering one's actions. On the other hand, this unjustified optimism is also grounded in a *voluntaristic moral legalism* that "manifests itself in the barely concealed belief that reason is unable to discern what is morally ordered or disordered in marriage."[63]

The proponents of contraception often claim to be pastoral in their approach. However, KD explains it differently. To argue, like these proponents do, that every conjugal act is always an act of self-gift or virtuous love, is naïve and *nonpastoral*: "Contemporary discussions of marital morality do not adequately recognize a point of which *every pastor is aware*, namely, that *the mere fact of entering into marriage does not cure the spouses of their tendency to moral disorder.*"[64] Against this false optimism, there needs to be an emphasis on the cooperation with the grace received from the sacrament. This proposal is a clear development of the conciliar attitude of participation. Such active and conscious participation in the sacrament will mature conjugal love in its being ordered to parenthood, thereby contributing to its virtuous development into a fully human love. It will do so within the sphere of Christian responsibility and the universal call to holiness in charity and imitation of God. Once again, KD takes up Wojtyła's interpretation of Vatican II and foreshadows the exact structure and argument that will be found in TOB.

Periodic Continence

At this point, KD needs to answer a couple of foundational questions: how is the number of children called into existence to be consciously decided by the spouses? What means are they to employ in order to cooperate with God and thus fulfill his will? KD explains that, according to medical science, periodic continence is "sufficiently certain, simple, and low cost so that every family of good will, with adequate

---

62. KD, 335; emphasis added. The implicit reference here seems to be the Council of Trent's Decree on Original Sin: "This holy Synod confesses and perceives that there remains in the baptized concupiscence of an inclination, although this is *left to be wrestled with*, it cannot harm those who do not consent, but *manfully* resist by the grace of Jesus Christ. Nay, indeed, 'he who shall have striven lawfully, shall be crowned' (2 Tim 2:5). This concupiscence, which at times the Apostle calls sin (Rom 6:12–14) the holy Synod declares that the Catholic Church has never understood to be called sin, as truly and properly sin in those born again, but because *it is from sin and inclines to sin*. But if anyone is of the contrary opinion, let him be anathema." DS 1515.

63. KD, 348.

64. Ibid., 346; emphasis added.

instruction, can use it."⁶⁵ Now, periodic continence is a completely different object of choice from contraception. It is not Catholic contraception. Periodic continence "consists in abstaining from sexual relations during the fertile phase, while engaging in these relations at other times according to the norms of conjugal life."⁶⁶ In this case, husband and wife "can fittingly express the parental character of conjugal life and of the love uniting the spouses. This is *entirely the opposite* of the conscious sterilization of the relationship, which, actively deprived of its proper role, cannot be the sexual expression of the love uniting two persons."⁶⁷

However, not every practice of periodic continence is morally right, because a good act can be vitiated by a bad intention. In this way, "the practice of periodic continence for the sake of not transmitting life without sufficient rational motives (for example, an aversion to children, pleasure alone, aesthetic considerations, etc.) bears witness to a disorder within one's psycho-sexual behavior."⁶⁸ The right use of periodic continence requires cooperation with the Creator, as well as the attitudes of faith and self-sacrifice for the common good of the family, society, and the church. For all of that, one needs to grow in virtue, especially in conjugal chastity.⁶⁹ As Wojtyła will express it in his philosophical anthropology, what is needed for the right practice of periodic continence is integration in the person (growth in virtue) and between persons (communion in authentic participation).

KD adds that integration in the person is especially needed on the part of the husband, for whom continence is usually more difficult. Indeed, within conjugal friendship, sexual difference is to be conceived under the light of an equality in dignity between the spouses, a fact that does not deny the greater responsibility of the male towards procreation. Indeed, in this matter, "there is no biological parity between the male and the woman. The just proportion of their common contribution to the regulation of births can only be found, therefore, when the male is able to *integrate* the dynamism of his instinct into the totality of his reason-dominated life, and to express his love by the sexual act in a reflective manner."⁷⁰ This is part of his basic Christian responsibility. If it remains unfulfilled, "the woman would be excessively burdened by sexual life and its consequences, or would simply become—at least to a certain extent—an object which her husband uses to satisfy his lust."⁷¹ Moreover, provided periodic continence is carried out with a good intention, it clearly shows that, some-

---

65. Ibid., 352.

66. Ibid., 353.

67. Ibid.; emphasis added.

68. Ibid., 354. HV 16 will speak of *iustae causae*. John Paul II had also located procreation under the virtue of justice in LR, 245–248. This argument will be expanded in TOB 122:3; 125:3–4.

69. See also LR, 241.

70. KD, 355; emphasis added. For an explanation on integration as growth in virtue, see my *De la experiencia*, 309–66.

71. KD, 355.

times, abstention from the marital act is a greater sign of mature conjugal love and responsibility than a consciously willed marital act. This reality is manifested visibly to married people by celibates, who practice permanent continence out of love. It is not in vain that, "there is a link between inadequate theological appreciation of celibacy and the defense of contraception."[72]

An Important Step Towards TOB

KD constitutes a very important step in the genesis of TOB. It makes evident the advocates of contraception's misunderstanding of the philosophical and theological dimensions of natural law. Thus, the document asks for a metaphysical view of the human person that makes those dimensions complementary. In this sense, KD is requiring what Wojtyła will develop philosophically in AP. This philosophical anthropology has to lay the foundations for a correct interpretation of the natural character of natural law. Moreover, this adequate anthropology needs to be compatible with the biblical revelation about the human person created in God's image. Based on that philosophy and theology of the human body as human, one can approach a close study of revelation and of the sacramentality of marriage, which theologically supports the conclusions outlined by KD in its treatment of the Christian responsibility for parenting.

In this sense, KD suggests TOB's very structural disposition. What is more, it places that same structural order within the conciliar initiation as studied. Indeed, the christocentric anthropology of GS, viewed from the ecclesiology of communion, and the moral attitudes that bring about the moral renewal in the sources proposed by Wojtyła are also latently present in KD. Hence, two steps need to be taken in order to elucidate in a more explicit manner the conciliar framework in which TOB was gestated: we need to analyze Wojtyła's interpretation of HV, and we need to explain synthetically the main coordinates of his philosophical view of the human person, highlighting the elements that will reappear in TOB.

---

72. Ibid., 356. See also Wojtyła, "La verdad de la Encíclica *Humanae Vitae*," 195.

3

Continuity between Vatican II and *Humane Vitae*

Two Structural Points of Continuity

From the summer of 1968 until his election to the papacy, Wojtyła wrote a series of articles directly concerned with an analysis of HV and its continuity with Vatican II. After HV's publication, the proponents of contraception thought that Paul VI had betrayed the novelty and originality of the so-called "spirit of the Second Vatican Council."[1] Wojtyła strongly disagreed with this accusation. Without a doubt, his own participation at Vatican II, as well as his work for its implementation, formed the background of his interpretation of HV in continuity with the previous magisterium.

In this chapter, I want to concentrate on two important points of Wojtyła's interpretation of this continuity, leaving the rest for chapter 12. First, our author argues for a continuity between Vatican II's personalism and HV's integral vision of the human person. Thus, according to Wojtyła, GS's christocentric anthropology, wherein man's substantial unity as well as his personal dignity are seen under the revealed doctrine of being created in God's image, corresponds exactly with HV 7's appeal for an integral view of the human person. Second, our author argues that there is continuity between Vatican II's theology of conjugal love and that of HV. GS's theology of conjugal love is informed by the classical doctrine of the goods of marriage, as it is manifested in GS 48 and 52. In preparation for the exposition of the inseparability principle, HV 8–9 follows this same doctrine. Wojtyła argues that it does so with a peculiar emphasis: concentrating on the laws that are founded upon those goods.

These two points of continuity between Vatican II and HV have a structural import for TOB. The entirety of John Paul's adequate anthropology, contained in the first three chapters of the book, unfolds that integral vision of the human person in exact continuity with GS's christocentric anthropology of man created in God's image. On the other hand, the next two chapters in TOB develop a theology of conjugal love from the viewpoint of the good of the sacrament, as it elevates the goods of offspring and fidelity. Finally, the pope uses all of that background in order to comment on

---

1. For a deep study on HV, see Smith, *Humanae Vitae*.

HV's understanding of the inseparability of the procreative and unitive meaning of the conjugal act, as a doctrine which defends the very integrity of conjugal love and its development in virtue.

Paul VI's Integral Vision of Man

Both Vatican II and HV base their teachings on conjugal love and procreation on an integral view of the human person that is non-reductionistic. Neither conjugal love nor procreation can be properly understood in their full human character apart from a vision of man's substantial unity, and apart from his dignity as a person. Since "the truth about man is at the basis of all the principles of morality,"[2] HV's total vision of man "permeates the whole content and the entire text from beginning to end."[3] As Wojtyła explains in another place, a "comprehensive ontology of marriage, an integral vision of the human being, a vision of man and woman as persons, is what best contributes to a true coordination of the ends of marriage."[4] Obviously, the same applies to HV's teachings on conjugal love: "[T]he place that the encyclical leaves for the psychology of conjugal love—although it does not become absorbed in this aspect—is *the fruit of the integral vision of the human being* that Paul VI has *constantly* before his eyes."[5] Moreover, Paul VI also connects his teachings on procreation with an adequate anthropology that takes into account the human person's *munus*.[6] Echoing GS 61, HV 7 explains that the question concerning procreation can be answered only by taking into account "the whole man [*totum hominem*] and the whole mission [*munus*] to which he has been called ... this [mission] pertains not only to his natural and earthly existence but also to his supernatural and eternal existence." In accordance with Vatican II, Paul VI's integral vision of man is one of *munus* and hence, one of communion. Consequently, without a proper understanding of man's substantial unity, neither procreation nor conjugal love can be understood in their *generically animal but specifically rational traits*.[7]

Yet, despite its importance for understanding conjugal love and procreation, HV does not make an explicit systematic exposition of its adequate anthropology. Wojtyła argues that Paul VI only outlines it, when dealing with the human being as *an acting person*, and when it concentrates on the reciprocal relationship between spouses in

2. Wojtyła, "Anthropological Vision," 732.
3. Ibid., 733.
4. PC, 314.
5. Ibid., 310; emphasis added.
6. See Smith, "The Importance of the Concept of 'Munus.'"
7. "To render judgment about questions that concern the person in the essence of his humanity, and also precisely there where procreation is at stake, that is, in a certain way the reproduction of humanity in every new human being through the cooperation of persons, man and woman, we must again *ascend to the concept of the humanity of man himself*." Wojtyła, "Anthropological Vision," 735; emphasis added.

the marital embrace.[8] Thus, the acts proper to marriage "reveal not only the masculinity and femininity of the acting subjects *but also their personal subjectivity*."[9] The way to unveil that personal subjectivity is to concentrate on the personal acts described by HV. Our "method of anthropological analysis must therefore be in a certain way *a posteriori*; it must be deduced from judgments on human action with this aim in view: to formulate judgments on man himself."[10] This method of *a posteriori* analysis would have to begin by considering that conjugal love pertains to both the *sensible* and the *spiritual* sphere in the human person. To the "make-up" of conjugal love belongs love as a sensible passion, as a spiritual sentiment, and as a rational choice of the free will made possible and conditioned by the judgment of the intellect.[11] Now, since the same man experiences himself as the ultimate subject of the spiritual and the sensible dimensions of the act of conjugal love, following the principle *operari sequitur esse*, one must conclude that the human person is a substantial unity, as it is explained in GS 14.[12]

Based on the spiritual and corporeal actions of man, one can also infer his being an individual substance of a rational nature; one can infer his dignity as a human person.[13] This dignity is natural or innate. It results from his peculiar degree of ontological participation in God as *the* good; it results from the simple fact of being human. Indeed, person is a name that denotes dignity.[14] It is not really a genus, but an *analogous* metaphysical notion that signifies a pure perfection.[15] Divine, angelic, and human persons are not persons in a univocal way: they are not equally perfect. Compare the Divine Persons to any other personal being. Yet, both angels and human beings, despite their different natures, cross a certain threshold of perfection, which only intellectual beings do. Thus, they are rightly and properly called persons.[16] In considering conjugal love and procreation, both GS and HV appeal not only to man's substantial unity, but also to his personal dignity. In so doing, these documents show "the intimate relationship between the ontology of man and his axiology: being and value together must be the hermeneutic principle of man."[17] Even if HV does not often use the noun person or the adjective personalistic, "it is difficult to understand this

---

8. See Wojtyła, "La verdad de la encíclica *Humanae Vitae*," in DA, 188.
9. Wojtyła, "Anthropological Vision," 734; emphasis added.
10. Ibid., 734.
11. See HV 9.
12. See Wojtyła, "Anthropological Vision," 740.
13. See PC, 73–94.
14. See *In I Sent.*, d. 10, q. 1, a. 5; d. 26, q. 1, a. 1.
15. See Millán-Puelles, *Lógica de los Conceptos Metafísicos*, 203–42.
16. See *ST* I, q. 29, a. 1, c.
17. Wojtyła, "Anthropological Vision," 737.

humanism in any other way than as personalistic."[18] Just as in GS, what is eminently human seems equivalent in HV to what is personal.[19]

Man's substantial unity and his being a person are contained in his being created in God's image. Considering Paul VI's integral vision of man from this perspective reveals its full personalistic significance. Indeed, Wojtyła explains that the "consideration of this value [the human being as created in God's image] allows us to understand *better the very being of man as person and gift*."[20] Man's being is understood as person and gift when viewed from the perspective of his being created in God's image, because then one envisions the human person's rational and social nature as healed, elevated, and perfected by sanctifying grace. It should be very evident by now that this whole teaching is at the heart of Wojtyła's interpretation of Vatican II. In its light, the future pope comments on HV, explaining that "this image and likeness concern not only his spiritual nature, by means of which he is constituted a person in his individual unrepeatableness, but also the dimension of relation, that is, the reference to another person inscribed within the interior structure of the person. This dimension reflects in a certain way the Trinitarian mystery of God."[21] In fact, the traditional theology of the *imago Dei* has always looked at these two perspectives: the human person images the one God but also the Trinity.[22]

Wojtyła explicitly declares that Paul VI's "integral vision of man was expressed in the pastoral constitution *Gaudium et Spes* of Vatican Council II, where almost the whole of part 1 *The Church and the Vocation of Man* was dedicated to this issue."[23] Our author's emphasis on the relational aspect of being created in God's image shows that, in his view, Paul VI's integral vision of man is in continuation with GS's christocentric anthropology of the *imago Dei* in its complementary relationship with LG and its ecclesiology of communion. This very connection was the key to envision the moral dimension of man's participation in Christ's threefold *munera*. Applying it to those who are married, this connection is also the key to envision the spouses' common *munus* identified by Paul VI in HV 7. Moreover, the christocentric character of this anthropology is located in GS 22. The mystery of Christ reveals man to man himself in the manifestation of his supreme calling to be a son in the Son. God not only makes the human person aware of this reality, he also empowers him to find himself in the gift of self, modeled after Christ's own spousal gift of self for the church.

Wojtyła asserts, without hesitation, that this same fullness of revelation to the human person about his identity and mission, which was "affirmed by Vatican II *was in the mind of the author of Humanae Vitae when he appealed to an integral vision of*

18. Ibid., 737.
19. See ibid., 738n7.
20. Ibid., 737.
21. Ibid., 738.
22. For an excellent traditional treatment, see Hübscher, *De Imagine Dei in Homine Viatore*.
23. Wojtyła, "Anthropological Vision," 736.

man."²⁴ The Holy Spirit, by imprinting the image of the Son, makes us participants of the mission of the Redeemer. This participation becomes the source whereby the human person can find his fulfillment in charity towards oneself and others in the sincere gift of self. According to Wojtyła, HV 7 speaks of this same reality when it asserts that the spouses seek, by means of their reciprocal gift, a communion of their being, a common *munus* that results in a *communio personarum*, as it is said in GS 12. For this reason, our author clearly holds that "the integral vision of man, to which the author of *Humanae Vitae* appeals from the very beginning of the document, is a vision of faith. It considers in the light of Revelation the full vocation of man."²⁵

Spiritualistic Cartesian Personalisms

Let us come back now to the accusation of the advocates of contraception as was previously mentioned. We need to conclude that the alleged opposition between Vatican II's personalism and HV should be rejected. Actually, the real contrast or opposition is between Vatican II's personalism and that of contraception's proponents. While HV is based on an adequate anthropology of the human person as a substantial unity created in God's image, those who oppose the encyclical letter have a reductionistic and Cartesian view of man utterly incompatible with GS.²⁶ They make one of the aspects of the human person, namely his consciousness, the absolute interpretative key of the *humanum*. And as our author explains, "the mistake of absolutizing an aspect [is] most serious both for anthropology and for ethics."²⁷ According to Wojtyła, this reductionism is a particular temptation for these Cartesian anthropological views, which are not only postmetaphysical but also a-metaphysical. Indeed, to the modern mentality belongs a *"division of a Cartesian type that opposes in man his understanding, his consciousness, and his body."*²⁸ This division leads theologians and philosophers alike "to *examine everything regarding the body as exclusively and solely in the light of somatic processes* that, as the progress of medical science shows, can be directed and *dominated artificially*. It is precisely here, among other things, that the problem of the practice and technique of contraception is situated."²⁹

Cartesian anthropological views tend to identify the human person with consciousness. Then, they oppose "person-consciousness" to "nature," understanding by "nature" what is subpersonal in man, namely, something not ruled by the laws

---

24. Ibid.; emphasis added.

25. Ibid., 750.

26. By Cartesian, I do not necessarily mean only the strict followers of Descartes, but those influenced by his philosophical anthropology. A profound analysis of the influence of Descartes in contemporary philosophy can be found in Malo, *Cartesio e la Posmodernità*.

27. Wojtyła, "Anthropological Vision," 746.

28. Ibid.; emphasis added.

29. Ibid.; emphasis added.

of the spirit but by those of biology and physics. Consequently, "nature" conceived in this manner is no longer something that manifests transparently the intention of the Creator. The natural law is not anymore a rational order and an order of virtues. Rather, nature is now reduced to the *raw material at the complete disposal of one's dominion*. Obviously, all these reductionisms imply a sort of destruction and division of the integrity of the human person, which has enormous consequences for sexual ethics. Rhonheimer rightly calls them a form of spiritualism. By this term, he signifies "an anthropology and ethics in which bodiliness and sensuality are granted *no constitutive moral significance in the context of human actions*; instead, through the dualistic antithesis of person and nature, all human acts are viewed as originally spiritual phenomena."[30] Human acts, inasmuch as they are spiritual, "are only subsequently allowed to express or incarnate bodiliness and sensuality on a plane that is itself subhuman or subpersonal, and indifferent toward such acts; this plane of expressive behavior is a material field for the soul, and lacks any proper moral significance; upon this field its shaping force can be disposed."[31]

Max Scheler's position is a paradigmatic instance of the spiritualism and contemporary Cartesian view just described.[32] It seems that divine providence was preparing Wojtyła to get acquainted with these kinds of anthropological issues, way before HV and its aftermath. Be that as it may, it is unquestionable that much of the following words could be viewed as a criticism of both the German Phenomenologist and the proponents of contraception:

> A being's essence, or nature, determines how free we are to behave with respect to that being, how we should or ought to behave when that being is an object of our activity. *This whole norm-generating aspect disappears when we conceive the person in a totally subjectivistic way as pure consciousness.* In Catholic ethics, including Catholic sexual ethics, we do not accept such a view of the person because *it is extremely one-sided and incompatible with reality*. The human person is not just a consciousness prolific in experiences of various content, but is basically a highly organized being, an individual of a spiritual nature composed into a single whole with the body (hence, a *suppositum humanum*).[33]

In a nutshell, one finds here a fuller explanation of the reductionistic anthropological vision held by most defenders of contraception. Interestingly enough, Wojtyła accuses them of a combined naturalistic and personalistic error. The naturalistic error of this reductionistic view consists in misunderstanding what human nature is all

30. Rhonheimer, *Practical Reason and Natural Law*, 102; emphasis added.

31. Ibid.

32. I have shown that at the heart of Scheler's ethical personalism, there is a rupture between person and nature, and an identification between person and consciousness as the one described above in my *De la experiencia*, 69–134.

33. PC, 286–287; emphasis added.

about. The advocates of contraception end up compartmentalizing, in a materialistic and biologistic way, the sexual urge within the nonspiritual sphere of the human person. This error springs from either ignorance or a complete misunderstanding of the metaphysics of the soul and man's substantial unity.

Lacking those two foundational pillars, they cannot understand the sexual urge as a rational and natural inclination in the human person, even if such an inclination has its roots in the vegetative and sensible realm as well. *The sexual urge in the human person is generically animal but specifically rational.* It is not exactly the same as the sexual urge of a monkey. We are not monkeys with an added spiritual or intellectual soul. Neither are we monkeys with reason and will. By virtue of our rational soul, we are human beings, rational animals. And what makes us generically animals but specifically rational is our very rational soul.[34] Thus, the sexual urge in the human person is from its very origin equipped with the real power to be integrated and become the subject of virtue.

Even if the image of the monkey's sexual urge with an added reason and will illustrates my point in caricaturesque fashion, it successfully conveys how the human sexual urge is conceived by the proponents of contraception. The sexual urge is treated by them unilaterally, without due consideration to its origin in the rational soul, and without due consideration to its real potency to be integrated in the truth about the good. Therefore, the "necessity of sin" is magnified in the sexual sphere without sufficient attention to the possibility of virtue. As a result, this naturalistic position ends up not seeing the specific dignity of conjugal sexual relations between *persons* of the opposite sex.

On the other hand, such a naturalistic compartmentalization of the sexual natural inclination brings with it a personalistic error, which leads to situation ethics. Indeed, from these premises, it follows a unilateral overemphasis on freedom and self-determination, at the expense of nature and truth. The human person is viewed here as an autonomous agent, capable to decide what is good and bad. He lacks due *subordination* to the intentions of the Creator, expressed in one's nature and accessible to one's understanding. Precisely for this reason, Wojtyła explains that this position leads to situation ethics, because the latter "arises when we conceive the person in a totally subjectivistic way as pure consciousness . . . The person then appears neither as a substantial subject (*suppositum*) of conscious and free acts nor as the basis of an objective norm."[35]

---

34. See *ST* I, q. 76, a. 6, ad 1.

35. PC, 286. In Scheler's case, his moral intentionalism is anthropologically rooted in his spiritualism and metaphysically anchored in his actualism *sui generis*, unable of conceiving the human person as a creature that is not pure act.

Conflict Between Personalism and Natural Law?

The spiritualistic Cartesian view of the person transposes the conflict between person, understood as pure spirit (*res cogitans*), and corporeal nature understood as pure matter (*res extensa*), to an alleged conflict between the person and natural law. In so doing, the proponents of contraception make HV's teaching utterly incomprehensible. Indeed, with this distorted understanding of human nature, it is impossible to properly perceive the natural character of natural law. Then, HV's argument in favor of the inseparability of the meanings of the conjugal act cannot be envisioned from the perspective of virtue. Wojtyła explains it with the following words:

> We saw this occur just recently with regard to the encyclical *Humanae Vitae*, when a discussion arose in the press—and not only in the press—concerning *the* extent *to which natural law can serve as a norm or as the basis of a norm for the person*. In this discussion, natural law was taken to mean merely the *biological regularity* we find in people in the area of sexual actualization. *This was said to be natural law*. Authors of various articles and publications spoke out in behalf of such a *misguided concept*, and they in turn imposed upon the Holy Father, and along with him upon the magisterium of the Church, an understanding of natural law that *in no way corresponds to the Church's understanding of it*.[36]

By eliminating the possibility of understanding the natural character of natural law, this reductionistic vision of man is incompatible with the foundations of Christian morality. Additionally, it denies the *intrinsice bonum et malum*. It also marginalizes the scriptures from the categorical realm of an alleged autonomous morality. According to this erroneous view, their a-metaphysical reason does not acknowledge Christ in this categorical realm. He is not recognized as God's *Logos* and Exemplar of Creation, as the foundation for both the metaphysical and biblical basis of Catholic moral theology. As I have been saying throughout the book, I am convinced that one finds here the primordial theological error of the proponents of contraception to which TOB responds from its christocentric anthropology of man created in God's image.

The grain of truth contained in the Cartesian view of nature goes back to the classical distinction between the mode of causality of nature and that of freedom.[37] What merely happens in man is different from what man does voluntarily. However, as we will see in our next chapter, Wojtyła is not willing to concede that everything which merely happens in man is sensible, and not spiritual. What merely happens in man also includes spiritual activations. Moreover, our author also argues that the irreducibility between these two modes of causality is only relative and not absolute. Both modes of causality can be reduced (lead back, *re-ducere*) to the substantial form of the human person. Thus, one can distinguish and unite person and nature within

---

36. Ibid., 183; emphasis added.
37. See *ST* I–II, q. 10, a. 1, ad 1.

the realm of operation (*actus secundus*), without undermining thereby the metaphysical foundations of the natural law.[38] Applying the principle *operari sequitur esse* to this experience, one can infer the substantial unity of the human person, distinguishing here at the level of first act (*actus primus*) between the human person and human nature. In this way, it can be shown that the human being is a person by nature. His nature, unlike the nature of subhuman beings, is a rational or personal nature with a real aptitude and inclination to be completed, perfected, or affirmed by free acts. Only then can one see how natural law corresponds to the human person and makes his dignity shine with the splendor of truth and humility that recognizes the superiority of God within an adequate metaphysical view of the created cosmos.[39]

According to Wojtyła, HV moves within this metaphysical view of the human soul, which is now part of perennial philosophy. For this reason, Paul VI "considers the body *not as an autonomous being, with its own structure and dynamic*, but as a component of the whole man in his personal constitution."[40] In accordance with the anthropology of GS 14 and with LG 36, the respect due to the body and to its procreative functions is then a boundary to man's possibility of dominion.[41] This boundary is not biological but ethical. It is not a matter of artificiality, but a matter of virtue or vice. It is a matter of either fostering the virtues that responsibly perfect conjugal love or of falsifying conjugal love by abandoning it to concupiscence and to the effects of original sin. For this reason, this boundary establishes the borderline between integration and dominion in the Lord (*Dominus*) versus disintegration and slavery to sin.[42] It really draws the line of demarcation between perfected or acquired freedom and the slavish subjugation of one's innate freedom to what is lower in man.[43]

As LG 36 explains, true or perfected freedom is that which subordinates everything lower in man to what is higher. At the same time, this good use of one's natural or innate freedom subordinates itself to the true good. This double subordination is

---

38. I have explained this distinction in greater detail in my *De la experiencia*, 290–308.

39. See PC, 184–85.

40. Wojtyła, "Anthropological Vision," 746; emphasis added.

41. See GS 34, 36; SR, 48–49.

42. See Rom 6:12; 8:21; LG 36; SR, 97–98; AP, 105–88.

43. "These unsurpassable limits of man's dominion over his own body are rooted in the *profound structure of personal being* and stand in relationship to a specific value, that is, the personal value of man. It is absolutely indispensable to put these structures and values into evidence, *if our aim is the interior correctness in the conjugal act that is destined, above all, to realize the communion of persons* (cf. *Humanae Vitae* 8). *It is this that creates the basis for a just criterion in this matter.* Man cannot exercise power over his own body by means of interventions or techniques that, at the same time, compromise his authentic personal dominion over himself and that even, in a certain way, annihilate this dominion. This way of exercising dominion over one's own body and over its functions, although effected with a method elaborated by man's intelligence, is in contrast with the profound and 'global' 'given' that man is himself, namely, a person with dominion over himself and that this dominion over himself enters into the integral definition of freedom." Wojtyła, "Anthropological Vision," 747. Wojtyła refers to chaps. 5–6 of *The Acting Person*, namely, to the entire part dedicated to the integration of the person in action. See ibid., 747n15. See my *De la experiencia*, 335–66.

the proper self-dominion that spouses should have, that integration within the person, which makes possible integration between persons: "The authentic donation, which must express and form the communion of persons, demands dominion over one's self."[44] Thus, by adhering to the natural law, husband and wife are faithful and truthful to God.[45] Thereby, they acknowledge that they are not subjectivistic autonomous arbiters. They acknowledge that, instead, they are ministers or stewards of God's design. The laws of this design are manifested to the human person both in his rational nature and in revelation. In both instances, what is being communicated in different ways is a "word" from the Father's *Logos*, the Son, the image of the invisible God, in whom the metaphysical and biblical foundations of Catholic morality converge.

HV and GS on Conjugal Love

According to Wojtyła, there is strict continuity between the philosophical and the theological anthropology of GS and HV. Moreover, HV's ethical teaching must also be read in accordance with Vatican II's intellectual formation and the attitudes therein implied: "We need to look at the encyclical *Humanae Vitae* according to that consciousness of the Church which the Second Vatican Council has formed."[46] Note the expression "consciousness of the Church" formed by Vatican II. It refers exactly to that understanding of the sources of revelation studied in chapter 1. Additionally, our author notes that GS's theological exploration on conjugal love "forms a kind of *background* for the subsequent teaching of Paul VI in his Encyclical *Humanae Vitae*, a background that the Holy Father *has before his eyes and to which he appeals in key elements*."[47]

In which sense does GS's doctrine on conjugal love offer a kind of background for HV? Having discussed the church's task in today's world, GS deals with some urgent problems, amongst which the promotion of the dignity of marriage and the family ranks first. Wojtyła is referring to this section of the document, which corresponds to paragraph numbers 47 to 52. For now, I would like to concentrate on two brief but very important sections from GS 48 and 52. In my view, these texts are two keys that further unlock our author's conciliar interpretation of HV: "God Himself is the Author of marriage. He has endowed marriage with various goods and ends."[48] Moreover, "Christians . . . should *actively promote the goods of marriage* and the family, both by the examples of their own lives and by cooperation with other men of good

---

44. Wojtyła, "Anthropological Vision," 747–48.

45. See HV 13; Wojtyła, "Anthropological Vision," 750.

46. Wojtyła, "Introducción a la Encíclica *Humanae Vitae*," 202.

47. PC, 302; emphasis added. The same point is also made very clear in Wojtyła, *Fruitful and Responsible Love*, 14–18; Wojtyła, "La verdad de la Encíclica *Humanae Vitae*," 187.

48. I have altered the translation in view of the original Latin: "Ipse vero Deus est auctor matromonii, variis bonis ac finibus praediti." GS 48.

will."⁴⁹ Vatican II footnotes Augustine, Thomas Aquinas, and *Casti Connubi* in the very first sentence from GS 48 to indicate which goods and ends are to be understood here. Hence, there is no doubt that GS refers to the goods of the offspring, fidelity, and the sacrament of marriage. These goods are ends as well, hence the paraenesis to actively promote them found in GS 52.

Now, let us read HV in light of the principle of integration developed by Wojtyła.⁵⁰ According to this principle, one should be able to reread Paul VI's document in light of the same doctrine that structured *Casti Connubi*, that is, the doctrine concerning the goods of marriage. Doing so provides the necessary background to understand why TOB takes in this same theme and develops it as an argument grounded in Vatican II.

The doctrine of the goods of marriage reappears without any explicit reference in HV 8–9. Following the same order as GS 48–49, HV 8 presents the scheme of the goods of marriage as a preparation to speak about the characteristics of conjugal love in HV 9, where this same scheme appears latently once again.⁵¹ HV 8 begins explaining the origin of conjugal love as instituted by God himself. Then, the document makes the following statement:

> As a consequence, husband and wife, through that mutual gift of themselves, which is specific and exclusive to them alone, develop that union of two persons in which they perfect one another [*bonum fidei*], cooperating with God in the generation and rearing of new lives [*bonum prolis*]. The marriage of those who have been baptized is, in addition, invested with the dignity of a sacramental sign of grace [*bonum sacramenti*], for it represents the union of Christ and His Church.⁵²

Wojtyła notices this same structure and explains that while GS concentrates more on the goods of marriage, HV looks at the obligations founded upon those goods.⁵³ Hence, the latter ought to be interpreted as a continuation of the former.⁵⁴ The goods of matrimony are goods in the first perfection of marriage. But they are also goods and ends as a second perfection of matrimony. Thus, HV's emphasis on obligations

---

49. "Christifideles ... bona matrimonii et familiae, tum propriae vitae testimonio tum concordi actione cum hominibus bonae voluntatis, diligenter promoveant." Ibid., 52; see also Wojtyła, *Fruitful and Responsible Love*, 32–33.

50. See SR, 40–41.

51. Other commentators, like Janet Smith, have also seen this internal logic in HV 8–9. See Smith, *Humanae Vitae*, 314–15.

52. HV 8.

53. See PC, 302.

54. John Paul II will similarly follow HV's way of interpreting the traditional teaching of the goods of marriage in FC. In this post-synodal exhortation, the *bonum fidei* is seen as the formation of the community of persons, thanks to virtuous conjugal love. The *bonum prolis* is viewed as service to life. And the *bonum sacramenti* is understood as the healing and elevation of marriage, thanks to supernatural grace as well as the origin of its participation in the mission of the Church. See García de Haro, *Marriage and the Family*, 351.

is based on the fact that "the ends [of marriage] established by God are, precisely, the goods promised by him; and he has established his laws in their service, as the active intimate principle and external guide for the successful attainment of those very ends."[55] For this reason, the ends of matrimony correspond to its goods. Conjugal moral laws find their source in these same goods. A true or perfect marriage is the one that conforms to God's eternal plan as the latter is abbreviated, as it were, in the *tria bona*. In this plan, the Exemplar is none other than the Father's Logos, the Son. In him, the eternal law—ultimate source of every moral law—was promulgated from all times.[56] In him, this eternal plan has been revealed to us, especially in his sacrificial and fruitful spousal gift of self for the church.[57]

HV 9 unfolds GS 49's teachings on conjugal love.[58] The good of fidelity is contained there as the conjugal love promised at the marriage celebration. This specific kind of love includes a peculiar *communion* of persons affected by the parenting *munus*, by the possibility of procreation and the mutual belonging resulting thereof. Thus, HV 9 explains that conjugal love *is* and *ought to be* human, total, faithful, and fruitful. *Conjugal love is and ought to be human*. Wojtyła interprets this characteristic, saying that it "proclaims the requirement of jointly *striving for the human perfection* that such love entails."[59] Keeping the metaphysics of the soul in mind, we can comprehend what this *human perfection* is all about. What is generically animal in conjugal love is also specifically rational. The physiological and the sensible (or passionate) dimensions of conjugal love are to be integrated into virtuous benevolent love as they truly have an aptness or potency for such an integration. Thus, conjugal love is inclined from its origin to become an integrated love, in which the sensible and sensual dimensions are subordinated to the spiritual. Moreover, the attitude of human identity already points to an ulterior perfection of conjugal love. For conjugal love to be fully human, it needs to be perfected by conjugal charity, by a real conformation to Christ's spousal gift of self for the church.

Conjugal love is and ought to be total. It constitutes a special form of friendship which requires the gift of self as a norm for action. That marriage is one specific kind of friendship, namely, conjugal friendship, is really the explicit teaching of GS 49. It is a very special friendship, because the gift of one's love within marriage is such a radical and serious gift that it entails the gift of one's entire life until the death of one of the spouses. Thus, Thomas argues that marriage is the maximum expression of human friendship.[60] For this same reason, Wojtyła explains that conjugal love implies sharing,

55. Ibid., 118–19; emphasis added.
56. See *ST* I–II, q. 91, a. 1, ad 2.
57. See Col 1:26; Rom 16:25; Eph 3:9, 5:25; Heb 1:1–3; John 14:6.
58. See García de Haro, *Marriage and the Family*, 123.
59. PC, 305; emphasis added.
60. See *ScG* III.123. For a superb exposition of the essence of friendship, see Ramírez, *De Caritate*, 22–65. For a good study on marriage in Aquinas, see Mortensen, *The Relation of the Juridical and the Sacramental in Matrimony*.

without egoism, one's material and *spiritual* possessions. "These are the requirements that true friendship places upon human beings, taking into consideration that *special form of friendship that occurs in marriage,* the special measure of the giving of self that is contained and realized in marriage, and that should, of course, be properly reciprocated."[61]

Conjugal love is and ought to be faithful. It is exclusive and indissoluble. Indeed, marriage is a form of friendship that establishes a bond that yokes together two persons of the opposite sex in a lifelong union. Thus, Wojtyła explains that "these traits [fidelity and exclusivity] are intimately connected with the previously mentioned trait of total love and its personalistic interpretation."[62] In other words, the exclusivity and indissolubility of marriage is better explained by the radical gift of self inherent in conjugal friendship, as a communion made possible by the sharing in the parental *munus*.

We come from the *bonum fidei*, described in the previous characteristics of conjugal love, to the *bonum prolis*. *Conjugal love is and ought to be fruitful.* Conjugal love ought to be open and willing to collaborate with the Creator in the transmission and education of human life. But this collaboration cannot be fully accomplished without the parents' testimony of mutual love. Parenting is a *munus* that perfects the communion characteristic of conjugal love. Thus, Wojtyła argues that procreation is so essential to matrimony that "it is *impossible* to maintain that a man and a woman (except in cases of acquired or innate sterility) are joined in matrimony *primarily* for the sake of mutually complementing or reciprocally supplementing one another (*mutuum adiutorium*)."[63] Wojtyła is clear and strong in holding this position: "[T]his would not be in keeping with the plan of the Creator either in order of nature and in the light of reason or in the order of grace and in the light of revelation."[64] Based on GS 50–51, our author argues that parenthood preserves conjugal love, so that it is free from its major enemies. Paul VI confirms the same core truth in HV 21. Responsible parenthood "fosters in husband and wife thoughtfulness and loving consideration for one another. It helps them to repel inordinate self-love, which is the opposite of charity. It arouses in them a consciousness of their responsibilities. And finally, it confers upon parents a deeper and more effective influence in the education of children."[65] Transmitting and educating human life frees conjugal love from egoism and utilitarianism. Thus, parenthood brings conjugal love to its integration or maturation in virtue. "Conjugal love is fulfilled by parenthood."[66] That is why, "following the same logic which is the logic of human conscience and Christian faith as well, *we accept the responsibility for*

---

61. PC, 305; emphasis added.
62. Ibid.
63. Ibid., 291; emphasis added.
64. Ibid.
65. HV 21.
66. Wojtyła, *Fruitful and Responsible Love*, 23.

parenthood as one of the elements, or rather as the constituting element of responsibility for love, for its conjugal shape and sense."[67] As we will see in chapter 12, this connection between the responsibility for parenthood and for conjugal love will be the bedrock that helps John Paul expose the moral evil of contraception.

All of these considerations bring us to the *bonum sacramenti*. According to Wojtyła, HV bears in itself the stamp of the Gospel. There, Paul VI offers a reflection founded on the natural law, but also enriched by divine revelation.[68] The attitudes inferred from Vatican II in light of the sacramentality of marriage as explained in LG 11 converge with the following passage from HV:

> [B]y the sacrament of marriage spouses are strengthened and, as it were, *consecrated* so that they might faithfully fulfill their duties [*munia*], so that they might bring their vocation to its perfect end and so that, as befits them, they might openly offer the world a *Christian witness*. To them the Lord entrusts [*committit*] the mission [*munus*] of making manifest to men the holiness and indeed sweetness of the law that unites their mutual love and generous service closely to the love of God, the author of human life ... Therefore, let the spouses willingly take up the labors that have been assigned [*destinatos*] to them, strengthened both by faith and by hope, which do not disappoint: because the charity of God is poured into our hearts through the Holy Spirit given to us ... It is by this way of life that spouses will be able to *advance toward perfection in their married life*.[69]

Conferring a specific grace, the sacrament of marriage *consecrates* the spouses to a particular exercise of their priestly mission (*munus*).[70] Its fulfillment implies a *Christian witness* informed by the theological virtues, a witness to which spouses have been predestined and called in Christ.[71] Consequently, one could also see in HV a synthesis of the moral attitudes that, according to Wojtyła, are required by Vatican II for married couples. The *mission* and the *testimony* of the spouses is based on their *participation* in the mission of Christ, thanks to the work of the Holy Spirit in the sacraments, especially that of matrimony. Hence, the moral law that unites the mutual love and generous service of the spouses to the love of God as the Author of human

---

67. Ibid., 24; emphasis added.
68. See HV 4; PC, 297.
69. HV 25; emphasis added. This passage will be quoted explictly in TOB 126:1.
70. See Wojtyła, *Fruitful and Responsible Love*, 22–23.
71. See Rom 8:30. One should note that HV is shorter and less descriptive than GS on this matter. Wojtyła also notes it. However, instead of opposition, one should see here complementarity: "In fact, the exposition of *Gaudium et Spes* on the subject of conjugal love (§ 49) and in turn on the fruitfulness of marriage (§ 50) is even more extensive than that of the encyclical *Humanae Vitae*. It also seems more analytical, while the encyclical treats the subject of conjugal life in a more synthetical way. The pastoral constitution uses a more descriptive method stressing the Christological and sacramental aspect of marriage and enriching the text with many parenthetical injunctions. It contains as it were the whole of Christian pedagogy and ethics." Wojtyła, *Fruitful and Responsible Love*, 15–16.

life (with whom they collaborate in the transmission and education of human life) is placed within the sphere of *Christian responsibility* as explained in GS 48.[72] Due to the sacramentality of marriage as a cause of grace and as a sign, spouses are to make present in a visible manner Christ's spousal charity and self-gift for the church by being just and faithful to their spousal love, and by their generous fruitfulness. This rendering visible Christ's spousal charity and self-gift for the church is the *prophetic testimony* that results from the *participation* of the spouses in Christ's priestly *munus* "through the sacraments and the exercise of virtues."[73] In turn, this testimony also implies sharing in his kingly mission, that is, it also implies the true freedom of those who reign with Christ by serving him, living out the precepts of charity.[74]

The Need for a Philosophical Clarification

Wojtyła's interpretation of HV has evidenced the need for a sound and adequate anthropology, wherein the biblical and metaphysical dimensions of conjugal morality are harmonized. From the philosophical viewpoint, there needs to be an elucidation of man's rational mode of being and of his substantial unity. Such a clarification has to take into consideration the human person's consciousness without reducing the whole of the person to this one aspect of his personality. Moreover, it needs to rediscover more of the metaphysical view of human nature. Without this philosophical clarification, the human phenomena of conjugal love and procreation cannot be properly understood. In short, Wojtyła's interpretation of HV manifests the need for a philosophical clarification against the proponents of contraception and their Cartesian personalism, so as to avoid their opposition between personalism and natural law. Moreover, this philosophical inquiry on the integral vision of man is also essential to properly understand the theology of the goods of marriage. I will try to show in the next chapter that AP offers such an integral view of the human person.

---

72. See ibid., 18–19.
73. LG 11. See SR, 97.
74. See LG 36; SR, 97–98.

4

Anthropology of Love

Proper Context

Wojtyła published the first edition of AP in 1969. He had been working on this book for a long time. Its remote origins could be traced back to 1949, to a series of talks about the essence of man, compiled in 1951 as a typescript, but not released for publication by John Paul II until 1999.[1] Without a doubt, AP is a much deeper and well thought-out book. It really is Wojtyła's most mature philosophical work. However, in my opinion, insufficient attention has been paid to the fact that AP's final redaction had been forged during the time that spanned from Wojtyła's direct involvement in Vatican II to the publication of HV. This chapter will concentrate precisely on this very point.

At Vatican II, Wojtyła not only participated as the bishop from Kraków on many of the documents, he was also part of the commission that worked directly on the redaction of GS.[2] As we know from our first chapter, Wojtyła had a very profound grasp of Vatican II. Many of the Council's insights had a great deal of philosophical implications, which will make their way into AP. For this reason, I think that the conciliar origins of AP should be placed in the preparatory stages of Vatican II, in the *vota et consilia*. Therein, Wojtyła clearly recommended distinguishing the Christian view of the human person from other personalisms whose vision of man is incompatible with the faith. To accomplish such a discernment, Wojtyła offered some non-negotiable truths from perennial philosophy: (1) man's substantial unity; (2) the spirituality

---

1. See Wojtyła, *Rozważania*. After returning from his graduate studies in Rome, during his second pastoral assignment, in 1949, Wojtyła founded a group of young people to study Thomas's *Summa* (see Boniecki, *Kalendarium*, 123). This book, dedicated to the essence of man, was the fruit of that group and of a series of talks delivered at San Florian's Parish (see ibid., 124). However, the book was completed during the time in which Wojtyła was working on his *Habilitationschrift* on Max Scheler (see ibid., 130–31). As important as this work is to properly understand AP, it is not well known. Partly, this is due to the fact that it was not until 1999 that Wojtyła released the manuscript to the publishing house. To my knowledge, there is no English translation of this work. I have had the opportunity to study it closely, and to evaluate its impact in AP in my *De la experiencia*, 201–58, 399–407.

2. For the text of Wojtyła's interventions at Vatican II, and a good commentary on them, see Skrzypczak, *Karol Wojtyła al Concilio Vaticano II*. For the typed conversations of the meetings of the commission that Wojtyła was part of in the redaction of GS, see González, *El Vaticano II en Taquigrafía*.

and immortality of his soul, and (3) his place of honor within the created cosmos by virtue of his rational mode of being (*esse*). This is how he put it:

> Man is a composed being. Through his body he is part of the material world. Nevertheless, through his spiritual and immortal soul he is distinguished from such a world. If this distinction comes from his soul, then it is a distinction that comes from his being [*esse*], because the soul is the form of the body [NB. Wojtyła is appealing here to the well-known Thomistic principle, *forma dat esse*]. The human body, due to its substantial unity with the spiritual soul, is higher than other bodies in the world. By means of the future resurrection, it seems that the body can participate, in some way, in the immortality of its soul. All of this, partially known through the natural light of reason but fully known by the light of revelation, demands a distinction between man as a person and the other visible beings in this world; the latter are not personal beings.[3]

Many of the themes suggested here were incorporated in GS 12–22.[4] Moreover, Wojtyła began to redact AP's actual text during Vatican II's working sessions. Initially, he wanted to offer an integral vision of man rooted in experience and in the perennial metaphysical truths about the human person. Such a view would serve as a philosophical support to GS's christocentric anthropology.[5] However, as Wojtyła began to work on the advisory commission to Paul VI, AP's scope began to be more and more related with HV, and its appeal for an integral vision of man. This is the time when he composed KD. As we know, this last document also expressed multifaceted concerns on the need to offer a vision of the human person to properly understand the philosophical and theological dimensions of the natural law. AP attempts to offer such a view. Thus, it disputes the identification between person and consciousness; it defends the substantiality of the human person; it reconciles the notions of person and nature, and those of person and natural law, and it demonstrates the spirituality of man's soul together with his substantial unity. Moreover, Wojtyła was very involved in the subsequent debate concerning HV, as we studied in our previous chapter. Therein, we saw the constant appeal to an integral vision of the human person in order to properly understand natural law, procreation, conjugal love, etc. This seems to be the *proper context* wherein to place AP. This context, often not taken into account by Wojtyła's commentators,[6] provides some fundamental interpretative keys for AP, which I would like to unveil based on the basic metaphysical principle that animates the whole of the book.

3. ACV, 741.
4. See PC, 220.
5. See Weigel, *Witness to Hope*, 168–69; Smith, "The Kraków Document," 367.
6. One paradigmatic example of this error is found in the work of Heaney, who argues that Wojtyła's phenomenological views on the unity of the human person in AP are incompatible with the philosophy of Thomas Aquinas. See Heaney, *The Concept of the Unity of the Person*.

Operari Sequitur Esse

Commentators of Wojtyła's philosophy dispute about the metaphysical import of AP. However, the best way to resolve that dispute is to take the words of our author seriously. In a letter to Henri De Lubac, Wojtyła clarifies that AP was dedicated to the *metaphysical* sense and mystery of the human person:

> I devote my very rare free moments to a work that is close to my heart and *devoted to the metaphysical sense and mystery of the person*. It seems to me that the debate today is being played on that level. The evil of our times consists in the first place in a kind of degradation, indeed in a pulverization, of the fundamental uniqueness of each human person. This evil is even *much more of the metaphysical order than of the moral order*. To this disintegration, planned at times by atheistic ideologies, we must oppose, rather than sterile polemics, a kind of "recapitulation" of the inviolable mystery of the person.[7]

True to his self-evaluation of AP, Wojtyła centers his entire book within the Thomistic and metaphysical principle *operari sequitur esse*: "In its basic conception, the *whole* of *The Acting Person* is grounded on the premise that *operari sequitur esse*: the act of personal existence has its direct consequences in the activity of the person (i.e., in action). And so action, in turn, is the basis for disclosing and understanding the person."[8] The *whole* and not only part of the book is grounded on this metaphysical principle. Allow me to show exactly how this is the case. In this way, what Wojtyła understands in AP by the integral vision of the human person will be better disclosed. This will also provide an opportunity to explain the title of the present chapter.

As AP unfolds, Wojtyła looks at different *aspects* of the experience of human action, which in turn reveal different *aspects* of man's personal mode of being. As he progresses, each aspect presupposes the ones developed before. For this reason, Wojtyła says that it is important not to reduce the human person to any one of those aspects: "From the particular moments or *aspects of experience* we have to pass to the whole and from the particular moments or *aspects of man* as the subject of experience to *the integral conception of man*."[9] Wojtyła's integral vision of man is a non-reductionistic view of the human person that is whole or complete, and that is based on man's experience of being perfected through his good actions. Indeed, Wojtyła's anthropology results from analyzing the experience of *ethical* actions. Yet, he notes, the ethical dimension of these actions is like a common factor left outside of the equation in order to simplify it.

> As to the position of the relationship of anthropology and ethics in this approach it may be formulated—by analogy to operations used in algebra—as

---

7. Wojtyła, "Letter to Henri De Lubac," 171–72; emphasis added.
8. PC, 260n6.
9. AP, 79. Translation altered. For this particular quote, see OC, 210.

> placing a term before brackets. We place outside brackets those factors of an algebraic expression which in one way or another are common to all the terms of the expression, that is, which are somehow common to everything that remains within the brackets. The aim is to simplify subsequent operations and not to reject what is withdrawn or sever the relations of what is outside to what remains in brackets. On the contrary, the operation underlines and enhances the significance of the factor isolated from the expression.[10]

Although he mentions brackets or parentheses, and placing the reality of the person and his action into those brackets, Wojtyła is not talking about Husserl and his *epoché* here.[11] To fully grasp Wojtyła's point, we need to go back not to phenomenology, but to our algebra studies in high school. As we recall, the equation $4x + 4y = 8$ could also be expressed as $4(x+y=2)$. The equation is thus simplified. As a consequence, the number four stands out to a greater extent. Something similar happens in AP. Instead of the number four, what is factored out of the parenthesis is the ethical dimension present both in human action and in the human person. If we were to express it in a sort of equation, it would look like this: ethical dimension (action + person). To be sure, this factoring out simplifies our study of human action and the person. But it does not deny that the human person is naturally an ethical being, or that every free human act is morally relevant in its execution. On the contrary, it ends up underlining and enhancing the most important element that *ethically perfects a human being*, namely, *genuine love*.

Wojtyła clearly affirms that love is the most important ethical dimension for both human action and for the human person: "[L]ove is the fullest realization of the possibilities inherent in man. The potential inherent in the person is most fully actualized through love. The person finds in love the greatest possible fullness of being, of objective existence."[12] For this reason, in AP, what is really factored out of the parenthesis is love as the ethical dimension that fully perfects the human person. Now, let us remember that, as Wojtyła just said, "the operation underlines and enhances the significance of the factor isolated from the expression."[13] Like the number four in our example, love should now stand out to a greater extent. Therefore, what this "pseudo-mathematical operation" conveys is quite profound: Wojtyła's philosophical anthropology is in reality *an anthropology of (genuine) love*.

This last conclusion justifies the title for this chapter. It is also central to understanding Wojtyła's integral vision of the human person. The five cumulative aspects which comprise that integral vision are consciousness, efficacy, transcendence, integration, and participation. In every one of them, the structural metaphysical principle

---

10. AP, 13.

11. Wojtyła argues that, although the Husserlian method could be fruitful in some areas of philosophy, it is inadequate for philosophical anthropology itself. See PC, 226.

12. LR, 82.

13. AP, 13.

is *operari sequitur esse*. Additionally, I am interested in showing that, in every single aspect of Wojtyła's anthropology of (genuine) love, we can also find a topic of contention with contraception's proponents. For clarity's sake, I will now offer a brief overview. The remainder of the present chapter will explain each aspect in more detail.

The first aspect of Wojtyła's integral anthropology looks at the experience of conscious acting. This experience is part of the human *operari* that reveals a certain facet of his *esse*. More concretely, it reveals the personal mode of consciousness in its proper ontological status. Additionally, this revelation implicitly responds to the advocates of contraception's identification between person and consciousness as the psychological subject of diverse lived experiences.

The second aspect of Wojtyła's integral vision of the human person is that of efficacy. It looks at the experience of causing an action, of being its efficient cause. That experience is the *operari* that reveals man's substantiality. Here, Wojtyła introduces a very important discussion about the classical definition of the human person as "an individual substance of a rational nature."[14] Moreover, concentrating on the relationship between person and nature, he looks at this definition at the levels of both first and second act. Thus, this whole aspect implicitly contends with the advocates of contraception's a-metaphysical understanding of human nature as that which is subpersonal and nonspiritual.

Now, the rational nature of the individual substance that is man is the object of study in the next three aspects. Indeed, the aspect of *transcendence* discloses that rational nature from a very peculiar viewpoint. It looks at the experience of acting freely. Freedom is understood here both as innate freedom (self-determination), and as acquired or perfected freedom (self-fulfillment). That whole experience of acting freely in both ways is the *operari* that reveals the spirituality of the soul, and thus of the human person. This entire section on transcendence is not only a refutation of materialism, or a philosophical defense of that participation in the *munus regalis* outlined in Wojtyła's interpretation of Vatican II, but also an implicit answer to the proponents of contraception's Kantian views on autonomy mentioned before.

The aspect of *integration* looks at the experience of being acted upon freely, of how one is the recipient of one's own free action, something that happens, for instance, in the formation of virtues. Thus, according to Wojtyła, the experience of being acted upon freely is the *operari* that reveals man's substantial unity. This whole aspect implicitly disputes with the proponents of contraception at different levels. It clearly responds to their deficient understanding of the unity of the human person. But it also disputes their naturalistic view of human inclinations, such as the one to procreation. Wojtyła offers the basis herein to refute their lack of understanding of human phenomena such as conjugal love or procreation in their human dimension, that is to say, as phenomena that are generically animal but specifically rational.

---

14. *ST* I, q. 29, a. 1, c.

Finally, the aspect of *participation* or integration between persons was added to AP as an appendix. It is certainly only an outline, not fully developed. Yet, it must be emphasized that this final aspect presupposes all of the others. It transports all of them to the realm of *intersubjectivity*. The aspect of participation looks at the experience of acting together with others. This experience is the *operari* that discloses the social nature inscribed and included in our rational mode of being. This entire section builds upon the anthropological import of the commandment to love one's neighbor, and upon Aristotle's understanding of friendship. Both elements allow Wojtyła to distinguish, in his anthropology of love, what are the attitudes that foster true and authentic participation, namely, that participation in which the human person finds his ethical fulfillment. Thus, in light of the conciliar framework, this section is a philosophical foundation of participating in the same *munus*. It philosophically supports what is theologically understood as the *communio personarum*. In this sense, against the advocates of contraception, this appendix offers a sketch of the essential principles for true and authentic communion among persons, including for persons who are married.

Conscious Acting and Consciousness

The conciliar framework is the proper context wherein to interpret AP. It reveals the tremendous value of Wojtyła's analysis of the human experience of conscious acting. An important philosophical dialogue takes place in this terrain, which has vast anthropological and ethical consequences. Contraception's advocates reduce the human person to consciousness.[15] They misunderstand the experience of conscious acting. Thus, they err in their explanation of consciousness' ontological status, making of consciousness the absolute interpretative key of the *humanum*. Consequently, Wojtyła catalogues their position as a form of spiritualistic Cartesian personalism,[16] which is highly problematic for Catholic sexual ethics.[17] This Cartesian personalism denies both the substantiality of the human person and the role of human nature as the basis of moral norms. As a result, it creates an alleged conflict between the notions of person and natural law, a conflict further used to critique the magisterium in general and Paul VI's HV in particular.[18]

Additionally, Wojtyła's philosophical analysis of the human experience of conscious acting will be essential to comprehend TOB's approach to the lived experience of phenomena accounted for in the scriptures, such as the experience of original solitude, the awareness of the spousal meaning of the body, the experience of shame, the awareness of the absence of shame in the experience of original innocence, etc. Since I

15. See KD, 326.
16. See Wojtyła, "Anthropological Vision," 746.
17. See PC, 286–87.
18. See ibid., 183.

have dealt with the topic of Wojtyła's theory of consciousness in other places, allow me to concentrate on a different dimension of this same question, that is, on a new formal aspect of this same subject matter.[19] I am now focusing on the double role played by Wojtyła's understanding of consciousness' ontological status and of consciousness' two functions. On the one hand, this understanding refutes the position of the proponents of contraception while, on the other, it provides for a solid basis to understand John Paul II's theology of the original experiences.

Adequate Ontological Status

As one is, so one acts. For this reason, one's acting also reveals one's being. Consequently, Wojtyła proposes to reflect on conscious acting in *voluntary action* in order to reveal the mode of being conscious proper to the human person. Wojtyła thinks that his theory of consciousness is latent in Thomas's understanding of the *actus humanus*. Indeed, the experience "acting consciously" refers to our freedom. However, it also includes our intellect. We can act freely precisely *because* we are capable of knowing the very essence or formula (*ratio*) of things. For this reason, we can judge different options as best under a certain aspect. This capacity for judgment makes freedom possible. It creates the necessary "space for choice," that is, for the will to remove the impediment between two judgments which in a way oppose each other: Option A is the best under this one aspect, and option B is the best under this other aspect.

The will always follows the last judgment of practical reason. But it is the will's choice that makes the judgment of practical reason inform that very choice *as last*. Thus, Thomas Aquinas teaches that freedom is rooted in the intellect.[20] It makes free choice possible. This fact is quite important for AP. Wojtyła argues there that the presence of the intellect in the will at the moment of voluntary action accounts for our conscious acting. Moreover, this very presence of the intellect also accounts for our consciousness of acting, that is, for the perception or experiential awareness (*notitia experimentalis*) concomitant to that act of the intellect that informs our choice.

---

19. I have already mentioned my treatment of consciousness under the formal aspect of its Thomistic foundations in "Karol Wojtyła's Thomistic Understanding of Consciousness." For the study of consciousness under the formal aspect of its role in Wojtyła's integral view of the human person, see my *De la experiencia*, 259–308. For the reasons described in these two studies, I would somewhat qualify Petri's opinion. He suggests that Wojtyła's theory of consciousness complements the objective ontology of Thomism. See Petri, *Aquinas*, 4–6. I would add that Wojtyła's theory of consciousness is *not* a supplement to Saint Thomas that comes from Scheler's personalism. Rather, its origins are also in Thomas Aquinas himself. Consequently, I disagree with Petri when he says that according to Wojtyła, "Aquinas's presuppositions were not suitable for a major discussion of human experience and consciousness." Ibid., 6. See also ibid., 115, 194. I also disagree with his final conclusions: "Aquinas did not offer a view of the experience of human consciousness." Ibid., 311.

20. See *De Veritate*, q. 24, a. 2, c. For an excellent treatment of this topic, see Bergamino, *La razionalità della libertà della scelta*.

To unveil the adequate ontological status of human consciousness, Wojtyła opposes the well-known thesis that consciousness is intentional. This statement may have a weird ring to it for someone familiar with phenomenology. However, Wojtyła does not deny the fact that consciousness is always consciousness of something. He would agree with phenomenologists on that point. But Wojtyła wants to adopt a more adequate understanding of act and action, a more metaphysical view. He argues that it is necessary "to adopt a different dynamic concept of the act," a different notion of act from the one present in phenomenology and closer to "the concept associated with the Aristotelian tradition."[21] Consequently, Wojtyła continues, we also need "a different concept of intentionality. We thus regard as *acts in the strict sense of the word only the manifestations of the real powers of the person*."[22] Hence, consciousness is not intentional in the sense that it does not have the intentionality of the power or faculty of the intellect.[23] Consciousness is not the full actualization of a power of the soul. Therefore, although we use the expression, it is technically incorrect to speak about acts of consciousness. When I intellectually know something reaching into its essence, concomitantly, I am aware of the object whose essence or meaning is being known. I am also aware of the act whereby I am knowing this object. And I am also aware of myself as the one doing the knowing. Consciousness is that being aware of myself, the act, and the object, which accompanies my intellectual knowledge. But consciousness does not have the capacity or power of the intellect to penetrate into the essences of things, conferring to them *intentional* or mental being.[24] For this reason, Wojtyła explains that "consciousness mirrors human actions in its own peculiar manner—the reflection intrinsically belongs to it—but *does not cognitively objectivize* either the actions or the person who performs them, or even the whole universe of the person, which in one way or another is connected with man's being and acting."[25]

Hence, strictly speaking, consciousness is not an act. It can neither be a faculty nor the proximate or the remote subject of an action. Thus, the correct understanding of conscious acting shows that the advocates of contraception, who in identifying person and consciousness reject thereby the substantial unity of man, incur the well-known fallacy *pars pro toto*. Consciousness is a dimension of our acts of knowledge. But it is neither a faculty of the human person nor the person himself. Consciousness is neither a subject nor a substance. Moreover, it belongs in the accidental order. An adequate comprehension of consciousness reveals it simply as a kind of *cum-scientia* that is concomitant to human knowledge. Placing consciousness in this accidental order, we are now able to adopt an experiential view of the human person that takes into account internal and external experience without prejudice to the substantial

21. AP, 304n16.
22. Ibid.; emphasis added.
23. See ibid., 33–34.
24. See ibid., 44.
25. Ibid., 35; emphasis added.

unity of man. Furthermore, Wojtyła can now develop what I would call his "realistic semantics." The main aspects of these semantics are found in the following text:

> [T]he acts of consciousness as well as their resultant are obviously related to everything that *lies beyond them* . . . This relation is established by means of the consciousness, which is constituted by the meanings of the particular items of reality and of their interrelationships. When we speak of the aspect of consciousness that refers to meanings, and at the same time state that consciousness as such has no power of cognitive objectivation, we come to the conclusion that the whole of human cognition—the power and the efficacy of active comprehension—closely cooperates with consciousness. Consciousness itself is thus conditioned by this power and efficacy—it is conditioned, so to speak, by the cognitive potentiality . . . The power and the efficacy of active understanding allows us to ascertain the meaning of particular things and to intellectually incorporate them, as well as the relations between them, into our consciousness. For to understand means the same as to grasp the meaning of things and their interrelations. Insofar as *all this is alien to consciousness* the whole process of active comprehending neither proceeds in it nor is owing to it. *The* meanings *of things and of their relations are given to consciousness, as it were, from outside as the product of knowledge*, which in turn results from the active constitution and comprehension of the objective reality and is accumulated by man and possessed by him by various means and to different degrees.[26]

This realistic semantics will be fundamental in order to grasp what is, according to Wojtyła, the correct relationship between ends and meanings in HV 12. Within this kind of semantics, the conceptual meaning of something is like a formal sign that signifies the thing as it is in its real nature. For this reason, Wojtyła argues that consciousness receives all of its signifying contents from the outside, namely, from the operation of the intellect whereby one objectifies something intentionally and apprehends its form as the form of another. Note well that here the human intellect is not the measure of reality. It is the other way around. The human intellect is measured by reality. That same reality, consequently, is the source of those meanings.

In this way, Wojtyła's reflections on HV's teaching on the meanings of the conjugal act are *transphenomenical*.[27] They are not restricted to phenomena given as objects of consciousness. They go *beyond* those phenomena. They attain the real and extra-mental realities signified by those mental meanings. They reach those realities as *esse reale in rerum naturae*. In other words, we attain the realities signified by those meanings in their very being, as they are, *independently* of one's knowledge and one's awareness of them. These realistic semantics establish the adequate link between lived experience and metaphysical notions. The latter are given in experience, even if

26. Ibid.
27. Wojtyła, "The Person: Subject and Community," 222.

they go beyond experience when they explain it by its causes. At the same time, these premises will also furnish the key to comprehend the way in which John Paul II relates the first and more metaphysical account of Creation with the second account. In the latter account, we will find the experiential terrain wherein the precise metaphysical and theological truth of being created in God's image and likeness is illustrated by means of the so-called original experiences.[28]

Two Functions

Man rationally experiences the world around him as well as his own self. This human or rational way of experiencing is manifested by the twofold function of consciousness: the mirroring and the reflexive functions. Mirroring consciousness focuses on the objective dimension of that which is experienced. It makes one aware of something other than oneself. Furthermore, the mirroring function of consciousness allows for introspection of the contents or meanings deposited in consciousness by the intellect.[29]

Instead, the reflexive function of consciousness presupposes the mirroring one. What is added now is that this reflexive function turns one's consciousness towards one's subjectivity.[30] Thus, I experience *myself* knowing; that I am the *one* aching; that I am willing something *for me*; that I am the *one* feeling, that this moral obligation I experience in my conscience binds *me*, etc. Wojtyła explains it by saying that "the *reflexive trait* or *reflexiveness* of consciousness denotes that consciousness, so to speak, *turns back naturally upon the subject*, if thereby the subjectiveness of the subject is brought into prominence in experience."[31] As Wojtyła also says, "thanks to this function, the experience of the human being (primarily as a determinate self) discloses the inwardness and in-selfness proper to concrete human *esse* and *operari*."[32]

Israel Pérez López has acutely apprehended the depth of Wojtyła's position.[33] Thanks to the reflexive function of consciousness, one's subjectivity is not only experienced, it is also made somewhat explicit, by being affected by some phenomenon as one's own or as the result of one's own state. In other words, reflexive consciousness helps to furnish the experience by which one is aware of one's own subjectivity or selfhood as affected by the objective reality that is known and experienced. By means of this function of consciousness, its objective contents are referred to one's I. I can say that "they are mine" or "for me": "Consciousness allows us not only to have an inner

---

28. See TOB 5:4.
29. See AP, 42–44.
30. See PC, 231.
31. AP, 43; emphasis added.
32. PC, 231.
33. See Pérez López, *Teoría de la Conciencia*.

view of our actions (immanent perception) and of their dynamic dependence on the ego, but also to *experience these actions as actions and as our own.*"[34]

As I hinted previously, this is the kind of experience we have when we have a headache or another physical pain. We are aware of the pain in reference to ourselves as its subject experiencing it. But I should emphasize once again that the reflexive function of consciousness also accounts for our lived experience of willing something *for me* and for the awareness of *feelings like shame*. This same function also accounts for the consciousness of *being morally obligated* and for the lived *experience of another person as another I*.[35] Explicitly and implicitly, TOB will appeal to this very function of consciousness in order to explain original solitude, original unity, original innocence, and some of the effects of original sin.

Causing an Action and the Person's Substantiality

The conciliar framework allows us to consider the aspect of efficacy developed in AP under a particular light. This entire section implicitly rebuts the proponents of contraception's a-metaphysical understanding of human nature as that which is subpersonal and nonspiritual. Wojtyła begins building upon his analysis of consciousness. He is particularly interested in showing the limited realm of being that is given in consciousness. To be does not equal to be perceived by the human mind or by human consciousness. There are beings that are not perceived by us, beings of which we have no actual consciousness. Although one has an awareness of one's own person, "not everything belonging to the human dynamism is reflected in consciousness."[36] Most of the vegetative dimension of the human dynamism escapes our conscious perception. Additionally, our psychic and spiritual life is so complex that one also finds there an entire subconscious realm that, by definition, is not mirrored in consciousness either. Our habits, let them be moral or mental, when they are not in act, escape the realm of our consciousness as well. Consequently, we find an indication here that a proper study of the human person cannot be restricted to one's internal lived experience.

Wojtyła applies this last conclusion to his study of the lived experiences "man-acts" and "something-happens-in-man."[37] Although these realities are perceived in consciousness, our author is interested in their correlative ontic structures within the human person, that is to say, in their *esse reale in rerum naturae*. As lived experiences, "man-acts" and "something-happens-in-man" are *meanings* deposited in consciousness by the intentional and objectifying act of the intellect. Such concepts, as it were, "silently" signify reality itself (the *res significata*).

---

34. AP, 42; emphasis added.

35. One could also add here the experience of making true judgments. This is also as an experience in which the reflexive function of consciousness is at work. See *De Veritate*, q. 1, a. 9, c.

36. AP, 60.

37. This distinction seems to be based on *De Virtutibus*, q. 1, a. 4, c.

The aspect of *efficacy* points to the fact that "when acting I have the experience of myself as the agent responsible for this particular form of dynamization of myself as the subject."[38] In this case, I experience the will actively using the faculties of the soul. Moreover, I experience that I am the one who "produces an effect [the action] and sustain[s] its existence, its becoming and its being."[39] In accordance with Wojtyła's realistic semantics, this experience should have an ontological structure that is objective in the sense that it has an *esse reale in rerum naturae*. Thus, our author says that "*objective efficacy* is the correlate of the experience of efficacy, for having this experience opens to our insight the structure of the efficacious ego."[40] In this manner, Wojtyła reaches the conclusion that the human person, as that objective efficacious ego, has a certain transcendence *with respect to* his own action and with respect to his own awareness of that same action.

Being the efficient cause of his actions, the human person has this certain transcendence with respect to them, because he belongs to *a different ontological level*. While his actions belong to the *accidental* level, the human person is a *substance*. There is a clear primacy of the existence of the person as a substance in first act (*esse substantiale*) over the existence of actions in second act (*esse accidentale*). Moreover, there is also a connection between these two orders. One must first exist in order to act. But also, one's mode of acting corresponds to one's mode of being. This last consideration leads to a very important conclusion: "It is in the subject *as a being* that *every* dynamic structure is rooted, *every* acting and happening."[41] At this point of his reflection, our author begins to implicitly address the advocates of contraception's a-metaphysical understanding of human nature as that which is subpersonal and nonspiritual.

> The existential relation between action and being with which we are here concerned allows us to clarify and grasp these relations not only in the order of existence. . . . The statement that action is subsequent or follows existence [*operari sequitur esse*] is meant to indicate a specific cohesion of the acting process and the acting agent. *This cohesion is impossible to express otherwise than by resorting to the conception of nature.* For nature is none other than the basis of the essential cohesion of the one who acts (though the acting agent need not be human) with his acting. To put it more generally and more precisely, we may say *nature provides the basis for the essential cohesion of the subject of dynamism with all the dynamism of the subject.* The attributive *all* is important, because it allows us *to reject once and for all that meaning of nature which exhibits it as only a moment and only one mode of the dynamization of the subject.*[42]

38. AP, 66.
39. Ibid., 67.
40. Ibid.; emphasis added.
41. Ibid., 72; emphasis added.
42. Ibid., 83; emphasis added.

The position that is to be rejected once and for all, mentioned here by Wojtyła, is clearly that of contraception's advocates. Against their position, our author makes very important distinctions. He first alludes to the grain of truth in their position. They are pointing at two different modes of dynamization, at two modes of causality. One could certainly distinguish between the personal or free mode of causality inherent in the structure "man-acts" and the natural mode of causality inherent in the structure "something-happens-in-man." Yet, *both of them are integrated at the level of second and first act*. Once again, Wojtyła is quite clever. He has implicitly led his reader to a point of dispute with both Scheler and authors influenced by him, who defend contraception. They have equated the opposition between the structures "man-acts" and "something-happens-in-man" to the opposition between person and nature.[43] Our author wants to show that instead of opposition, one should speak of integration.

Creator and Material of One's Moral Identity

Against the position of the proponents of contraception, Wojtyła explains in which sense person and nature are integrated at the level of second act. Such integration results in a consideration of the human person as both "creator" and "material" of his own moral identity. In reality, within the level of operation or second act, "man-acts" and "something-happens-in-man" are only *two modes of acting*.

> Emphasizing some moments in experience we may miss and disregard the transition between man's nature and his person, and we may fail to grasp their integrity . . . person and nature would then denote practically nothing more than a certain mode of acting and hence also a certain form of the dynamism proper to man, but would not in any significant way denote the subject of this dynamism and acting.[44]

Hence, the person cannot be reduced to the psychological subject given in consciousness in the experience of man-acting. In turn, human nature cannot be simply opposed to the human person. What is natural in man, in the sense of being spontaneous and not chosen, does not oppose the human person, but only free acting. And it opposes free acting only under a certain aspect (*secundum quid*), and not absolutely speaking (*simpliciter*). But there is a more foundational meaning of nature, a more metaphysical view: the essence of man as the root of all dynamisms in the the order of operation. Wojtyła explicitly compares these two views on nature, pointing at the very limited character of the first view: "When so conceived nature presents itself as *a strictly defined moment of the dynamism proper to man rather than as the basis of*

---

43. In Scheler, this opposition runs parallel to the one between acts and functions. See Scheler, *Formalism*, 398.

44. AP, 79.

all this dynamism. It is manifested solely in the activation of the man-subject, while actions show him to be a person."[45]

However, even at this level of second act, there is an integration between these two modes of acting. Such integration is conceived thanks to the understanding of action as the real relation between *agent* and *patient*. Wojtyła implicitly appeals to the idea that "human acts can be considered in both ways [as actions and passions], since man moves himself, and is moved by himself."[46] Additionally, he also uses some ideas here which are almost imperceptible in any translation. It is necessary to appeal to the original Polish text of AP.

Making a reference to artistic productions, Wojtyła speaks of the human being as author or *creator* of his action (człowiek-*twórca*). This is the perspective of the acting person as agent in which human acts are viewed as actions. But as such, the human person is not a creator *ex nihilo*. Man creates using some materials already constituted in their nature. For this reason, human actions could be considered from another perspective, from the perspective of being acted upon. In this other sense, I am considered as patient of the act. I am like the recipient, the material for this work of art which is the moral life. Think about the formation of virtues: my feelings of anger are the material out of which I can be the creator of the virtue of meekness; my fear and daring are the material for the creation of the virtue of fortitude; my feelings of hope are the material for the creation of the virtue of humility, etc. Within this context, one can also consider nature *secundum principium activum sive formale* or *secundum principium passivum sive materiale*, that is to say, either as a principle and capacity to act in a certain manner, or as a principle and capacity to be acted upon in a given way.[47]

Now, note the play on words. Wojtyła refers to this other dimension of my own dynamism as the man-material that is informed by this action (człowiek-*tworzywo*).[48] This is the perspective of the person as patient, in which human acts are viewed as passions. Thus, the creator (*twórca*) and his material (*tworzywo*) are the key to understanding the integration between person and nature at the level of second act. I experience all these "materials" as merely happening in me. At the same time, they are not a subhuman *raw* material whose meaning is totally dependent upon my freedom. They already have from their very origin the real aptness or potency to be formed into all these virtues. In fact, the passions of irrational animals do not have that same real potency or aptness. Mine, on the other hand, because of that real potency, are the apt material out of which I can build my own moral identity.

This last conclusion is very important for sexual ethics. With this metaphysical understanding, it is impossible to consider as *raw material* things like the end of the human reproductive faculty in its basic orientation towards procreation, or the

---

45. Ibid., 78–79.
46. *ST* I–II, q. 1, a. 3, c.
47. See AP, 83; *ScG* III. 23; *ST* I–II, q. 6, a. 5, ad 2; *ST* III, q. 13, a. 1, c. *De Potentia*, q. 5, a. 5, c.
48. See AP, 69–70. John Paul II's *Letter to Artists*, 1.

sensible passions of love meant to be integrated into virtuous conjugal love. They are not raw materials. They are the apt or adequate materials for those virtuous behaviors. They are ready to become so from their very origin. This is quite significant because not every material is apt to receive one given form. Think about another example. One cannot make statues out of water, unless this water is frozen. Similarly, that which happens in man already has an inclination from its origin, a real potency that needs to be freely affirmed. Both inclinations and freedom are rooted in the one rational soul of the human person as in their origin. They owe to the rational soul their reciprocal configuration and aptness for each other. Wojtyła conceives the integration between person and nature at the level of second act in this way: as the *free affirmation of our own rational nature*. It really consists in bringing to fulfillment the direction of integration of our natural inclinations.[49]

In reality, Wojtyła is appealing to another Thomistic distinction regarding nature and the natural. Like Wojtyła, Thomas acknowledges a certain opposition between nature and freedom. Aquinas also explains another way in which these two integrate. Interestingly enough, Thomas does all that while explaining in which sense *matrimony* is natural. He compares it to the way in which *virtues* are natural. There can be a natural inclination to marriage as a human phenomenon, like there can be a natural inclination to the virtues, or a natural inclination to procreation in all its human distinctiveness. All of those natural inclinations are truly natural and rooted in our one rational soul. Yet, they need to be integrated by the exercise of our freedom. Without freedom, they do not reach their fulfillment. They remain only in potency.

> Something is said to be natural in two ways. In one way, something is natural as resulting of necessity from the principles of nature. In this way, upward movement is natural to fire, etc. And in this way, matrimony is not natural, nor are any of those things that are fulfilled [*complentur*] through free-will. Secondly, something is said to be natural in another way, as that to which nature inclines although it is fulfilled [*completur*] by free-will, just as the acts of virtue are called natural; and in this way matrimony is natural, because natural reason [*ratio naturalis*] inclines thereto.[50]

Aquinas continues on in this text explaining one of those natural inclinations, which is quite rational: one's inclination to the *bonum prolis*. I do not think that it is a coincidence that Thomas gives the very understanding of procreation that is present in LR in this precise text, within this exact context. Nor do I believe it to be a coincidence that Wojtyła's anthropology of love gives a solution to a metaphysical problem implicitly relying on a Thomistic text that explains why conjugal love is natural. Be that as it may, Thomas continues in this text saying that we are naturally inclined to the principal end of matrimony, "which is the good of the offspring. Nature does

---

49. See AP, 116.
50. *In IV Sent.*, d. 26, q. 1, a. 1, c.

not intend only their generation, but also their upbringing and advancement [*traductionem et promotionem*] to the perfect state of man as man, that is, to the state of virtue."⁵¹ We are already inclined towards that by our rational nature or natural *ratio*. However, this inclination finds its fulfillment in collaboration with our freedom because the human person is substantially permanent, but accidentally perfectible.

These conclusions already direct our attention to the level of first act. The question that has already emerged is the following: what is the origin of these inclinations that come to fulfillment through the intervention of our freedom? This question transports us to an even more metaphysical view of the structures man-acts and something-happens-in-man. Obviously, this view requires transcending these structures as meanings of consciousness. It requires attaining their real being, as I keep repeating, their *esse reale in rerum naturae*.

Metaphysics of the Soul

In fact, Wojtyła is already indicating the metaphysics of the soul described above, especially at it relates with the principle *operari sequitur esse*. Our substantial form, the one that gives us our rational mode of being (*esse*), is the one responsible for these inclinations to the virtues. More importantly, it is also responsible for that inclination to procreation. We find now, at the level of first act, the implicit but direct refutation of the advocates of contraception's a-metaphysical understanding of human nature as that which is subpersonal and nonspiritual. Even at this level of first act, one can still distinguish person and nature. Indeed, in one sense, there is also a distinction *secundum rem* between this human person (Socrates, Bob, or Cathy), and human nature. Bob is not human nature. He is not humanity either. Moreover, human nature does not act; only the concrete subject that is the *suppositum* does so. In fact, human nature is a formal part of the human person. Separated from a person, human nature would not have real *esse*.

Additionally, the distinction between the two modes of acting in the structures "man-acts" and "something-happens-in-man" is reduced or lead back to the *suppositum*. Wojtyła appeals once again to the metaphysical principle *operari sequitur esse*. Hence, all the *operari* of the human person comes from its mode of being (*esse*) given by his substantial form. Thus, the human form understood as nature is the basis for the dynamic cohesion of the person: "The first and foremost dynamization of any being appears as being derived from its existence, from its actual being."⁵² Moreover, against contraception's advocates, Wojtyła concludes that *all of man's dynamism is personal*.

> Hence, *every form of dynamization* of the subject, every operation—whether it consists in acting or in happening, that is, in activation—if really related to

---

51. Ibid.
52. AP, 83.

humanness, to nature, *must also be really personal*. The integration of human nature, of humanness, in and by the person has as its consequence the integration of all the dynamism proper to man in the human person.[53]

This view, which accounts for the integration between person and nature at the level of first and second act, equips Wojtyła with a way of explaining how the human person is naturally free. "This *must* be the strongest argument for the metaphysical conception of human nature. The human being is a person by nature."[54] Moreover, rooted in the metaphysics of the soul as the giver of personal being (*esse*) to man, it also allows him to explain how the so-called direction of integration corresponds to that aptitude which is to be affirmed freely in order to attain self-fulfillment. Wojtyła will devote his discussion of transcendence and integration to explaining these two things.

Acting Freely and The Human Soul's Spirituality

As a *suppositum* who consciously is the efficient cause of his actions, the human person's proper mode of acting is to act freely. Wojtyła's account of the transcendence of the acting person concentrates on this very experience in order to understand and explain it in terms of the spiritual nature of the will and thus of the human soul. As it was mentioned, this entire section also finds its proper context in the conciliar framework and in the debates around HV. Wojtyła is going to implicitly dispute with the advocates of contraception on their Kantian views on autonomy and moral conscience. He will do so by elucidating the intimate connection between human freedom and truth. Thus, our author will also provide a philosophical foundation for man's participation in the *munus regalis*, for the attitude of Christian responsibility, and for what he will call in TOB the "freedom of the gift of self."

Wojtyła uses the term "transcendence" for different reasons. First of all, it signifies a going *beyond one's self towards an object of choice* that occurs when the human person acts in accordance with the truth about the good. Additionally, since the section will conclude with a proof of the spirituality of man's rational soul, the term "transcendence" is also quite fitting. Inasmuch as it is spiritual, the human soul *transcends* not only the world of matter, but also the immaterial level of sensibility characteristic of other animals. Thus, Wojtyła says that "transcendence is the spirituality of the human being revealing itself."[55]

Let us begin with the first sense in which Wojtyła uses transcendence, that going beyond oneself towards an object of choice. Such transcendence has two dimensions. In reality, they are based on the two objects of rational love. As Thomas says, "an act

53. Ibid.
54. PC, 225.
55. Ibid., 233.

of love always tends towards two things; *to the good* that one wills, and *to the person* for whom one wills it."[56] The "vertical" dimension of transcendence concentrates *on the person*. It looks at the fact that when loving something good other than one's ego, at the same time, man loves *himself* and configures *his moral identity*, thanks to the impact of his action upon his own self. The "horizontal" dimension of transcendence, instead, concentrates on *the good*. It looks at the direction of one's choice towards something other than one's ego. It pinpoints the harmony between the specification of the intellect and the efficient causality of the will in the moment of election.

It is very important to note that Wojtyła explains that his analysis of the two dimensions of transcendence advances progressively. He is going to begin with the vertical dimension and continue with the horizontal. The relationship between these two is contained in the following programmatic text:

> The consecutive steps of this analysis will, so to speak, unveil deeper and deeper levels of that transcendence of the acting person in which the person's structure, in its existential status of reality, is manifested experientially. The outer, overlying layers of this reality, those we can uncover and objectify first, are conditioned by the inner ones, and as we proceed in depth each will tell us more about the person, about his specific structure. They will allow us to define more and more fully the person's specificity and his spiritual nature.[57]

Wojtyła offers in this text his program for this section of AP. He is moving from the most easily known or superficial layers to the deeper ones. He is going to *dig deep into* the explanation of these phenomena. Once again, there is an implicit Polish reference here. The verb Wojtyła uses is *wydobyć*. It means to explain. But it literally conveys the image of explaining by excavating or mining something. And precisely because the deeper layers are the explanation of the more superficial ones, Wojtyła says that the deeper layers *condition* them. Considering the big picture, we can identify three main layers. The first stratum or layer of the transcendence of the acting person is the structure of self-determination. This corresponds to the use of our innate freedom. Within this same structure, we find both dimensions of transcendence already mentioned. Now, the whole structure of self-determination is conditioned by the second and deeper layer. It corresponds to the structure of self-fulfillment. At the same time, those two layers give access to a deeper, third one: the spiritual nature of the rational soul.

Once again, Wojtyła is tacitly appealing to the principle *operari sequitur esse*. Indeed, in acting freely, the human person experiences his own self as the ultimate subject of operations of a spiritual nature. Consequently, these operations reveal the spirituality of the intellect and the will as the powers involved. Additionally, these same operations also manifest the spirituality of the formal principle in which these

---

56. *ST* I, q. 20, a. 1, ad 3; emphasis added. See also *ScG* I.91.

57. AP, 124.

faculties inhere, the same formal principle that gives substantial *esse* or first act of existence to the human person, and out of which springs all of his *operari*: the rational soul.

The Use of Innate Freedom

Within self-determination as the use of our innate freedom, Wojtyła distinguishes two dimensions that correspond to vertical and horizontal transcendence, namely, freedom in its fundamental sense and freedom in its broader or extended sense: "By autodetermination we mean the moment of freedom not only in the fundamental sense of self-reliance of the person but also in the broader sense when it refers to the possible objects of willing."[58] Freedom in its fundamental sense is characterized by two different stages in the comprehension of the phenomenon of self-determination: self-decision and self-dependence (or self-reliance).

Inasmuch as freedom implies a decision about oneself when choosing to do something, it constitutes the foundation of the moral becoming (*fieri*) of man: "When willing something even beyond myself I thereby also in one way or another *bring back the discretion of the will upon myself*."[59] As he also says: "The turning to any external object that is seen as an end or a value implies *a simultaneous fundamental turn toward the ego as the object*."[60] As agent and efficient cause of my own action, I am capable of causing something formally within myself. In the experience of the formation of virtues, for instance, the person who fulfills an action, at the same time, fulfills himself in that action. He becomes the kind of person who would act in this way.

Wojtyła does not imply that the human will has itself or one's ego as its first intentional and most excellent object. The human will cannot will itself without wanting something other than oneself. Neither is the will the *Sumum Bonum* that one naturally desires. Wojtyła is simply elucidating one superficial dimension or layer of the experience of acting freely. It is one of those experiences in which the reflexive function of consciousness is present. This function turns our awareness towards our own self without our own self being the direct object of the action. I think this is the best way to explain Thomas's understanding of the double object of rational love, when adopting the perspective of the first person, in which I will something good *for me*.

For those who have studied Latin or any other language that declines, it is helpful to think of this phenomenon as a sort of "psychological dative." Not to misunderstand our author, we need to concentrate on this *for me* in every willing *something*. In a sense, we need to zoom in on this indirect object. We need to leave for later the analysis of every other aspect of "I am willing something." That ulterior step will be a deeper explanation of this psychological dative. After all, this is only the first layer

---

58. Ibid., 140.
59. Ibid., 161; emphasis added.
60. Ibid., 110; emphasis added.

conditioned by deeper layers in the analysis of the experience of acting freely. Zooming into that indirect object, Wojtyła explains his position in the following manner: "[I]n this action the person is, owing to self-determination, an object for himself, in a peculiar way being the immanent target upon which man's exercise of all his powers concentrates, insofar as it is he whose determination is at stake. He is in this sense, the primary object or the nearest object of his action."[61]

The ego is the primary and nearest object in a very precise sense. As it was explained, within the intellectual and intentional knowledge of something, there is a concomitant and non-intentional consciousness of the same act, of its content or object, and of one's subjectivity. Similarly, willing something intentionally is concomitantly accompanied by a non-intentional but conscious willing of oneself. This willing of oneself, however, is not to be confused with the capacity of the will to intentionally and consciously objectify itself. This last phenomenon is not only conscious, but also due to the intellect's capacity to reflect upon itself. Thus, I can will to will something. Wojtyła is not interested now in this last kind of reflexivity of the will. He is only looking at the "for me" in the experience of "willing something for me." Pinpointing this precise case and making reference to the reflexive function of consciousness, our author affirms that "the acting ego also *experiences the awareness* that he is the one who is determined [as patient] by himself [as agent]."[62] Therefore, self-decision evinces the way in which the human dynamism can be the material out of which one configures one's own moral personality, *even when one does not think explicitly and intentionally about it*.[63]

We move now into a deeper layer in the analysis of self-determination: *freedom as self-dependence*. It implies the structures of self-governance and self-possession. Indeed, self-dependence signifies the capacity to affirm one's natural inclinations (the direction of integration explained above) *in strict dependency with the truth about the good*. Non-rational animals move themselves by virtue of an internal principle and with some sensible knowledge of their end. But they are governed by instincts and by an external rationality. Thus, their fulfillment is, as it were, *independent* of themselves. It is not strictly dependent on them. Since they lack intellectual knowledge, instinct integrates and orients their action. Alternatively, the human person enjoys intellectual knowledge and can deliberate about himself. He possesses and governs himself with lordship over his own actions, with a capacity to use his own free will. Hence, first and foremost, *freedom should not be characterized as independence but as self-dependence*.

---

61. Ibid., 108.

62. Ibid., 113; emphasis added.

63. This is important for Wojtyła for two reasons, first, because of Scheler's accusation of classical ethics of amounting to Phariseeism. And second, it is important because of Scheler's incapacity to give a proper account of ethical perfectivism. See my *De la experiencia*, 87–88, 127–130, 220–224, 250–55, 296, 363–65.

As we will see in a moment, man's self-dependence will help us to understand why the rational soul of man is not only form, but also mover and administrator of the body.

We move now into an even deeper layer of the analysis: horizontal transcendence. Here, the experience of acting freely is captured in its broader or extended sense. Inasmuch as we are in a deeper layer, freedom in its broader or extended sense as horizontal transcendence *conditions and makes possible freedom in its fundamental sense as vertical transcendence*. In reality, horizontal transcendence includes vertical transcendence in one and the same voluntary act of self-determination. We are concerned here with the experience "I will *something*." In this experience, the human person consciously decides to do something and, *simultaneously*, decides about himself. Vertical transcendence looked at the deciding about myself. Wojtyła concentrates his analysis now on the experience of intentionally deciding *something*. The human will is then revealed as a moved mover that, nevertheless, is not dragged necessarily by the finite good presented by the intellect in its specifying role. Avoiding both intellectual and voluntaristic determinism, and harmonizing the movement of specification and that of exercise, Wojtyła explains how the practical judgment of the intellect is the sufficient, but not the necessary, cause of the decision of the will.[64]

I already made a brief allusion to this topic when I explained the presence of the intellect in voluntary action. Allow me to expand a bit here for the sake of clarity. Once the will is moved to love goodness itself by the intellect, and after the comparative counsel concerning particular goods, the human will moves actively towards the particular good chosen by using oneself to decide, based on the last judgment of practical reason. Such *usus* establishes the line of demarcation between the experience "man-acts" and "something-happens-in-man." To be sure, for Wojtyła there is no act of the will that is not preceded by an act of the intellect. Every decision has a *motive*, for it is made possible by the last judgment of practical reason. However, as I said, the will makes this judgment to be the last one.[65] And this is exactly what a decision is all about. The intellect moves the will like a formal and final cause. But the intellect does not move the will in the mode of an efficient cause. Thus, a decision is all about that nucleus of efficient causality (efficacy) which is an active answer of the will and not of the intellect.

Perfected or Acquired Freedom

Wojtyła leads us now to an even deeper layer of the experience of acting freely. He is leading us to the fulfillment or perfection of freedom in its good use. This layer is deeper in the sense that whatever is more final is more formal. Since we are looking at the end or perfection of innate freedom, we can discover in its most intimate core a natural orientation towards its fulfillment. We have already seen the great connection

---

64. See ibid., 140–41; *De Veritate*, q. 24, a. 2, c.
65. See AP, 136–39.

between innate freedom and truth. Without our capacity for truth, we would not have free choice. Freedom is rooted in the intellect. It is made possible because of our capacity for truth. Wojtyła wants to go deeper now. He wants to explain that our freedom is not only made possible by the intellect; it is also *conditioned* by its reference to the truth. I refer to this stage as perfected or acquired freedom precisely because Wojtyła speaks about using well our natural freedom by choosing the true and not merely the apparent good.[66] Thus, the structure of self-fulfillment studies how the human person finds fulfillment in genuine love. Wojtyła's implicit dispute with the advocates of contraception on their Kantian views on autonomy and moral conscience will reach its apex. Additionally, in light of the conciliar framework in which TOB was gestated, this whole section also provides a philosophical foundation for man's participation in the *munus regalis* expressed in LG 36, for the attitude of Christian responsibility, for the freedom of the gift of self, and the freedom that is characteristic of God's children in the ethos of redemption.

The structure of self-fulfillment concentrates on how the human person as agent has the active power to be *the cause of his own obedience to the moral law*. In this manner, the human person attains the fulfillment of his vocation responsibly and in collaboration with the Creator. Indeed, to *subordinate* oneself to the truth about the good means to properly love one's self, in being good friends with one's interior man.[67] It also means to subordinate to the Creator as *the* Author of nature. For this reason, establishing a foundational premise to his entire moral theology,[68] Wojtyła argues, that "human freedom is *not fulfilled by subordinating truth to itself but by subordinating itself to the truth*. The dependence upon truth marks out the borderlines of the autonomy appropriate to the human person."[69] The borderlines of the autonomy that is appropriate for the human person consist in being a collaborator with the Creator, and freely obeying him by virtue of one's reason and will. The fulfillment of freedom consists in choosing the true good as opposed to the merely apparent one. When the human person subordinates himself to the truth about the good, thanks to his moral conscience, only then is his freedom perfected.

As we know, after Vatican II, a number of theologians in favor of contraception advanced a view of moral conscience influenced by Kant. This view of autonomy

---

66. For a study on the true good in John Paul II see Giertych, "Verum Bonum."

67. See *ST* II–II, q. 25, a. 7, c.

68. For instance, Wojtyła interprets in TOB the state of original justice based on this very idea. See TOB 16:3–19:5.

69. AP, 154. I have altered the translation. See OC, 370. The emphasis of the realization or fulfillment of freedom and its due subordination to truth will be very important for understanding in TOB the central role of the freedom of the gift, and the freedom that belongs to the ethos of the redemption of the body (see TOB 15:1–2; 49:2–4), especially when one reads this whole doctrine under the light of John of the Cross, for whom perfected or true freedom consists in being able to love God with all of one's strengths, namely, with all of one's faculties or powers (*potentiae*). See *Cántico* B 28, 5; *Noche* II. 11, 4–5; *Subida* I. 4, 6.

relies on a detachment from this intrinsic connection and subordination to the truth. Wojtyła's analysis of moral conscience, right at this level of the fulfillment of freedom in the truth about the good, is in strict continuity with GS, DH and KD. At the same time, it anticipates the full development of the relationship between freedom and truth present in VS from a theological viewpoint. From the metaphysical viewpoint, we already know that the soul is responsible for the coordination of this subordination of the lower faculties to the higher ones. It is also responsible for the very nature of the human will and its freedom. It is responsible for its *natural inclination* to be dependent of or subordinated to the truth about the good. This is the direction of integration of our will and of our innate freedom. For this reason, implicitly appealing to the principle that what is more final is more formal, our author explains that man's "fulfillment is based on self-determination, that is to say, on freedom. Freedom, on the other hand, *carries within itself the surrender to truth*, and this fact is most vividly brought into prominence in man's conscience."[70]

Wojtyła moves now to oppose the advocates of contraception in their Kantian understanding of conscience based on autonomy. But he does so with a great weapon at hand: the intrinsic and natural connection between human freedom and truth. Our author conceives conscience quite differently from Kant and from contraception's proponents. First of all, for Wojtyła, conscience is not a faculty but an *act* of practical *reason*. More concretely, it is a *judgment*. By means of this act of practical reason, one judges the morality of an action. One can judge an action either already performed or about to be performed. Wojtyła's emphasis is quite important: judgments are acts based on truth. Truth is found in them. Consequently, the judgment about the morality of one's actions is a judgment concerned with truth. Thus, freedom of conscience is all about *finding the truth about the good in order to freely subordinate to it*. For this reason, Wojtyła argues, against Kant, that the judgment of conscience is based on the truth *found*, and not created by man's intellect. As he explicitly says, "there is no question of assigning to the conscience, as Kant argued, the power to make its own laws—followed by an identification of this power with the notion of autonomy and thus in a way with an unrestricted freedom of the person. The *conscience is no lawmaker; it does not itself create norms; rather it discovers them, as it were, in the objective order of morality or law*."[71]

Indeed, the laws that are inherent in this judgment are not made by human reason. Our conscience is like a tribunal. It applies laws in its judgment. But these laws are not made by us. They come from God. He has promulgated such laws naturally, that is to say, by the very creation of the rational creature. Such laws that we *find* within ourselves are commanded by God. The *natural* promulgation of the eternal law in the creation of the rational creature relies on the fact that, first and foremost, God's command is an *intellectual order*. Only secondarily is it an expression of his will. Thus,

70. AP, 156. See PC, 234–35.
71. AP, 165; emphasis added.

we are capable of finding this order before we get a mature knowledge of the Creator as the proper authority that wills and legislates such laws. This is the whole point of *natural* as opposed to *positive* promulgation.

Truth has such a prominence in Wojtyła's proposal precisely because he holds this non-voluntaristic view about command (*imperium*). Something is commanded because it is truly good and not vice versa.[72] In this way, moral conscience is the subjective measure of the morality of one's actions that ought to be well-formed. Consequently, moral conscience is not the supreme or highest norm of human conduct, but only the closest understanding the subject has concerning the morality of one's actions. Within one's conscience, one experiences moral obligation as resulting from a good to be done or an evil to be avoided.[73] Moreover, such an obligation is in reality an interpersonal experience wherein one is called to a *rationabilem obsequium* to God-the-Creator. Note that Wojtyła has spoken precisely in these terms when describing our participation in Christ's priestly *munus*. He said at that time that the entire heart of Vatican II was therein contained. In his philosophy, he argues a parallel point when talking about the interpersonal or personalistic dimension of moral obligation. Moral obligation implies a certain sacrificial offering of oneself out of love.

> The tension arising between the objective order of norms and the inner freedom of the subject-person is relieved by truth, by the conviction of the truthfulness of good. But it is, on the contrary, intensified and not relieved by external pressures, by the power of injunction or compulsion. This is best formulated in St. Paul, in his demand of *rationabile obsequium*, which is the personalistic synonym of obligation.[74]

Greater consciousness of the truth about the good leads to a greater and more intimate awareness of one's moral obligations. Moreover, Wojtyła speaks about this sacrificial offering of oneself out of love, in the context of moral conscience, because the latter is not limited in applying universal certain knowledge to particular cases. Moral conscience also has an important role in the *discernment* of one's unique moral vocation. Such a discernment is the key to conform one's life to the divine Exemplar, to the truth about man. These ideas constitute, as it were, a philosophical pillar that sustains the christocentric view of TOB in consonance with Thomism and Vatican II.

The Spirituality of the Human Person

We arrive at the moment of *metaphysical reduction* within AP's methodology. All of the previous considerations provide phenomena that need to be explained by its

---

72. See Wojtyła, *Max Scheler*, 135; *De Veritate*, q. 17, a. 3, c and ad 3.

73. See AP, 156–58; *In II Sent.*, d. 24, q. 2, a. 4, ad 2; *De Veritate*, q. 17, a. 1, ad 4.

74. AP, 166. For an explanation of this thesis in light of its sources, see my *De la experiencia*, 160–63.

causes or roots. Wojtyła argues that the spirituality of the substantial formal principle of the human person is exactly that explanation. The intellect's act which makes freedom possible and points to the fulfillment of the latter, in the subordination to the truth about the good, must belong to a faculty that is not intrinsically dependent upon the matter of the human organism.[75] According to the principle of sufficient reason and non-contradiction, there must be something in the human person whereby he is what he is, and not another thing. This something that allows him to act in such a way must be his spiritual soul.

> In tracing that expressive whole of the experience of man we cannot limit our quest solely to an acknowledgment of the manifestations of spirituality without seeking to reach its roots. In point of fact, it appears that all the manifestations of the spiritual nature of man lead by the thread of their genesis to showing the real immanence of the spirit and of the spiritual element in man. Man could not exhibit the spiritual element of his nature had he not in some way been a spirit himself. This point of view refers to the fundamental principles of understanding the whole of reality: the principle of non-contradiction and the principle of sufficient reason.[76]

Wojtyła offers this anthropological proof for the spirituality of man's soul. But he also connects the spirituality of the human person with the Pauline and moral theme of the interior or higher man, to which I alluded before. Wojtyła's anthropology of love cannot be silent on this foundational topic. The entire order of love is based on this distinction. One is to love others as another I. However, to love them in the proper way, one needs to love oneself correctly. Thus, one needs to be friends, so to speak, with one's interior or higher man. One needs to will what is truly good for him:

> This distinction has often been used in the history of Christian ethics and ascetics; it derives from St. Paul. In the present context, the higher man refers to the subject who manifests himself in the experience of both transcendence and integration, thus the lower man applies to the same subject—if he manifests himself as such—who because of the transcendence appropriate to the actions of a person still requires integration.[77]

Wojtyła well knows that this is more a moral than a metaphysical distinction. There are not two real human persons in each one of us, a higher and a lower one. This Pauline distinction is often used in order to explain the order of charity. More concretely, it is employed to explain how one ought to love oneself. Now, we should not be surprised to see Wojtyła appealing to these notions. His anthropology, after all, is an anthropology of love. This connection, not sufficiently attended to by commentators, will be key for the proper comprehension of both his philosophical anthropology

---

75. See AP, 184.
76. Ibid., 183–84. For more on this, see my *De la experiencia*, 333–35.
77. AP, 315n74. See Rom 7:15–24; 6:6; 1Cor 15:47–49; *ST* II-II, q. 25, a. 7, c.

and his theological reflections in TOB concerning proper self-love as a foundation for an adequate love for others.[78] However, in order to have a fuller view of this reality, we need to explain the aspect of integration. As Wojtyła says, the person who loves himself properly is the one who reaches self-fulfillment and integration. And rather, the person who lacks this proper love of self is the one who is in need of integration.

Being Acted Upon and Man's Substantial Unity

The freedom of the human person as a being who is *dominus sui acti* uncovers another complementary aspect to the transcendence of the acting person. In the experience of action, the same person freely moves himself as agent and is moved by himself as patient. The same human person is the one who governs himself and is being governed by himself. He is the one who possesses himself and is being possessed by himself. This consideration unveils again how deep are AP's Thomistic and metaphysical foundations.[79] We can uncover Wojtyła's Thomistic understanding of action, wherein the act of agent *qua* agent is in the patient.[80] This view is also important to understand the way in which the human person *uses* one's body as an instrument, based on the Thomistic idea that the soul is not only the form of the body, but also its mover and administrator in view of one's end.[81]

The synthesis between these active and passive dimensions, between this *agere* and *pati*, corresponds to the aspect of integration within the person.[82] This aspect captures how human action manifests and perfects the unity within the human person. It *manifests* the substantial unity of his spiritual soul and the matter of his organism. But it also fulfills or *perfects* such a unity in a twofold subordination: the subordination of the sensible dynamisms within man to the spiritual ones, and the subordination of the latter to the truth about the good. In Wojtyła's anthropology of love, integration within the person is "the realization and the manifestation of a whole and a unity emerging on the basis of some complexity rather than the assembling into a whole of what was previously disconnected."[83]

---

78. In fact, this topic is abundantly present in TOB (see TOB 4:16; 24:4; 25:3; 28:5; 31:5; 39:2; 40:1; 41:6; 44:1; 48:3; 48:4; 50:1 51:1; 51:4; 58:5; 88:1; 130:4). Hence, Wojtyła's explicit connection between integration and transcendence with this Pauline doctrine is a very esteemed interpretative key to the whole of his Thomistic argument. This classical doctrine is a key to understanding the communion of persons in love within the experience of original unity, but also the way in which the Holy Spirit, in the ethos of redemption, strengthens the interior man (see DVi, 55–60).

79. See *ST* I–II, q. 1, a. 3, c.

80. See Aristotle, *Metaphysics* IX.1, 1046a19–22 in AP, 306, note 26. For Thomas's commentary on this passage, see *In IX Meta.*, lect. 1, n. 1776.

81. See *De Spirit., Creat.*, q. un., a. 3, ad 7; *Q. De anima*, q. un., a. 8, c; *ST* I–II, q. 12, a. 5, c.

82. See AP, 62–63.

83. AP, 191.

The aspect of the transcendence of the acting person concluded with a proof of the spirituality of the human person from a twofold perspective. We found there a psychological or anthropological perspective that inferred the spirituality of the soul of the human person. But we also saw in that aspect a moral perspective, in which the spirituality of the human person served as the anthropological basis to understand the proper love of self as friendship with one's own interior or higher man. Likewise, the aspect of integration also has two dimensions. It manifests the substantial unity of his spiritual soul and the matter of his organism from a psychological or anthropological perspective. But it also realizes or perfects such a unity from the moral perspective by the proper subordination of the exterior to the interior man.

Integration of Human Action in the Person

Wojtyła's argument begins with a distinction between the integration of human action in the human person, and the integration of the human person in action.[84] The first signifies a double subordination: the subordination of the sensible dynamisms within man to the spiritual ones, and the subordination of one's intellect and will to the truth about the good. Both aspects are key in proper self-love as friendship with one's interior man.[85] From this experience, one arrives at the integration of the human person in action as the aspect that manifests his substantial unity and the increase of such unity by becoming more perfect.[86]

Indeed, the integration of human action in the human person studies the active relationship of man's freedom with his nature as that which merely happens in him. Nature thus conceived is like the material out of which man builds his own moral identity. In so doing, the human person transforms what merely happens in him into an ally of his self-fulfillment or happiness. In this context, Wojtyła offers a sort of "map" of the somatic, psychic, and spiritual dimensions of what merely happens in man. This "map" is based on a Thomistic interpretation of Saint Paul's tripartite anthropology, which distinguishes different kinds of dependencies of man's potencies on matter.[87] While the spiritual faculties have an *external dependence* on the matter of the organism for their proper functioning, the sensible and vegetative faculties have an *internal or intrinsic dependence* on this same matter. Only the sensible and vegetative faculties have an organ, properly speaking.

Thus, within that which merely happens in man, one is to distinguish: (1) a material dimension corresponding to the somatic-vegetative dynamism; (2) a psychic and immaterial dimension internally or intrinsically dependent on the matter of the

---

84. See ibid., 225.

85. This will be key to understand the integration of eros "by means of a further truth of love." TOB 113:4.

86. See *ST* III, q. 73, a. 2, c; *ScG* II.68; De Finance, *Persona e valore*, 111.

87. See 1 Thess 5:23; *Super Heb.*, cap. 4, lect. 2, n. 222; *In I De anima*, lect. 10, nn. 157–60.

organism corresponding to sensible powers such as the concupiscible and irascible appetites, and (3) a spiritual dimension extrinsically dependent on the matter of the organism corresponding, for instance, to the spiritual affections of the will. As is manifested in the experience of the formation of virtues, the will can use in different ways and degrees what happens in the human person at these three different levels, subordinating it to the truth about the good.[88] In this way, what is experienced as passive and natural in man may become an ally to his self-fulfillment.

Integration of the Human Person in Action

The integration of human action in the human person just described furnishes Wojtyła with enough material to look at the roots of these phenomena. He does so thanks to his metaphysical reduction or explanation through causes. Applying his realistic method that looks for the ontic structures subjacent to the lived experiences "man-acts" and "something-happens-in-man," our author reaches some important conclusions. The first one is more a confirmation and recapitulation of something already seen: the same formal principle which gives personal and substantial *esse* to man is responsible for everything that happens in him. This principle is the one that confers this passive dimension of the human dynamism with a real aptitude to be integrated by the human person as active agent that moves, governs, and possesses himself. Such aptitude reveals a potential capacity for the actual and habitual integration of that which happens in the human person for the benefit and happiness of the same human person.

The second conclusion has to do with the experience described before as the integration of human action in the human person. Such an experience provides Wojtyła with the sufficient elements to show the substantial unity of the human person. Our author bases his reasoning on the following Thomistic principle: thanks to the reflective and reflexive function of consciousness, the same person experiences himself as the ultimate and remote subject of spiritual and sensible faculties and acts. As Thomas said, the same man perceives himself to understand and to sense (*ipse idem homo percipit se et intelligere et sentire*).[89] Indeed, the human person is aware of being the one subject of all of his dynamism mapped out before. Now, Wojtyła reaches a third conclusion. But we really need to study it in more detail, for it constitutes the heart of what I would call his "philosophy of the human body".

Philosophy of the Body

The experience of integration of human action in the person gives a certain predominance to the act of the will called *usus*.[90] From man's experience of having his own

---

88. See PC, 235.
89. See *ST* I, q. 76, a. 1, c. Pérez López, *De la experiencia*, 229–238 and 360–62.
90. Inexplicably, the English translation of AP omits the direct reference to the Latin *usus*, to St.

body, Wojtyła concludes that in a certain sense, *the human person is his own body*, especially when the human body is viewed as matter informed by the spiritual soul.

> He [man] then appears in the field of our integral experience as somebody material, as corporeal, but at the same time we know the personal unity of this material somebody to be determined by the spirit, by his spiritual nature and life. Indeed, the very fact that the personal—as well as the ontic—unity of the corporeal man is ultimately commanded by man's spiritual factor allows us to see in him the ontic composite of soul and body, of the spiritual and the material elements.[91]

Yet, the body must also be seen *as an instrument that the human person has*. In this sense Wojtyła affirms: "The body is not a member of the subjective ego in the way of being identical with the ego; man is *not* the body, he only has it . . . Man has his body in a special way and also in a special way he is aware of his possession, when in his acting he employs *his* body as a compliant *tool* to express his self-determination."[92] Note the reference to one's body as a tool (*instrumentum*). It will become quite important in a bit. For the moment, note also that this teaching explains the way the person rationally and freely *uses* his own body as instrument of communication. Then, "the human body is in its visible dynamism the territory where, or in a way even the medium whereby, the person expresses himself."[93] Not only is the use of the body for the benefit of the soul, but the powers that do have an organ also have a disposition or real aptitude to be integrated in contribution to the person's fulfillment.[94]

Let us return to Wojtyła's reference to one's body as a tool (*instrumentum*). As is known, an instrument must have a useful property in relation to the principal agent who, by its own form, moves the instrument in view of its end.[95] The agent provides the instrument with an operative power that the same instrument does not have on its own.[96] The instrument, in turn, extends the power of the principal agent by virtue of a property of its own. The instrument does so by a disposition that it has in itself to partake in the action of the principal agent.[97] Consequently, an instrument has a twofold power: (1) its proper power which will extend the power of the principal agent,

---

Thomas, and the Scholastic distinction between *usus activus* and *usus passivus* in AP, 206, 212–13. Instead, the original reads: "Through the obedience of the body, that Thomists express with the term *usus passivus*, the integration of the human person in action is accomplished." OC, 488.

91. AP, 185.

92. Ibid., 206; emphasis added.

93. Ibid., 204. See ibid., 314, note 65. We could also distinguish the body as an instrument of the will from the body as a means of expression of the human person independently of one's choices. Consider the way our body expresses our emotions. Often such an expression occurs independently from our will. In fact, in most cases, when one attempts willing to express an emotion one ends up faking it.

94. See *ScG* IV.73.

95. See *ST* III, q. 62, a. 4, c.

96. See ibid., I, q. 18, a. 3, c; I, q. 45, a. 5, c.

97. See ibid., q. 45, a. 5, c; III, q. 62, a. 1, ad 2.

and (2) an added virtue given by the principal agent to which the instrument has a disposition. Thus, for instance, the saw has the property of being able to cut. But on its own, the saw would not be able to cut the tree. It must be elevated with a new virtue that comes from the principal agent. This "added" power is a power passing into the instrument that need not be permanent. However, it is not necessary that the instrument achieves a disposition in the object acted upon or that it produces something *ex parte rei operata* through its own virtue. It is sufficient that the instrument modifies the action of the principal agent *ex parte modi operandi*.

Now, when Wojtyła follows Thomas in his claim that the human "soul is not only the form of the body but also its mover and end,"[98] he is not fully accepting Plato's position, which reduces the soul's unity with the body to one of contact between mover and moved.[99] To understand Wojtyła's position, we need to recall what was said about integration being the complementary aspect of the transcendence of the acting person. We need to recall that complementarity is within the understanding of action as the real relation between agent and patient, mover and moved. The self-movement of any animal implies a distinction that, strictly speaking, is not the distinction between body and soul, but rather the distinction between one *animated* part that moves, and another *animated* part that is moved. In any animal, the soul is the formal cause of its being and of the configuration of matter into its body. However, in irrational animals, the composite and not just the soul is the efficient cause of their action. In the case of the human person, there is a distinction to be made. The rational soul is not completely immersed in matter. The operations of the intellect and the will do not depend intrinsically on a corporeal organ. Thus, these spiritual faculties, which account for the transcendence of the acting person, can be considered as *movers of the same body that results from the information of the soul*. In this sense, Wojtyła spoke about freedom as self-decision and self-dependence. Then, within this perspective, the body is an instrument of the soul with regard to the exercise of the spiritual powers moving the body.

However, the human body should not be thought of as a *raw* material, as a sort of inanimate matter. Rather, the rational soul, through the intellectual powers, moves a human body, made *already human by the very same soul* that gives substantial *esse* and configures prime matter into this human body. Thus, the human body is seen as an instrument that is not separated but *conjoined*.[100] And it is in this sense that Wojtyła's opinions on the relationship between transcendence and integration, and the body as a property that the person has, is founded on Thomas's claim that *the administration of the body is a function of the soul*, inasmuch as it is a mover and not inasmuch as it is form.[101] From this viewpoint, the integration of the human person in action

---

98. *Q. De anima*, q. un., a. 8, c.
99. See *ST* I, q. 76, a. 7; TOB 66:6.
100. See *ST* III, q. 62, a. 5, c; *ST* III, q. 2, a. 6, ad 4.
101. See *De Spirit. Creat.*, q. un., a. 3, ad 7.

is the complementary dimension of the transcendence of the acting person as self-fulfillment. Indeed, the body and all the potencies that are intrinsically dependent on it (the exterior man) serve the intellect and the will (the human *mens* or the interior man). The body is for the soul. The union with matter of the rational soul is for its own proper functioning and benefit, so that the human person may be able to know and to love. The body serves the intellect as an instrument inasmuch as the latter needs the mediation of the senses in order to operate. And although the will does not need to use an instrument in order to exercise its proper act, it can move as an efficient cause and use instrumentally almost any power of man with the mediation of the *imperium* or command of the intellect.[102] Nevertheless, the power of the will is not absolute. Its efficacy is *limited by the nature of the instruments or powers moved.*

Wojtyła and Thomas differentiate between despotic and/or political rule over these "instruments."[103] Sensible powers, which are partly in the body as their subject, when moved by the will, become instruments of the soul and rational through participation. The instruments used extend the power of human *mens* as the principal agent. In this way, they *express the interior life of the soul.* In this sense, we say that one's face is the mirror of one's soul. Being an instrument of the soul, the body expresses the thoughts and affections of the human spirit (*mens*), its interior life. Thomas sees this reality when he argues that the intellectual soul is so clearly seen in man's face that the scriptures say that the breath of life was breathed into the face of man.[104] Alternately, the sensible powers as instruments receive the impression of a quality from the same *mens*, thereby *becoming rational by participation.*[105]

These clarifications will allow us to see more clearly the Thomistic foundations of Wojtyła's position. Even if man's being consists in soul and body, the body's being depends on the soul and not vice versa. The body is for the soul as matter is for form, and the instrument for the mover.[106] The union of the soul with the body is for the perfection of the rational nature.[107] An instrument is improved when it is all the better for the end it is meant to serve.[108] Since the soul is the end of the body,[109] the human body is meant to be, by the Divine Artist, a well-adapted instrument.[110] A moral theology of the human body must explain an "administration" or use of the body worthy of its dignity and role in man's life. Such administration is what Wojtyła means by his

102. See *ST* I, q. 82, a. 4, c; I, q. 76, a. 1, c; I–II, q. 17, a. 8, c; I–II, q. 16, a. 1, c.
103. See *In Polit.*, lect. 3, n. 34; AP, 315n72.
104. See *ST* I, q. 91, a. 4, ad 4.
105. See ibid., I–II, q. 56, a. 4, ad 1.
106. See ibid., I–II, q. 2, a. 5, c.
107. See *Q. De anima*, q. un., a. 2, ad 14; a. 10, ad 9. Thomas argues that precisely because it is ordained to the soul, the body must be serving the soul and not be an obstacle to its development. See *ScG* III.129.
108. See *ST* II–II, q. 188, a. 7, ad 1.
109. See *Q. De anima*, q. un., a. 8, c.
110. See *ST* I, q. 76, a. 5, c; *ST* I, q. 91, a. 3, c; Aristotle, *Physics* VIII.2, 252b; *ST* I, q. 91, a. 1, c.

teaching on integration. As we will see in TOB, such administration or integration, especially when dealing with sexual morality, should take into account that the body is for the Lord, and that the Lord is for the body.[111]

Therefore, it becomes quite clear now that this whole aspect implicitly antagonizes the proponents of contraception for their deficient understanding of the unity of the human person. But it also opposes their naturalistic view of human inclinations, such as the one to procreate or to engage in conjugal love. These inclinations are not a raw material at the complete disposal of an arbitrary freedom. They are *human* inclinations which spring from the soul as form and mover of the body. They should be understood as generically animal but specifically rational. They already have a certain orientation to be completed by the exercise of one's freedom in order to reach self-fulfillment.

Acting Together with Others and Man's Social Nature

As I mentioned before, the aspect of participation or integration between persons was added to AP as an appendix. Although it is only an outline not fully developed, it is quite important for our purposes to delineate its main coordinates.[112] The aspect of participation or integration between persons transports all of the previous aspects into the realm of intersubjectivity. Keeping in mind all the elements already studied in Wojtyła's anthropology of love, this last aspect focuses on the experience of acting together with others as the *operari* that discloses the social nature inscribed and included in our rational mode of being.

The reason why I keep referring to the aspect of participation as integration between persons is found in LR. In this book, Wojtyła emphasizes the interpersonal dimension of the aspect of integration. He does so, concentrating on the education of love to its virtuous state. In this context, Wojtyła speaks about the maturation of love as "the integration of love *in* the person and *between* persons."[113] At this interpersonal level, integration also denotes "the realization and manifestation of a whole and a unity emerging on the basis of some complexity."[114] But now, the manifestation of unity refers to the kind of (accidental) union between human persons, who love each other, and love a common good. It refers to the communion of persons resulting from partaking in a common *munus*. The realization or perfection of this unity denotes the fulfillment of the person and of the communion of persons in this same kind of love and sharing in the same *munus*. In this way, Wojtyła's reflections on integration

---

111. See ibid., II–II, q. 153, a. 3, ad 2.

112. Wojtyła will develop this part of AP during the same time in which he is working on the text of TOB. See the articles written between 1975–1976 in PC, 209–17, 219–61. I will come back to these articles in my explanations of original unity.

113. LR, 140; emphasis added.

114. AP, 191.

between persons as participation point to the fact that the human person attains happiness and flourishes in the communion of persons resulting from the fulfillment of the commandment of love or personalistic norm.

In this sense, the aspect of integration between persons as participation not only reveals that the human person is a being capable of communion, but also transports all of the aspects treated before into this interpersonal dimension. For this reason, our author explains that "participation corresponds to the person's transcendence and integration in the action because it is that property which allows man, when he acts together with other men, to realize thereby, and at once, the authentically personalistic value—the performance of the action and the fulfillment of himself in the action."[115] Perhaps this is the place where Wojtyła's anthropology is most clearly seen as an anthropology of love.

In this final aspect, participation is understood in two complementary ways.[116] It is a property of the person to endow his existence and activity with an interpersonal dimension. But it is also "a positive relation to the humanity of others."[117] This positive relation entails something greater than just affirming a concept, the concept of humanity. It also entails acknowledging and affirming the other as a *concrete* and *particular* personal self that is like me, that is another *I*. For this reason, Wojtyła focuses on extracting the anthropological conclusions of the commandment of love: to love one's neighbor *as oneself*.[118] He speaks about the theoretical and normative significance of such a commandment. It has a theoretical significance inasmuch as it allows for a study of interpersonal communion based on a system of reference where the other is viewed as one's neighbor, that is to say, as another "I." Wojtyła argues that his notion of integration between persons as participation "was already explained to a considerable degree by Aristotle."[119] He refers later on to Aristotle's philosophy of friendship.[120] This is a very important topic for this book because, following Aristotle, both Wojtyła and Thomas Aquinas view marriage as one special kind of friendship. And let us remember that this is also the view present in Vatican II. On the other hand, the commandment of love has a normative significance inasmuch as it carries with it the obligation to love the other as one should love oneself. For this reason, the integration between persons as participation not only manifests the social nature of the human person, but based on that nature, it also prescribes the way in which to bring it to fulfillment.

Wojtyła considers *alienation* to be the very opposite of participation or integration between persons. It really destroys both significances of the commandment to

---

115. Ibid., 327.
116. See PC, 237.
117. Ibid.
118. See Mark 12:31; Matt 22:9, 7:12; Gal 5:14; Rom 13:9–10; 1 John 3:11.
119. PC, 204.
120. See ibid., 207n11.

love. Against Marxism, our author argues that the true alienation of the human person is the incapacity to love and to be perfected by loving in this manner. Indeed, alienation is "the negation of participation, for it renders participation difficult or even impossible. It devastates the I—other relationship, weakens the ability to experience another human being as another I, and inhibits the possibility of friendship and the spontaneous powers of community (*communio personarum*)."[121] Any human community that damages or destroys the system of reference of being a neighbor is dehumanizing and is ultimately destined to annihilation.[122]

This last point will be important in understanding the doctrine of TOB. Since marriage is a special kind of friendship, therein the love for the other as one's neighbor is based on the proper love of self.[123] In this same line, Wojtyła argues that the path that leads to true participation goes from the person to the community, from a proper self-knowledge and self-love to a correct appreciation and love towards the other and another I. For this reason, this last aspect of Wojtyła's integral vision of man presupposes all the aspects treated so far, envisioning them from the viewpoint of intersubjectivity and man's capacity for communion. In light of the conciliar framework, this last aspect could be seen as a philosophical understanding of the *communio personarum*. It will become quite relevant to comprehend Wojtyła's theology of procreation as the common good that specifies and perfects conjugal friendship. Wojtyła concludes this final aspect by offering some detailed explanations on the nature of the common good as well as the authentic and inauthentic attitudes for true participation, which I have explained elsewhere in great detail.[124] However, with what has been said so far, we already have the essential philosophical underpinnings for a correct interpretation of TOB's theologically adequate anthropology. I will come back to this same topic in my own analysis of original unity.

Narrative of a Conciliar Genesis

Up to this point, we have seen something like a narrative of TOB's conciliar genesis. This narrative will become very useful in the analysis of TOB in parts II and III of this book. It provides the main hermeneutical coordinates for John Paul II's understanding of the spousal meaning of the body and its relationship with procreation. His position was gestated around his interpretation of Vatican II and his contribution to and interpretation of HV. Indeed, the narrative of TOB's conciliar genesis contextualizes this work as an attempt to supplement and explain the teachings of Paul VI's HV. The narrative of this conciliar genesis also shows that TOB attempts to supplement and explain those teachings in continuity with the teachings of Vatican II, as interpreted

---

121. PC, 206.
122. See AP, 297–99.
123. See TOB 109:4.
124. See my *De la experiencia*, 375–97.

by Karol Wojtyła. Now, in order to develop a conjugal moral theology in accordance with directives from that same Council, there is a need to harmonize the biblical and metaphysical dimensions of the natural law. In implicit dialogue with the advocates of contraception, Wojtyła's anthropology of love has offered the philosophical support needed.

We are now equipped to undergo a thorough analysis of TOB's understanding of the spousal meaning of the body and its relationship with procreation. Our next task will be to show the Thomistic and conciliar foundations of John Paul II's understanding of the spousal meaning of the body.

Part II: Spousal Meaning of the Body

5

In God's Image

Ends and Beginnings

In order to effectively accomplish my goal in this second part of the book, I need to begin by showing *synthetically* that John Paul II's understanding of the spousal meaning of the body is grounded in Vatican II and in Aquinas's theology. LG 40 teaches that *charity is the essence of holiness*. Since all men are called to holiness, one can easily conclude that it is the very meaning of our human existence, our very vocation.[1] Likewise, Aquinas identifies charity as the measure of Christian perfection. Since it is "charity that unites us to God, who is the last end of the human *mens* . . . *the perfection of the Christian life consists radically in charity*."[2] Grounded by these sources, John Paul II also links the vocation, capacity, and responsibility to charity with our being created in the image and likeness of God. As is known, FC is the document produced at the Synod of Bishops which TOB was meant to accompany. TOB begins and ends referring to this synod and to the document that it produced.[3] Some of TOB's main teachings are summarized in FC, including John Paul II's understanding of the spousal meaning of the body: "Creating the human race in His own image and continually keeping it in being, God inscribed in the humanity of man and woman *the vocation, and thus the capacity and responsibility, of love and communion. Love is therefore the fundamental and innate vocation of every human being*."[4]

Following Vatican II's christocentric view, RH speaks about Christ as the Exemplar and Exemplum for this human vocation to charity. First, the pope underlines something that is true at both the natural and the supernatural level: "[M]an cannot live without love. He remains a being that is incomprehensible for himself, his life is senseless, if love is not revealed to him, if he does not encounter love, if he does not experience it and make it his own, if he does not participate intimately in it."[5] But in

---

1. See also SR, 194.

2. *ST* II–II, q. 184, a. 1, c; emphasis added.

3. See TOB 1:1, 1:5, 124:3, 133:2, 133:4.

4. FC 11. See Marengo, "La antropología adecuada." McGovern, "The Christian Anthropology." Clavell, "L'antropologia integrale."

5. RH 10.

Christ we have encountered love, not just natural but *supernatural* and divine love, a love that heals and elevates all of our human and natural aspirations. It is also in Christ that we have experienced that marvelous love and are empowered to participate in it.[6] Thus, John Paul II concludes that this "is why Christ the Redeemer fully reveals man to himself. If we may use the expression, this is the human dimension of the mystery of the redemption. In this dimension man finds again the greatness, dignity, and value that belong to his humanity."[7]

TOB reaches this same position and captures it with the expression, "the spousal meaning of the body." First, John Paul II explains that his understanding of the spousal meaning of the body is the end of a long process of reflection which began with the analysis of Christ's words concerning divorce, adultery in the heart, and the Resurrection: "Christ's words, which flow from the divine depth of the mystery of redemption, allow us to discover and strengthen the bond that exists between the dignity of the human being (of the man or the woman) and *the spousal meaning of his body*."[8] John Paul II evokes both his understanding of one's participation in the *munus regalis* of Christ and his philosophical view that supports it, namely, his theory of self-fulfillment as acquired or perfected freedom. Thus, the pope closely associates the notion of the spousal meaning of the body with a form of perfected, mature, or royal freedom: the freedom of the gift. All men are called to participate in it. Those who are married and those who are virgins for the sake of the Kingdom fulfill this same vocation to charity as gift of self in different but complementary ways.

Note how John Paul II again appeals to GS 22, pointing at Christ as the one who makes clear the spousal meaning of our bodies, our *supreme vocation*: "On the basis of this meaning [the spousal meaning of the body] they [Christ's words] allow us to understand and bring about the *mature freedom of the gift*, which expresses itself in one *way in indissoluble marriage and in another way by abstaining from marriage for the Kingdom of God*. In these different ways, Christ "fully reveals man to man himself and makes his supreme vocation clear" (Gaudium et Spes 22:1)."[9] The pope continues explaining that "this *vocation is inscribed in man* according to his whole psychophysical *compositum* precisely through the mystery of "the redemption of the body."[10] Consequently, John Paul II clearly identifies here the spousal meaning of the body as the vocation that is inscribed in the human person as a unity of body and soul, a vocation which results from being created in God's image. It is a vocation to find one's fulfillment in that freedom perfected by supernatural love, the freedom of the gift of self modeled by Christ's spousal love for his church.

---

6. See 1 John 1:1–4; Rom 5:8, 8:37–39; Eph 2:4–5; 2 Pet 1:4.
7. RH 10.
8. TOB 86:8.
9. Ibid.; emphasis added.
10. Ibid.; emphasis added.

Now, this synthetical exposition is *not the end but only the beginning* of our analyses. Our explanatory analytical method will be quite enriching. Wojtyła arrives at these conclusions only after a long study of Christ's words. To follow the pope down this path will show that there are some important nuances in his position, which need to be further explained in order to be adequately understood. In this book, I am particularly interested in appreciating the depth of his theology, by showing its extreme continuity with Vatican II and Thomas Aquinas. Thus, we will understand its "originality" in going back to the origins or sources of tradition in order to answer contemporary questions. I am especially concerned with elucidating this continuity, but not out of blind loyalty to a particular school of thought. I am interested in this formal aspect because *it best unveils the genius of John Paul II*. It shows the way in which TOB overcomes the chief limitation of the proponents of contraception's moral theology.

John Paul II's theological analyses contain an entire theology of the *imago Dei*, which fulfills Vatican II's requirements for the renewal of moral theology by adopting a perspective that is at the same time philosophical, biblical, and theological. As Ratzinger points out, John Paul II manages to harmonize here the biblical and metaphysical foundations of a christocentric moral theory. Such theory is compatible with the natural law and is grounded on the substantial unity of man as a being created in God's image.[11] Thus, in TOB, John Paul II overcomes the two great errors found in many post-conciliar attempts to renew moral theology according to the directives of OT 16: pure biblicism and the anti-metaphysical attitude of different moral theologies, especially those consequentionalist theories of the fundamental option.

John Paul's point of departure is Christ's words. Particularly, Wojtyła begins with Matthew 19:3–9. Disputing with the Pharisees about the indissolubility of marriage, Jesus points to Creation as a first disclosure of the Father's plan for man's salvation, namely, to be sons in the Son (*filii in Filio*).[12] This is truly "the beginning" that John Paul II keeps alluding to in his catecheses. The pope argues that, in these words, one can find Jesus himself solving a question of conjugal morality by appealing to a sound anthropology of the *imago Dei*.[13] We should do the same. Hence, we will also start our analysis at that point. My goal or end for these next two chapters is to make evident for the reader the following idea. Grounded in Aquinas and Vatican II, John Paul II's understanding of the spousal meaning of the body in the accounts of Creation offer an example of how to harmonize the biblical and metaphysical foundations of moral theology. The pope accomplishes such a task by positing a complementary relationship between the two accounts found in Genesis.[14] This present chapter will

---

11. See Benedict XVI, *John Paul II*, 39–41; Kurz, "The Scriptural foundation." Ognibeni, "Juan Pablo II ante la Sagrada Escritura"; Séguin, "The Biblical Foundations."

12. See Eph 1:3–15.

13. See TOB 1:4.

14. See Gen 1:1–31, 2:4–25; MD 6; Martin, "Male and Female."

look at the more metaphysical account. I will make explicit its latent metaphysical doctrine. Moreover, I will concentrate on the most important points that are in need of clarification in order to evince the Thomistic and conciliar coordinates of John Paul's theological anthropology.

Theological and Metaphysical

The first account of Creation, found in Gen 1:1–31, "has a *theological* character."[15] It really "contains hidden within itself *a powerful metaphysical content*."[16] Its anthropology relates man's *esse* to the phenomenon of procreation as a sign of man's contingency. The human person "is defined in it primarily in the dimensions of being and existing (*esse*)."[17] The dimension of being and existing is expressed in Gen 1:1–31 by man's being made in God's image. But "to the mystery of his creation (in the image of God he created him) corresponds the perspective of procreation (be fruitful and multiply), of coming to be in the world and in time, of *fieri*, which is necessarily tied to the metaphysical situation of creation: of contingent being (*contingens*)."[18]

Additionally, this entire metaphysical view of the human person's rational mode of being, and of his becoming as a contingent being, is based on two key and interrelated metaphysical claims. Both are foundational, not only for anthropology, but also for ethics. They are also axial for a sound moral theology. These metaphysical principles are the convertibility between being (*ens*) and good (*bonum*), and our participation in God as *the* Good.

Precisely in this metaphysical context of the description of Genesis 1, one must understand the entity of the good, that is, the aspect of value. In fact, this aspect returns in the rhythm of almost all of the days of Creation and reaches its high point after the creation of man, "God saw everything that he had made, and indeed, it was very good" (Gen 1:31). This is why one can say *with certainty* that the first chapter of Genesis has formed *an incontrovertible point of reference and solid basis of a metaphysics and also for an anthropology and an ethics* according to which "*ens et bonum convertuntur.*" Of course, all this *has its own significance* for theology as well, and above all *for the theology of the body.*[19]

This way of commenting on the scriptures is clearly reminiscent of Thomas Aquinas's own biblical commentaries. Take his commentary on John as an example. Following a very similar modus operandi, John Paul II offers in this text a very strong indication about his intent to harmonize the biblical and metaphysical foundations of moral theology. He restricts his scope to the theology of the body, especially to the

---

15. TOB 2:5.
16. Ibid.
17. Ibid.
18. Ibid., 2:5.
19. Ibid.; emphasis added.

biblical, theological, and metaphysical doctrine of man's being created in God's image and likeness. However, this text raises some questions that remain unanswered in TOB: what exactly are the other metaphysical truths contained in the first account of Creation but hidden in the *locus theologicus* of man's creation in God's image? What is their significance for ethics and for the theology of the body?

The pope is presupposing here quite a bit from his readers. He is implicitly appealing to a key philosophical position of his: the role of metaphysical participation and exemplarity for ethics.[20] The *imago Dei* in the human person is at the core of this key metaphysical theme. But it is seen from the perspective of the principle *ens et bonum convertuntur*. Indeed, participation and exemplarity explain through ultimate causes—that is, metaphysically—the innate and acquired goodness of the human person. And this philosophical doctrine is exactly what the text quoted beforehand identified as the core metaphysical content *hidden* in the first account of Creation. It is exactly the point of contact between metaphysics, anthropology, and ethics.

As John Paul II notes, after the creation of the human person, we read in Gen 1:31—"God saw everything that he had made, and behold, it was very good." Wojtyła sees a lot of metaphysics here because to explain in which sense something or someone is good, our author would appeal to *the centrality of form* as the immanent and transcendent measure of a being (*ens*). He would do so calling to mind the connection between efficient and exemplary causality. Once again, we encounter here Thomas's metaphysical view of the human soul as the one substantial form in man. For this reason, John Paul II has said that the first account of Creation is so crucial for the theology of the body. It offers the same metaphysical key that triumphs over the advocates of contraception's reductionistic view of the human person in Wojtyła's anthropology of love. To make this whole point a bit more apparent, I need to explain in which way Thomas's and Wojtyła's metaphysics of the soul offer a basic understanding of man's creation in God's image, viewed from the perspective of the metaphysical principle *ens et bonum convertuntur*.

In the case of the human person, Wojtyła would argue that a man is good, firstly, by virtue of his substantial form, by virtue of his rational soul created directly by God. Since every agent produces something like itself (*omnes agens agit sibi simile*), this form has a certain likeness to God as Supreme Good. Man's substantial immanent form—that is to say, his rational soul—is the basis for this metaphysical participation. And since man has an intellectual nature similar to that of God, he is the being in the *visible* world who resembles him the most. Thus, the human being is made in God's image.[21] For this reason, God says "and behold, it was *very* good." The innate indelible dignity and value of every human person, a dignity inherent to the simple fact of being

---

20. See PC, 73–94.
21. See Wojtyła, *Rozważania*, 77.

human, finds its source right here, in this kind of metaphysical participation in God as *the* Good.[22]

As we know from Wojtyła's anthropology of love, man's substantial form inclines the human person naturally. It does so in accordance with his rational and social mode of being. In the human person, there are natural inclinations to the acquisition of virtues.[23] Hence, we find another sense in which the human person is good. We find here another metaphysical explanation for God's declaration in Gen 1:31: "[B]ehold, it was *very* good." The human person is good in second act (*actus secundus*) because of the *conformity* to God as extrinsic form or Supreme Good. In other words, the human person is morally good because of his conformity to God as the final end and *the* Exemplar. As Thomas would say, a person is good in *actus secundus* if he conforms to the "truth of life," namely, to what the divine intellect has ordered him to do.[24]

Indeed, imitation of God as *the* Exemplar (*measure of the truth*) of the *imago Dei* in man is key for moral theology. Without a doubt, it is foundational for John Paul II's theological anthropology and moral theology. In this regard, TOB is clearly based on Vatican II because that imitation of God as *the* Exemplar of the *imago Dei* in man is the whole point of GS 22 and 24. Additionally, this same metaphysical and theological structural nerve of TOB is definitely Thomistic. It is the very foundational *locus* upon which Thomas builds *his entire moral theology,* as well as his theological anthropology as found in the *Secunda pars* of the *Summa theologiae*.[25] Such an important theological foundation is biblical, metaphysical, and theological. Since its biblical and theological character is now more evident, allow me to point to another metaphysical principle behind it: "[A]n image is related to that of which it is the image as what is measurable is related to its measure."[26]

The human person is substantially permanent but perfectible in the accidental order. Hence, when he lives a virtuous life conforming to the Divine Exemplar, he resembles God even more. Indeed, a virtuous person looks more like God than a morally deprived one. This is the sense in which *likeness*—in the expression in God's image and *likeness*—means the perfection of the *imago Dei*.[27] Moreover, the theological realm opens up new vistas. It opens a whole new supernatural dimension to the metaphysical considerations previously made. Thus, the metaphysical and biblical basis for John Paul II's christocentricism find their theological *locus*. The Son is especially the Divine Exemplar because Word is his personal name.[28] Thus, he is especially

---

22. See SR, 284 and 312; PC, 265.
23. See *ST* I, q. 76, a. 6, ad 1; I–II, q. 94, a. 3, c.
24. See *ST* I, q. 16, a. 4, ad 3; II–II, q. 109, a. 2, ad 3; SR, 15 and 420.
25. See *ST* I–II, prologue. See Abbà, *Lex et virtus*.
26. *In V Meta.*, lect. 17, n. 1003.
27. See PC, 45–56, 48, 74; *ST* I, q. 5, a. 1; q. 93, a. 9, c; I–II, q. 18, a. 1. For a clarifying explanation on this topic, see Brock, "Quanti atti di essere ha una sostanza?"
28. See John 1:1–5; *ST* I, q. 34, a. 2, c; *Super Io.*, cap. 1, lect. 1, nn. 25–29.

the Truth.[29] Everything was created in him and for him. The Son is the image of the invisible God,[30] and the human person is an icon in *the* icon (*ad imaginem*). Christ is the measure for the perfection of God's work of art in Creation. Consequently, the human person more closely resembles his Divine Exemplar by becoming *a son in the Son*.[31]

For these biblical and metaphysical reasons, following Thomas and Vatican II, Wojtyła connects the *imago Dei* in man and its perfection in the order of grace within the theme of filiation and conformity with Christ.[32] The natural, infused, and theological virtues, the Gifts of the Holy Spirit, together with the sacraments, conform the human person to Christ.[33] In this manner, they perfect, in the accidental order, his being in the image and likeness of the triune God. The vocation to holiness is nothing but a call to this conformity.[34] Such a call is ultimately perfected in glory, in the beatific vision.[35] Indeed, with the aid of supernatural grace, the more one knows and loves God, also by knowing and loving one's neighbor in God and because of God, the more one resembles the Divine Exemplar.[36] The moral growth in God's image and likeness is inseparable from the missions of the Son and the Holy Spirit. To enable us to imitate the Father and be perfect, the Son became for us both a *moral* and an *ontological* exemplar.[37] Christ "showed unto us in his own Person the way of truth."[38] He showed the way to God and led us to him because, in his humanity, Christ is *the* Way. He did so by giving an example and by empowering us to walk in the way towards union with God. His humanity is the instrument through which we receive the grace of the Holy Spirit. Thus, as Torrell explains, "conformity to Christ is necessarily part of conformity to God, and is obtained through the grace of the Holy Spirit."[39] Just like creation, the *new* Creation is a trinitarian event as well.

In general terms, this is the sketch of that theological and metaphysical content that John Paul II argues lies hidden in the first account of Creation. It undoubtedly has a conciliar and a Thomistic flavor. However, there are two points of clarification that I should address here. They all have to do with two possible obstacles to the goal of this chapter. Within this theological and metaphysical view, John Paul II posits that

29. See John 14:6; *Super Io.*, cap. 14, lect. 2, nn. 1867–1872.

30. See Col 1:16; *ST* I, q. 32, a. 2, c.

31. See *ST* III, q. 45, a. 4; Wojtyła, *Rozwżania*, 109–10; Anderson and Granados, *Called to Love*, 83–86.

32. See SR, 83.

33. See Cessario, "The Image of God."

34. See SR, 193.

35. See ibid., 189; *ST* I, q. 93, a. 4, c.

36. See *De Veritate*, q. 23, a. 7, ad 9; *ST* II–II, q. 26, a. 7, ad 2; *In III Sent.*, d. 29, q. 1, a. 6, ad 2; *Cántico* 39, 4–5.

37. See Matt 5:48; *Super I Cor.*, cap. 11, lect. 1, n. 583.

38. *ST* III, prologue. See John 14:6; *Super Io.*, cap. 14, lect. 2, nn. 1867–1872.

39. Torrell, *Christ and the Spirituality*, 123.

the human body participates in the similitude of image, and that the Trinity is the exemplar for the human communion of persons, including the communion in marriage between male and female. Are these two positions at odds with the theology of Thomas Aquinas? Are they to be considered as theological novelties?

The Human Body Images God

In the summary I just offered of Wojtyła's teachings on participation in *the* Good and on the *imago Dei*, the metaphysics of form occupies a definitive place of honor. Therefore, one may be surprised to read in TOB that the human *body* participates in the similitude of image: "Man, whom God created male and female, bears *the divine image impressed in the body* from the beginning."[40] Within the context of the life of grace and purity, John Paul II explains that we should keep our bodies holy by abstaining from unchastity. In this way, we will grow in our experience of the love inscribed by God "in the *whole human being* and thus *also in his body according to the image and likeness of God himself.*"[41] Thus, the pope claims that the human body reveals in the world God's eternal plan of salvation.[42] Can we find here a discrepancy with Aquinas?

Analyzing the more popular presentations of TOB, I always get the impression that, in fact, we can find such a discrepancy. Often, popular presentations claim that this is one of the "novelties" of John Paul II. But even at the scholarly level, there are also reasons in favor of this conflict.[43] An initial reading of some texts would strongly suggest such an opposition. For instance, Thomas explicitly says that "we find in man a likeness to God by way of an image *in his mind*; but *in the other parts* of his being by way of a *trace*."[44] Elsewhere, he also affirms that "man is said to be after the image of God, *not as regards his body*, but as regards that whereby he excels other animals . . . Now man excels all animals by his reason and intelligence; hence it is according to his intelligence and reason, which are incorporeal, that man is said to be according to the image of God."[45] Reading these and other similar affirmations, one could conclude that in Thomas's view, the human body does not participate in the similitude of image. John Paul II would then be in direct opposition to the Angelic Doctor.

However, instead of a direct opposition, I see here an opportunity to go deeper into this matter. In my opinion, John Paul II's proposal goes *back to the origins* or sources of traditional theology, leading us to a less one-sided reading of Thomas's own view. An attentive reading of Aquinas's theological anthropology unveils an important

---

40. TOB 13:2.
41. Ibid., 57:3; emphasis added.
42. See ibid., 19:4.
43. Both Scola and Kupczak seem to propose such a conflict. See Scola, *The Nuptial Mystery*, 47; Kupczak, *Gift and Communion*, 154–55.
44. *ST* I, q. 93, a. 6, c; emphasis added.
45. *ST* I, q. 3, a. 1, ad 2; emphasis added.

distinction. One could consider the human body only from the standpoint of that which it has in common with other corporeal creatures. From this perspective, it does not make the body part of God's image in man, because a body *as such* is not of an intellectual nature. Hence, from this viewpoint, corporeity is only a trace (*vestigium*) of God. However, one could adopt a different but non-contradictory perspective, and I think that this is the stance that John Paul II takes against the proponents of contraception's reductive anthropology. Instead of looking at the body in its corporeity, that is, in its similarities with irrational bodies, we could consider it as a *human* body. The emphasis is now different. We are focusing on what makes the human body human, on what makes it dissimilar from irrational bodies. Of course, the dissimilarity is that the human body is human *because of the one rational soul in man*. The body of a dead human person is a "body" without a soul. It is really not a human body but a cadaver.[46] Again, in a sense, the human body is generically animal but specifically rational. Thomas would agree. As we saw, he teaches that our human body has its proper accidents or essential qualities precisely because of our one rational soul.[47]

Hence, John Paul II's position in TOB seems to square perfectly with Thomas's metaphysics of the human soul. It turns out, then, that the pope was being very precise in saying that "*the divine image* [has been] *impressed in the body*."[48] But I think I can take it a step further. John Paul's view is *identical* to Thomas's explicit teaching found in another less well-known text. In his *Commentary on Peter Lombard's Sentences*, Aquinas adopts the very perspective alluded to in my second distinction. He says: "Indeed, the rational soul, in which the image of God is found, is the form of the human body. Therefore, *in the human body, inasmuch as it has the soul*, there is *not only the similitude of trace but also the similitude of image*."[49] Consequently, John Paul II's teaching according to which the human body participates in the similitude of image is not a theological novelty in opposition to Thomas Aquinas. It is clearly Thomistic. The pope acknowledges in TOB that the body shares in the *imago Dei* because of the human person's spiritual soul. Commenting on the shame experienced by our first parents in Gen 3:10, John Paul II explains that this experience makes man aware "for the first time that his body has ceased drawing on the power of *the spirit, which raised him to the level of the image of God*."[50]

---

46. See Aristotle, *De anima*, II.1, 412b10–24; *In II De anima*, lect. 1, n. 226.

47. See *ST* I, q. 76, a. 6, ad 1.

48. TOB 13:2.

49. *In III Sent.*, d. 2, q. 1, a. 3, qc. 1, ad 2; emphasis added. In light of this text, I would also qualify what Petri says in this respect: "For Aquinas, the image of God in each human person resides in the soul, not in the body." Petri, *Aquinas*, 220.

50. TOB 28:2; emphasis added.

PART II: SPOUSAL MEANING OF THE BODY

The Human Communion of Persons Images the Trinity

Another important clarification concerning the theological and metaphysical meaning implicit in the first account of Creation has to do with a question that I raised in the first chapter. Commenting on John 17:20–23 and GS 24, Wojtyła suggested an analogy between the Trinity and the communion of human persons. This same analogy is present in MD, with a special mention of Adam and Eve. My question really descends to the specific terms of this analogy. Both popular presentations on TOB and some scholars posit that, according to John Paul II, in the human family, the husband images the Father, the wife images the Son, and the offspring image the Holy Spirit.[51] Were John Paul to defend that thesis, his trinitarian theology and his theological anthropology would be in direct opposition to that of Aquinas and Augustine.[52] At the same time, this also seems to be the fitting context to address another related common misunderstanding in more popular presentations on TOB. To my knowledge, John Paul II has never taught that intra-trinitarian love is *free* and that it models conjugal love in *that* precise trait, namely, in being a love freely chosen. Obviously, conjugal love is not the question here. It is clear that, by its very nature, conjugal love is free.[53] The real question is whether or not God's eternal self-love is free. Is there any text in which John Paul II holds that position?

New Relational Vistas

Our discussion should begin with an analysis of GS 24. According to the Austin Flannery English edition, Jesus's prayer in John 17:20–23 "opened new horizons closed to human reason." The original Latin reads, "*prospectus praebens humanae rationi impervios.*" A more literal translation would say that Jesus "presents an inaccessible view to human reason." In a more periphrastic translation, one could also say that Jesus "opens up vistas closed to human reason." My point, however, is that the adjective *new* is nowhere to be found in the Latin text. But I am convinced that the use of this adjective has contributed to an important misunderstanding. It seems to have obscured the precise meaning of this expression. Thus, some of John Paul II's interpreters have been led astray by the idea of *newness*.

Some authors seem to conclude that the relational dimension of being created in God's image is something new, a development only present in some schools of *contemporary* philosophy and theology. Thus, for instance, Coll goes as far as accusing Wojtyła of ignoring these whole new relational vistas: "[O]ne cannot speak in Wojtyła of a true relational conception of the human person founded on a metaphysics of

---

51. See, for example, Rossetti, *Novissimus Adam*, 153; West, *Theology of the Body explained*, 108–9.
52. See *ST* I, q. 93, a. 6, ad 2.
53. See HV 9.

being as love, or even as likeness of God."[54] Such an objection is resolved, at a philosophical level, when one considers Wojtyła's anthropology of love and its study of the experience of acting together with others. Moreover, Thomas Aquinas argues that all of the relational virtues treated in the *Secunda Pars* are also a philosophical and theological manifestation of man's being created in God's image.[55] At the theological level, Wojtyła explicitly says about the *imago Dei* that "this image and likeness concern not only his [the human person's] spiritual nature, by means of which he is constituted a person in his individual unrepeatableness, but *also the dimension of relation*, that is, the reference to another person inscribed within the interior structure of the person. This dimension reflects in a certain way the Trinitarian mystery in God."[56] Furthermore, Coll's objection will also be explicitly answered in TOB, more particularly, in the experience of original unity.

Other authors are fascinated with the idea of theological newness for very different reasons, which lead to the heart of our discussion about the Trinity as *the* Exemplar of the human communion of persons. For instance, West seems to interpret these new vistas or horizons as "a *dramatic development* of catholic thought." This is actually the subheading title under which he is commenting on TOB 9:3 in light of GS 24. According to West, the resembling of the Trinity in the communion of human persons, especially in the communion between husband and wife, is not something we can *explicitly* find in traditional theology. West argues that until GS 24 and John Paul II's TOB, there is no explicit text which plainly holds this position:

> Not only as a rational individual does the human person image God (not only in the experience of original solitude), but also in the communion formed by man and woman (the experience of original unity). This marks *a bold theological development* on the Pope's part. Positing the divine image in the male-female communion—although it can be found under the surface of various texts in the theological tradition—*has not been the explicitly held perspective.*[57]

Notwithstanding the many merits of his very dedicated, zealous, and enthusiastic work on John Paul II's theology, West's opinion interests me mostly as an illustration. It reflects a common ethos in TOB's interpretation. Reading some of these commentators, one has the impression that the value of John Paul's theological position is directly proportional to its innovative character. This same ethos may have lead some to read newness into GS 24. But we cannot fall into the Kantian temptation of searching for originality and novelty to the detriment of the value of tradition.

At first, West's words appear to be unclear or imprecise. On the one hand, he says that no theologian explicitly held this perspective. On the other hand, he makes

---

54. Coll, "Karol Wojtyła," 220.
55. See *ST* I–II, prologue.
56. Wojtyła, "Anthropological Vision," 738; emphasis added.
57. West, *Theology of the Body Explained*, 108–9; emphasis added.

a direct reference to Augustine's explicit treatment of the matter in *De Trinitate* XII, 5 and to Thomas's in *ST* I, q. 93, a. 6, ad 2. Hence, West obviously knows that the resembling of the Trinity in the communion of husband and wife was *explicitly upheld* by some theologians in the fourth century. Augustine rejected the specific theological way in which this resembling was described with very harsh words. According to him, those who hold that view do not "advance a probable opinion."[58] Moreover, this "erroneous opinion" contains only one single grain of truth found in the scripture: Eve is from Adam and he is not her father. Augustine says that "all the rest of this opinion is in truth *so absurd*, nay indeed *so false*, that *it is most easy to refute it*."[59]

Why then did West say that this theological position was not explicitly upheld in the past? My only explanation is that he really argues that John Paul II explicitly holds it with approval. In other words, the reader of West's explanation of TOB is lead to believe that the pope accepts the very position which Augustine so forcefully rejects, the very same opinion that Aquinas also disregards. One is especially lead to believe it, particularly after reading how West appeals to MD 7 in order to conclude the following: "[T]hrough his Wednesday audiences, and even more authoritatively in later statements, John Paul brings *the once dismissed idea* that man and woman image God *in and through their communion* into the realm of official magisterial teaching."[60] West's affirmations sound quite serious. Is he saying that John Paul II dared to elevate to the rank of magisterial teaching of the church a position explicitly rejected by two of the greatest Doctors of the Church, a position said to be absurd, false, and most easy to refute? Did the pope actually do that?

To shed some light on this matter, we need to go back to clarify the precise meaning of the Council's expression "*prospectus praebens humanae rationi impervios*." This expression does not say that GS 24 is offering a new teaching with respect to traditional theology. It only points at what can be known about God's image in man *beyond* the natural light of human reason. In other words, it shows where philosophy stops and where theology begins. These new *theological* vistas include the relational aspect of God's image in the human person. However, as we know, there is also a natural dimension of being created in the image of God, which captures, in its own way, such a relational aspect as well. As was said, that natural dimension not closed to human reason is accessible when one studies man's social nature in his acting together with others. Hence, we get to the precise meaning of the Council's expression: *What is inaccessible to the natural light of reason is the healing and elevation of this relational and natural dimension of being created in God's image to the supernatural level*. These are the "new" relational vistas closed to human reason and its natural light. GS 24 makes perfectly clear the *supernatural* dimension of the communion of human persons being

---

58. Augustine, *On the Trinity*, XII, 5.
59. Ibid.; emphasis added.
60. West, *Theology of the Body Explained*, 109; emphasis added.

considered here. Thus, it speaks about a common "union among the sons of God, a union in charity and truth (*unionem filiorum Dei in veritate et caritate*)."

It is also very important to note that the analogy established between the Divine Persons and the communion of human persons works for *any* communion of human persons in *charity and in truth*. A convent of nuns who live in charity and truth image the Trinity in the exact manner described by GS 24. The same is true for a monastery of Carthusians living in charity and truth or for married couples living under the same conditions. It is indifferent whether they have children or not. It is also indifferent for this imaging whether the human persons involved are male or female.[61] What is absolutely determinant for GS 24 is that they are sons and daughters of God and that they are living in charity and truth. With these clarifications at hand, the whole question concerns now the exact terms of this analogy. GS 24 already hints at some points. Since the Triune God is charity and truth, those who partake of his divine life as adopted children, and live their moral lives in charity and truth, image this same Triune God. Now, in order to get a more detailed exposition of the exact terms of this wonderful analogy, we need to turn to MD 7.

One in Nature and Love

John Paul II begins in MD 7 by appealing to the image of Creation. He emphasizes that all men and women are made in God's image by virtue of their rational nature, which empowers them to know and to love God. Thus, "every individual is made in the image of God, insofar as he or she is a rational and free creature capable of knowing God and loving him."[62] The pope continues speaking of the relational dimension of man's rational nature. Still within the image of creation, John Paul II argues that every individual human person images God inasmuch as we exist in relation to other human beings, whom we can love as another *I*. He appeals to Adam and Eve to illustrate this point: "Moreover, we read that man cannot exist alone (Gen 2:18); he can exist only as a unity of the two, and therefore in relation to another human person. It is a question here of a mutual relationship: man to woman and woman to man. Being a person in the image and likeness of God thus also involves existing in a relationship, in relation to the other *I*."[63]

John Paul II moves now to the new relational vistas. He appeals to the image of grace as it perfects our relational or social human nature, thereby becoming icons of the Trinity. Thus, the pope is about to explain why the image of grace is the foundation

61. According to Lobato, human persons who actually love each other in charity and truth (let them be married or not), are a visible sign of God's intra-trinitarian *communio*. This commentator explains that this position is not excluded by Aquinas. See Lobato, "La famillia y la *communio personarum*." On this topic, Aranda does not see either opposition between John Paul II and Aquinas. See Aranda, "Ley natural e imagen de Dios," 42.

62. MD 7.

63. Ibid.

of the entire *Christian* ethos as an ethos of *charity*. Indeed, to love one's neighbor with charity is to grow in conformity with the Divine Exemplar. And this is precisely the biblical and metaphysical foundation of the most important moral norm, which contains all moral norms and brings them to perfection: Jesus's new commandment.[64]

> Man and woman, created as a "unity of the two" *in their common humanity*, are called to live in a *communion of love*, and in this way to mirror in the world the *communion of love that is in God*, through which the Three Persons love each other in the intimate mystery of the one divine life. The Father, Son, and Holy Spirit, one God through the *unity of the divinity*, exist as persons through the inscrutable divine relationship. Only in this way can we understand the truth that God in himself is Love (cf. 1 John 4:16).[65]

Note the four terms of this analogy that explains how the human communion of persons images the Trinity. John Paul II argues that the union of nature in common humanity images the unity of the divinity. Moreover, he says that the human communion of love images the communion of love that is God. Those are the exact terms of this wonderful analogy: one in nature and love. Thus, John Paul II is applying GS 24 and the unity of the sons of God in charity and truth to the unity of the two, the unity of man and woman. But he is pointing at the exact way in which this analogy should be constructed. In both analogies, of course, the dissimilitude is greater than the similitude.

The axial terms of the analogy have to do with being one in nature and one in love. But there is no mention of sexual differentiation in the analogy itself. There is no analogical relation between human and divine persons based on that. Being sexually distinct as male and female does not image one person of the Trinity over another. If the actual sexual union between husband and wife images the Trinity, it does so only because it is a union of two human persons in charity and truth. It does not image the Trinity because of any sexual dimension proper to the conjugal act as an act between one male and one female human being. The union between Adam and Eve, which does image the Trinity, is a union in their common humanity and their common charity.

The image and likeness of God in man, created as man and woman (in the analogy that can be presumed between Creator and creature), thus also expresses the "unity of the two" *in a common humanity*. This "unity of the two," which is a sign of interpersonal communion, shows that the creation of man is also marked by a certain likeness to the divine communion ("*communio*"). This likeness is a quality of the personal being of both man and woman, and is *also a call and a task*. The foundation of the whole human "ethos" is rooted in the image and likeness of God which the human

---

64. See John 13:34.
65. MD 7; emphasis added.

being bears within himself from the beginning. Both the Old and New Testament will develop that "ethos," which reaches its apex in *the commandment of love*.[66]

One more time, in this section of MD 7, John Paul II unfolds the same explicit terms of the analogy. It is all about a twofold perspective on unity. On the one hand, there is an analogous relationship in the unity of nature that is found in the Divine Persons and in the unity of nature between human persons. On the other hand, there is also an analogous relationship between the unity in love in the Divine Persons and the unity in love between human persons who fulfill the commandment of love as their vocation and moral task. Consequently, Adam and Eve are *not* seen in this analogy in their sexual differentiation but in their *common humanity and in their charity*. They could very well be considered as brother and sister. That is in fact, as we will see, one of the most foundational meanings of original unity. It is, according to John Paul II, the first sense of Gen 2:23—"This at last is bone of my bones and flesh of my flesh."[67]

Hence, MD 7 is also applicable in exactly the same terms not only to man and woman, to Adam and Eve, but also to other communions of human persons. The convent of nuns or the monastery of Carthusians perfectly fit into the same analogy as well. Furthermore, nowhere in the text does John Paul II say that Adam images the Father and Eve the Son. The position adopted here by John Paul II has no resemblance to the one rejected by Aquinas. It has no resemblance to the position Augustine considered "absurd" and "so false, that it is most easy to refute."[68] Consequently, I do not think that this text brings the once dismissed idea by Thomas and Augustine into the realm of official magisterial teaching. In fact, I think that the very *opposite* is true. If John Paul II is bringing into the realm of official magisterial teaching any theological position, it is exactly the one found in Thomas's explicit commentary on John 17:11–12. And this, of course, is a very important point for this book.

Allow me to briefly analyze Thomas's commentary. He interprets Jesus's prayer as asking for our (moral) perfection. As we know, Aquinas understands this perfection as conformity with God, who is love.[69] Thus, he can confidently say that *"our entire perfection lies in a unity of spirit."*[70] At this point, Thomas raises a very important objection. The unity of human persons and the unity of Divine persons cannot be put on a par. The Father and the Son are one in essence. They are two Persons but one God. Instead, the unity of two human persons does not result in one single being. It does not matter how much love there might be. It does not matter how supernatural that love is. They will always be two separate human beings. Such an objection forces Thomas to spell out the exact terms of the *analogy* between the communion of Divine

---

66. Ibid.
67. See TOB 8:4.
68. Augustine, *On the Trinity*, XII.5.
69. See 1 John 4:8.
70. *In Io.*, cap. 17, lect. 3, n. 2213. See Eph 4:3; Ps 133:1.

Persons and the communion of human persons included in Jesus's prayer. In so doing, Aquinas will show what the fourth Lateran Council taught in 1215: "[B]etween the Creator and the creature so great a likeness cannot be noted without the necessity of noting a greater dissimilarity between them."[71]

Thomas begins by placing the analogy in the context of his theology of the *imago Dei*. We are good to the extent that we resemble God by participating in *the* good. Hence, our unity contributes to our perfection because it shares in God's unity: "[T]he perfection of each thing is nothing but sharing a *likeness* to God; for we are good to the extent that we resemble God [*Deo assimilatur*]. Accordingly, our unity contributes to our perfection to the extent that it shares in the unity of God."[72] Having placed this doctrine in the right context, namely, that of the *imago Dei* and its perfection, let us look at how Thomas describes the exact terms of the analogy.

Now there is a twofold unity in God. There is a unity of nature: "I and the Father are one" (John 10:30); and a unity of love in the Father and Son, which is a unity of spirit. Both of these unities are found in us, not in an equal way, but with a certain likeness [*per similitudem quamdam*]. The Father and the Son have numerically the same nature [*sunt eiusdem naturae numero*], while we have the same specific nature. Again, they are one by a love which is not a participated love and a gift from another; rather, this love proceeds from them, for the Father and Son love themselves by the Holy Spirit. We are one by participating in a higher love.[73]

In God, there is *unity of nature*. Accordingly, there is a certain similitude in the unity of human persons. We also share the same specific nature. However, note that the dissimilarity is even greater. While the Divine Persons in the unity of their nature are one being, human persons, in the unity of their specific nature, remain different beings. In other words, the union of human persons, also in the supernatural realm, is destined to belong to the accidental and not the substantial level.[74]

Now, in God there is also a spiritual *unity of love*. There is a certain similitude in the spiritual loving union of human persons. However, once again, the dissimilarity is even greater. The unity of love in the Divine Persons is not given by another and it is not participated from another. Instead, the union or common union in charity between human persons that images God in the supernatural realm is a gift received from sanctifying grace. It is given by God. Moreover, it is a participation in God. Furthermore, it is a union with other human persons because of our communion with God. For this reason, commenting on this same passage, John of the Cross says that Jesus's prayer is brought to fulfillment in the following way: "The Father loves them

---

71. DS 804. See also Num 23:19; Hos 11:9; Isa 40:18, 46:5; MD 8.
72. *In Io.*, cap. 17, lect. 3, n. 2214.
73. Ibid.
74. Thomas also argues, in another place, that human persons image God better than the angels under the aspect of being the principle of things. The one God is the principle of all things. Similarly, all human beings come from one man. See *In I Sent.*, d. 3, q. 3, a. 1, ad 4; *ST* I, q. 93, a. 3, c.

by communicating to them the same love he communicates to the Son, though not naturally as to the Son, but as we said, through unity and transformation of love."[75]

The similarities between MD 7 and Thomas's commentary are really remarkable. Both texts establish the same analogy within the context of man's being good in accordance with his being created in God's image. Both texts establish an analogous relationship in the unity of nature that is found in the Divine Persons and in the unity of human persons. Both texts draw another analogy between the unity in love in the Divine Persons and the unity in love between human persons as a moral task accomplished by God's grace. In both texts, the explanation for Jesus's prayer lies in the similitude and greater dissimilitude between the unity of the Divine Persons in their divinity and love, and the unity among human persons in their humanity and their communion in charity and truth. Consequently, GS 24 and MD 7 are extremely close, if not identical, to Thomas's position here.

In none of those passages is the position rejected by Augustine found. In fact, to my knowledge, there is no clear text in which John Paul II adopts that rejected position. His explicit teaching concerning the human communion of persons imaging the Trinity applies not only to marriage but also to other kinds of friendships. Consequently, John Paul II's position is clearly Thomistic and clearly grounded in Vatican II. MD 7 seems a good example of the pope's *modus operandi*: to go back to the sources of tradition to answer new questions, and to do so harmonizing the biblical and metaphysical foundations of moral theology.[76]

Freedom In God's Eternal Self-Love?

In a former edition of his work, West rightly argues that Catholic sexual teaching is based on a solid anthropology of man created in God's image. He then provides his readers with very important advice for sexual morality: "[I]n order to determine what is good, we only need to ask *a simple question*: Does this sexual attitude, thought, or action truly image God's free, total, faithful, and fruitful love?"[77] Of course, this "simple question" is based on HV 9. There, Paul VI identified these essential traits of conjugal love listed by West. The difference, however, is that West applies them to

75. *Cántico* 39, 5.

76. Thus, I would also qualify Petri's comment: "The pope argues that being in the image of God is the equivalent of being called to a community of persons ... Here the pope does not disparage the tradition of seeing the *imago Dei* only in the intellectual faculties of intellect and will. Rather, *he supplements the tradition* by incorporating a biblical anthropology which he has drawn from a reading of the Genesis narrative." Petri, *Aquinas*, 168; emphasis added. See also, ibid., 194. In light of what has been explained, if Petri means that John Paul II *supplements* Aquinas because the former does not offer an explicit theology of the communion of human persons imaging the Trinity, I would disagree. Petri seems to rely on Spinello, *Genius of John Paul II*, 75; and on Shivanandan, *Crossing the Threshold of Love*, 141–70. However, Petri also acknowledges that he has not looked at the issue with all the attention it deserves. See Petri, *Aquinas*, 194n146.

77. West, *Theology of the Body* [1st ed.], 167; emphasis added.

God. Is this application correct? Within the parameters of analogy, there is a certain sense in which they are. One form of God's love is especially free, total, faithful and fruitful: Christ's love for his church. In this sense, West *is absolutely right*. Christ has freely given his life for the church.[78] Moreover, he has totally given himself to us,[79] in faithful obedience to the Father's will.[80] Jesus will always be faithful to his church.[81] And Christ's love for the church is also fruitful. Indeed, he is the grain of wheat that has fallen into the ground, out of love, and has given abundant fruit.[82] Thus, after dying for us, being in the tomb, and rising on the third day, Jesus, in his love, has given us his Holy Spirit and its first fruits.[83] Living already in these first fruits, we look forward to their ultimate perfection, eagerly awaiting for the Second Coming of the Lord and for the fullness of the redemption of our bodies.[84]

However, West could be misunderstood. His advice could lead to the following reasoning: HV 9 clearly states that freedom is one essential characteristic of conjugal love; but conjugal love images the Trinity; therefore, the element of freedom that is natural to conjugal love must also be present within Trinitarian love, even before the Incarnation.[85] From the logical viewpoint, the major and minor premises of this syllogism are indisputable. However, the conclusion does not really flow from them, unless the minor premise is reversed. Only if the Trinity were to image conjugal love, would it follow that freedom belongs necessarily to God's eternal self-love. But both the inversion of the minor premise and the conclusion of this syllogism seem utterly incompatible with John Paul's theology. The inversion of the minor premise denies TOB's foundational principle. Instead of upholding that the human person is made in *God's* image, the pope would be defending that God is in *man's* image. This is absurd![86] Feuerbach would happily applaud, cheering from the sidelines: theology would be nothing but anthropology. But this is certainly not John Paul's position. On the other hand, the conclusion of the syllogism is also incompatible with John Paul's theology. Before the Incarnation, there is only one will in God. From all eternity, its object is the ineffable divine essence. In a most simple way and simultaneously, this ineffable essence is God's own being (*esse*), infinite goodness, and God's own will. To affirm that

---

78. See John 10:18.
79. See Gal 2:20; Eph 5:25.
80. See Phil 2:8; Luke 22:42.
81. See 2 Tim 2:13.
82. See John 12:24.
83. See John 20:22.
84. See Rom 8:23.

85. See Ashour, *Theology of the Body*, 7. After personal conversations with this author, she has changed her opinion on this issue. Although Ashour claims not to be influenced by West, it seems that her former position was closely associated with a misunderstanding quite close to the one just described.

86. West explicitly denies such an inversion in *Good News*, 19–20.

God's eternal self-love is free would entail the denial of God's simplicity, perfection, and unity.

In his catecheses on the Creed, John Paul II offers an example of how he views a correct analogy between communion in the Trinity and human freedom. "The relations which distinguish the Father, Son, and Holy Spirit, and which really relate them to one another *in their same being*, possess in themselves all the richness of light and life of the divine nature, *with which they are totally identified*. They are subsisting relations, which by virtue of their vital impulse go out to meet one another in a communion in which each is completely open to the other."[87] The Divine Persons are subsisting relations related *in their same being*. The *divine attributes* are predicated of that same ineffable being. God is all of them at one and the same time, and without any composition whatsoever. Thus, Father, Son, and Holy Spirit, all of them "possess," so to speak, *all the richness of life of the divine nature*. Furthermore, they are totally *identified* with that same nature. The Father is goodness itself, and so is the Son and the Holy Spirit. This model and archetype serves to illumine what is authentic in any communion of human persons in love, also in that communion present in marriage. But John Paul II does *not* affirm freedom in the love among the Persons of the Trinity. He only affirms that the human freedom inherent in human interpersonal love is modeled by the eternal love between the Divine Persons. "This loving communion is a *supreme model* of the sincerity and *spiritual liberty* which should characterize human interpersonal relations, which are always so far removed from this transcendent model."[88] Hence, conjugal love cannot become the rule and measure of intra-trinitarian love. It is actually the other way around. The love among the persons of the Trinity is *the* exemplar for human freedom. It is also *the* exemplar for that freedom inherent in conjugal love. As we know, the metaphysical principle at play here is very Thomistic: "[A]n image is related to that of which it is the image as what is measurable is related to its measure."[89]

The Trinity is the supreme and transcendent model for the perfection of human freedom because perfected human freedom images this one precise aspect of the Trinity's eternal self-love, namely, the simplest identification between love, truth, and goodness. Indeed, God's self-love is love for truth and goodness coinciding in the same and most simple being. This same divine simplicity and perfection is the reason why God's eternal self-love is necessary and not free. Consider our own will to be happy. We will to be happy without a choice about it. We want goodness itself without freedom, because goodness itself is the natural object of our own will. The will is not freely but naturally inclined to its proper object.[90] Thus, Thomas explains that "the divine will has a necessary relation to the divine goodness, since that is its

---

87. John Paul II, *Father and Creator*, 183; emphasis added.
88. Ibid., 183–184.
89. *In V Meta.*, lect. 17, n. 1003.
90. See Augustine, *On the Trinity*, XIII.5; *ST* I, q. 94, a. 1, c; *In IV Sent.*, d. 49, q. 1, a. 3, c.

proper object. Hence God wills his own goodness necessarily, even as we will our own happiness necessarily, and as any other faculty has necessary relation to its proper and principal object, for instance the sight to color, since it tends to it by its own nature."[91] As he later says, distinguishing God's freedom in loving *creatures* from God's eternal self-love: "Since then God necessarily wills his own goodness, but other things not necessarily, as shown above, he has free will with respect to what he does not necessarily will."[92] To my knowledge, John Paul II has never taught something to the contrary.

This whole discussion concerning the first account of Creation has lead us to make more explicit that metaphysical and theological content "hidden," as it were, in Gen 1:1–31. It has also provided an opportunity to make important clarifications, which evince not only John Paul II's Thomism but also his theological and philosophical genius. It is time now to show how the second account of Creation complements and illustrates the first, by means of the psychological experiences witnessed from the viewpoint of consciousness. These original experiences are also interpreted by Wojtyła within the coordinates of Thomistic theology and his anthropology of love. They illustrate the meaning of man being created in God's image. They offer an experiential view of some of the theological and metaphysical truths latent in Gen 1:1–31. Our author harmonizes in TOB what is biblical, philosophical, and theological. And, he keeps doing so by offering a Thomistic argument grounded in Vatican II.

---

91. *ST* I, q. 19, a. 3, c.
92. *ST* I, q. 19, a. 10, c.

6

Original Experiences

Understanding Original Experiences

John Paul II explains the complementary relationship between Genesis 1:1–31 and Genesis 2:4–25 in the following terms: "Genesis 2 presents the creation of man especially in the aspect of his subjectivity. When we compare the two accounts, we reach the conviction that *this subjectivity corresponds to the objective reality of man created in the image of God.*"[1] As he says elsewhere, "the text of Genesis 2:18–25 helps us to understand better what we find in the concise passage of Genesis 1:27–28. At the same time, if it is read together with the latter, it *helps us to understand even more profoundly* the fundamental *truth* which it contains *concerning man* created as man and woman in the image and likeness of God."[2] The complementarity between these two accounts of Creation hinges upon the connection between the original experiences and the theological and metaphysical teachings on God's image in the human person explained in chapter 5. Based on these original experiences, Adam and Eve *became aware of the spousal meaning of their body*. Hence, a set of very crucial questions appear before our eyes: what are these original experiences? What makes them original? How do we get to know them? How do they relate to each other? How does John Paul II arrive at the conclusion that, based on these original experiences, Adam and Eve became aware of the spousal meaning of their bodies? How does each one of these original experiences concretely illustrate our being created in God's image? How is this whole argument Thomistic and grounded in Vatican II?[3]

These experiences are original in that they have to do with the *first experiences* the human person had. They refer to the first time a human being experienced something. However, they are also original because they *originate* or cause a deeper (pre-scientific) understanding about the human person.[4] The first sense of original points to a simple awareness or consciousness about something new. The second, on the other

---

1. TOB 3:1; emphasis added.
2. MD 6.
3. By answering these questions, I intend to supplement Petri's brief explorations in, *Aquinas*, 165–75.
4. See PC, 240.

119

hand, refers to a certain understanding of that awareness, to an act of self-knowledge. Thus, this second account of Creation highlights man's subjectivity. In its own peculiar way, Gen 2:4–25 offers a description of man's lived experience or consciousness, and of the understanding of his own personal identity from that internal viewpoint.

We know about these original experiences mainly through revelation. Yet, our own human experience and understanding of similar experiences are also helpful.[5] Certainly, we do not share in Adam and Eve's state of justice before the fall. Nevertheless, we do share in the same human nature, and our own experience of living in the state of grace also helps us to indirectly understand some of their original experiences. Although limited and indirect, this other point of access to the original experiences explains why Wojtyła's anthropology of love plays such a crucial role in the pope's interpretation of Gen 2:4–25. In his commentary, the specific way in which the biblical, the theological, and the metaphysical go together is found in the intimate connection between the original experiences. They are all linked in the same way by the different layers of transcendence related to each other in chapter 4. The original experiences will be *manifestations* of the *imago Dei* in the human person. In turn, the *imago Dei* will be the theological and metaphysical *explanation* of these same experiences. Thus, in this instance as well, the "phenomenological analyses based on the assumptions of the philosophy of consciousness begin to work in favor of an *enrichment* of the realistic image of the person."[6] In this chapter, I am interested in revealing the internal logic of this interconnection, explaining why this whole argument is Thomistic and grounded in Vatican II.

Original Solitude

The experience of original solitude is so important in illustrating man's creation in God's image that the pope says: "[W]ithout that deep meaning of man's original solitude, *one cannot understand and correctly interpret* the whole situation of man, *created in the image of God*, which is the situation of the first, in fact primeval, covenant with God."[7] This allusion to the primeval covenant situates us in the right context. In truth, original solitude is preceded in the biblical text by two other experiences, which have their own significance and input into Adam's consciousness. They are "motives and circumstances *that explain more deeply the meaning of man's original solitude*."[8] As he is placed in the garden of Eden, Adam experiences that he has the *munus* of cultivating the earth.[9] He experiences himself as a *cultural* being. In connection with his

---

5. See TOB 4:4,11:1.
6. PC, 220; emphasis added.
7. TOB 6:1; emphasis added. For a monographic study of this experience, see Shivanandan, *Original Solitude*.
8. See Gen 2:5; 1:18; TOB 5:4.
9. See Gen 2:15.

being cultural, Adam also experiences that he is a moral agent.[10] God establishes with him a covenant. Thus, Adam experiences that he is capable of being the free cause of his own obedience to the Creator.[11]

At this point in the account, God says that it is not good for man to be alone. He then further declares his intention to create a helper fit for man.[12] However, before he does, Adam has an experience of the truth signified by God's words regarding solitude. This new lived experience takes place when Adam names the irrational animals.[13] He brings to this experience the self-knowledge acquired by the reception of his *munus* of collaborating with the Creator in cultivating the garden and in being the free cause of his obedience to the first covenant. Hence, comparing and contrasting the essence of irrational animals with his own capacity to name them, and with the self-knowledge acquired in these two previous experiences, Adam has an awareness of his own solitude. Not only does he come to know *his own essence* and *vocation* as different from that of irrational animals, at the same time, he also experiences *his need for human friendship*. Such an internal experience of solitude evokes or *originates* some further reflection. It leads to a deeper understanding of Adam's own identity and mission. He is "*before God* in search of his own being."[14] While naming the irrational animals, Adam *understands* that he is a rational animal, a human person, in need to share with other human beings the gift and mission (*munus*) received from God.

This whole experience illustrates two peculiar aspects of being created in God's image. It manifests the human person as an individual substance of a rational nature, capable of knowing and loving God, and of being his partner. Additionally, this same experience manifests the relational dimension of being created in God's image. There is a longing here for friendship with another human being. Man is alone in the visible world for the following four reasons. First, Adam is the only one who is conscious of his rationality, thanks to his capacity for self-knowledge. Second, he is the only one on earth who is a partner of the Absolute. Third, Adam is the only one who is a substantial unity of matter and a spiritual rational soul, called to find authentic self-fulfillment in subordinating his own actions to the truth about the good. Fourth, Adam is the only one in the visible world capable of friendship. Thus, "man is alone: this is to say that through his own humanity, through what he is, he is at the same time set into a unique, exclusive, and unrepeatable relationship with God himself. The anthropological definition contained in the Yahwist text in its own way approaches *the theological definition of man that we find in the first creation account (Let us make man in our image and our likeness* (Gen 1:26)."[15]

10. For this understanding of culture and morality see PC, 263–78.
11. See Gen 2:16–17; TOB 5:4.
12. See Gen 2:18.
13. See Gen 2:19–20.
14. TOB 5:5.
15. Ibid., 6:2; emphasis added.

Consequently, within the experience of original solitude, "in relatively few sentences, the ancient text sketches *man as a person* with the subjectivity characterizing the person."[16] In very few sentences, we find "*almost all of the elements* of the analysis of man to which modern, and above all *contemporary philosophical anthropology* is sensitive."[17] It is no surprise, then, that the pope's interpretation of this experience is highly philosophical. It really presupposes the reader's familiarity with a great deal of Wojtyła's anthropology of love. For this reason, John Paul II acknowledges herein that almost all of the elements of contemporary anthropologies like his own are at play. If we look closely at the four reasons why Adam experiences solitude, we can easily see in them most of the aspects of Wojtyła's integral vision of man (consciousness, efficacy, transcendence, integration, and participation). The one aspect that is only hinted at in original solitude is that of participation. It will be part of original unity.

Consciousness and Self-knowledge of the Human Body

In the experience of original solitude, we find "the first witness of human consciousness."[18] We find a witness of human consciousness in its interrelationship with self-knowledge. Original solitude is not just about having an awareness of an experience. It is also about Adam having consciousness of his self-knowledge and of its *results* as *meanings* deposited in consciousness.[19] For this reason, in the experience of solitude, "man gains consciousness of his own superiority, that is, that he cannot be put on a par with any other species of living beings on the earth."[20] The Thomistic understanding of consciousness found here is that concomitant perception or experiential awareness (*notitia experimentalis*), whose two functions Wojtyła already explained. Both functions are key in order to account for this original experience. The reflective function is present in all of the parts of original solitude, reflecting as in a mirror, all the *objective* contents of Adam's experience. The reflexive function, on the other hand, turns to the *subject* experiencing. It refers all these objective contents to Adam's ego.[21] Following the principles of Aquinas's epistemology, John Paul II argues that these two functions are activated when Adam knows something other than his own act of knowing. Additionally, these same two functions, inherent in the act of knowing something, also forge the experiential terrain penetrated later by another act, by Adam's intellectual self-knowledge. Let us pay close attention to the following text:

16. Ibid., 6:1. See *ST* I, q. 29, a. 3, c; Ciccone, *Uomo-Donna*, 31–32; Shivanandan, *Crossing the Threshold*, 95–101.
17. TOB 5:6; emphasis added.
18. Ibid., 3:1.
19. See AP, 35.
20. TOB 5:4.
21. See AP, 43.

> Self-knowledge goes hand in hand with knowledge of the world, of all visible creatures, of all living beings to which man has given their names to affirm his own dissimilarity before them. Thus, *consciousness reveals man* as the one who possesses the *power of knowing* with respect to the visible world. With this knowledge, which makes him go in some way outside of his own being, man at the same time *reveals himself to himself in all the distinctiveness of his being.*[22]

Why does John Paul II say that self-knowledge goes hand in hand with knowledge of the world? Obviously, because Adam is comparing himself with other beings. In so doing, he is discerning his own essence by affirming his dissimilarity with irrational animals. However, the pope is also alluding here to an important epistemological principle: "[O]ur spirit [*mens*] comes to a knowledge of itself through apprehension of *other things*."[23] It is not possible for man to know the nature of his own act of knowledge without knowing *first* something other than itself. "One *perceives that he understands* only from the fact that he understands something. For to understand something is *prior to understanding that one understands.*"[24] *Within* the same act of knowing something, Adam has an awareness or concomitant consciousness of his own knowing. This awareness provides a lived experience, a perception, or a *notitia experimentalis* of his own act of knowledge.[25] This principle is really applicable to all the powers of the soul directed in some way by the command of the intellect and the will.[26] "Those things which are in the soul by their essence, are known through *experimental knowledge* in so far as through his acts man has experience of their inward principles."[27] This perception or experimental knowledge becomes, as it were, the terrain upon which another act of knowledge reflects. In this way, one understands that he understands, that he wills, that he feels, etc. In other words, one grasps the nature of his own acts, of his faculties, and of his own essence.[28] The results of this induction are like *meanings* deposited in consciousness.[29]

This is why John Paul says in the text that *consciousness* reveals man as the one who possesses the power to intellectually know reality. He is not saying that consciousness performs the self-knowledge. Wojtyła would never hold that position. He says in another place that while he agrees "with Husserl that these acts [knowledge and self-knowledge] are in consciousness, it is quite another thing to say that they are proper to consciousness."[30] Hence, what John Paul II is arguing, instead, is that

22. TOB 5:6; emphasis added.
23. *De Veritate*, q. 10, a. 8, c; emphasis added.
24. Ibid.
25. See *ST* I, q. 43, a. 5, ad 2; Aristotle, *Nichomachean Ethics*, IX. 9, 117a27–1170b1.
26. See *ST* I–II, q. 17.
27. Ibid., I–II, q. 112, a. 5, ad 1. Translation slightly altered.
28. See *De Veritate*, q. 10, a. 8, c.
29. See AP, 35.
30. PC, 227.

the meanings resulting from self-knowledge are deposited in consciousness. As a result, Adam is aware not only of the *existence* of his power of knowing but also of its *essence*. This is the case because "consciousness interiorizes all that the human being cognizes, *including everything that the individual cognizes from within in acts of self-knowledge*, and makes it all a content of the subject's lived experience."[31] *Consciousness* reveals man as the one who possesses the power to intellectually know reality. The essence of Adam's power of knowing is rational. Such an essence or nature is deposited as a meaning in consciousness by Adam's self-knowledge. The adjective rational is the best one we have to signify our dissimilarity with respect to other animals. Thus, the adjective rational is given to man's soul not only to signify the power of reason; above all, it is an adjective that modifies the *whole* human soul, whose perfection is clearly manifested in the power of intellectually knowing reality.[32] Consequently, based on these precisions, John Paul II argues that, in this entire process, man reveals himself to himself as different from other animals, not only in his power but above all, *in his being*.

The human person finds himself before God in quest of an understanding of his own essence. He is looking for his definition or, as we would say today, for his "identity." While the human person knows that he is *not* an irrational being, he also acknowledges that he is a living body among others, that he is generically animal and part of the visible world. "Man, formed in this way, belongs to the visible world; he is a body among bodies."[33] On the other hand, original solitude also reveals that specifically speaking, man is rational or personal. He is alone in this regard. There is no other being like him in the *visible* universe. Man's animal nature (his sensibility and sensuality) is permeated by this specific difference, by his rationality. That is why, "*the body*, by which man shares in the visible created world, makes him at the same time aware of being alone."[34] Based on the Thomistic understanding of the soul previously explained, John Paul II argues that unlike the body of other animals, Adam's human body is rational.[35] Thus, against the advocates of contraception's anthropology, John Paul II argues that it is Adam's *human body* that makes him aware of being alone, of his solitude and of his unique relationship with God.

Partner of the Absolute

Adam's original solitude also entails a deeper layer. It includes the revelation of the human person as a "subject of the covenant" and "partner of the Absolute."[36] Being

---

31. Ibid.; emphasis added.
32. See *ST* I, q. 77, a. 1, ad 7.
33. TOB 6:3.
34. Ibid.
35. See *ST* I, q. 76, a. 6, ad 1.
36. TOB 6:2.

God's partner means to be able to *freely* collaborate with him. No one in the visible world can do that except Adam. He is alone in this regard as well. Thus, this capacity for free collaboration is inherent to his self-knowledge as generically animal but specifically rational. Adam's search for his own definition or identity reveals him as a human person. Indeed, the pope explains that "this process [man's awareness of his *genus* and his specific *differentia*] also leads to the *first delineation* of the human being *as* a human *person*, with the proper subjectivity that characterizes the person."[37]

In fact, the power of knowing both the visible world as well as his own self is already a proof of man's transcendence. It is a clear manifestation of his spirituality.[38] Based on this capacity for intellectual knowledge, man's going beyond himself also manifests his spiritual nature in his capacity for culture or dominion over his own actions and over irrational beings. Adam has the power of freely causing actions.[39] He belongs to a different ontological level than those actions. He is not an accident but a substance. He is substantially permanent but perfectible in the accidental order. However, Adam is not just a substance. He is a rational substance with the power to act freely. Thus, Adam is a moral and cultural being because, in a sense, he is both the creator and the material of his own moral identity. Therefore, against the spiritualistic Cartesian anthropology of the advocates of contraception, man is not a consciousness suspended in the void. His subjectivity consists in being an individual substance (*suppositum*), which has a similarity and a dissimilarity with other substances of the visible world by the fact of having a rational nature. All of his dynamisms spring from his one and only rational soul, which confers his peculiar personal *esse*. In short, man becomes aware of being a person (*individua substantia rationalis naturae*) in the visible world.

Being a partner of the Absolute also implies three additional interrelated characteristics peculiar to the human way of being a person. First, Adam is a non-autonomous person; second, he is subject to death, and third, Adam exists and lives in strict dependence on the Creator. In truth, God has already commanded Adam not to eat from the tree of knowledge of good and evil. This commandment establishes the limitations of human cognition against Kant's claims of autonomy. The human person's intellect is to conform to reality as its measure. Good and evil are rationally found or *discovered in the very nature of things made by the Creator*. The values of good and evil are *not* created by man's conscience.[40] For this reason, the human person is not to eat from the tree of knowledge. He is not to establish himself as the autonomous subject that creates values. At the same time, this exact command from God makes man aware of his own capacity for self-determination. This is another aspect of the human person's spirituality or transcendence. His freedom becomes, as it were, the

---

37. Ibid., 5:6. See *ST* I, q. 29, a. 1, c; Lombo, *La persona en Tomás*.
38. See *ST* I, q. 75, a. 2, c.
39. See TOB 6:1; AP, 67; PC, 228.
40. See AP, 165; *De Veritate*, q. 17, a. 3, ad 3; q. 17, a. 5, c.

living testimony of his mode of being and individuality.[41] Freedom expresses who the human person is as an *individum*, that is, as a being that is one (*unum*) and undivided (*indivisum*), as a being that is distinct from other beings. Freedom expresses the human person's individuality even better than just sheer knowledge, because it expresses *more essential qualities* about the human person. Freedom includes *both* the intellect and the will in their governance of other powers. Hence, it is a greater manifestation of the human rational soul.

Additionally, the connection between cultivating the garden and cultivating one's moral identity is found in this, that the human person's lordship or dominion over his own actions—and thus over his moral identity—transpires outwardly in a dominion over the visible world. But it is always *a lordship in the Lord*. The human person is, hence, a cultural being in collaboration with the Creator. Acting together with God, Adam can cultivate the formation of his own personality and the development of the world around him.[42] Moreover, being a partner of the Absolute does not imply that one is to be considered on a par with God. Rather, it means a proper *subordination* that is in accordance with our rational nature. It implies a strict dependence on the Creator for one's own life and happiness. Indeed, Adam is a creature that can experience death if he disobeys God. When God said to man that if he ate of the tree of knowledge of good and evil he would die, man understood death as the radical antithesis of all that he had been endowed with. "The words of God-Yahweh addressed to the man *confirm a dependence in existing*, so that they show man as a limited being and, by his nature, susceptible to nonexistence."[43] As God's partner, the human person experienced the possibility of losing the fulfillment of the meaning of his being a rational body, that is to say, the fulfillment of his being *capax Dei*.[44]

At the same time, as partner of the Absolute, Adam's relationship with God is very unique in the visible world. He is alone on this earth in that kind of relationship. No other animal has it. For this reason, John Paul II has said that original solitude reveals Adam's dignity as a human person. In reality, we are going back to GS 24. Vatican II explains therein that the human person is the only creature on earth, in the visible world, that God has willed for his own sake (*in terris sola creatura est quam Deus propter seipsam voluerit*). Adam is alone in that kind of relationship with God and Creation. As a result, he also experiences solitude. Even if the human person is corporeal, he is capable of knowing and loving freely, whence his solitude in his dominion over irrational beings, which are incapable of such foundational knowledge and love, that same knowledge and love which allows for man's characteristic relationship with God as *the* Legislator.

---

41. See TOB 6:2. See Dewan, *Form and Being*, 229–48.
42. See PC, 263–78.
43. TOB 7:3.
44. See Granados, *La ética esponsal*, 204.

The conciliar context of this aspect of original solitude is of the utmost importance. Think of it in light of the proponents of contraception's anthropology and in light of their understanding of conscience. Against their view on autonomy, John Paul's explanations of how original solitude *originates* an understanding of the human person as partner of the Absolute speaks "directly about the *submission* and *dependence* of man-creature on his Creator."[45] As we saw in chapter 1, consciousness of creation reveals that the human person has a lordship over creation that is *in* the Lord. Man must cultivate his own moral identity and the world around him in accordance with God's intelligible design of his own rational nature. The human person must dominate nature neither against these laws of rational nature nor against the Creator as their author. Rather, Adam is to exercise his dominion by participating or collaborating with God through the fulfillment of the natural and revealed law.

The Meaning of the Body

Original solitude also *originates* Adam's perception of the very *meaning of his body*. He gains consciousness of the meaning of his body as understood by his intellect in the acts of self-knowledge described thus far. Understanding his own essence in contrast with irrational animals, and understanding his own personhood and his *munus* as a partner of the Absolute, brings about a deeper realization of Adam's own *identity and mission*. Thus, "one can affirm with certainty that man thus formed has at the same time *the awareness and consciousness of the meaning of his own body*. Moreover, he has *based this on the experience of original solitude*."[46] According to Wojtyła's realistic semantics, the meaning of the body signifies the real identity and ontic constitution of the human person, as is deposited in consciousness after being apprehended by the intellect. Moreover, the meaning of the body also signifies the orientation of man's very nature, whom he ought to be because of his rationality, his vocation and mission. John Paul's understanding of the meaning of body entails a twofold perspective, reminiscent of his *anthropological* and *ethical* considerations on the aspects of transcendence and integration.

On the one hand, the pope speaks at this point about Adam's self-knowledge of his substantial unity. "Consciousness of the body seems to be identical in this case with the discovery of the complexity of one's own structure, which in the end, based on a philosophical anthropology, consists *in the relation between soul and body*."[47] Genesis does not offer a metaphysical explanation of the human soul. It speaks, rather, of man's composition in terms of body and life. However, from the text of Genesis, one can infer a subjective understanding of this relationship from the perspective of lived experience. Indeed, in the text, man experiences that he is the same conscious

---

45. TOB 6:2; emphasis added. See SR, 50; LR, 246–47; AP, 165.
46. TOB 6:3; emphasis added.
47. Ibid., 7:1.

subject of bodily and spiritual actions. Thereby, the human person has an awareness or consciousness of the unity of his body and soul. However, according to John Paul II, this same awareness has an *ethical* significance. It reveals both who man *is* and who he *ought* to be. This is how the pope begins his argument from the *anthropological* viewpoint:

> If the original description of human consciousness reported by the Yahwist text includes also the body in the whole account, if it contains, as it were, the first witness of the discovery of one's own bodiliness (and even, as we said, the perception of the meaning of one's own body), all of this reveals itself not on the basis of man's sufficiently clear concrete subjectivity. *Man is a subject not only by his self-consciousness and by self-determination, but also based on his own body.* The structure of this body is such that it permits him to be the author of genuinely human activity. In this activity *the body expresses the person.*[48]

From the *anthropological* viewpoint, John Paul II is appealing to the principle that the human person is a subject of spiritual acts, like self-determination. These acts are intrinsically independent from matter. But the human person is not to be identified with his intellectual consciousness nor with his free self-determination. The human person is not a pure spirit. In truth, the human person is also a subject based on his own body. He is also the conscious subject of actions that are intrinsically dependent on matter. There are not different souls in the human person, but only one that is responsible for his entire dynamism. Otherwise, we could not explain why we are not able to study when we have a severe fever or a headache. If we had more than one soul, those things would not be impediments. Hence, according to the principle *operari sequitur esse*, the human person is a substantial unity of matter and spiritual soul.[49] Moreover, John Paul views the soul not only as the form of the body, but also as its mover and end. Although there is a sense in which the human person is his body, there is another sense in which the body is the *instrument* used by the person to express himself.

On the other hand, from the *ethical* viewpoint, the pope speaks about who man *ought to be* in accordance with his rational nature. The body's materiality was "penetrable and transparent, as it were, in such a way as *to make it clear who man is (and who he ought to be) thanks to the structure of his consciousness and self-determination.*"[50] The pope finds the grounds for this moral obligation inscribed in the very lived experience (consciousness) and nature of self-determination. To follow this reasoning, once again, we need to go back to the attitude of Christian responsibility and to Wojtyła's anthropology of love. The human person experiences his acting freely, and consequently, his capacity for self-determination. His freedom is made possible and perfected by his *capacity for truth*. Such capacity is measured by reality. Ultimately, this

---

48. Ibid., 7:2; emphasis added.
49. See *ST* I, q. 76, a. 1, c.
50. TOB 7:2; emphasis added.

moral capacity for truth is measured by the Creator's intelligible order. It is measured by his eternal plan, as inscribed in man's own rational nature, and as made superiorly known through revelation. As a result, at this point, Adam is aware that the meaning of his body is this: *to freely subordinate to the truth about the good, and to the Creator.*[51] As subject of the covenant, Adam can choose between death and immortality. The bad use of his freedom means privation of all that the Creator has given him.[52] The right or good use of his freedom, on the other hand, means happiness and self-fulfillment. Once again, Adam is alone. No one in the visible world is like him. No earthly creature can freely love as he can.

Fellowship of Friendship

By virtue of all the dimensions just analyzed, the experience of original solitude *originates* an even deeper understanding of Adam's identity and vocation. He now knows himself as a being *capable of human friendship*. Unlike the irrational animals, Adam knows that he can be part of a manifested and reciprocal benevolent relationship with another human being that is habitual and founded upon the sharing of goods, especially the sharing of the *munus* received from God.[53] But he is alone in this regard: there is *no other human being* with whom to share this great gift and good work. Thus, he feels solitude. To be sure, Adam was created in the state of grace. Moreover, he has experienced himself as partner of the Absolute. Hence, we need to ask the following questions: is God not enough for Adam? Does he not walk with God in the garden as with a friend? Why then does he long for friendship with fellow humans? The answer to these questions is found in man's rational, social, and dependent nature. For this reason, despite his friendship with God, Adam still feels the need to have *fellowship of friendship* with another human being in order to be happy on this earth. Borrowing MacIntyre's expression, we could say that Adam knows himself as a *dependent* rational animal.[54] His experience reflects an objective, real, and true need that springs from the relational dimension of being created in God's image. Fellowship of friendship is crucial not only for man's natural happiness, but also for his supernatural happiness in this life.

No one should be bewildered by the fact that Thomas Aquinas shares this vision. On the one hand, Aquinas argues that the *imago Dei* in man reveals his relationality and capacity for friendship. All of the relational virtues in the *Secunda Pars* are nothing but a manifestation of how the human person perfects his being created in God's image.[55] On the other hand, in perfect agreement with John Paul II, Thomas also ex-

51. AP, 154; *Cántico* B 28, 5; *Noche* II. 11, 4–5; *Subida* I. 4, 6.
52. See TOB 7:3.
53. See Ramírez, *De Caritate*, 38–39.
54. See MacIntyre, *Dependent Rational Animals*.
55. See *ST* I–II, prologue.

plains that the human person needs friendship with other human beings to be happy. Aquinas argues that he needs friends to be happy, even if he already lives in charity as friendship with God. The human person needs friends not only for his *natural* happiness as considered by Aristotle; he also needs them for his *supernatural* happiness on this earth.[56] Thus, Thomas explains that "if we speak of the happiness of this life, the happy man needs friends . . . not, indeed, to make use of them, since he suffices himself; nor to delight in them, since he possesses perfect delight in the operation of virtue."[57] Adam needs human friends "for the purpose of a good operation, namely, that he may do good to them; that he may delight in seeing them do good; and again that he may be *helped by them in his good work*."[58] Besides God, Adam also needs a *human* friend to share with and to communicate in his God-given *munus*, in his good work. Thus, his longing for friendship is a longing for a common union that results from sharing in that *munus*, a communion which makes him grow in his likeness to God.[59]

I have not spoken yet about marriage. The reason is quite simple. John Paul II distinguishes two different meanings of solitude: "[O]ne deriving from man's very nature . . . and the other deriving from the relationship between male and female."[60] The pope has chosen to concentrate on the first over the second. Obviously, they are both interconnected. However, it is very important to distinguish them as well. The first meaning refers to every human being, not just to male human persons. As we know, God says that it is not good for man to be alone before all these experiences take place.[61] Since man is not considered as male until the creation of woman,[62] "when God-Yahweh speaks the words about solitude, he refers with them to *the solitude of man as such and not only to that of the male*."[63] As the pope clarifies in the footnote, "man was thus alone even *without reference to sex*."[64] John Paul II concentrates on the longing for a unity in human nature and in human love, without dealing yet with the specific character of conjugality.

The pope is actually laying a very important foundation. Conjugal love is in fact founded upon the dignity of the human person as distinct from irrational animals and as a being capable of friendship because of that dignity. Indeed, marriage is one specific kind of friendship and communion founded upon the sharing of the procreative or parenting *munus*. The second sense of original solitude speaks about the

---

56. See Ramírez, *De Hominis Beatitudine*, 459–64.
57. *ST* I–II, q. 4, a. 8, c.
58. Ibid.
59. See *Super Ga.*, cap. 2, lect. 6, n. 107.
60. TOB 5:2.
61. See Gen 2:18.
62. See Gen 2:21–22.
63. TOB 5:2; emphasis added.
64. Ibid., 5:2, n9; emphasis added.

specific longing for conjugal friendship. However, since both man and woman, male and female, partake of the same human nature, even *the second meaning of solitude is based on the first.* John Paul II will not concentrate on the second meaning of solitude until he deals with the second meaning of original unity.

Original Unity

The interconnection between original solitude and original unity is very profound. The second presupposes the first. Moreover, this interconnection resembles the relationship between all of the original experiences and the theology of the *imago Dei*. On the one hand, original solitude *manifests* original unity. Indeed, Adam's understanding of solitude leads to his awareness of his own need for friendship and unity. Moreover, this same understanding will also lead Adam to the recognition of Eve as another self. For this reason, John Paul II argues that "the *meaning* of original solitude enters and becomes part of the *meaning* of original unity."[65]

The pope does not say that original solitude, as a sheer lived experience or awareness, enters into the experience of original unity. Rather, he is saying that the *understanding* of original solitude—namely, its *meaning*—is what enters into the *meaning* or the understanding of original unity. The truths discovered by Adam about his own identity and mission are now transported to the interpersonal dimension of original unity. On the other hand, original solitude is *conditioned* by original unity. The latter fulfills the deepest desires inherent in solitude. Original unity, therefore, is like the end that satisfies those desires. In this sense, the understanding of original unity conditions the very meaning of original solitude. Man would not feel alone in this respect had he not experienced his longing for friendship as a longing for original unity. But most importantly, as we will see, original unity perfects the *imago Dei* manifested in original solitude.

Original experiences *originate* a deeper understanding of man's identity and mission. They lead towards a greater understanding of the meaning of the body. The experience of original unity will also bring about this deeper understanding. It will reveal the *unitive meaning of the body*. In accordance with solitude's first meaning, original unity's first meaning will concentrate on the unity in human nature and love existing between Adam and Eve as a *communio personarum*. In turn, in accordance with solitude's second meaning, original unity's second meaning will concentrate on the marriage or conjugal friendship existing between our first parents as they share the procreative *munus* given to them by the Creator.[66] Both meanings of original unity illustrate our being created in God's image and likeness. For this reason, John Paul II reminds us in this exact section that "following the Yahwist text, in which the creation

---

65. Ibid., 8:1; emphasis added.
66. See Gen 1:28.

of woman is described separately (Gen 2:21–22), we should have before our eyes at the same time that image of God of the first creation account."⁶⁷

Unity in Nature and Love

The first account of Creation expresses succinctly the relational or social nature of the human person, created in God's image, by pointing out that both male and female were created at one and the same time. The second account, instead, offers a more psychological description of this same phenomenon. In truth, the second account follows a progressive reasoning in which the meaning of different experiences accumulate in Adam's consciousness. They progressively increase his own self-knowledge and understanding of the meaning of his body. For this reason, original unity presupposes original solitude and the understanding it has originated in Adam's consciousness. Moreover, we find a confirmation of the primacy of the personal subject in relation to the community.⁶⁸ This primacy is metaphysical. Without individuals, there is no community. But more importantly, this primacy also has another dimension. To be able to say something philosophically and theologically meaningful about the community, we need to proceed from the subject. In TOB's language, we need to proceed from solitude to unity, and not vice versa.

We have already seen that Adam is aware of being a rational animal and God's partner. Moreover, he identifies himself with his spiritual soul as substantially united to the matter of his organism. Both elements together constitute his body as human. The ethical meaning of his human body or his moral vocation consists thus far in subordination to the truth about the good and to the Creator. Adam has also become aware of his need for friendship with another human being in order to attain happiness on this earth. In this way, in his need for fellowship, he has already begun to perceive and to understand his dependent social or relational nature. The meaning of his body in now enriched. It already points to man's need for communion with other human persons. Thus, Gen 2:20 concludes after the experience of naming the irrational animals: "The man gave names to all cattle, and to the birds of the air, and to every beast of the field; but for the man *there was not found a helper fit for him*."

Original unity's first meaning begins here, right where original solitude finished. Original unity's first meaning is closely connected with the aspect of participation. Remember that the latter is the aspect that contains all of the other aspects of Wojtyła's integral vision of man in view of intersubjectivity. Studying the experience of acting together with others leads to an understanding of the human person's social nature. In this study, Wojtyła distinguishes between authentic and inauthentic attitudes for true participation. The authentic attitudes delineate the path towards the adequate fulfillment of man's longing for communion. To understand and to treat the other as

---

67. TOB 8:2.
68. See PC, 237.

one's neighbor is essential for this fulfillment.[69] But this is exactly what is contained in Gen 2:23. For this reason, based on the conciliar attitude of human identity, on his philosophy of participation, and on some further reflections on community and alienation, John Paul II proceeds to the theological exploration of Adam's words at the sight of Eve: "This at last is bone of my bones and flesh of my flesh."[70]

What is investigated here is the *common unity* or the community formed by Adam and Eve. The focal point is not just the material fact of two human beings existing and acting together. The term community speaks about something more. It designates the peculiar unity that exists among them. From the metaphysical viewpoint, this unity belongs to the accidental order. It is determined and specified by the good or *munus* that is shared in common. At this point, the following question emerges: what is contained in this metaphysical understanding of community from the viewpoint of lived experience and consciousness? From the viewpoint of lived experience, every common unity of persons or community has two dimensions: the *I–thou* dimension and the *we* dimension. The first dimension corresponds to Adam's recognition of Eve as another *I*.[71]

Another I

Gen 2:23 is an exclamation contrary to alienation. There is no dehumanization of Eve whatsoever in Adam's words and attitude. Instead, these words express Adam's awareness of Eve as a personal self, as a human person, as another *I*. "The Biblical text provides sufficient bases for recognizing the essential equality of man and woman from the point of view of their humanity. From the very beginning, both are persons, unlike the other living beings in the world about them. *The woman is another I in a common humanity.*"[72] Thus, Adam is participating in the humanity of Eve according to the theoretical and normative dimensions of the commandment of love. Such participation is not only a matter of emotions and spontaneity; the will is also present. In other words, Adam freely affirms Eve as a person. His understanding of her personhood is so transparent that his will follows upon that knowledge almost spontaneously. Effortlessly, Adam's will is moved, by that knowledge of the truth about the good, to love Eve as another self. This kind of love is really what is meant by the willful affirmation of Eve's personhood. But note that, sometimes, this "affirmation" is not experienced as a free choice resulting from a difficult deliberation and an arduous decision. Rather, it is almost spontaneous. Yet such spontaneity does not negate that, for Adam and for us, the willful affirmation of another's personhood is both a free choice and a moral task. Emotions are certainly involved in this process. In Adam's case, they all seem to

---

69. See AP, 350–55.
70. Gen 2:23. See SR, 309; Bird, "Bone of My Bones and Flesh of My Flesh."
71. See PC, 238–40.
72. MD 6. See TOB 14:4.

be in perfect alignment with the truth about the good. In our case, as we know from experience, they may help or hinder this moral task.[73]

After this initial description, we need to ask: how exactly does Adam get to know and willfully affirm Eve as "another I"? Adam does not get to this knowledge through a syllogism. The interpersonal acknowledgement and affirmation of Eve as another *I* is not the result of discursive reasoning. It is, rather, an indirect intellectual apprehension based on a lived experience: "[T]he reality of the other does not result principally from categorical knowledge, from humanity as the conceptualized essence "human being," but from an even richer lived experience, one in which I as though *transfer what is given to me as my own I beyond myself to one of the others*, who, as a result, appears primarily as a different *I*, another *I*, my neighbor."[74] Evidently, understanding the essence of humanity, even in a pre-scientific way, is not an obstacle but an aid in the discovery of the other as another *I*. However, our author is trying to go back to the more precise lived experience of intersubjectivity. It includes the notion "human being" as contained in one's self-knowledge. But this notion is part of a richer awareness that generates the *I–thou* relationship. This whole process "starts from the lived experience of one's own *I*."[75] One cannot experience another's *I* with the same immediacy as one experiences his own ego. "I cannot experience another as I experience myself, because my own *I* as such is nontransferable."[76] Nevertheless, there is a way for me to "*understand* that the other is constituted in a *similar fashion*, that the other is also an *I*."[77] Such an intellectual apprehension or understanding is necessary for Adam's exclamation in Gen 2:23. It is the condition to experience Eve as a person with the same properties he discovered about himself in original solitude.

Note very well that Adam now has that exact experience of Eve's self *through the mediation of her body*. Looking at her corporeal constitution, he exclaims that she is truly bone of his bones and flesh of his flesh. This reference is not without philosophical significance for the theology of the body. Recall that the soul is not only the form of the body but also its mover and end. Recall also that it was Adam's human body that made him aware of his own solitude. It is Eve's human body expressing her *I* that will make Adam aware that he is not alone, that she is a fellow human being. Although Adam does not experience Eve's *I* with the same immediacy as she experiences herself, he experiences Eve's ego *indirectly*, thanks to the mediation of her human body as a territory of expression of her own self.[78] There is also a special role played here by particular reason, also known as the *vis cogitativa*.[79] Adam's particular reason appre-

---

73. See PC, 203–204.
74. PC, 200–201; emphasis added.
75. Ibid., 201.
76. Ibid., 202.
77. Ibid., 200.
78. See AP, 204, 206, and 314n65.
79. Wojtyła implicitly refers to this faculty in AP, 4–8. However, for a fuller treatment of this power

hends Eve's substance as the center of reference for the sensible qualities of her body. Particular reason apprehends the meaning behind Eve's bodily gestures. It apprehends Eve's body as human, as informed by her rational soul. Thus, Wojtyła says that "as human beings, we are capable of participating in the very humanity of other people, and because of this every human being can be our neighbor."[80] This peculiar conscious participation arises "from my awareness that this being is another *I*, which means also also an *I*."[81] Perceiving or experiencing the other as oneself implies, on Adam's part, recognizing in Eve all the elements he came to know about himself in the experience of original solitude. In this way, "the *thou* stands before my self as a true and complete other self, which, like my own self, is characterized not only by self-determination, but also and above all by self-possession and self-governance. In this subjective structure, the *thou* as another self represents its own transcendence and its own tendency toward self-fulfillment."[82]

Yet, there is another philosophical key that further unlocks this original experience: the reflexive function of consciousness. Of course, this reflexive function is transported here into the interpersonal realm. The interpersonal encounter between Adam and Eve contains the experience of Eve's *I* in relationship to Adam's. Consciousness not only mirrors Eve's personal self as the content perceived through her human body by Adam's particular reason and intellect. In its reflexive function, consciousness also refers this objective content back to Adam's subjectivity. "The particular reflexivity of this relation is also revealed here. The relation to a *thou* is in its essential structure always a relation to another, and yet, because one member of this relation is an *I*, the relation—in a peculiar way to itself—demonstrates the ability to return to the *I* from which it proceeded."[83] In this way, there is a new rediscovery and affirmation of Adam's own personal identity in the very encounter with Eve. Hence, "the *I–thou* relationship, far from leading me away from my subjectivity, in some sense more firmly grounds me in it."[84] Although it is fundamental, this experience does not yet form a community. It does not yet constitute participation. The reason is simple: it is unilateral; it lacks the reciprocity of the *thou-I* relationship.

Common Unity

The biblical text speaks directly about Adam's experience of Eve's body as human. That is the most literal meaning of Gen 2:23. However, based on the one flesh union

---

of the soul, see Millán-Puelles, *Objeto Puro*, 431–50. For a monographic study on the *vis cogitativa*, see García Jaramillo, *La cogitativa*.

80. PC, 200.
81. Ibid.
82. Ibid., 245.
83. Ibid., 242.
84. Ibid., 243.

described in Gen 2:24, we could also infer that the experience is *reciprocal*.[85] This new factor adds a different dimension. Through that same mediation of the body, Adam would experience that Eve is able to experience his own ego in a similar way as he does. Hence, there can be an interpersonal encounter of dialogue and communication between them. There is, properly speaking, a community; there can be *communio* because there can be communication and partnership in the same *munus*.[86] With this reciprocity in mind, we also discover the *thou-I* relationship. Adam experiences Eve experiencing him. For clarity's sake, allow me to express this phenomenon in the first person: "I experience that the other is experiencing *me*." This turning to one's subject suggested in the sentence by "experiencing *me*" is also the result of the reflexive function of consciousness. In the interpersonal encounter, I perceive myself as experienced by the other. Eve *faces* Adam in such a way that they both experience each other. In this new experience, Eve is revealed as a being with whom Adam can *dialogue*, a being with whom Adam can freely *collaborate*. She is a fellow human partner. Like him, she is another human being capable of friendship or communion. Adam is not alone anymore in this regard. In the person of Eve, he has found the *fellowship of friendship* with another human being that he was longing for.

For this reason, John Paul II argues that Gen 2:23 expresses the fulfillment of the longing inscribed in the first meaning of solitude, the fulfillment of Adam's capacity and expectation for the communion of persons, a "desire of finding a being similar to himself," a "second I."[87] As the pope also says: "The man's solitude in the Yawhist account presents itself to us not only as the first discovery of the characteristic transcendence proper to the person, but also as the discovery of an adequate relation to the person, and thus as opening toward and waiting for a communion of persons."[88] Such communion is fulfilled in the original unity between Adam and Eve as neighbors. This is the most basic meaning of Eve's creation from Adam's rib.[89] It is also the basic and first meaning of Gen 2:23. What this text indicates "is the *homogeneity* of the whole being of both . . . Thus, the woman is created in a certain sense based *on the same humanity*."[90] This original unity has both an anthropological and an ethical meaning. "In interpersonal *I–thou* relationships, the partners should not only unveil themselves before one another in the truth of their personal reality, but they should also *accept and affirm one another in that truth*. Such acceptance and affirmation is an expression of the moral (ethical) meaning of interpersonal community."[91] Adam and Eve are

---

85. John Paul II explains this reciprocity again in light of original nakedness in TOB 17:5.

86. Following Aristotle, Thomas Aquinas speaks of *communicatio* as an important factor specifying different kinds of friendship. See *In VIII Ethic.*, lect. 9, n. 1661.

87. TOB 8:3.

88. Ibid. 9:2.

89. See Gen 2:21.

90. TOB 8:4; emphasis added.

91. PC, 245; emphasis added.

mutually responsible for one another. Their community, based on their unity of nature and love, is marked by their abiding "in a mutual affirmation of the transcendent value of the person."[92] This kind of community is really applicable, as Wojtyła explicitly acknowledges, to any community formed by human persons, let them be married or not.[93] The foundations of this kind of community or common unity are sharing in the same human nature—hence, also in the same dignity—and sharing in the affirmation of the value and dignity of the human person. It is a community based on the unity of nature and love. These are, in reality, the theoretical and normative dimensions of the commandment of love.

This reasoning has solid foundations in Vatican II, especially in the attitude of human identity studied above. Moreover, John Paul's position is also based on Thomas's theology of marriage. I would like to appeal to what I would call Aquinas's *personalistic* argument against polygamy. Pay close attention to the following text:

> [F]riendship consists in an *equality*. So, if it is not lawful for the wife to have several husbands, since this is contrary to certainty as to offspring, it would not be lawful, on the other hand, for a man to have several wives, for *the friendship of wife for husband would not be free, but somewhat servile*. And this argument is corroborated by experience, for among husbands having plural wives the wives have a status like that of *servants*. Furthermore, strong friendship is not possible in regard to many people ... Therefore, if a wife has but one husband, but the husband has several wives, *the friendship will not be equal on both sides*. So, the friendship will *not be free, but servile* in some way.[94]

Note how Thomas's argument is based on the *equality in dignity and love* between man and woman, on their sharing the *same human nature*, on their being in this sense brother and sister, and capable of friendship. Polygamy excludes true friendship and good parenting. It destroys *equality* and *liberality* among spouses. It particularly violates the personal dignity of the wife. It dehumanizes and alienates her by establishing a relationship of servitude or slavery. Thus, polygamy is contrary to the commandment of love as the first precept of the natural law.[95] It reduces the friendship between husband and wife to a utilitarian level, in which the woman is not treated as another self, as one's neighbor. Indeed, for both Wojtyła and Thomas, friendship is possible only among those who are equal in the dignity of being persons. Both authors claim that marriage is the *maximum* expression of human friendship in view of a common good.[96] Both Adam and Eve are human persons. Both share the same dignity. Thomas expresses it in another place, in a manner which resembles John Paul II's

---

92. Ibid., 246.
93. See ibid., 244.
94. *ScG* III.124; emphasis added.
95. See *ST* I–II, q. 100, a. 3, ad 1.
96. See *ScG* III.123; LR, 214.

understanding of original unity: "[T]he woman was not formed from the feet of the man as a servant, nor from the head as lording it over her husband, but *from the side as a companion,* as it says in Genesis (2:21)."[97] This same dignity is to be respected for their friendship to be virtuous, that is to say, for the communion of persons to occur.

Thomas's emphasis on friendship, equality, and liberality as opposed to servitude, and on companionship, is really a basis for John Paul II's strong emphasis on the first meaning of unity as the foundation for the second. Before one considers the conjugal relationship between Adam and Eve, one needs to dwell on its generic base. The original unity between our first parents is *generically friendship and specifically conjugal.* The first meaning of original unity concentrates on the genus, while the second meaning focuses on the specific difference. Thus, the pope stresses that Eve is a fit help for Adam, first as his *sister.* Only afterwards is Eve looked at as Adam's *bride.* Consider the following undelivered text, in which John Paul II is commenting on Song 4:9, where one reads: "[Y]ou have ravished my heart, *my sister, my bride.*"[98]

At this point, those sentences of Genesis 2:23–25 can come to mind that seem to reveal for the first time the experience of the masculine and the feminine "I," born from the common sense of *belonging to the Creator as their common Father.* Before him, in all the truth of their masculinity and femininity, *they were above all "brother" and "sister" in the union of the same humanity* . . . And this reciprocal relation of "brother" and "sister" is constituted in them as the *first foundation of the communion of persons*—in a certain sense as the *constitutive condition* of their reciprocal destiny, also in the dimension of the vocation by which they were to become "husband and wife."[99]

Within this foundational level, which prevents the danger of alienation, Eve is a fit help because, unlike irrational animals, she can be Adam's friend; she can be loved as another *I.* Genesis 2:23 expresses Adam's joy at the inherent and honest goodness found in Eve as another member of the human race, as his sister, as his neighbor. "In this way, for the first time, the man (male) shows joy and even exultation, for which he had no reason before, due to the lack of a being similar to himself. Joy for *the other human being,* for *the second I,* dominates in the words the man (male) speaks on seeing the woman (female). All of this helps to establish the full meaning of original unity."[100] This is the first testimony of the axiological lived experience of the value of the human person as such. Thus, we have sufficiently explained the first and generic meaning of original unity. Its second and specific meaning concentrates on its conjugal character. It focuses on their being yoked together in their relationship as a *we* to the procreative *munus* as their specific common good.

---

97. *Super I Cor.,* cap 7, lect. 1, n. 321.
98. See also Song 4:10,12, 5:1,2.
99. TOB 110:3; emphasis added.
100. Ibid., 8:4.

Conjugal Unity and the Common Good of Procreation

Original unity's second meaning has to do with the *specific* way in which Adam and Eve form a *we*, a married couple. It concentrates on the one-flesh union. Man and woman are participants of the same human nature. However, they are also two distinct yet complementary ways of being a human body: male and female. As John Paul puts it: "[T]hey communicate in the fullness of humanity, which shows itself in them as *reciprocal complementarity* precisely because they are 'male' and 'female.'"[101] Therefore, the logical sequence of treating original unity, first in its genus and then in its species, proves itself to be quite foundational. It clearly shows why John Paul II rejects what Prudence Allen has described as the reductionistic views of "sex identity" and "sex polarity."[102] "Sex identity" preserves the equality between man and woman, but it denies their differentiation. On the other hand, "sex polarity" preserves their differentiation to the detriment of their equality. John Paul proposes an alternative: a theory of complementarity between man and woman. Thanks to his analysis of the first meaning of original unity, he assumes what is true in sex identity. John Paul II is able to retain Adam and Eve's equality in their common dignity as persons, neighbors, and participants of the same human nature. In turn, thanks to his analysis of the second meaning of original unity, the pope is also able to assume what is true in sex polarity. He retains Adam and Eve's sexual differentiation but under a new light, namely, that of complementarity. The pope is able to retain these two true elements under this new light by virtue of an adequate view of their mutual relationship and of the human person's hylomorphic substantial unity. Thus, Adam and Eve are, for one another, complementary ways of being a human body, two complementary ways of being a human person.

Let us concentrate on the conjugal community formed by Adam and Eve. Every community is a *we* that has a shared common good.[103] The relationship to this common good is of the utmost importance for the very specific nature of the community. In fact, the relation to the common good determines the very *meaning* of that community. What is more final is, in a sense, more formal. In this instance, what is more final defines more intimately the core specific difference of the one-flesh union as a community. For marriage, the community's final cause is the cause of the causality of the community's formal cause. In even more metaphysical terms, "the end is the cause of causes, because it is the cause of the causality in all causes."[104] Allow me to explain the application of this metaphysical principle to a human community that forms a *we*.

Human persons are the agents or efficient causes of the community's existence. They constitute that community because they act together with each other in view of

---

101. Ibid.; emphasis added.
102. See Allen, "Man-Woman Complementarity."
103. See *In IV Sent.*, d. 27, q. 1, a. 1, qc.1, c.
104. *De Principis Naturae*, cap. 4.

their common end. They are also the cause of their end coming into existence. But they are not the cause of their end's being an end. Most importantly, their end is the very cause of their acting together with each other united in a community, as a *we*. Consequently, their end is the *munus* that binds them and specifies their common union in its core essence. An experiential example may illustrate this extremely metaphysical point. For instance, the formation of future priests is the end which unites and intimately defines the very core essence of a seminary community. The formation of future priests is the very cause of the seminary's members acting together with each other and being united in a community as a *we*. Although the formation of future priests comes into existence because of the (efficient) agents of formation, priestly formation is not an end because of their efficient causality. It is a lovable end in and of itself, independently of what the agents of priestly formation know or do. Yet, their active and conscious pursuing of this end intimately defines the very axial essence of their community of persons as a *seminary community*. Consequently, the relation to the objective common good determines the community's specific and objective nature. Thus, the final cause is the cause of the causality in the formal cause of the community. But it is so through the mediation of the efficient cause.

Wojtyła articulates this very Thomistic and metaphysical point but focuses on its correlate in one's lived or conscious experience. According to him, the common good is an objective end that becomes a conscious and subjective purpose of the agents establishing the community. It becomes part of the subjective participant's awareness and aspirations. Thus, "by virtue of this relation [to their common good], the people involved in it [the community], while experiencing their personal subjectivity—the factual multiciplicity of human *I*'s— are *aware that they form a specific we, and they experience themselves in this new dimension.*"[105] As we will study in chapter 10, Wojtyła clearly identifies a very rich and personalistic understanding of procreation as the objective end and common good of marriage.[106]

In order to explain the original character of this second meaning of unity, what interests me most, at this time, is to explain why this common good *originates* a new understanding of Adam and Eve's personal identity and mission. Why does Wojtyła say in the text just quoted that the people involved in the community experience themselves in the new dimension opened by their common good? Because "in this relation [to the common good] the *I* and the *thou* also find their mutual relationship in a new dimension: they find their *I–thou* through the common good, which establishes a new union between them. The best example of this is marriage."[107]

As we know, original solitude *originated* an initial understanding of the meaning of the human body as the substantial unity between the spiritual soul and the matter

---

105. PC, 247; emphasis added.

106. See LR, 30. A development of this same doctrine can be found in John Paul II, *Letter to the Families*, 10. For Thomas Aquinas's theology, see *In IV Sent.*, d. 33, q. 2, a. 1, ad 4.

107. PC, 247; emphasis added.

of the organism. Moreover, it revealed the human body's meaning as man's vocation to find fulfillment in the perfection of self-determination, in subordination to the truth about the good. The experience of original unity also *originates* a new process of self-knowledge, in which the meaning of the human body is enriched. Within original unity's first meaning, Adam's self was rediscovered and affirmed in his encounter with Eve. Adam discovered the *unitive meaning of his body* as a fulfilled capacity for friendship with a fellow human being. John Paul explains, for this reason, that in Genesis 2:23, there is "a *new* consciousness of the meaning of one's body. This meaning, one can say, consists in reciprocal enrichment" in the communion of persons.[108]

Additionally, within original unity's second meaning, Adam and Eve's self-knowledge will also be augmented in light of the sexual differentiation as it relates to the common good of procreation. Adam and Eve's own personal self is also rediscovered and affirmed in the encounter with the conjugal *we* in which they are immersed with one another. This new rediscovery will take place in light of the procreative *munus* as the common good, which specifies the common union between Adam and Eve as husband and wife. In a sense, Adam and Eve discover a new facet of their own personal identity. Original unity's second meaning effects or originates an understanding of how the meaning of the body can be fulfilled within the one–flesh union described in Gen 2:24. It makes Adam and Eve aware of their relationship as conjugal friendship. This is one specific way—although not the only one—of overcoming original solitude in the fulfillment of the unitive meaning of the body as one's vocation for interpersonal communion. It is also one specific way of reciprocally affirming in one another the personal dignity discovered in that same solitude. Thus, "the meaning of man's original unity through masculinity and femininity expresses itself as an overcoming of the frontier of solitude and at the same time as an affirmation—for both human beings—of everything in solitude that constitutes man."[109]

The generic unitive meaning of the body, expressed in the first meaning of original unity as a longing for communion, belongs to any human person, married or not. But there is one specific way of fulfilling it: the peculiar *communio personarum* within marriage in which God is present as a common Father. This accounts for a singular and special way of living out the unitive meaning of the body within the context of the parenting attitude or the procreative *munus*. Although this second and more specific sense of the unitive meaning of the body is closely connected with the unitive meaning of the conjugal act, they should not be confused. John Paul II argues that Gen 2:24 speaks about this second sense of the unitive meaning *of the body*. It also refers to the unitive meaning of the *conjugal act*, because the conjugal act is *one more* act within conjugal life. But certainly it is *not the only one*. "That unifying meaning should be understood not only in reference to the unity that the man and the woman were to constitute as spouses by becoming one flesh (Gen 2:24) through the conjugal act, but

108. TOB 9:5; emphasis added.
109. Ibid., 9:2.

also in reference to the communion of persons itself, which was the proper dimension of the existence of man and woman in the mystery of creation."[110]

Our considerations thus far explain why that what best clarifies the second sense of the unitive meaning of the body is the consideration of Adam and Eve's procreative *munus*. The first account of creation includes it as a *mandatum* expressed in Gen 1:28. John Paul II argues that, in the second account, Gen 4:1 should be read as a parallel to that *mandatum*. Gen 4:1 should, in reality, be included within the second meaning of original unity.[111] We read in that last biblical text that "Adam knew Eve his wife, and she conceived and bore Cain, saying, I have gotten a man *with the help of the Lord*." Note the reference here in the text to the help of the Lord. It reveals the specifically human way of procreating. Adam and Eve *procreate* in collaboration with the *Creator* as partners of the Absolute, partners who can be the free cause of their obedience to the *mandatum*. Their conjugal union, their one-flesh union, is a union in which God is always present. As we already know, the completion of the unitive meaning of the body is a fulfillment found in charity. But charity among neighbors, who also are husband and wife, is a supernatural love *in* God and *because of* God. Thus, Gen 4:1 should be connected with Gen 2:24, with conjugal charity, and with the resulting one-flesh union. In light of this new connection, there can be no doubt: the union in the flesh of man and woman also refers to the union "that is expressed and realized in the conjugal act."[112] In this sense, John Paul II explains that their sexual differentiation allows Adam and Eve "to place their whole humanity at the same time *under* the blessing of fruitfulness."[113]

Note again the precise language of the pope. The blessing of fruitfulness is the common good *under which* the humanity of Adam and Eve is specifically united in a union which we call marriage. It is *under* that blessing because Adam and Eve conceived Cain *with the help of the Lord*. They collaborated with God. But since they cannot be put on par with God, their collaboration is always a *subordination* to the Creator and to the intelligible order bestowed by him on the realities of marriage and human sexuality. Moreover, Adam and Eve's humanity is placed *under* the blessing of fruitfulness because the latter is a shared common good for both of them. As a common good it also has a certain superior character: "[T]he common good's superior character and the greater fullness of value it represents derive ultimately from the fact that *the good of each of the subjects* of a community that calls itself a *we* is *more fully expressed and more fully actualized in the common good*. Through the common good, therefore, the human *I* more fully and more profoundly discovers itself precisely as a human *we*."[114] Adam and Eve's good as spouses is more fully expressed by procreation.

110. Ibid., 29:3; emphasis added.
111. See ibid., 2:1.
112. Ibid., 10:2.
113. Ibid.; emphasis added.
114. PC, 250; emphasis added.

The placing of their humanity *under the blessing of fruitfulness* actualizes more fully their self-fulfillment as husband and wife.

The fact that the pope refers to their *whole humanity* as placed under this blessing is also quite important. John Paul II begins pointing at the correct exercise of human sexuality in light of its original meaning or intended intelligible nature given by the Creator. Such intelligible nature and correct exercise presuppose that Adam and Eve, as brother and sister with one common Father, have the same dignity. Hence, the conjugal act cannot be separated from the personalistic norm or the commandment of love. The same personal dignity revealed in original solitude and rediscovered anew in original unity must be the axis for the correct exercise of human sexuality. For this reason, John Paul II explains that in the conjugal act, "one takes upon oneself the solitude of the body of the second *I* as one's own."[115] The pope does *not* mean that in the conjugal act spouses help one another not to feel lonely. Although that may be *sometimes* true, what the pope really means here is something much more important and radical. He means that *for the conjugal act to be truly unitive* it needs to be solidly grounded on the first meaning of original unity. In that act, one should acknowledge and affirm the dignity of the spouse as one's own.[116]

In other words, for the conjugal act to be truly unitive, one should take upon oneself the solitude of the body of the second *I* as one's own, that is, one should take upon oneself all the truths about personal identity and dignity discovered in original solitude; then, these truths are to be reciprocally acknowledged and freely affirmed. Only in this way can the conjugal act express and be part of a true conjugal communion of persons, specified by a gift of one's soul and body, masculinity and femininity, and placed *under the blessing of fruitfulness.* This is the conjugal act's meaning and nature intended by the Creator from the beginning. This is how the pope synthetically puts it: "This communion had been *intended* to make man and woman mutually happy through the search of a simple and pure *union in humanity*, through a reciprocal offering of themselves, that is, through the experience of the gift of the person *expressed with soul and body*, with *masculinity* and *femininity*—"flesh of my flesh" (Gen 2:23)—and finally through the *subordination* of such a union to the *blessing of fruitfulness with procreation*."[117] I will come back to this topic in the third part of this book.

Image of the Trinity

The whole experience of original unity illustrates a certain completion of man's creation in the image and likeness of God, who is love.[118] Once again, John Paul II appeals to the intimate connection between the two accounts of Creation. To be sure, the

---

115. TOB 10:2.
116. See PC, 245.
117. TOB 30:3. See McCarthy, "El amor esponsal."
118. 1 John 4:8.

second account does not explicitly speak of the *imago Dei* as the first account does. Yet, this second account "reveals, in the manner proper to it, that the complete and definitive creation of man (subject first to the experience of original solitude) expresses itself in giving life to the *communio personarum* that man and woman form."[119] Very similarly to the way in which MD 7 develops GS 24, TOB also presents an analogy between Adam and Eve and the Trinity. The exact terms of the analogy are the following: "[M]an became the image of God not only *through his own humanity,* but also *through the communion of persons,* which man and woman form from the very beginning."[120]

Note the twofold perspective: the human person's humanity and his actual communion with other human persons. The individual human person's *humanity* is itself an imitation of God that belongs to the *imago Dei*. However, the *imago Dei* images God as one and as Trinity. As Thomas explains, "to be to the image of God by imitation of the Divine Nature does not exclude being to the same image by the representation of the Divine Persons: but rather one follows from the other."[121] Hence, Adam and Eve's *communion of persons* is also an imitation of the Trinity that flows precisely because their humanity images God's nature. Without that human nature, they could not establish that communion of human persons that images the Trinity. In this sense, John Paul II explains that "man becomes an image of God *not so much in the moment of solitude as in the moment of communion.* He is, in fact, from the beginning not only an image in which the solitude of one Person, who rules the world, mirrors itself, but also and essentially the image of an inscrutable divine communion of Persons."[122]

John Paul II's words also suggest a certain order of perfection. The moment of communion seems to image God even more. Is the pope offering here something new or contrary to the thought of Thomas Aquinas? Far from it. The capacity or potency to know and to love inherent in human nature is *actualized* in the communion of human persons in charity and in truth. To be sure, "first and chiefly [*primo et principaliter*], the image of the Trinity is to be found in the acts of the soul," especially "inasmuch as from the knowledge which we possess, by actual thought we form an internal word; and thence break forth into love."[123] There is no doubt, then, that for both Thomas Aquinas and John Paul II, charity *perfects* the *imago Dei* in the human person far more than the sheer existence of the powers of the soul and their potency to know and to love not yet actualized. The *actual* communion of human persons is a greater imitation of God. As we know, original unity's first meaning already reveals that Adam and Eve's union of nature in common humanity images the unity of the Divinity. Even within this first meaning of unity, there is also a generic apprehension of their mutual love as friendship. In their state of original grace, we can easily say that their love is in

---

119. TOB 9:3; emphasis added. See Wilder, "Community of Persons."
120. TOB 9:3; emphasis added.
121. *ST* I, q. 93, a. 5, c.
122. TOB 9:3; emphasis added.
123. *ST* I, q. 93, a. 7, c.

charity and in truth. Hence, Adam and Eve's human communion of love images the communion of love that is God, also within the first meaning of unity.

However, the second meaning of unity should not be left out from this same analogy. It really contains the first as its genus, but it brings about a further specification. Hence, the communion of persons founded upon *conjugal* charity also images the Trinity. It does so for the same reasons just mentioned.[124] One could additionally ask the following question: is there a distinctive way in which the conjugal union of husband and wife, specified by the common good of procreation and informed by charity, images God? To my knowledge, John Paul II does not offer a clear and explicit answer in TOB. Based on John Paul's theology and that of Thomas Aquinas, I personally think that the second meaning of original unity also images God in a peculiar way. In my opinion, it illustrates how marriage as conjugal friendship, specified by the procreative *munus*, imitates God's paternity and providence.

I think that this is how one could interpret Ephesians 3:14–15.[125] Saint Paul says there: "For this reason I bow my knees before the Father, from whom every *patría* in heaven and on earth is named." I have left untranslated the Greek word *patría*.[126] It could mean paternity, family, homeland, or clan. All of these meanings are acceptable, as long as we acknowledge in them a certain priority and posteriority. In the text, *patría* really refers to a subject that is a principle of being. Parents, families, homelands, and clans are all principles of being. But they are not so in the same way. Paul is explaining that there is one principle of being from whom all of the rest receive their name. God, *the Father*, is the *principium sine principio*. He is Fatherhood in person.[127]

---

124. We have already studied how Thomas Aquinas understands the communion of human persons imaging the Trinity. Marriage is one possible instance that perfectly works for Aquinas's analogy. One does not need to get very far beyond the surface of his text to realize this fact. It is right there to see for anyone who acknowledges that marriage truly is one of the many possible communions of human persons in charity and in truth. Hence, I cannot fully agree with West's claim regarding the originality or novelty of John Paul II's position. Remember, West said that "positing the divine image in the male-female communion—although it can be found *under the surface* of various texts in the theological tradition—*has not been the explicitly held perspective*" (West, *Theology of the Body Explained*, 108–9). Moreover, taking a closer look at John Paul's understanding of the original unity, I cannot agree with West in his other dubious affirmation. Remember, West claimed that "through his Wednesday audiences, and even more authoritatively in later statements, John Paul brings *the once dismissed idea* that man and woman image God *in and through their communion* into the realm of official magisterial teaching" (ibid., 109). The idea of the communion of human persons imaging the Trinity—also that communion present in marriage—was clearly defended by Aquinas, not dismissed. If West means that Thomas dismissed it, I simply cannot agree with him. The only thing Thomas dismissed was an opinion already rejected by Augustine. But neither can I agree with West, if he means that John Paul II is accepting that absurd and false opinion. The pope is not bringing this opinion into the realm of official magisterial teaching. That false opinion is simply absent in TOB and in MD 7. There is no mention of it in either text.

125. A similar interpretation can be found in MD 8.

126. See also Luke 2:4; Acts 3:25.

127. *ST* I, q. 33, a. 2, c.

Absolutely no one is a father like he is. No one else is a principle without a principle.[128] In this sense, we should call no one father except him.[129] Can we call father the Son of God? Can we call the Holy Spirit father as well? The Son proceeds from the Father; the Son is not a *principium sine principio*. Yet, without denying the distinction between the Divine Persons, the Son is not only our brother, but also a father to us.[130] The Holy Spirit is not the *principium sine principio*; he comes from the Father and the Son. Yet, he is also a father to us inasmuch as he is giver of life. Thus, as we pray in the *Veni Sancte Spiritus*, the Holy Spirit is the father of the poor (*pater pauperum*).

Any creature who participates in being a principle of life and education shares in God's *patría*. Priests are fathers for this very reason. Thus, Paul considers himself as a father in 1 Cor 4:15. But Adam and Eve, in their original unity as husband and wife, also partook of God's *patría*. They were meant to be principles of both natural and supernatural life. In procreation, they were meant to collaborate with God in order to transmit to their offspring both human nature as well as the state of grace.[131] Additionally, they were meant to be a principle of education in the natural and supernatural virtues for their children, *providing* for them what was necessary for their full development. Like any other married couple, they were meant to exercise a *prudential* or *providential* parenting for heaven. I think that, in doing all these things, they image God's *patría*. In their prudential governance of the family in educating their children, they also seem to image God's providence. No one in this visible world could imitate God in this way. For these reasons, it seems that for married couples, God's paternity and providence is *the* measure and model of how to be their children's principle of being and right conduct. He is *the* Exemplar of how to be a parent and of how to educate one's children, providing for them that which is necessary for their salvation.[132]

Be that as it may, John Paul II concludes his reflections on original unity arguing that the conjugal friendship between Adam and Eve also has a sacramental significance, understanding sacrament here in a broad sense.[133] Such a friendship becomes *the first visible sign* that foretells God's eternal plan for the salvation of man as it will be expressed in Ephesians 5:29–32. For this reason, as we will see, the pope speaks of marriage as the *primordial sacrament*. I will come back to this topic in chapter 11. For the moment, we are interested in explaining the internal connection between the original experiences and how they lead to Adam and Eve's awareness of the spousal

---

128. See ibid., I, q. 33, a. 4, c.

129. See Matt 23:9.

130. In Mark 10:24, Jesus calls *tékna*, little children, his own disciples. As Jesus explains in John 14:9, he reveals God's *patría*. Jesus's beloved disciple will also call children (*paidia*) his own disciples, as we read in 1 John 2:18. See also 1 Pet 1:23; Heb 4:15; Isa 9:6–7; 2 Cor 5:16.

131. See *ST* I, q. 100, a. 1, c. In ad 2, Thomas explains that the state of grace would have resulted from God's direct infusion of the rational soul in collaboration with our first parents.

132. This fact could be inferred from *Super Eph.*, cap. 3, lect. 4; *ST* I, q. 33, a. 2, ad 4; II–II, q. 101, a. 1, c; q. 106, a. 1, c; I, q. 22; II–II, q. 47.

133. See TOB 93:5; 98:7; *ST* III, q. 60, a. 2, c.

meaning of the body. To continue to do so, we need to advance to the next original experience, the experience of original nakedness.

Original Nakedness

Original unity already manifests the experience of original nakedness insofar as the latter deepens into that ease and harmony experienced by our first parents in their interpersonal encounter of communion in the Lord. The experience of original nakedness digs into the theological explanation of this phenomenon: the peculiar graces of original justice. Such a prelapsarian state is especially manifested by Gen 2:25. The image of grace in the human person accounts for why, even if Adam and Eve were naked, they experienced no shame. It also explicates the interconnection between the meaning of the body and charity. In conjunction with the meaning of the other original experiences, the meaning of Adam and Eve's original nakedness reveals that the human "soul is *naturally capable of grace*; since from its having been made to the likeness of God, it is fit to receive God by grace."[134] Thus, once again, we see the complementarity between the two accounts of Creation. Being created in God's image ultimately explains why, in our first parents' original justice, their interpersonal community of love was a communion in charity founded upon their relationship to the Lord. The meaning of original nakedness further illustrates that being created in God's image implies having a capacity for God himself, which is fulfilled in the order of grace through charity.

In this theological reasoning, there are three successive steps of ever-greater understanding of the human person's identity and mission. First, the experience of original nakedness deepens into the specific dependence and subordination to the Creator, present in Adam's original solitude as God's partner. Against the advocates of contraception's views on autonomy, such a dependence will be further explicated as a threefold subordination within the human person. Second, the experience of original nakedness reveals an even deeper understanding of the human body than the one offered in the meaning of original solitude. Understanding original nakedness adds to the revelation of man's substantial unity a greater manifestation of the intimate degree of spiritualization of the body as it manifests itself in the complete absence of antecedent passions. Third, the meaning of original nakedness also deepens the understanding of the *communio personarum* inherent in original unity by exposing its foundation in the theology of the *imago Dei*. God's image in man is the measure and foundation for the unitive meaning of the body as one's vocation to charity in its proper order.

---

134. Ibid., I–II, q. 113, a. 10, c.

PART II: SPOUSAL MEANING OF THE BODY
Threefold Subordination

Adam and Eve's lack of shame does not imply blindness or ignorance with respect to the nakedness of the other. It rather points to the lived experience of the true meaning of one's body before the Creator and creatures, "God made man upright."[135] Within this state in which Adam and Eve were created, to acknowledge and to freely affirm the dignity and vocation of the human person as being created in God's image was easy. It was evident and transparently manifested through the mediation of the body. Such an acknowledgement and affirmation occurred without error or effort. No passion whatsoever was an obstacle or a hindrance in any way to that acknowledgment and free affirmation. There was no awareness of any disordered and dishonest concupiscence of which one should be ashamed. There was no awareness in oneself or in the other of a threat to one's personal dignity and value. There was no fear for one's *I* in the face of the second *I*.[136] Consequently, Adam and Eve's absence of shame points to something deeper, namely, to the characteristic innocence of their state of original justice.[137]

This original experience is best explained in light of Wojtyła's anthropology of love. The aspect of integration looks at a peculiar phenomenon in the formation of virtues: how the human person, as the material of his own moral identity, is being acted upon by his own self as creator of this same moral identity. Thus, in the integrated human person, the lower faculties of his dynamism (sensibility and sensuality) are subordinated to the higher ones (intellect and will). Moreover, the integrated person subordinates his intellect and the exercise of his will, in the use of itself and other potencies, to the truth about the good. Thereby, against the Kantian claim for autonomy, the human person subordinates to the Creator and to the intelligible order of creation. Founded upon these philosophical pillars, John Paul II looks at the experience of original nakedness in retrospect from our present condition, from the situation of historical man. Even if we have been wounded by sin, we are also aided by grace in the practice of virtue. As a result, we can experience a similar growth in our internal unity. We can grow in integration by allowing the most spiritual dimension of our soul to rule over the other faculties, always subordinating what is higher in us to the Creator. This experience of the life of grace is John Paul's *indirect* point of reference to understand Adam and Eve's lived experience of their original state of justice. The pope knows that our historical experience is not exactly the same. Thus, he says that in the state of original justice, there was "a degree of spiritualization of man that differs from the one about which the text speaks after original sin (Gen 3) and which we know from the experience of historical man. It is a different measure of spiritualization that

---

135. Qoh 7:29.
136. See TOB 12:1; 13:1. For secondary literature on this topic, see Larrú, "El significado personalista." Latkovic, "Pope John Paul II's 'Theology of the Body.'"
137. See TOB 16:4; 17:1.

implies another composition of inner forces in man himself, *another body-soul relation, as it were, other inner proportions between sensitivity, spirituality, and affectivity, that is, another degree of inner sensibility for the gifts of the Holy Spirit.*"[138]

To elucidate his position, John Paul makes an explicit reference to Adolph Tanquerey's classic work on Thomistic dogmatic theology.[139] Hence, the pope's text just quoted should be interpreted in light of Aquinas's understanding of the state of original justice.[140] It is not a coincidence that Wojtyła's view on integration parallels exactly the threefold subordination posited by Aquinas in order to explain the state of integrity of Adam and Eve. "God bestowed this favor on man in his primitive state, that as long as his spirit [*mens*] was subject to God, the lower powers of his soul would be subject to his rational spirit [*mens*], and his body to his soul."[141] This is the theological explanation for the original experience of nakedness. Adam and Eve had a government of their lower powers unknown to historical man. It is unknown even to those who, wounded by original sin, live in the state of grace on this earth. What is so different about the power of Adam and Eve's spirit over their lower faculties and over their bodies? Why does John Paul II say that their body-soul relationship is different than ours, even when we live in the state of grace on this earth?

Spiritualized Body and Antecedent Passions

One direct way of illustrating this difference consists in explaining that Adam and Eve did not feel shame because, unlike anyone who lives on this earth and has been affected by original sin, they experienced no antecedent passions. They had no sudden passions that *preceded* or were *not caused* by their rational judgment and their free choice. Conversely, all of their feelings were a *consequence* of their rational judgment and of their willful choice.[142] Their emotions were always extremely docile allies of their virtues. They were never potential or actual rebellious enemies to the acknowledgement and free affirmation of their mutual personal dignity.[143] Adam and Eve never experienced a passion "hampering the judgment of reason necessary in choosing."[144]

John Paul II is very perceptive in his description of their body-soul relationship: there was a greater *spiritualization* of their body. The biblical basis for this expression seems to be found in 1 Cor 15:44. Paul speaks herein about the resurrection of the body. He describes the human body in the state of glory as a "spiritual body" (*soma pneumatikón*). Our first parents' inner unity was greater than historical man's

138. Ibid., 18:2.
139. See ibid., 18:2, n29.
140. For an excellent study on this topic, see Van Roo, *Grace and Original Justice*.
141. *ST* II–II, q. 164, a. 1, c. See also *ST* I, q. 95, a. 1; q. 97, a. 1.
142. See ibid., I–II, q. 24, a. 3, ad 1.
143. See *ST* I, q. 95, a. 2, c.
144. *De Veritate*, q. 26, a. 7, ad 3.

in this metaphysical sense: there was less matter or material to be conquered by their spiritual or rational form than in our case.[145] This understanding of our first parents' affectivity explains their absence of shame and it roots such an absence in their state of original justice. But let us be completely clear: Adam and Eve's bodies were *not* in the state of glory. However, they were affected by the preternatural gifts. Thus, their spirit enjoyed a mastery over their sensible and vegetative faculties unknown to us now. In this sense, their bodies and their emotions resembled more of what we hope for in the state of glory.

This theological reasoning is profoundly Thomistic. Indeed, in accordance with John Paul II, Aquinas compares the way Adam and Eve experienced their emotions to the blessed in heaven. Thomas even includes the earthly Christ in this comparison. He says that "in the blessed, in man in the first state, and in Christ as subject to our infirmity, such passions are *never sudden*, seeing that because of the *perfect obedience of the lower powers to the higher* no movement arises in the lower appetite *except at the dictate of reason.*"[146] Christ experienced hunger because he willed to do so. He experienced fear by willing to do so.[147] In short, he experienced only *consequent* passions. Now, "the same is to be understood of the blessed after the resurrection *and of men in the first state.*"[148] Yet, Adam and Eve's emotions were different from the ones in Christ during his earthly life. The Son of God had to suffer for us and for our salvation. Instead, in our first parents, there is "*no passion except with regard to good*, as love, joy, and the like, but not sadness or fear or anger or anything of the sort."[149] Hence, Adam and Eve experienced no shame for these two reasons: there were no antecedent passions in them, and their passions were only with regard to the good.

The Measure of the *Imago Dei* and Charity

There is an innocence inherent in the experience of original nakedness.[150] Such an innocence has to do with the state of purity of *the human will*.[151] John Paul II also uses *the biblical metaphor of the heart* in order to signify this same reality. To avoid confusion, allow me to briefly explain the metaphor. As a physical organ, the heart is an *essential and interior principle of human life*. As a metaphor, it really signifies *the deepest and most interior principle of our life*. It signifies our one rational soul. But in signifying our soul, it appeals to its most interior, intimate, and spiritual dimension. Thus, the heart corresponds to the intellect and the will in their reciprocal immanence

---

145. See *ScG* II.68; De Finance, *Persona e valore*, 111.
146. *De Veritate*, q. 26, a. 8, c; emphasis added. See also *ST* I, q. 95, a. 2, c.
147. See Gondreau, *The Passions of Christ's Soul*.
148. *De Veritate*, q. 26, a. 8, c; emphasis added.
149. Ibid.; emphasis added.
150. See TOB 16:4.
151. See *ST* I, q. 95, a. 1, c.

and synergy.[152] The intellect and the will's reciprocal immanence and synergy is exactly and in all rigor the most interior and intimate dimension of man's soul. No angel or demon can "enter" into that innermost dimension of our soul.[153] Only God can directly move from within the human intellect and will without violating our nature. As a result, it is very fitting to use the metaphor of the heart to refer to the synergy of these two faculties. They are, in reality, the most intimate or interior dimension of our true and most radical principle of life, our soul. John Paul II uses two other ways of referring to the "heart," to the intellect and the will in their reciprocal immanence and synergy. Sometimes, with more philosophical precision, John Paul calls it the human spirit (*mens*). Other times, in a more metaphorical and biblical manner, the pope also uses the Pauline expression, "the interior man."[154] They all mean the same thing. In the thought of John Paul II, heart, spirit, and inner or interior man signify one single and precise thing *in rerum naturae*: the reciprocal immanence and synergy between the human intellect and will.

The theological and philosophical clarification of this biblical metaphor allows us to read correctly the pope's description of original innocence as "the *interior* state of the human *heart*, of the human *will*."[155] This interior state includes a certain moral consciousness of innocence before the knowledge of good and evil. Since our first parents' spirit (*mens*) was subordinated to the Creator, their moral conscience did not accuse them. Within the context of the covenant and as God's partners, they were innocent. They had not rebelled against God, claiming autonomy. They had not subverted their due subordination by eating from the tree of knowledge of good and evil. Because of the Holy Spirit poured into their hearts, their acknowledgement of being inferior to God, and their subordination to him in their heart or spirit, was paired with the subordination of their lower powers to their intellect and will.[156] Since they felt no disobedience in their flesh, no disordered concupiscence, they experienced no shame. Exactly like the pope, Thomas points to the absence or presence of shame as the indicator of the presence or absence of original innocence. Here, Aquinas is also following Augustine: "Augustine says that, as soon as they [Adam and Eve] disobeyed the Divine command, and forfeited Divine grace, they were ashamed of their nakedness, for they felt the impulse of disobedience in the flesh, as though it were a punishment corresponding to their own disobedience."[157] The pope adopts this same position but from the subjective perspective of lived experience, from Adam and Eve's awareness of the meaning of their original justice. Such a lived experience results in the consciousness of original innocence. This innocence is "that which radically, that is, *at its very roots, excludes the*

---

152. See PC, 80.
153. See *ST* I, q. 111, aa. 1–2.
154. See TOB 31:5; AP, 315, note 74; *ST* I, q. 75, a. 4, ad 1; II–II, q. 25, a. 7, c.
155. TOB 16:4; emphasis added.
156. See *De Malo*, q. 4, a. 8, c.
157. *ST* I, q. 95, a. 1, c.

shame of the body in the relation between man and woman, that which *eliminates the necessity of this shame in man*, in his *heart* and his *conscience*."[158]

John Paul argues now that Gen 2:25 also *originates* a *deeper awareness of the meaning of the body*. "Original innocence is revealed by man's *consciousness* concerning the *meaning of his body* as described in Gen 2:25; original innocence signifies that "mysterious gift made to man's innermost being—to the human heart—that allows both the man and the woman to exist from the beginning in the reciprocal relationship of the disinterested gift of self."[159] Because of their purity of heart, Adam and Eve enjoyed a perfected freedom. They had a sort of habit to use well their natural freedom or innate capacity for self-determination. They had the sound operative habit of choosing the true good. They were able to love each other within that very context. Hence, Adam and Eve were capable of the interior freedom of the gift. In their purity and innocence, they were able to experience the *meaning* of the primary gift of the world. They were conscious of the objective intended nature of the visible world as a gift to them from the Creator. Their subordination to the Creator also made them aware of their place of honor in that world.

Above all, such an immense gift made them aware of God's love for them. Adam and Eve also experienced the *meaning* of the reciprocal gift among persons. They were conscious of another facet of the human person's objective intended nature by God. They were aware of an enriched meaning of the body. At this point, they were aware of being a creature who finds fulfillment in love, especially in that love inherent in the free gift of self.[160] According to our experience, shame is absorbed by love.[161] Thus, it makes sense that Adam and Eve did not experience shame. They lived in a mutual love in God and because of God. This mutual charity prevented them from feeling shame in their original nakedness. But it also revealed the meaning of their body in a peculiar way. It revealed original innocence as a grace given by the Creator through which man is capable "to live the meaning of *the primary gift of the world* and in particular *the meaning of reciprocal gift of one person to the other* through masculinity and femininity in this world."[162] The unitive meaning of the human body is now inserted in the context of charity and the gift of self.

Original nakedness is an experience that brings the unitive meaning of the body to a deeper level of reflection. It *originates* an even deeper understanding of the meaning of the body rooted in the *imago Dei*. At this deeper level, the fundamental premise is that God's grace, poured into their hearts, gave Adam and Eve a righteous intention in their mutual gift of self. The process itself has three major parts. First, the woman is given to man by the Creator. She is a gift that shows God's love. Adam accepts her as a

---

158. TOB 16:4; emphasis added
159. Ibid., 16:3; emphasis added
160. See TOB 16:5; GS 24.
161. See LR, 181–85.
162. TOB 16:4; emphasis added.

gift, as a great good, non-merited, and given gratuitously to him by the Creator. Adam also acknowledges and affirms her personal dignity, participating in her humanity as his sister. In so doing, Adam also partakes in God's willing Eve for her own sake. Second, this acknowledgement and affirmation causes in Eve a profound process of self-knowledge whereby she finds herself. She knows herself, in turn, as a person, as a being willed by God for her own sake. Eve comes to this realization because of Adam's affirmation of her dignity in both her humanity and in her femininity. This finding of her own identity is the very source of the discovery of the meaning of her body, of her vocation to love Adam in God and because of God. Third, Adam's acknowledgement and affirmation of Eve's personal dignity is the source of her gift of self to him. This third part reveals Adam's peculiar *responsibility*. He is called to receive Eve as a gift. She is entrusted to him. He is responsible for affirming her dignity and thus, assuring her giving of herself.[163]

At this precise moment of his reasoning, the pope brings up the notion of the spousal meaning of the body. He argues that original innocence is a "particular purity of heart preserving interior *faithfulness to the gift according* to *the spousal meaning of the body*."[164] The work of grace in the intellect and the will accounts for Adam and Eve's fidelity to their mutual gift of self. But why is that fidelity "according to the spousal meaning of the body"? This fidelity is in accordance with the spousal meaning of their body not only because Adam and Eve are perfecting their marriage in that gift of self. Although that perfection is truly taking place, their fidelity is in accordance with the spousal meaning of body above all *because of their relationship to the Creator*. Adam and Eve are loving each other *in God and because of God.* In our first parents, there was a fullness of exterior perception in physical nakedness looked at from an interior "vision of man in God, that is, *according to the measure of the image of God*."[165] Adam and Eve had "an inner dimension of a share in the vision of the Creator himself."[166] Thus, their "nakedness signifies the original good of the divine vision."[167] What is the measure of God's image?

As Thomas explains, "the likeness we have to God precedes and causes the likeness we have to our neighbor: because from the very fact that we share along with our neighbor in something received from God, we become like to our neighbor. Hence *by reason of this likeness we ought to love God more than we love our neighbor.*"[168] Thus, the measure of the *imago Dei* is the foundation for the love towards oneself and towards one's neighbor. It is the measure whereby we love God more than oneself and more than our neighbor. John Paul II argues that, in their original justice, Adam and Eve

163. See TOB 17:5.
164. Ibid., 16:5; emphasis added.
165. Ibid., 12:5; emphasis added.
166. Ibid., 13:1.
167. Ibid.
168. *ST* II–II, q. 26, a. 2, ad 2; emphasis added.

saw each other *according to this measure*. They had a purity of heart according to the spousal meaning of their bodies because such purity helped them to *well-orderedly live their vocation to charity*. They loved each other with an order of charity (*ordo amoris*), in which their mutual love was referred back to God as the only one who should be loved above all things, and above all created persons, including oneself.

Open Questions

The understanding of the original experiences originate the human person's awareness of the spousal meaning of his body. Founded on GS 24 and Thomas Aquinas, John Paul explains how Adam and Eve experienced a unity in charity and in truth, a communion of persons loving each other in God and because of God, which images the Trinity. Within this conjugal communion, the two meanings of original unity are present. They participated in each other's humanity and they experienced the complementarity of their sexual differentiation. Indeed, "seeing and knowing each other in all the peace and tranquility of the interior gaze, they communicate in the fullness of humanity, which shows itself in them as reciprocal complementarity, precisely because they are male and female. At the same time, they communicate based on the communion of persons in which they become a mutual gift for each other, through femininity and masculinity. In reciprocity, they reach in this way a particular understanding of the meaning of their bodies."[169] The understanding of the original experiences has been cumulative. As we progressed, the current experience presupposed the precedent one. Thus, the experience of original nakedness has drawn the understanding of original solitude and unity into the dimension of charity. Adam and Eve experienced their conjugal communion as a way to fulfill their vocation to charity, as a way to live out the spousal meaning of their bodies.

It is evident now that John Paul II's understanding of the spousal meaning of the body is a cumulative argument based on the original experiences. They have originated a progressive understanding of the meaning of the human body. This process of self-knowledge and discovery of one's identity and mission has led to one's call to charity, to love God and neighbor. It is also evident the way in which this argument, up to this junction, is Thomistic and grounded in Vatican II. Thus, John Paul II reconciles in this peculiar way the biblical, metaphysical, and theological foundations of a moral theology centered around the *imago Dei*. However, at this point, a series of new questions arises: why does John Paul II use the term *spousal* to characterize the meaning of the human body if that meaning is not exclusively fulfilled in marriage? More importantly, why use the adjective 'spousal' to characterize the meaning of the human body if that meaning is perfectly fulfilled in heaven where there is no marriage? Is this choice Thomistic? Is it grounded in Vatican II?

169. TOB 13:1.

7

Why Spousal?

Spousal Love as Gift of Self

Wojtyła explains that "the person finds in love the greatest possible fullness of being, of objective existence."[1] This is Aquinas's position exactly and that of Vatican II.[2] In TOB, in order to speak about our vocation to charity, John Paul II concentrates on one particular form of love, on spousal love. Thus, he speaks about the spousal meaning of the body as our supernatural vocation to charity. Looking chronologically at Wojtyła's works, this choice of words finds its roots in LR. In this book, our author characterizes one peculiar form of love with the adjective *oblubieńczy*. This Polish adjective could be translated into English either as bethrothed or as 'spousal'. To fully understand John Paul II's position in TOB, it is important to *reread* LR in light of the conciliar framework developed in the previous chapters, and in light of his teachings on spousal love in MD. It is germane to pay close attention to Eph 5:25's central role in both Wojtyła's christocentric interpretation of Vatican II and in MD's understanding of the Christian vocation to charity. This scriptural text is the key to understand both marriage and continence for the sake of the Kingdom: "[T]o clarify what the kingdom of heaven is for those who choose voluntary continence for its sake, *the revelation of the spousal relationship between Christ and the Church* has particular significance. Among other texts, therefore, the *decisive one* is Eph 5:25–33."[3] As the pope clarifies, "this text is *equally valid* both for the theology of marriage and for the theology of continence for the kingdom, the theology of virginity or celibacy."[4] In Eph 5:25–33, we find Christ who "having taken on human nature, definitively illumines it in its constitutive elements and *in its dynamism of charity towards God and neighbour*."[5]

As is known, Eph 5:25 uses the spousal analogy in order to present Jesus's charity for the church as the root and norm for the charity which ought to exist among sacramentally married people. Jesus's spousal charity finds its greatest expression in his gift

---

1. LR, 82.
2. See LG 40; *ST* II–II, q. 184, a. 1, c; II–II, q. 23, a. 6, c; II–II, q. 23, a. 8, c.
3. TOB 79:7; emphasis added.
4. Ibid.; emphasis added. See *In IV Sent.*, d. 38, q. 1, a. 5, c.
5. VS 53; emphasis added.

of self in his passion and death. The Greek *paredoken*, from the verb *paradidomi*, suggests a sacrificial gift, an offering, a certain surrender.[6] The reflexive emphasis leaves no room for doubt: what is being sacrificed, what is being offered, and what is being surrendered is Jesus's very self (*eauton*). Yet, how does Christ concretely surrender his own self? What does he do in order to bring into effect such a surrender and gift of self? Phil 2:8 provides the right context to answer these questions: Jesus's *obedience* unto death. Within the context of obedience, the adherence of Christ's human will to the divine will is *the paradigm* and *exemplar* for one's gift of self in charity. Christ gave himself *by giving his own human will* to God, by being obedient to the Father. He did so out of love for God and for us, loving unto his death.[7] As John Paul II teaches, "Christ is the Bridegroom because he has given himself."[8] Similarly, as a member of the Church—the bride of Christ—the human person's self is being surrendered in the sacrificial offering and giving of one's will that is effected out of love for God and others. Moreover, Heb 10:5–7 is another scriptural hermeneutical key, which further unveils Wojtyła's interpretation of Vatican II. It speaks of Jesus's sacrificial self-gift, expressed in his obedience to the divine will out of charity, as *the* priestly action of Christ. Our participation in that act of charity is a *communion* with God. It is a participation in Christ's priestly *munus*. Thus, in Rom 12:1, Paul teaches how to partake in that priestly *munus*, by presenting our "bodies as a living sacrifice, holy and acceptable to God," thereby offering a "spiritual worship."[9] We already know that Wojtyła appeals to this precise text to explain authentic moral obligations.

This reading of Eph 5:25 seems to correspond exactly with Wojtyła's interpretation of Vatican II. Indeed, as we saw in chapter 1, Wojtyła argues that Eph 5:25 describes the greatest *priestly* action of Jesus Christ. Our participation in it constitutes the simplest and most complete conciliar moral attitude. Such a moral attitude is the one synthesized in GS 24. For this reason, Wojtyła said that our participation in Christ's self-offering, as described in Eph 5:25, really "expresses the vocation of the person in its existential nucleus [charity!]—a vocation referred to by *Gaudium et Spes* in the words to which we must constantly return."[10] (Wojtyła refers to GS 24.) Hence, participating in this attitude, the human person follows the example of the Virgin Mary in her "virginal gift of self to God, the Bridegroom."[11] Thus, the human person gives himself and offers the world to God in the manner of a sacrifice that is a true spiritual worship (*rationabilem obsequium*).[12] In this *priestly* attitude, one fulfills

---

6. See also Eph 5:2; Ga 2:20; Rom 8:32, 4:25. John 15:13; 19:30.

7. See John 15:13; 13:1.

8. MD 26.

9. Phil 2:17 also speaks in this very context of being poured out as a libation upon the sacrificial offering of the faith of the community. See MD 27.

10. SR, 224.

11. Ibid., 198–99. See also MD 27.

12. See Rom 12:1; PO 2; SR, 223.

the gift of self or self-offering inherent in the obedience of faith and expressed as the ethical conclusion of the christocentric anthropology of man created in God's image.

This theological context clarifies why, from the philosophical viewpoint, LR envisions spousal love as a particular form of love within the genus of friendship, as a particular kind of love whose essence is summarized in the following words: "[T]he essence of betrothed [or spousal] love is self-giving, the surrender of one's *I*."[13] Indeed, spousal love is all about self-gift. However, as it is explained in 1 Jn 4:19, "we love, because he [God] first loved us." Hence, there is an *order* between the spousal love of the bridegroom and the bride: "The Bridegroom is the one who loves. The Bride is loved: it is she who receives love, in order to love in return."[14] In this manner, the spousal analogy highlights God's *initiative and our responsibility*.

In Wojtyła's philosophy and theology, betrothed or spousal love is not restricted to marriage. Its *primum analogatum* is Christ's love for the church and her answer to that love.[15] To be sure, in the order of knowledge, we first know the reality of married love since, as Thomas Aquinas teaches, marriage is the greatest of friendships.[16] Then, this human reality is used in God's revelation as an analogy that we can understand, as a way of speaking of God's love for his people and of Christ's love for the church. However, in the order of being, the primacy belongs to Christ's love for the church. Thus, the pope explains Eph 5:25 with the following words: "That gift of self to the Father through obedience to the point of death is at the same time, according to Ephesians, an act of giving himself for the Church. In this expression, *redeeming love* transforms itself, I would say, *into spousal love*."[17]

For Wojtyła, when one speaks of Christ's spousal love, or when one calls Christ the Bridegroom, one is not speaking metaphorically but analogically. Without a doubt, Eph 5:25–27 also uses metaphorical language. The analogy present in Eph 5:25–27 establishes a proportion of similarity and dissimilarity among the love between Christ and the church and the love between husbands and wives. Yet, within this analogy, there are also metaphors used. For example, in Eph 5:27, the church is said to be presented "without spot or wrinkle." Those spots and wrinkles are clearly metaphors that represent moral defects. As John Paul II says, "it is significant that the image of the glorious Church is presented, in the text quoted, as a bride all beautiful in her body. Certainly, *this is a metaphor*, but it is a very eloquent one and testifies how deeply important the body is in *the analogy of spousal love*."[18]

---

13. LR, 96.

14. MD 29.

15. See LG 9 and 64.

16. "Between husband and wife, there seems to be the greatest friendship [*maxima amicitia esse videtur*]." *ScG* III.123.

17. TOB 90:6.

18. Ibid., 92:2. Wojtyła uses the concepts of analogy and metaphor in a Thomistic sense, reminiscent of the developments from the Scholastics. See García López, *Metafísica Tomista*, 33–35.

Were Christ's spousal love only a metaphor, Christ would be the bridegroom like he is the morning star.[19] As Thomas teaches, "all names applied metaphorically to God, are applied to creatures primarily rather than to God, because when said of God they mean only similitudes to such creatures."[20] Strictly speaking, Christ is no more a star than God is a rock. Rock and star are both predicated primarily of creatures, but they are predicated of God only metaphorically. But it does not seem true that spousal love, as defined by Wojtyła, belongs primarily to creatures. In fact, this kind of love, whose essence is self-gift, seems to be "applied primarily to God rather than to creatures."[21] God is the one who most eminently gives himself in love. He is gift.[22] By the power of God's grace, the rational creature alone is capable of receiving God as such, as a gift. Moreover, although gift is a personal name of the Holy Spirit, it is also predicated appropriately of the Son, who is given to us by the Father, and it is also predicated appropriately of the Son who gives himself out of love for us.[23]

Perhaps it may be helpful to compare how we predicate of God both paternity and spousal love. In the order of knowledge, paternity is first known by us in created reality. For this reason, one could initially see in the use of paternity a certain anthropomorphism. It is a name first applied *by us* to the visible created realm, the same realm out of which we form our concepts. But we should not conclude from this fact that paternity is only a metaphor. *Every* name used to speak of God always has this kind of imperfection. As Thomas explains, "with reference to the mode of signification there is in every name that we use an imperfection, which does not befit God, *even though the thing signified in some eminent way does befit God*."[24] Thus, John Paul II says that "it is not possible to attribute human qualities to the eternal generation of the Word of God."[25] In fact, the pope clearly affirms that "divine fatherhood does not possess masculine characteristics in a physical sense."[26] Yet, the creatural mode of signification, which belongs to the order of our knowledge, should not obscure that, *in the order of being*, first and foremost, paternity belongs to God. He is *the* principle

---

19. See Rev 22:16.
20. *ST* I, q. 13, a. 6, c.
21. Ibid.
22. See *ST* I, q. 38, a. 1, c.
23. See John 3:16; *ST* I, q. 38, a. 2, ad 1; DV, 10. John Paul II further explains Christ's gift of self through the Holy Spirit. He begins to treat this topic in DV, 23–24. Later on, in the same document, he concludes: "The Son of God Jesus Christ, as man, in the ardent prayer of his Passion, enabled the Holy Spirit, who had already penetrated the inmost depths of his humanity, to transform that humanity into a perfect sacrifice through the act of his death as the victim of love on the Cross. He made this offering by himself. As the one priest, he offered himself without blemish to God: In his humanity he was worthy to become this sacrifice, for he alone was without blemish. But he offered it through the eternal Spirit, which means that the Holy Spirit acted in a special way in this absolute self-giving of the Son of Man, in order to transform this suffering into redemptive love." DV, 40.
24. *ScG* I.30; emphasis added.
25. MD 8.
26. Ibid.

of another's being. God's fatherhood is the model and exemplar of every *patría*.[27] As the pope also says, we must "seek in God the absolute model of all generation among human beings."[28] Consequently, although known by us through creatures, the names father and son are *not* predicated of God metaphorically.[29]

John Paul II's choice of words suggests that something similar happens in the spousal analogy.[30] Spousal love as gift of self is first known to us in the marriage between a man and a woman. In this way, this analogy has a mode of signification which belongs to creatures. Thus, it even includes a certain anthropomorphism. But we should not conclude from this fact that we are dealing here with sheer metaphor. In the order of being, spousal love belongs first and foremost to God. He is the supreme model and measure for the gift of self in love. Thus, God is the archetype of being a bridegroom. Just as every *patría* receives its name from the Father, so every spousal love finds in Christ its supreme model and exemplar. Christ is *the* Model and Exemplar of spousal love because he is *the* Bridegroom. Following Wojtyła's christocentric theology of the *imago Dei*, we could say that in giving himself up for the church, Jesus Christ is the measure and exemplar of the gift of self inherent in every form of spousal love, let that spousal love find its expression in the vocation to marriage or in the vocation to virginity for the sake of the Kingdom.[31] It is from this ontological primacy that the very fulfillment of one's union with Christ in heaven, where there will be no conjugal union between man and woman, sheds light on the vocation to marriage.[32]

As a result, Wojtyła insists that the very specific essence of spousal love is not intrinsically determined by factors which only belong to the conjugal union of one man and one woman. Instead, the very intrinsic essence of spousal love is, according to our author, the gift of self, a self-surrender out of love, which finds its own expression in one's vocation to marriage, but also in another's vocation to continence for the sake of God's Kingdom. Similarly, Thomas also argues that carnal marriage between a man and a woman partially represents Christ's spousal union with the church. While

27. See Eph 3:15.
28. MD 8.
29. See *ST* I, q. 33, a. 2, ad 3.
30. See Wojtyła, "On the Meaning of Spousal Love," 284; TOB 94:6–8; MD 23, 25, and 29; John Paul II, *The Church*, 113–14; John Paul II, *Jesus*, 418–22.
31. Petri rightly comments: "Precisely because the spousal meaning of the body entails freedom for a self-gift in love, it is not entirely surprising that the pope holds that vocations other than marriage are capable of living out that spousal meaning in a non-conjugal way. The spousal meaning of the body can be lived in these various ways of life because Christ's redemptive love is a spousal love. His redemptive love embraces all these vocations, and each mirrors that love in its own way." Petri, *Aquinas*, 183.
32. "The truth about the union of the human person with a personal God, which will be fully accomplished within the dimensions of eternity, at the same time illuminates more fully and makes plainer the value of human love, the value of the union of man and woman as two persons. Significantly the Old and the New Testament both speak of marriage of God with mankind (in the chosen people, or in the Church), and the writings of mystics of the conjugal union of the human soul with God." LR, 173. See also TOB 68:3.

marriage between man and woman best represents the fecundity of the marriage between Christ and the church, the spiritual marriage of those who are continent for the sake of the Kingdom best represents its integrity and purity.[33] In both vocations, Wojtyła teaches that one's gift and surrender to God is not to be viewed on equal footing with one's gift and surrender to others. Strictly speaking, a total or complete self-surrender is due *to God alone*. This is another aspect particularly highlighted by the spousal analogy. God is the Bridegroom and any attempt to love anyone or anything above him is seen in the scriptures as a sort of adultery. No other being but God should be loved in this way: "In accordance with the First commandment, the commandment to love, man may surrender himself *completely* in love to God *alone*, so that giving himself to another human being must be simultaneously a way of giving himself *completely* to God."[34] The human person should love only God more than himself.[35] When the human person loves his neighbor as himself and donates himself to him or her, this gift is simultaneously a gift to the Creator.

Keeping this theological context in mind, there is still a philosophical need to explain in which sense one can surrender one's own self, in which sense one person can be possessed by another. From the *metaphysical* perspective, the human person possesses and governs himself. He does so in such an intimate way that no one else can take his place in making a free choice. Even God respects this very dignity. The human person is *alteri incomunicabilis*. Thus, from this viewpoint, "it makes no sense to speak of a person giving himself or herself to another."[36] However, from the *moral* perspective, the human person is able to freely decide to surrender his own free will to another. Moreover, one can do that out of charity, that is, out of love for God and others. It is from this moral perspective that the gift of self is understood in the scriptures with the image of spousal love. The reciprocal possession between persons, of which we read in Song 2:16—"My beloved is mine and I am his"— must be interpreted from this exact moral perspective.[37] Such a possession implies no violation of one's personal dignity but rather its ethical fulfillment. From this very perspective, John Paul II understands the spousal meaning of the body. Wojtyła explains that, in this moral sense, "one person can give himself or herself, can surrender entirely to another, whether to a human person or to God, and such a giving of the self creates a special form of love which we define as betrothed [or spousal] love."[38] Relating betrothed or spousal love with Matthew 10:39 and anticipating GS 24, Wojtyła argues in LR that the apparent paradox of finding one's life in giving it contains what perfects man, that

---

33. See *In IV Sent.*, d. 38, q. 1, a. 5, c.
34. LR, 295 note 20; emphasis added.
35. See *ST* II–II, q. 26, a. 3, c.
36. LR, 96.
37. See TOB 31:3; 110:8.
38. LR, 97.

is to say, that which gives meaning to his existence.³⁹ Obviously, this kind of love presupposes maturity or integration in the human person. No one can give what he or she does not possess. As a result, "in giving ourselves we find clear proof that we possess ourselves."⁴⁰

Retractatio

Fourteen years after the publication of LR, in 1974, Karol Wojtyła wrote an article to clarify some controversy originated by his previous treatment of spousal love.⁴¹ Although he calls his article a *retractatio*, our author argues that he is *not* changing his initial position.⁴² Instead, Wojtyła offers a *re-tractatio* in its most etymological sense: he is *treating again* the same topic, offering further precisions about spousal love which do not alter his original position but rather enrich and deepen it. For our purposes, this article offers an appreciated hermeneutical key for TOB. It was written after Vatican II and it appeals to the teaching of the Council on this matter. Moreover, this article is also very valuable to our study because it was composed at the same time in which our author was working on TOB.

Wojtyła appeals in his article to GS 24 as the text which best expresses the law of the gift inscribed in man's being.⁴³ This law is at the heart of the gift of self that is inherent in spousal love, and understood "as the choice of a vocation in the dimension of the whole life."⁴⁴ Our author continues to explain: "[T]he entire tradition, which we do not present here in its full extent, but rather limit ourselves to mentioning it, advocates *ascribing an analogous meaning to spousal love*."⁴⁵ We will see in this chapter in what way Thomas Aquinas and John of the Cross are part of that tradition mentioned by Wojtyła. For the moment, let us note how our author explains that there is a law within ourselves according to which we find the full meaning of our lives in the gift of self. Such a gift of self is inherent in the acts of the virtues, especially as they are elevated and concentrated in charity. Wojtyła explains that "this gift of self, which man can and should make in order to fully find himself, is realized through particular virtues and

---

39. "Christ gave expression to this in a saying which is on the face of it profoundly paradoxical: 'He who would save his soul shall lose it, and he who would lose his soul for my sake shall find it again' (Matthew 10:39) . . . We have already stated that this self-perfection proceeds side by side and step by step with love. The fullest, the most uncompromising form of love consists precisely in self-giving, making one's inalienable and non-transferable *I* someone else's property." Ibid.

40. LR, 98. Following a similar reasoning, Thomas explains that the spouses are the ministers of the sacrament of marriage. They have the sufficient self-possession to make a gift of themselves through consent. See Aquinas, *In IV Sent.*, d. 28, q. 1, a. 3, ad 2; *In IV Sent.*, d. 36, q. 1, a. 3, sc; TOB 15:2.

41. See Wojtyła, "On the Meaning of Spousal Love."

42. See ibid., 275.

43. LG 44 is also referenced to explain that virginity is also to be understood as spousal love.

44. Wojtyła, "On the Meaning of Spousal Love," 285.

45. Ibid., 289–90; emphasis added.

through each of them."⁴⁶ He then clarifies that the law of the gift inscribed in the being of the person "is realized in various forms *through every act of love* (in order to avoid all misunderstandings, we could say: through every act of true love)."⁴⁷ But our author reminds us immediately that "the act of every virtue is such an act because *all virtues find in love their common root, their full sense and ultimate expression.*"⁴⁸

Within the analogy of spousal love, from the ontological viewpoint, the *primum analogatum* is not marriage but Christ's love for the church. For this reason, Wojtyła explains again that, in this earthly life, spousal love finds two expressions that participate in this *primum analogatum*. Indeed, "in accordance with Christ's teaching, this love is realized *in one way* in the exclusive self-giving to God alone, and *in another way* in marriage through the reciprocal self-giving of human persons, of a man and a woman."⁴⁹ But these two vocations, considered in themselves, are *not* equal in dignity. Wojtyła is also crystal clear about it: "The Gospel and the Church's teaching that follows it emphasize continuously the *superiority* of the former vocation over the latter."⁵⁰

Obviously, Wojtyła is not implying that the sheer fact of following one's vocation makes one person more perfect than another. What accounts for such a perfection is the degree of one's charity and not one's absolute vocation to virginity or to marriage. But this very point evidences something common to both vocations. In both of them, there is a gift of self which is proper to God alone and his *dominium altum*. In both of them, there is a gift to God as he who is loved above all things and persons. In both of them, there is charity. Indeed, Wojtyła wants to dispel the error according to which he who is married has, by necessity, a divided heart that cannot love God above all things. Consequently, he says that some err by thinking "that the reciprocal self-giving of persons in marriage, of a man and a woman, in a sense takes away these people from God, precludes their self-giving to God, or severs them from him."⁵¹ It is no wonder that our author reacts against this error. Think about the Virgin Mary. She was truly and perfectly married.⁵² Yet, she loved God with great charity and without any division in her heart. From our viewpoint, charity as spousal love is a response from the human person who has been loved first by Christ, the Bridegroom. Thus, in his interpretation of Vatican II, the future pope found a moral example of this ecclesial and spousal dimension of charity in the Blessed Virgin Mary. He described her relationship with Christ in terms of the gift of self and using the spousal analogy.

46. Ibid., 284.

47. Ibid.

48. Ibid.; emphasis added. See *ST* II–II, q. 23, a. 8, c.

49. Wojtyła, "On the Meaning of Spousal Love," 290; emphasis added. See Aquinas, *In IV Sent.*, d. 38, q. 1, a. 5, c.

50. Wojtyła, "On the Meaning of Spousal Love," 290; emphasis added.

51. Ibid.

52. See *ST* III, q. 29, a. 2, c.

In this manner, with Mary's example of receptive response and responsibility to God's initiative, the vocation to holiness in charity of the members of the church acquires a "spousal" dimension that is referred to Christ.[53]

In keeping with this view and reacting against the error already mentioned, Wojtyła forcefully explains that "the entire tradition of Christian thought, which draws its inspiration from the Gospel, does not allow such an understanding."[54] Indeed, grounding his reflections in Vatican II, our author continues to explain that "by reciprocally giving and receiving each other (*Gaudium et Spes*, 48) in this shared vocation of theirs and in its realization throughout their whole life, *the spouses at the same time realize*, together and each of them separately, *that gift of the person which is directed to God alone*."[55] The experiences of original unity and nakedness manifested that Adam and Eve loved each other *in God* and *because of God*. Their conjugal relationship was founded upon their relationship as brother and sister with God as their Father. Their relationship before original sin is an example for us today because, as our author explains, "this belonging of persons who are spouses to each other finds its source and its confirmation in the belonging of each of them to God alone."[56]

Wojtyła also comes back to some important clarifications on the exact meaning of the gift of self. First, he differentiates again between the metaphysical and the ethical dimensions. Second, he distinguishes the non-personal from the personal status of possession. At the metaphysical level, we belong to God alone. As Psalm 100:3 says, "Know that the Lord is God! It is he that made us, and we are his." However, even then, there is a certain *incommunicability*. The Creator cannot decide in place of the human person.[57] As Augustine says, "God made you without you. You did not, after all, give any consent to God making you. How were you to consent, if you did not yet exist? So while he made you without you, he does not justify you without you. So he made you without your knowing it, he justifies you with your willing consent to it."[58] However, at the ethical level, a human person can freely decide that another governs him. He can make a gift of that which is most valuable to him, namely, his own will.[59] In doing so, he does not violate his own personal dignity. He belongs to another in a personal way. In this manner, the free gift of one's will to another does not amount to a non-personal status of possession.

---

53. See SR, 198–99.
54. Wojtyła, "On the Meaning of Spousal Love," 290–91.
55. Ibid.
56. Ibid., 287.
57. See ibid., 279.
58. Augustine, Sermon 169, 13 in *Sermons 151–183 (III/5)*.
59. See *De perfectione*, cap. 10.

The Gift and the Spousal Meaning of the Body

The previous clarifications on the nature of spousal love aid our analysis of TOB's understanding of the spousal meaning of the body. At this point of his argument, John Paul recapitulates the original experiences in light of what he calls the "hermeneutics of the gift." This hermeneutics leads to the discovery of the spousal meaning of the body as present in all of the original experiences. As the pope says, "the dimension of gift is decisive for the essential truth and depth of the meaning of original solitude-unity-nakedness."[60]

In light of 1 John 4:8, God's act of Creation should be viewed as an act of love.[61] The visible world is given to the human person as *a sign of love*. In the visible world, only the human person, created in God's image, can understand the meaning of God's gift: "[I]n the account of the creation of the visible world, giving has meaning only in relation to man."[62] Understanding such a meaning makes the human person aware of being not only the recipient of God's gift but also a *beloved* partner called to collaborate with the Creator. Indeed, as Aristotle says, a gift is a gratuitous donation, something given without having the intent of being repaid.[63] Since we give gifts like this to those whom we love, the first gift given to them is the gift of our love. Thus, love is the first and most *primordial gift*: it is the gift whereby all other gifts are given gratuitously.[64] John Paul II is saying that Adam and Eve understand God's gift under this very light of love as the primordial gift. Thereby, they attain consciousness of a relationship with the Creator based on love as the most primordial of God's gifts. As it was explained, the spousal analogy highlights God's gratuitous initiative and our responsibility.[65] Note how in John Paul's rereading of the original experiences under the hermeneutics of the gift, the initiative belongs to God. He is the one who loved them originally, who gave himself to them with the gift of his grace. He is the Bridegroom. In turn, Adam and Eve receive God's love as a gift. Thus, they are called to love him and each other in return.

Hence, John Paul II notes that the human person is "able to respond to the Creator with the language of this understanding."[66] The human person experiences the need for the fellowship of friendship as a call to live out the gift of self to God in giving oneself to another human being. Thus, in original solitude, Adam realizes that "none of these beings (*animalia*), in fact, offers man the basic conditions that *make it possible*

---

60. See TOB 13:2.
61. See Gen 1:31; 1 Cor 13:6.
62. TOB 13:4.
63. See Aristotle, *Topics*, IV. 4.
64. See *ST* I, q. 38, a. 2, c; *In I Sent.*, d. 18, q. 1, a. 2, c.
65. See TOB 95b:4; MD 29.
66. TOB 13:4.

to exist in a relation of reciprocal gift."[67] This experience manifests that the fulfillment of being created in God's image consists in living in a relationship of a reciprocal gift, where one lives for another.[68] In this way, original unity originates the understanding of Creation and of the other human person as a gift from God. It also originates an understanding of the very meaning of human existence. This meaning is essentially the gift of self to God and to others. Since the very essence of spousal love is gift of self, John Paul II rightly calls this very meaning of human existence, the *spousal* meaning of the body. Thus, the pope claims that "this beatifying beginning of man's being and existing as male and female is connected with the revelation and the discovery of the meaning of the body that is rightly called spousal."[69]

As we know, original nakedness places this acknowledgement and interpersonal encounter within the context of supernatural grace, within the context of original justice.[70] Consequently, John Paul II signifies, with the spousal meaning of the body, the *supernatural* meaning of our human existence, what most perfectly brings to fulfillment our being created in God's image. The pope is truly speaking about charity. To be sure, the first discovery of the spousal meaning of the body takes place in Adam and Eve's awareness of their vocation to charity *within the context of their marriage.*[71] Yet, although the meaning of their body is discovered and known in the context of marriage, such a meaning is not called spousal by John Paul II *only* because of the *conjugal* character of their union. Our previous clarifications of the *primum analogatum* of spousal charity help us to understand that, above all, the meaning of their body is *spousal* because it signifies a call to live out the gift of self to God in their reciprocal gift of self to each other.[72]

Because of their original justice, Adam and Eve experience an interior freedom which makes possible the fulfillment of such a vocation to the gift of self. This freedom is called by John Paul the freedom of the gift. He explains that "*this freedom lies exactly*

67. Ibid., 14:1.
68. See ibid., 14:2.
69. Ibid., 14:5.
70. See ibid., 15:2.

71. Note once again that the pope views *procreation* as the end which specifies their union as conjugal. Conjugal union orders "man's masculinity and femininity to an end, in the life of the spouses-parents. Uniting so closely with each other that they become one flesh, they place their humanity in some way *under the blessing of* fruitfulness, that is, of *procreation.*" Ibid., 14:6; emphasis added.

72. In light of the clarifications made so far, I would like to comment on Smith's affirmation: "John Paul teaches that the meaning of the body is *a sexual meaning*, one that is truly expressed through a nuptial union. This nuptial union of communion of persons that Man is, is made possible by the nuptial meaning of the body and is accomplished through a kind of giving, a giving of male and female to each other." Smith, Humanae Vitae, 253; emphasis added. These affirmations are correct, but they could lead someone to think erroneously that the nuptial or spousal meaning of the body is spousal or nuptial *because it is a sexual meaning in that it entails the actual exercise of sexuality*. As it is fulfilled in marriage, the spousal meaning of the body informs the exercise of the conjugal act. However, it is spousal for a very different reason: because of the gift of self inherent to charity. Christ's *virginal* love for the church and not marriage is the *primum analogatum* of the spousal meaning of the body.

at the basis of the spousal meaning of the body."[73] Obviously, the freedom in question here is *perfected* freedom. Wojtyła's anthropology of love and the original experiences show that the human person's freedom is *dependent* and *conditioned* by its reference to the truth. Thus, the perfection of that freedom must consist in acting in accordance with the truth about man. According to the christocentric anthropology of GS 22 and 24, this truth is found in Christ and in the sincere gift of self. As a result, John Paul II calls this perfected freedom "the freedom of the gift."

Since spousal love is all about self-gift, Adam and Eve's experience of this kind of freedom in the state of original justice is the foundation for their conscious awareness of the spousal meaning of their bodies, that is, of their supernatural vocation to charity. They experience their vocation to give their own will to God and to each other because of God. Remember, that is exactly the Thomistic understanding of original justice, the same threefold subordination which informs John Paul II's views on original nakedness.[74] The freedom of the gift presupposes integration within the person. It presupposes self-mastery and self-possession because to give oneself, one must possess oneself. As the pope says, "self-mastery is indispensable *in order for man to be able to give himself,* in order for him to become a gift, in order for him (referring to the words of the Council) to be able to find himself fully through a sincere gift of self [*Gaudium et Spes*, 24:3]."[75] This kind of freedom is what "makes possible and qualifies the spousal meaning of the body."[76]

As we can see, in his hermeneutics of the gift, John Paul II rereads the original experiences in light of GS 24. God created the human person as the only creature in the visible world willed for himself.[77] This dignity is the condition of possibility for the fact that the human person can find himself through the disinterested gift of self. Because the human person is willed for his own sake, he is capable of self-possession and self-surrender. Moreover, this personal dignity must be mutually affirmed so that the communion of persons may be possible. Indeed, Adam and Eve welcomed each other as creatures willed for their own sake by the Creator. This acceptance or welcoming made possible Adam's ordered love for Eve and vice versa.[78] Fulfilling the law of the gift inscribed in man's heart made them aware of their vocation to find themselves in the gift of self.

Hence, the relationship between the spousal meaning of the body and the freedom of the gift could be expressed in the following way. In the order of being, the spousal meaning of the body is perfected in charity as the act that springs from the freedom of the gift of self. In turn, in the order of knowledge, the experience of this

73. TOB 15:1.
74. See ibid., 16:4; 17:1; *De Malo*, q. 4, a. 8, c; *ST* I, q. 95, a. 1; q. 97, a. 1; II–II, q. 164, a. 1, c.
75. TOB 15:2.
76. Ibid.
77. See *ScG* III.113.
78. See TOB 15:3.

same freedom in act makes Adam and Eve aware of the spousal meaning of their body. Because of this awareness, John Paul II says that their bodies become, as it were, a witness to creation as a fundamental gift, that is, as a sign of God's love: "[T]his is *the body: a witness* to creation as a fundamental gift, and therefore a witness *to Love as the source from which this same giving springs.*"[79] Indeed, the experience of the freedom of the gift manifests that the human person is created to love. The origin of this vocation is God himself, who creates out of love and who has endowed the human person with gifts also out of love. Therefore, the spousal meaning of the body "points to a particular power to express the love in which man becomes a gift."[80] It has to do with the supernatural sense or meaning of human life: that same love revealed to us by Christ and his spousal gift of self for the church. John Paul II claims a great centrality to this kind of love. Thus, he declares that "the consciousness of the *spousal* meaning of the body constitutes the *fundamental component of human existence in the world.*"[81] It really refers to the capacity whereby the human body is able "to express the love by which the human person becomes a gift, thus *fulfilling the deep meaning of his or her being and existence.*"[82]

The spousal meaning of the body plays an important role not only in our relationship with God but also in our relationship with our neighbors. Moreover, it also permeates the vocation to marriage. As a result, the spousal meaning of the body played an important role in the relationship between Adam and Eve. Note at this point how John Paul II concentrates again on their relationship as brother and sister, as neighbors. The pope explains that the spousal meaning of the body refers in their interrelationship "to a power and deep availability for the affirmation of the person, that is, literally, the power to live the fact that the other—the woman for the man and the man for the woman—is through the body someone willed by the Creator for his own sake, that is, someone unique and unrepeatable, someone chosen by eternal Love."[83]

Rooted in the Thomistic Tradition

Amicitia Caritatis

John Paul's theology of the spousal meaning of the body is clearly grounded in Vatican II, especially in GS 22 and 24. However, Wojtyła also implied that his understanding of spousal love is rooted in tradition: "[T]he *entire tradition*, which we do not present here in its full extent, but rather limit ourselves to mentioning it, advocates *ascribing*

---

79. Ibid., 14:4. John Paul seems to be appealing implicitly to *ST* I, q. 38, a. 2, c; *In I Sent.*, d. 18, q. 1, a. 2, c.
80. TOB 15:4.
81. Ibid., 15:5; emphasis added.
82. Ibid., 32:1; emphasis added.
83. Ibid., 15:4.

an analogous meaning to spousal love."[84] It is time now to show in which manner the pope's views are also Thomistic. In Wojtyła's interpretation of Vatican II, the human person perfects his being made in God's image, within the ecclesial context of *communio*, by partaking of the missions of the Son and the Holy Spirit.[85] This participation brings about one's union in truth and charity with God and neighbor. Such a relationship is proper to persons only, and traditionally it has been understood as a friendship of charity (*amicitia charitatis*), that is, a friendship with God.[86] John Paul's theology of the spousal meaning of the body is rooted in this same Thomistic tradition, which conceives paternity, filiation, brotherhood, and conjugality as different kinds of friendships.[87] As we see in scripture, they all serve as *analogies* to speak of charity as human and divine friendship: Jesus taught us to call God our Father; we are God's children by adoption; the only Son of God is said to be our brother, and he is also the Bridegroom of the church.[88] Therefore, it is useless and even erroneous to see them as antagonistic; all of these analogies are complementary. They all highlight one specific aspect of the virtue of charity.

Any of these analogies could be considered as contained in Christ's words: "No longer do I call you servants, for the servant does not know what his master is doing; *but I have called you friends*, for all that I have heard from my Father I have made known to you."[89] However, John Paul II explains the spousal analogy appears especially in relationship with Christ, the *Redeemer* of man. "*The first dimension of love and election,* as a mystery hidden from ages in God, *is a fatherly dimension not a conjugal one.*"[90] As he continues to clarify: "[T]he analogy of spousal love and of marriage appears only when the Creator, the Holy One of Israel manifests himself as Redeemer."[91] Thus, John Paul's emphasis on the spousal analogy should be interpreted in light of his christocentrism but never in rivalry with being sons in the Son. Conformity with Christ is the whole point of his moral theology. There is a relationship of complementarity here. John Paul underlines that "the analogy of spousal love contains a characteristic of the mystery that is not directly emphasized by the analogy of merciful love, nor by the analogy of fatherly love (nor by any other analogy used in the

---

84. Wojtyła, "On the Meaning of Spousal Love," 289–90; emphasis added.

85. See SR, 61.

86. See DV 2; SR, 54; PDV, 46; VS 20, 86; FR, 10; TOB 109:3–4; *ST* II–II, q. 23, aa. 1 and 5; q. 25, a. 3. Also see Torrell, *Christ and Spirituality*, 45–64.

87. For paternity and maternity as friendship see, for example, *In VIII Ethic.*, lect. 12, n. 1706. In turn, for filiation as friendship see, for instance, ibid., lect. 12, n. 1715. Among other texts, brotherhood is also a kind of friendship according to ibid., lect. 11, n. 1695. For marriage as conjugal friendship see, for example, ibid., lect. 11, n. 1694 and GS 48.

88. See Matt 6:9; Rom 8:15, 29; Eph 5:25.

89. John 15:15; emphasis added.

90. TOB 95:4.

91. Ibid., 95:6.

Bible to which we could have appealed)."[92] The specific characteristic of the mystery directly manifested by the analogy of spousal love is the whole order of created *grace as God's radical and irrevocable gift of self in Christ and to man*, whereby the human person participates in divine nature.[93] This gift is *total* inasmuch as "it is in some sense all that God could give of himself to man, considering the limited faculties of man as a creature. In this way, the analogy of spousal love indicates the radical character of grace: of the whole order of created grace."[94]

Let us clarify first the analogy with friendship in general. A Thomistic reading of John 15:15 conceives this supernatural friendship as a habitual, reciprocal, and mutually known benevolence between Christ and his disciples, a benevolence founded upon a certain "*communicatio*."[95] Our Lord is not referring here to an act of love that takes place once, but refers rather to a habit.[96] It is not a fixed routine. Instead, it is a firm and stable inclination to love with a creative spontaneity, which also includes ease and delight.[97] The love in question is neither a sensible passion nor a spiritual affection of the rational appetite.[98] It is an *elective* love of the will, a freely chosen act, whose objects are both the good of the other as well as the good things willed for him.[99] In this kind of elective love, we have two different *terminus ad quem*. There are two objects that specify two different kinds of love. The first object is the person loved (one's own or another). The second object is the "thing" that is loved for this person. We love the person for their own sake, while we love the "thing" *for the person*. Hence, we can speak of two kinds of elective love inherent in friendship: love for the person and love for "things."[100] Friendship is the habitual form of elective love towards the person of the other, for whom one wills good "things"—understanding by "things" herein any sensible substance or any sensible or spiritual accident.[101]

Quite clearly, the Lord freely loves our person and wills for us good "things." Yet, his benevolence is very special. In our experience, we may will someone's good for different reasons.[102] Perhaps we want it because he or she is useful to us in some way, or because he or she is the cause of some form of pleasure. In these two instances, the *degree* of friendship is unmistakably low. Still, there is a third and more perfect degree

---

92. Ibid., 95b:3.
93. See 2 Pet 1:4.
94. TOB 95b:4.
95. See Ramírez, *De Caritate*, 38–39; Aquila, "The Priest as Man of Charity," 39–44.
96. See *In VIII Ethic.*, lect. 5, nn. 1596, 1603, 1604.
97. See *In III Sent.*, d. 27, q. 2, a. 1, c.
98. See *ST* I–II, q. 26, a. 3, c.
99. See ibid., II–II, q. 27, a. 2, c.
100. See García López, *Tomás de Aquino*, 210–12.
101. See *ST* II–II, q. 25, a. 3, c.
102. See *In VIII Ethic.*, lect. 3, n. 1563.

of friendship, wherein the good of the other is willed for its own sake.[103] Hence, we can rightly speak of an analogous sense of the word friendship. It is found first and foremost, not in the love of utility or pleasure, but in the love which aims at the good of the other for its own sake. Indeed, "these [loves] do not differ in kind as three equal species of a genus but are *classified by priority and posteriority.*"[104] Now, the highest degree of friendship, often called virtuous friendship,[105] is the one elevated to the supernatural level in our relationship of charity with God. This is the kind of friendship that God has for us. He wills our good for our own sake. He does not subordinate his love for us to some sort of usefulness or pleasure.

In fact, it is not possible for God to love us with sheer love of utility. Before God's infinite goodness and perfection, we will always be useless (*achreioi*) servants.[106] Whatever good we can give God, was given to us by him beforehand: "[W]ho has given a gift to him that he might be repaid?"[107] As Paul teaches elsewhere, "What have you that you did not receive?"[108] The concrete way by which God loves our good for its own sake is by willing our sanctification or salvation and the things needed to that end.[109] God loved the world and sent his only Son not to judge the world but to save it.[110] Christ came so that we may have life and have it in abundance.[111] In this relationship, as was noted before, it was God who loved us first. *His is the initiative, ours is the responsibility.*[112] God teaches how to love by loving us, especially when we were sinners.[113] Jesus, *the* Teacher, gave his own life for us, for his friends.[114] Each and every one of us can say with St. Paul that Christ "loved me and gave Himself up for me."[115] As a result, we are called to respond: to love *as* Christ has loved us.[116]

Further, our friendship with Christ is mutually known and reciprocal. Indeed, two people "cannot be friends while they are unaware of one another's feelings."[117] And friendship is all about loving and being loved. Consequently, "we say friendship is benevolence with corresponding requital inasmuch as the one loving is loved in

---

103. See ibid., lect. 2, n. 1558.
104. Ibid., lect. 3, n. 1563; emphasis added.
105. See ibid., lect. 3, n. 1575.
106. See Luke 17:10.
107. See Rom 11:35.
108. 1 Cor 4:7.
109. See 1 Thess 4:3.
110. See John 3:16–17.
111. See John 10:10.
112. See MD 29.
113. See Rom 5:8–9.
114. See 1 John 3:16.
115. Gal 2:20.
116. See John 13:34.
117. *In VIII Ethic.*, lect. 2, n. 1560.

return."¹¹⁸ So, our friendship with Christ must be a reciprocal love known to both parties.¹¹⁹ That this love is mutually known can be seen from the very words of our Lord in John 10:14: "I am the good shepherd; I know my own and my own know me." We have already seen the way in which God wills our good. The question that arises now, however, is in what measure can we will God's good? To be sure, we cannot add any good to God's infinite perfection, but we can certainly will to manifest and communicate it. To will God's goodness means for us, then, to seek God's greater glory, to will its manifestation and communication.¹²⁰

Of course, utility and pleasure have their own place in this habitual, reciprocal, and mutually known benevolence between God and the human person. Just as the highest degree of human friendship integrates utility and pleasure without making of them its main motive, so our friendship with God makes us useful to him under a certain aspect (*secundum quid*). Without usefulness being the main motive for love, in charity, we are useful to the Lord under a certain aspect just as God is useful to us.¹²¹ Similarly, we can make a case for pleasure. God's friends delight and rejoice in him.¹²² In turn, God is also well-pleased in those who love Him.¹²³

Our friendship with Christ is founded upon a certain *communicatio*. The Father, who gave us his only Son, will also give us every sort of good that grants us access to God's intimate life.¹²⁴ Thomas explains that "we are made lovers of God by the Holy Spirit."¹²⁵ The Spirit conforms us to Christ, making our friendship with him possible. As Thomas explains (following Aristotle), "men are accustomed to call friends those who *share in any common undertaking*."¹²⁶ In accordance with Wojtyła's interpretation of Vatican II, thanks to the grace of the Holy Spirit, the Christian is made an adoptive son of God who can share in Christ's *tria munera*. Sharing in divine life and in that common *munus*, we are called to fellowship (*societas*) with the Son.¹²⁷ Such a participation brings about a communion of friendship, in which the human person shares secrets with the Lord, and is of one mind and heart with him.

Indeed, "friendship seems to exist among people to the extent that they share with one another."¹²⁸ Thus, friendship with Christ is also founded upon the communication of secrets. Aquinas explains: "[T]his is the proper mark of friendship: that one reveals

---

118. Ibid., lect. 2, n. 1559.
119. See *ST* I–II, q. 65, a. 5, c.
120. See ibid., I, q. 19, a. 2, c; II–II, q. 132, a. 1, c.
121. See 2 Tim 2:21; Titus 3:7–8; Wis 8:16.
122. See Ps 33:9; Phil 4:4.
123. See Prov 8:31; *ScG* IV. 22.
124. See Rom 8:32; *In II Sent.*, d. 26, q. 1, a. 1, ad 2.
125. *ScG* IV. 21.
126. *In VIII Ethic.*, lect. 9, n. 1659; emphasis added.
127. See Eph 3:6; John 14: 23; 1 John 4:16; 1 Cor 1:9.
128. *In VIII Ethic.*, lect. 9, n. 1659.

his secrets to his friend. For, since charity unites affections and makes, as it were, one heart of two, one seems not to have dismissed from his heart that which he reveals to a friend."[129] For this reason, while for some Christ's message appears in parables, the secrets of the Kingdom have been revealed to us.[130] No human eye has seen and no human ear has heard what God has prepared for his children; yet, "God has revealed to us through the Spirit. For the Spirit searches everything, even the depths of God."[131] In turn, we are also to have a hidden life in Christ, so as to taste of the intimacy that friends enjoy.[132] The Holy Spirit conforms us to Christ, making us capable of the contemplation of God and conversation with him. Accordingly, Aquinas also explains that "this appears to be especially proper to friendship: really to converse with the friend. Now, the conversation of man with God is by contemplation of Him . . . Since, therefore, the Holy Spirit makes us lovers of God, we are in consequence established by the Holy Spirit as contemplators of God."[133]

Moreover, friendship with Christ consists in a love whereby there is a communication or communion of intellect and will. Thomas often uses the word *concord* to signify such a communion of intellect and will. Indeed, concord nominally means 'with [the same] heart' (*concordia*). As we know, both Thomas and John Paul II use the heart as a metaphor to signify the will and the intellect in their reciprocal immanence. As a result, to be of one heart with Christ amounts to have a *communicatio* of intellect and will. Thus, "concord, properly speaking, is between one man and another, in so far as *the wills of various hearts agree together in consenting to the same thing*."[134] In this hidden and intimate life in Jesus, in this supernatural friendship with him, the Christian is called to think with the mind of Christ, to have the same feelings as Jesus, to freely will what Christ wills, and to educate accordingly one's thoughts and feelings.[135] As Thomas explains, "it is proper to friendship to consent to a friend in what he wills. Of course, the will of God is set forth for us by His precepts. Therefore, it belongs to the love by which we love God that we fulfill His commandments . . . Hence, since we are established as God's lovers by the Holy Spirit, by Him, too, we are in a way driven to fulfill the precepts of God."[136] Jesus expresses it simply but profoundly: "You are my friends if you do what I command you."[137] The Lord is asking us to make a gift of our own will to him. He is asking the same kind of spousal love he has shown by suffering

---

129. *ScG* IV. 21.
130. See Mark 4:11.
131. 1 Cor 2:9–10.
132. See Col 3:3.
133. *ScG* IV. 22. See Phil 3:20; 2 Cor 3:18.
134. *ST* II–II, q. 29, a. 1, c; emphasis added.
135. See 1 Cor 2:16.
136. *ScG* IV.22. See John 14:15; Rom 8:14.
137. John 15:14.

and dying for the church. Once again, the gratuitous initiative belongs to God; ours is the responsibility.

Through his own obedience to the Father, Jesus gives himself, making the gift of self for the church, that is, for each and every one of her members. And Aquinas explains that, "we are related as to ourselves to those whom we love in that love, thereby *communicating ourselves to them in some way*."[138] Thomas explains that John 3:16 "indicates the immensity of the divine love. For in giving eternal life *he gives himself*, since eternal life is nothing other than enjoying God. To give oneself is an *indication of great love*."[139] The Father gives us his Son who, in turn, gives himself for the church in the sacrifice of the cross. Together with the Father, the Son gives us the Holy Spirit (the giver of life), he for whom Gift is his proper personal name.[140] Thus, Christ takes the initiative to *communicate* or give himself as bridegroom to his bride, so that in gratitude and responsibility we may give ourselves to him, giving to the Lord the treasure we value the most, namely, our own will, by loving him above all things and persons.[141]

Centrality of the Spousal Analogy

The analogy of spousal love builds upon all the elements of friendship just explained. This analogy seems to especially underline the order of charity, God's gratuitous gift of self to us through grace, and our response or collaboration with that grace. As a result, it is made more evident that God alone is to be loved above all things and above all persons, and in charity, the initiative belongs to God while the responsibility belongs to us. Obviously, these elements emphasized, as well as the analogy itself, are found in Sacred Scripture. As is known, Thomas was not a philosopher by profession, but a teacher of the sacred page (*magister in sacra pagina*), a commentator of Sacred Scripture, a theologian—as we would say today.[142] His insightful biblical commentaries usually begin with a general division of the text, in which he identifies the main thesis of the book being commented upon. Following this same *modus operandi*, in his inaugural lecture in Paris, Thomas proposes a division of Sacred Scripture as a whole. In this division, spiritual marriage occupies a place of honor, namely, the place of honor reserved to final causality.

Indeed, the Old Testament's point of arrival, in Aquinas's view, is the song on spousal love in the Song of Songs, which teaches about "the virtues of the purified soul, whereby a man, completely cleansed from worldly cares, delights in the contemplation

---

138. *Super Io.*, cap. 15, lect. 4, n. 2036.

139. Ibid., cap. 3, lect. 3, n. 480; emphasis added. See Waldstein, "John Paul II and St. Thomas," 129.

140. See John 3:16; Eph 5:25; *ST* I, q. 38, aa. 1–2.

141. See *De perfectione*, cap. 10.

142. See Torrell, *Saint Thomas Aquinas: The Person and His Work*, 54.

of wisdom alone."¹⁴³ This spousal love comes about as a mature love of God above all things and persons. In turn, Thomas sees three parts to the New Testament: one on the origin of grace, another on the power of grace, and the last one on the completion or execution of that same power. Commenting on this third part, Thomas speaks about the final end of the church and its members in terms of a spiritual marriage with Christ. Thus, the highpoint of arrival of the entire New Testament, the completion of God's grace in the church, is the wedding feast of the Lamb. Thus, "the *end* of the Church, with which the whole content of Scripture concludes in the Apocalypse," consists in "the spouse in the chamber [*in thalamum*] of Jesus Christ sharing the life of glory, *to which Jesus Christ himself conducts*."¹⁴⁴ Thomas also places the initiative in Christ. His is the gratuitous initiative; ours is the responsibility.

Thomas delivers in another place this same teaching by explaining that the marriage between Christ and the believing members of the church "will be consummated when the bride, i.e., the Church, is *led into* [*introducetur*] the bridal chamber of the groom [*in thalamum sponsi*], i.e., into the glory of heaven."¹⁴⁵ He also applies this same doctrine to every believing member of the pilgrim church: "[T]hrough faith the Christian soul makes, as it were, a certain marriage with God [*quoddam matrimonium cum Deo*]."¹⁴⁶ In the final consummation of the spousal meaning of our existence, faith and hope will pass away.¹⁴⁷ However, charity will remain. Thus, it is in charity where the spousal union between the soul of the just and God finds its perfection.¹⁴⁸ In this sense, it can rightly be said that John Paul's theology of the spousal meaning of the body is Thomistic.

This last conclusion should not be a surprise to anyone. The biblical basis for both Thomas's and John Paul II's position are beyond doubt.¹⁴⁹ The Old Testament

---

143. See *De Commendatione*, 1207; Waldstein, "John Paul II and St. Thomas," 119.
144. See *De Commendatione*, 1208; emphasis added.
145. *Super Io.*, cap. 2, lect. 1, n. 338; emphasis added. See also LG 6.
146. *In Symbolum Apostolorum*, prom. See also *De Veritate*, q. 28, a. 3, sc 4.
147. See 1 Cor 13:13.
148. See *De Virtutibus*, q. 2, a. 12, arg. 24, ad 24; *De Veritate*, q. 28, a. 8, arg. 7, ad 7.
149. Matthias Scheeben, an author known to John Paul II, explains:

> To conceive of the integration of all members of the Church in Christ under the notion of a mystical marriage with the God-man, as the Apostle does, is merely to express the truth in another way. By the Incarnation Christ has assumed our nature in order to yoke Himself with us. The Fathers view the Incarnation itself as a marriage with the human race, inasmuch as it virtually contains everything that can lead to the full union of the Son of God with men. But the relationship of unity it sets up comes to full fruition only in the Church. Man is to attach himself to his divine bridegroom by faith; and the bridegroom seals His union with man in baptism, as with a wedding ring. But both faith and baptism are mere preliminaries for the coming together of man and the God-man in one flesh by a real Communion of flesh and blood in the Eucharist, and hence for the perfect fructifying of man with the energizing grace of his head. By entering the Church every soul becomes a real bride of God's Son, so truly that the Son of God is able, in the Apostle's words, not only

appeals to the spousal analogy within the context of God's covenant with his people. Isaiah 54:5 explains it beyond ambiguity: "[Y]our Maker is *your husband*, the Lord of hosts is his name; and the Holy One of Israel is your Redeemer, the God of the whole earth he is called." The prophets use this same analogy to call to conversion the people who have not loved God above all things and persons, but rather have been unfaithful to him and to the covenant.[150] They have been idolaters, "adulterers," as it were. They have abandoned their true husband and looked for other gods. Jesus takes up the very same theme of the covenant and merges it with the spousal analogy. He identifies himself with the bridegroom.[151] Moreover, Jesus also speaks of himself as the new and eternal covenant between God and humanity, in which the God-Man fulfills both parts of the contract. This may be one reason why, although Christ identifies himself with the divine bridegroom, he never mentions the bride: the hypostatic union is that very marriage covenant with humanity, that new and eternal covenant which cannot be broken.[152] Saint Paul has taken up this very teaching of the Lord and has unfolded its meaning, applying it to the church as the body of Christ.[153] This marriage is made once and for all. However, at the same time, the individual members of the church have need to be brought to Christ for this marriage to be effected in their lives. This is exactly how Paul understands his mission, and thus, he says in 2 Cor 11:2: "I feel a divine jealousy for you, for I betrothed you to Christ to present you as a pure bride to her one husband."

The Bridegroom and the Bride

Thomas's and John Paul's commentaries on these relevant scriptural passages are in strict continuity with each other. Both of them unfold a rich theology of the spousal analogy. Let us begin with some passages from the synoptic gospels, especially from Matthew. As is known, in Matt 9:14–17, on the occasion in which Christ talks to John's disciples about fasting, our Lord clearly identifies himself with the bridegroom. Thomas comments on this text, explaining that Christ is "the bridegroom of the entire

---

to compare His love and union with the Church and her members with the unity achieved in matrimony, but can even propose it as the ideal and model of the latter. If the Church in all its members is thus the body of Christ and the bride of Christ, the power of its divine head, the Spirit of its divine bridegroom, must be gloriously operative in it. In all its members the Church is a temple of the Holy Spirit, who dwells in it as the soul in its own body, and manifests His divine and divinizing power in it.

Scheeben, *The Mysteries of Christianity*, 543–44.

150. See Hos 2:20.

151. See Mark 2:18; Matt 9:14; Luke 5:33–35; John 3:29; Matt 22:2, 25:1–13; Luke 12:36; Rev 19:7. TOB 79:9.

152. See Galot, *Who is Christ?*, 110.

153. See Eph 5:25.

Church and *is its source*."¹⁵⁴ The same order presented in MD 29 is emphasized by Thomas: the gratuitous initiative is God's; the responsibility is ours. Jesus has the bride because, in his love, he is her origin, the origin of the new law and the life in the Spirit. The Bridegroom has taken the initiative to be the Redeemer of the human person. Similarly, Pope John Paul teaches that "with this answer Jesus made it clear that the prophetic message about God the Spouse, about the Redeemer, the Holy One of Israel, was fulfilled in himself. He revealed his awareness of being the bridegroom among his disciples."¹⁵⁵

Aquinas offers a more detailed commentary about Jesus's parable on the king's invitation to the marriage of his son presented in Matt 22:1–14. He begins by clarifying who is who in the parable: "[L]et us see who this man the King is. And it is said that he is God, and the person of the Father is understood, because he speaks of his son ... The son is Christ."¹⁵⁶ John Paul II follows this same interpretation: "Everything in the parable makes it clear that Jesus is speaking of himself, but he does so in the third person, which is a feature of his discourse in the parables."¹⁵⁷ Now, it is noteworthy that Thomas accepts a plurality of complementary interpretations on who the bride is and in what this marital union consists.

Firstly, this marriage may stand for "*the unity of the human nature with the divine*; that human nature might be the bride, the womb of the Virgin became the bridal chamber."¹⁵⁸ In another place, the Angelic Doctor explains that one of the reasons why it was fitting that the conception of Christ was announced to the Virgin Mary was to "to show that there is a certain spiritual marriage between the Son of God and human nature. Wherefore in the Annunciation the Virgin's consent was besought in place of that of the entire human nature."¹⁵⁹ In this interpretation, the theology of the body is eminently present. The Incarnation itself is seen as a spousal union between God and humanity. Once again, we could quote John Paul II's words. Because of the Incarnation, "the body entered theology ... through the main door."¹⁶⁰ Through the Incarnation, *both* the human body as well as its spousal meaning have entered theology through this main door. Moreover, in complete agreement with John Paul II, Aquinas sees in the Virgin Mary the paradigm for our response to Christ's spousal love. While Christ shows the divine initiative in charity, Mary exemplifies human responsibility in one's collaboration with supernatural grace.

---

154. *In Matt.*, cap. 9, lect. 3, n. 769; emphasis added.
155. See John Paul II, *The Church*, 109. See Isa 54:5.
156. *In Matt.*, cap. 22, lect. 1, n. 1755.
157. John Paul II, *The Church*, 110.
158. *In Matt.*, cap. 22, lect. 1, n. 1756.
159. *ST* III, q. 30, a. 1, c.
160. TOB 23:4.

Secondly, Thomas explains that it "can [also] be said that this bridegroom is the Word incarnate; the bride, the Church."[161] Obviously, this answer is not in contradiction with the first. The church is both the body and the bride of Christ.[162] Thirdly, this marriage can be interpreted as the spousal union between Christ and the individual members of the church. Thus, Thomas explains that it could refer to "the marriage of the Word himself to our soul. For the soul becomes a partaker of God's glory through faith, and in this way our marriage comes about."[163] Fourthly, this marriage could stand for the eschatological fulfillment of our betrothal in faith with the Lamb. Thus, "there will be a marriage in the common resurrection. And Christ is the way of this resurrection . . . There will be a marriage at that time, when our mortal body is swallowed up by life."[164] In another place, Aquinas also alludes to the teaching on spiritual marriage in order to speak of the blessed in heaven. Distinguishing dowry from beatitude, he identifies the spousal union between Christ and the soul in heaven with the latter. Instead, he considers that in heaven, the dowry corresponds to that which disposes the soul to beatitude as the perfect operation, whereby Christ and the soul are united in that spiritual marriage.[165]

Thomas continues in his explanation of the parable, concentrating on why the text says that, despite the rejection of those invited, the wedding is *ready*. It is so because, "the Son is incarnate."[166] The disciples preached everywhere, fulfilling this parable. Thus, the wedding was filled with guests, that is, with the faithful. The person not having a wedding garment is actually missing union with Christ in charity: "[T]o have a wedding garment is to put on Christ through good works, through a holy life, *through true charity*; and if one of these is lacking, it is bad."[167] John Paul II adopts this same interpretation, adding an interesting note: "[I]t seems that in Israel's world on the occasion of great banquets the clothes to be worn were made available to the guests in the banquet hall."[168] Thus, Christians who do not have this wedding garment will be held responsible: "This is the case of those who maintain and profess that they are followers of Christ and members of the Church, without obtaining the wedding garment of grace, which engenders a living faith, hope, and love."[169]

Thomas interprets Matt 25:1–13's parable of the virgins waiting for the bridegroom in light of 2 Cor 11:2. These virgins are the faithful of whom Paul says: "I have espoused you to one husband that I may present you as a chaste virgin to Christ." The

---

161. *In Matt.*, cap. 22, lect. 1, n. 1756.
162. See John Paul II, *The Church*, 115.
163. *In Matt.*, cap. 22, lect. 1, n. 1756.
164. Ibid.
165. See *In IV Sent.*, d. 49, q. 4, a. 2, c, ad 2.
166. *In Matt.*, cap. 22, lect. 1, n. 1770.
167. Ibid.; emphasis added.
168. John Paul II, *The Church*, 110.
169. Ibid. See Rev 19:7–9.

lamps of the virgins, in turn, are an image for the light of faith and for their works that shine among men. Then, explaining in more detail who is the bridegroom and who is the bride, Aquinas offers a twofold interpretation reminiscent of his previous remarks. The text could be referring to "the marriage of divinity to flesh, which was celebrated in the womb of a virgin... The bridegroom is the Son himself, the bride human nature; hence, to go out to meet the bridegroom and the bride is nothing other than to serve Christ."[170] However, the text can also be referred to "the marriage of Christ and the Church... Therefore, those who prepare the lamps intend to please the bridegroom, i.e., Christ, and the bride, i.e., Mother Church."[171]

The Angelic Doctor explains why the text says that Christ comes, when the virgins were going to him. His twofold explanation depends on how one understands the meaning of Christ's bride, either as his human nature or as the church. In the first case, Aquinas explains that the bridegroom is said to come, because "at the judgment the bride, i.e., the flesh of Christ, will be taken up unto glorification."[172] Instead, if the bride is viewed as the church, the bridegroom is said to come because, "she will then be perfectly united to the bridegroom through adherence."[173] Thomas is referring, in this second case, to the church's eschatological fulfillment in the wedding feast of the Lamb.[174]

Redemptive Messianic Mission of the Bridegroom

Moving now to John's Gospel, we find another important passage in John 3:27–32, where John the Baptist identifies himself as the friend of the bridegroom. John Paul II comments on this text, explaining that "the spousal tradition of the Old Testament is reflected in the awareness that this austere messenger of the Lord had of his mission in relationship to Christ's identity."[175] Thomas also clearly explains that in this text, "the groom is Christ."[176] Gleaning from Saint Paul's development, Aquinas identifies in this text the church as the bride: "His bride is the Church, which is joined to him by faith: 'I will espouse you to myself in faith.'"[177] Thus, in a sense, John the Baptist anticipates Paul's words in 2 Cor 11:2, identifying himself as the best man.[178]

As we know, in this last text, Paul explains to the community how he feels about them. Thomas explains Paul's "jealousy" by appealing to our human experience. He

---

170. *In Matt.*, cap. 25, lect. 1, n. 2014.
171. Ibid.
172. Ibid., cap. 25, lect. 1, n. 2028.
173. Ibid.
174. See John Paul II, *The Church*, 117–20.
175. Ibid., 108–109.
176. *In Io.*, cap. 3, lect. 5, n. 518.
177. Ibid. See Hos 2:20.
178. See John Paul II, *The Church*, 109.

points out that "a person is sometimes jealous for his wife, to keep her for himself."[179] Paul is not the bridegroom. However, he "was jealous on behalf of his people, whom he saw prepared for a fall and, although espoused to Christ, wished to be prostituted to the devil."[180] Once again, we find here the emphasis of the spousal analogy in loving God above all else. Paul speaks of divine jealousy because "he would not permit Christ, the true spouse, to suffer their being shared with the devil."[181] John Paul II also remarks that "in this text Paul presents himself as the best man, whose burning concern is to encourage the bride's complete faithfulness to the marriage union."[182]

Neither the Baptist nor Saint Paul identify themselves with the bridegroom. Instead, they bring the bride to Christ as his friends. "Although John had said earlier that he was not worthy to unfasten the strap of Jesus's sandal, he here calls himself the friend of Jesus in order to bring out the faithfulness of his love for Christ. For a servant does not act in the spirit of love in regard to the things that pertain to his master, but in a spirit of servitude; while a friend, on the other hand, seeks his friend's interests out of love and faithfulness."[183] Thomas contrasts this care for Christ's bride in fidelity to the Lord with "those evil prelates who do not follow Christ's command in governing the Church."[184] Paul, instead, is faithful. Following his example, "whoever converts the people by faith and charity, espouses them to Christ."[185]

Another important passage in John is found in the wedding at Cana. John Paul II remarks that the sign that Jesus performed in Cana was meant to prove his messianic mission, his being the Redeemer of man. "One may interpret his action as an indirect way of making it understood that the bridegroom announced by the prophets was present among his people, Israel."[186] Thomas offers a more mystical interpretation in complete consonance with John Paul II. The Angelic Doctor presents a summary of the relevance of the spousal analogy and its significance in understanding the Christian vocation. Thus, "in the mystical sense, marriage signifies the union [*coniunctio*] between Christ and His Church, because as the Apostle says: 'This is a great sacrament [*sacramentum*]: I am speaking of Christ and his Church.'"[187] Aquinas continues his commentary, harmonizing the different senses in which the bride could be interpreted. For this reason, he points out that "this marriage was begun in the womb of the Virgin, when God the Father united a human nature to his Son in a unity of person. So, the bridal chamber [*thalamus*] of this union was the womb of the Virgin."

---

179. *Super II Cor.*, cap. 11, lect. 1, n. 375.
180. Ibid.
181. Ibid.
182. John Paul II, *The Church*, 115.
183. *In Io.*, cap. 3, lect. 5, n. 519.
184. Ibid., cap. 3, lect. 5, n. 520.
185. *Super II Cor.*, cap. 11, lect. 1, n. 376.
186. John Paul II, *The Church*, 111.
187. *Super Io.*, cap. 2, lect. 1, n. 338. See Eph 5:32.

[188] Thomas makes a reference to Matt 22:2, noting the parable to signify "when God the Father joined a human nature to his Word in the womb of the Virgin."[189]

However, this marriage between Christ and human nature was *secret*, so to speak. "It was made public when the Church was united [*conjuncta*] to him by faith: 'I will bind you to myself in faith'. We read of this marriage: 'Blessed are they who are called to the marriage supper of the Lamb.'"[190] Yet, although now public, this marriage is not fully consummated for those who belong to the pilgrim church. "It will be consummated when the bride, i.e., the Church, is led into the bridal chamber of the groom [*in thalamum sponsi*], i.e., into the glory of heaven."[191] Furthermore, Thomas explains that this marriage took place on the third day, in order to signify the time of grace. In turn, it took place in Cana, which means "zeal," and in Galilee, which means "pass over," in order to signify that the marriage with Christ is "celebrated in the zeal of a pass over, to suggest that those persons are most worthy of union [*conjuctione*] with Christ who, burning with the zeal of a pious devotion [*piae devotionis ferventes*], pass over [*transmigrant*] from the state of guilt to the grace of the Church . . . And they pass from death to life, i.e., from the state of mortality and misery to the state of immortality and glory: 'I make all things new.'"[192] Consequently, the first of Christ's signs at Cana of Galilee signifies his messianic redemptive mission as the Bridegroom.

Inspired in John of the Cross

There are many possible reasons as to why Thomas's commentaries on the passages mentioned before essentially coincide with those of John Paul II. However, there is at least one historical reason which is important to consider now. The first contact that John Paul II had with the theology of Thomas was mediated by John of the Cross. As I have shown in another book of mine, John of the Cross is a continual source of inspiration for John Paul's Thomism.[193] This is also the case with respect to the spousal analogy. Consequently, it is now useful to explain briefly how John of the Cross develops Thomas's affirmations concerning spiritual marriage, unfolding them in his view of the spiritual life, and the process of deification.[194] Therein, the Spanish mystic connects the doctrine of spiritual marriage with the *imago Dei* in its relationship with

---

188. *Super Io.*, cap. 2, lect. 1, n. 338. See Ps 18:6.

189. *Super Io.*, cap. 2, lect. 1, n. 338. See Hos 2:20; Rev 19:9.

190. *Super Io.*, cap. 2, lect. 1, n. 338.

191. Ibid.

192. Ibid., cap. 2, lect. 1, n. 338. See Rev 21:5.

193. See Pérez López, *De la experiencia*, 39–69; 399–406.

194. For two good introductory works on John of the Cross, see Frost, *Saint John of the Cross*; and Ruíz, *Introducción a San Juan de la Cruz*. For a study of the Thomism of the Spanish mystic, see Del Niño Jesús, *El tomismo de San Juan de la Cruz*. For the influence of John of the Cross in Karol Wojtyła/John Paul II, see Huerga, "Karol Wojtyła, comentador de San Juan de la Cruz." Bosco, "Giovanni della Croce nella lettura di Karol Wojtyła." Castellano, "La rilettura della fede in Giovanni della Croce."

the moral life and the sacraments. In so doing, we may get a bit closer to John Paul II's Thomism, in his theology of the spousal meaning of the body.

John of the Cross distinguishes two different levels in which the spousal union between man and Christ takes place: at God's pace and at man's pace. Within the first level, at God's pace, there are two different moments: when God immediately accomplishes the spousal union at the Incarnation and the Redemption in the Cross, and when such a union is bestowed on each one of us in the life of the church, thanks to the sacraments, especially that of baptism. In the second level, the deifying spiritual marriage between Christ and man refers to the moral and spiritual life. More concretely, it signifies the dynamic and gradual perfection of the *imago Dei* (already perfected to a certain degree by the sacraments), thanks to the cardinal and theological virtues, as well as the gifts of the Holy Spirit. Thus, in the *Spiritual Canticle*, indicating this second level, John of the Cross explains that "the espousal [*desposorio*] made on the cross is not the one we now speak of. For that espousal is accomplished immediately when God gives the first grace, which is bestowed on each at Baptism."[195] The *Spiritual Canticle* is not primarily concerned with this first level, which takes place at God's pace. Rather, it concentrates on the moral and supernatural development of the human person which occurs at man's pace. Thus, John of the Cross clarifies that "the espousal of which we speak bears reference to perfection and is not achieved, save gradually and by stages. For though it is all one espousal, there is a difference in that one is attained at the soul's pace, and thus little by little, and the other at God's pace, and thus immediately."[196]

In his plan from all eternity, the Father decreed that the church might share in the loving union *ad intra* of the Persons of the Trinity.[197] The eternal processions, in their connection with the missions of the Son and the Holy Spirit, are the foundation and pattern for the spiritual marriage between God and the human person.[198] This is a plan fulfilled by the obedience of the Son, and his own *fiat* to the Father's will. With the aid of a poem, John of the Cross expresses such a *fiat* in the following terms: "I am very grateful the Son answered; I will show my brightness to the bride you give me, so that by it she may see how great my Father is, and how I have received my being from your being. I will hold her in my arms and she will burn with your love, and with eternal delight she will exalt your goodness."[199] The burning in the Father's love refers to the mission of the Holy Spirit as a living flame of love. This is the result of the redemptive Incarnation in which, as Thomas said, Christ espoused humanity.

---

195. *Cántico* 23.6.

196. Ibid.

197. See Eph 1:3–12.

198. See *Romance* 1.6–11. The way in which the Spanish mystic expresses himself about the inner life of God clearly resembles the poem of the *Dark Night* 5, where he speaks about the union of the human person with God. See also *De Potentia*, q. 9, a. 9, c.

199. *Romance* 3.

Echoing Aquinas's commentary on the wedding of Cana, John of the Cross says that "when the time had come for him to be born, he went forth like the bridegroom from his bridal chamber, embracing his bride, holding her in his arms."[200]

The Son's redemptive Incarnation is closely connected with the creation of the human person in God's image. According to Thomas, friendship exists among persons who share a certain equality. Thus, for the marriage between Christ and the human person, there needs to be a certain *communicatio*. This *communicatio* explains many of the arguments for the fittingness of the Incarnation in Thomistic theology.[201] Moreover, this same *communicatio* is interpreted by John of the Cross under the theological keys of the *imago Dei* and the new law. He begins by ascribing to the Father a description of the need for Christ's bride to be redeemed or ransomed: "[T]he time had come when it would be good to ransom the bride serving under the hard yoke of that law which Moses had given her, the Father, with tender love, spoke in this way: Now you see, Son, that your bride was made in your image, and so far as she is like you she will suit you well; yet she is different, in her flesh, which your simple being does not have."[202] Having pointed out the great dissimilarity between the Son and the bride, John of the Cross explains the need for a certain equality for friendship to exist between men and God. Thus, in his poem, the Father explains that "in perfect love this law holds: that the lover become like the one he loves; for the greater their likeness the greater their delight. Surely your bride's delight would greatly increase were she to see you like her, in her own flesh."[203]

I have referred to the Son's *fiat* before. Obviously, in reality, before the Incarnation, there is but one will in God, the divine will. Before the Incarnation, strictly speaking, there is no obedience of the Son to the Father.[204] For this very reason, John of the Cross is quite careful in describing the Son's reply to the Father's plan in his poem. First, he focuses on the identity of the Father's and the Son's divine will. Second, he mentions the future manifestation of Christ's goodness—his glory—in the obedience of Christ's *human* will to the Divine will: "My will is yours, the Son replied, and my glory is that your will be mine."[205] Moreover, John of the Cross has the Son offer a description of the fittingness of the Father's plan for the Incarnation: "This is fitting, Father, what you, the Most High, say; for in this way your goodness will be the more evident, your great power will be seen and your justice and wisdom."[206] The Son seeks the Father's glory, the manifestation of his infinite goodness. Thus, he continues: "I will go and tell the world, spreading the word of your beauty and sweetness and of

---

200. Romance 9.
201. See *ST* III, q. 1, a. 2, c.
202. Romance 7.
203. Ibid.
204. See White, *The Incarnate Lord*, 236–307.
205. Romance 7.
206. Ibid.

your sovereignty. I will go seek my bride and take upon myself her weariness and labors in which she suffers so; and that she may have life, I will die for her, and lifting her out of that deep, I will restore her to you."[207]

Consequently, for John of the Cross, the burning in the Father's love of the bride is accomplished by the Son's gift of self for the church in his obedience to the Father.[208] Thereby, the incarnate Lord becomes the exemplar and *exemplum* of the entire moral perfection of the *imago Dei* in the human person. On the cross, it is well manifested how Jesus Christ loved the Father with all his mind, all his heart, and all his strength, that is to say, with all his potencies or powers.[209] Thus, John of the Cross teaches that, in this way, Christ broke down the barriers built up through original sin between God and man. Furthermore, in this manner, "the Son of God redeemed human nature and consequently *espoused it to himself, and he espoused each soul by giving it through the cross grace and the pledges for this espousal.*"[210]

John of the Cross argues that the spiritual marriage carried out in Christ's paschal mystery is granted to the human person within the church's sacramental structure.[211] The Spanish mystic gives special attention to the sacrament of baptism. In this way, not only does he underline the universal call to holiness, but also another fact extremely influential in John Paul II's theology: holiness consists in *conformity with Christ* as the perfection of being created in God's image. Baptism confers a presence of the beloved in the soul. In the *Spiritual Canticle*, John of the Cross uses the following metaphor to describe it: "The soul experiences within herself a certain sketch of love, which is the sickness she mentions, and she desires the completion of the sketch of this image, the image of the Bridegroom, the Word, the Son of God, who as St. Paul says, is the splendor of His glory and the image of His substance."[212] Just like Thomas Aquinas and John Paul II, the Spanish mystic conceives the entire moral life in light of a christocentric anthropology of the *imago Dei*. Christ's sketch in the human soul seeks to be completed throughout life by means of *conformation* with the Son, thanks to all the virtues and the gifts of the Holy Spirit. Thus, John of the Cross argues that this "sickness of love is not cured except by your [God's] very presence and image."[213] As a result, the soul "feels she is like wax in which an impress is being made, but not yet completed. She knows too that she is like a sketch or the first draft of a drawing and calls out to the one who did this sketch to finish the painting and image."[214]

---

207. *Romance* 7.
208. See *Cántico* 3.5; Eph 5:25.
209. See 2 *Subida* 7. 9–12.
210. *Cántico* 23.3; emphasis added.
211. See *Cántico* 23.1–6. Cadrecha, *San Juan de la Cruz: Una Ecclesiologia de Amor*.
212. *Cántico* 11.12—12.1. See Heb 1:3.
213. *Cántico* 11.12—12.1.
214. Ibid.

This is the general framework within which John of the Cross speaks of the dark night of the soul as *an experience of integration*, in which all the potencies or powers of the human person are ordered to love God above all things and all created persons.[215] Such integration fulfills at man's pace his own spousal vocation to the gift of self. In this manner, man responds to the loving divine initiative with a love for God above anything else. Moreover, the human person, created in God's image and likeness, finds in this experience of integration the incipient fulfillment, the pledge of his spiritual marriage with Christ in heaven.[216] Just as John Paul II did and in perfect congruency with Thomas Aquinas, John of the Cross appeals to Matt 22:1–14 in order to describe the theological virtues as the wedding garment of one's soul. "The soul, then, touched with love for Christ, her Spouse, and aspiring to win his favor and *friendship*, departs in the disguise that more vividly represents the affections of her spirit. Her advance in this disguise makes her more secure against her adversaries: the devil, the world, and the flesh."[217] The garment is described in this text as a disguise. It equips the human person to live in spousal friendship with God, to give full consent to God, offering him in charity the most treasured gift that one has, namely, his own will. "The livery she thus wears is the three principal colors: white, green, and red. These three colors stand for the three theological virtues: faith, hope, and charity, by which she not only gains the favor and good will of her Beloved but also advances very safely, fortified against her three enemies."[218]

The progress described so far consists in the attainment, at man's pace, of the state of spiritual betrothal. "We should call to mind for the sake of a clearer understanding . . . that this spiritual flight denotes a high state and union of love in which, after much spiritual exercise, the soul is placed by God. This state is called spiritual betrothal with the Word, the Son of God."[219] At this stage God gives many gifts to the human person. He "beautifies her with grandeur and majesty, adorns her with gifts and virtues, and clothes her with the knowledge and honor of God, as the betrothed is clothed on the day of her betrothal."[220] Such betrothal can be completed only after death. Only in death can the human person give to God not only his will, but also his own flesh.[221] In perfect concomitance with John Paul II, this complete gift of self is interpreted by John of the Cross as the perfection of freedom. In this sense, it is true freedom, the freedom of God's children, who are able to imitate Christ in his own gift of self.[222]

215. See 3 *Subida* 16.2; *ST* I–II, q. 100, a. 10, ad 2.

216. I have explained the philosophical implications of this process and their influence on Wojtyła's understanding of integration in my *De la experiencia*, 39–68.

217. 2 *Noche* 21.3–5. 11; emphasis added.

218. Ibid.

219. *Cántico* 14.2.

220. Ibid.

221. See ibid., 14.30.

222. See 2 *Noche* 9.2; 3 *Subida* 16.3; 2 *Noche* 4.2; *Cántico* 1.18.

A Meaning for all Persons?

It seems certain by now that John Paul II's choice of the term "spousal," in the expression "the spousal meaning of the body," is a reference to man's supernatural vocation. Moreover, it is also evident that this is a Thomistic way of understanding man's supernatural vocation to charity as the virtue which unites us with God, within the christocentric anthropology of GS previously explained. Furthermore, it is also clear why the spousal meaning of the body is not to be confused with the unitive meaning of the conjugal act. Rather, it should be identified with one's vocation to the gift of self in charity. In fact, consecrated people live such a meaning in their own state of life. What is more, their state of life signifies, in a fuller and more perfect way, the ultimate fulfillment of the spousal meaning of the body. It signifies in a more perfect way the beatific vision of heaven, where there will be no conjugal act, procreation, or marriage between man and woman.[223]

At this point of our analysis, we can address an objection raised by Charles Curran. In his opinion, the pope's theology of the body "clearly cannot serve as a theology for all persons and all bodies," because, in Curran's view, "there are many people for whom the nuptial [or spousal] meaning of the body he [John Paul II] develops are not appropriate."[224] This American theologian thinks that John Paul II's theology of the spousal meaning of the body is a *utopia*. He further argues that, in that theology, "the elderly are missing. But also most obviously, the unmarried—people who are single, people who are widowed, and homosexuals."[225] Consequently, Curran finds *unconvincing* the pope's theology of the spousal meaning of the body.

In my opinion, Curran misses the point. John Paul's theology of charity is *not* a utopia. With God's grace, it is something attainable. Moreover, the pope's theology of charity does not exclude the elderly, those who are single, widowed, or homosexuals. In John Paul's theology, all of them are called by God to love with the same kind of love with which God loves them. Curran's critique would be partially correct were marriage the *primum analogatum* in John Paul's understanding of the spousal meaning of the body. If that were the case, those not married would be left out of the spousal meaning of the body. The entire Christian vocation would be intrinsically linked with the exercise of human sexuality in marriage. However, John Paul II's choice to speak about the spousal meaning of the body implies no sexualization of the Christian vocation. As we already know, from the ontological perspective, marriage is *not* the *primum analogatum* for our call to charity. Christ's spousal love for the Church, instead, is that *primum analogatum*. This is the exact perspective under which spousal love is essentially defined by John Paul as gift of self.

---

223. See Prieto, *Hacia una ética*, 125.
224. Curran, *The Moral Theology of John Paul II*, 168.
225. Ibid.

In light of this important precision, one can understand why those who do not marry, but follow a different vocation making a gift of self for the Kingdom of heaven, show "in turn and *perhaps even more* that the freedom of the gift exists in the human body. This means that this body possesses a full spousal meaning."[226] Moreover, this signifies that such a meaning has to do with God's image in man, which will be ultimately perfected in the state of glory, in the beatific vision. What the adjective spousal adds here is not the exercise of the reproductive faculty—as Curran seems to assume—but something much broader. It signifies the human person's power to express supernatural love in the gift of oneself. It signifies what truly "fulfills the very meaning of his being and existence."[227] For this reason, John Paul II said in RH, that the human person is unintelligible to himself apart from love.[228]

To be sure, the lived experience of the spousal meaning of the body at the "beginning" is somewhat different from the one man has after the fall. However, original sin has not destroyed this meaning. The spousal meaning of the body, as the conscious awareness of being created in God's image and called to imitate the same God who is love, remains in man even after the fall as a desire which cannot be completed, except with the gift of redemption and supernatural grace. Sin distorts man's awareness of his final end. It affects his consciousness of the spousal meaning of the body. However, objectively speaking, such an end remains intact. Moreover, even man's awareness of his supernatural call, though bedimmed, is not completely erased from his heart. For this reason, "in the whole perspective of his own history, man will not fail to confer a spousal meaning on his own body."[229] John Paul II acknowledges that this meaning will undergo many distortions. However, the spousal meaning of the body "will always remain at the deepest level, which demands that it be revealed in all its simplicity and purity and manifested in its whole truth as a sign of the image of God."[230]

It is clearer now why the awareness of the spousal meaning of the body results from the understanding born by the original experiences. These experiences disclose the human person's capacity to love one another in God and because of God, thereby offering to each other and to God a gift of self. Hence, the pope says that the experience of original nakedness, inasmuch as it presupposes the other ones, "allows us to identify that spousal meaning of the body *in actu*."[231] However, John Paul II acknowledges that reading this meaning as spousal springs from a certain perspective. He calls it "the prism of our historical *a posteriori*."[232] It really results from understanding Adam and Eve's mutual charity in light of the new Adam, in light of Christ's gift of

226. TOB 15:5; emphasis added.
227. Ibid., 15:1.
228. See RH 10; FC 11; TOB 15:5.
229. TOB 15:5.
230. Ibid.
231. Ibid., 15:3. See also 16:3.
232. Ibid., 16:5.

self for the Church as described in Eph 5:25. In this sense, there is a certain historical *a posteriori* based on Vatican II's teaching on God wisely arranging that "the New Testament be hidden in the Old and the Old be made manifest in the New."[233] It is from this same perspective that John Paul II claims that the (spousal meaning of the) body is a sort of *primordial sacrament*. It is the first visible sign of God's eternal and invisible plan of holiness for the human person.[234] As the pope explains, "original innocence, connected with the experience of the spousal meaning of the body, is holiness itself, which permits man to express himself deeply with his own body, precisely through the sincere gift of self [*Gaudium et Spes*, 24:3]."[235] The very human body becomes, in a very broad sense, a sacrament: "[C]onsciousness of the gift conditions in this case the sacrament of the body: in his body as man or woman, man senses himself as a subject of holiness."[236]

---

233. DV 16.
234. See TOB 11:4–5.
235. Ibid., 11:5.
236. Ibid.

8

Redemption of the Human Heart

Pessimistic and False Optimism

John Paul II's theology of the spousal meaning of the body continues to unfold a christocentric anthropology of the *imago Dei*, concentrating at this juncture on how this image is obscured by original sin and restored by the work of redemption.[1] This theological anthropology does not intend to be complete. Rather, it consists in a selection of topics made in light of the conciliar framework explained heretofore and in light of a very precise goal: to lay the foundations for HV's moral analysis from the perspective of the theology of the body as pedagogy.[2] Indeed, the pope is interested in offering a peculiar synthesis of theological anthropology meant to stand as the bedrock for a commentary on HV. His commentary intends to adopt the *theological* viewpoint of what is specifically Christian. In so doing, Wojtyła opposes the majority report and its claim for an *autonomous* morality. Moreover, with his selection of topics, John Paul II is also going to respond to the advocates of contraception's paradoxical error concerning the effects of original sin and the power of grace. Remember, Wojtyła already noted how the proponents of contraception's proposal was animated by a *false optimism* regarding human nature. At the same time, this false optimism concealed, in its core, a *profound pessimism* with respect to the power of supernatural grace. In short, their proposal was animated by what I would describe as a "pessimistic and false optimism."

Indeed, contraception's advocates did not seem to account for the fact that, even after redemption, the embers of sin are present in us. We must *always* reckon with their power; we must *always* be on guard.[3] Whence, the proponents of contraception's argument according to which, every conjugal act is always an act of self-gift or virtuous love, is the result of a false optimism. As Wojtyła already clarified, this position is not only naïve but also nonpastoral.[4] Paradoxically however, this false

---

1. See Hittinger, "Human Nature."

2. See TOB 133:4; Petri, *Aquinas*, 188. As Petri rightly notes, TOB should *not* be read as a work that stands sufficiently on its own. See ibid., 195–96.

3. See KD, 335.

4. See ibid., 346; emphasis added.

optimism is really grounded in a deep and latent theological pessimism, incapable of acknowledging the power of the new law, that is, the power of the redemption of the human heart. In this pessimistic view, even after redemption and the aid of supernatural grace, the human person would be *practically incapable* of ordering his actions so as to conform to the Gospel's ideal. Thus, contraception's advocates thought that the minority report, and later on HV, proposed a beautiful ideal for marriage and conjugal morality. However, their concealed pessimism considered such an ideal to be an *unreachable utopia* to most people. Consequently, they viewed this "utopian ideal" as a nonpastoral and nonpractical solution, which lacked mercy towards those who were frail, a solution that only brought discouragement and disillusionment for the weak and the wounded. Curran has expressed a very similar idea about TOB. Moreover, the current theological debates around the last two Synods on the Family have manifested that this same false and pessimistic optimism is very much alive in this day and age. It is a real threat yet present in our church. For this reason, John Paul II's theology of love offers a real and pastoral answer to this problem, which is still very valuable for us today.

Concupiscence and the Spousal Meaning of the Body

Original sin does not completely destroy the human person's consciousness of the spousal meaning of the body. Even if it distorts man's awareness of his final end, objectively speaking, such an end remains intact.[5] Its consciousness also remains after the fall as a desire that can only be fulfilled thanks to the redemption of the human heart. Even if the human person still retains his natural capacity and attitude to know and love God and others, this capacity coexists with concupiscence, that is to say, with an alteration of the integrated equilibrium and harmony between what is higher and lower in the human person, an alteration of the proper and due order between the spiritual and the sensible faculties, between the inner and the outer man.[6]

In order to illustrate Christ's redemption of the human heart as affected by concupiscence, John Paul II appeals to Jesus's words: "You have heard that it was said, 'you shall not commit adultery.' But I say to you that everyone who looks at a woman lustfully has already committed adultery with her in his heart."[7] This biblical passage is the starting point of a canonical interpretation, which concentrates at first on the biblical and theological dimensions of that lustful look or desire, relating it to the threefold concupiscence mentioned in 1 John 2:16: "For all that is in the world, the

---

5. See TOB 15:5.

6. See *ST* II–II, q. 25, a. 7, c; AP, 315, note 74.

7. Matt 5:27–28. For an exegetical study of this passage within the overall structure of the Sermon on the Mount, see Lambrecht, *The Sermon on the Mount*.

concupiscence of the flesh and the concupiscence of the eyes and the pride of life, is not of the Father but is of the world."[8]

John Paul implicitly follows Thomas's explanation of this threefold concupiscence as an inordinate self-love, manifested in disordered love for the finite good. For Thomas, the concupiscence of the flesh corresponds to the disordered love of "natural" concupiscence, namely, the desire for the goods that sustain the body (food, drink, and sexuality). The concupiscence of the eyes, instead, refers to the disordered love of "spiritual" concupiscence, namely, the disordered desire for goods that are delightful through their intellectual apprehension, such as the disordered desire to possess money. In turn, the pride of life refers to the disordered love and hope for the arduous good, especially for one's excellence.[9] The pope follows this same doctrine, as it becomes evident in his treatment of the masters of suspicion, and their correspondence with the threefold concupiscence. Thus, Freud relates to the concupiscence of the flesh, Marx to the concupiscence of the eyes, and Nietzsche to the pride of life.[10]

Moreover, these texts from Matthew and John become an interpretative key to understand the experiences found in the third chapter of Genesis. Therein, one finds the first conflict between what is higher and what is lower in the human person, between the intellectual and the sensible powers, the inner and the outer man. There arises an "opposition between the spirit and the body that was born—together with sin—in the human heart."[11] The serpent casts a doubt in man's heart concerning the Creator.[12] As a result, man disobeyed and experienced for the first time the alienation from God's original love. The human person detached his heart from that which comes from the Father and turned to what comes from the world.[13] He did not accept to be the subordinated partner of the Absolute. Rather, he aspired to become the *autonomous measure* of truth and goodness. But this external rebellion against God found a parallel internal rebellion within man's very being, which is especially disclosed by the experience of original shame: "[T]hat shame is, as it were, the first source of the manifestation in man—in both the man and the woman—of what does not come from the Father but from the world."[14]

The turning away (*aversio*) from what comes from the Father carried with it that being deprived of grace, of the supernatural and preternatural gifts. The resulting turning towards the world (*conversio*) damaged humanity in the original fullness of the image of God, but it did not entail the loss of the image of creation.[15] Original

---

8. See TOB 25:5; 26:1; 26:3.
9. See *ST* I–II, q. 77, a. 5, c.
10. See TOB 46:2.
11. Ibid., 33:5.
12. See Gen 3:5.
13. See TOB 26:4; Cokeley, "Shame." Latkovic, "Pope John Paul II's 'Theology of the Body.'"
14. TOB 26:5. See Gen 2:25; 3:6.
15. See TOB 27:2; *ST* I, q. 93, a. 4, c.

sin destroyed neither the principles of which human nature is constituted nor the properties that flow from them, such as the powers of the soul. However, original sin entirely destroyed the gift of original justice, and diminished significantly the human person's natural inclination to virtue.[16] Once again, John Paul II's interpretation of the turning away (*aversio*) from what comes from the Father, and the resulting turning to (*conversio*) what comes from the world, parallels Thomas's understanding of original sin in its relation to the threefold subjection of original justice explained already. Moreover, John Paul II's implicit reference to Aquinas's doctrine also explains the importance given by the pope to concupiscence. Both Thomas and John Paul II seem to conceive concupiscence as the quasi-material element of original sin. Considered formally, original sin consists in the privation of original justice as a consequence of the will's turning away (*aversio*) from God. Instead, considered materially, original sin consists in concupiscence, broadly understood here as the disorder of the soul's powers in their turning towards (*conversio*) the mutable good.[17] Following a very similar idea, John Paul II refers to the man of concupiscence throughout TOB and explains that concupiscence emerges as a privation of order "that plunges its roots into the original depth of the human spirit."[18]

The internal disharmony of the fallen human person is in clear contrast with the state of justice revealed in the understanding originated by the experience of original nakedness. Original sin affects the ease and harmony inherent to Adam and Eve's first interpersonal encounter. "Its consequences make themselves felt in the reciprocal relation of persons, whose unity in humanity has from the beginning been determined by the fact that they are man and woman."[19] Now, it will be much harder to acknowledge the personal dignity of the other and to freely affirm it, thereby forming a communion of human persons in the Lord. Indeed, "from the moment in which another law at war with the law of the mind installed itself in man, there exists an almost constant danger of a way of seeing, of evaluating, of loving such that the desire of the body shows itself stronger than the desire of the mind."[20] Such an experience of internal and interpersonal disharmony gives rise to three interrelated phenomena closely analyzed by John Paul II: original shame, the insatiability of the union, and the "corruption" of the spousal meaning of the body.

Original Shame and the Birth of Human Concupiscence

Genesis 3:8–10 points to Adam's state of consciousness in the words, "I was afraid, because I was naked, and I hid myself." Here, "the need to hide shows that, *in the depth*

---

16. See ibid., I–II, q. 85, aa. 1 and 3.
17. See ibid., I–II, q. 82, a. 3, c; *De Malo*, q. 4, a. 2, c. Mateo Seco, "Muerte y pecado original."
18. TOB 27:2.
19. Ibid.
20. Ibid. See Rom 7:23.

of the shame they feel before each other as the immediate fruit of the tree of knowledge of good and evil, a sense of *fear before God has matured*: a fear previously unknown."[21] In congruency with the pope's words, Thomas also points out that shame may be directly linked with fear of reproach as a penal disgrace.[22] In our own experience, the more one values a person's attestation, the greater shame one feels in his presence when one's mistakes or faults are manifested. For Adam and Eve, God was the greatest cause of shame because of the immense weight of the Creator's attestation due to his infinite wisdom, knowledge of, and closeness to them.[23]

Genesis 3:8–10 also manifests another radical change with respect to the understanding effected by original nakedness. Adam and Eve's pride affects *their knowledge of God's image* expressed in the body.[24] Once more, the argument is clearly grounded in Thomistic thought. The Angelic Doctor explains that pride can be a serious obstacle to the *knowledge of the truth*. Pride removes the cause of *speculative knowledge*. Unlike the human person in original justice, the proud person does not subject his intellect to God to receive truth from the Creator. Such a person does not allow others to teach him either. Moreover, pride directly hinders *affective knowledge*, that is, the knowledge that is either fostered or impeded by one's passions. Thus, the proud person *delights* in his own excellence to the point of disdaining the excellence of truth.[25] As a result, pride contributes to the collapse of the original acceptance of the body as a sign of the human person's place of honor in the visible world, as the only being therein created in God's image.

Before the fall, Adam and Eve knew, with certainty and without effort, the spousal meaning of their bodies. After original sin, that certainty has vanished: "[M]an in some way loses the original certainty of the image of God expressed in his body. He also loses in a certain way the sense of his right to participate in the perception of the world, which he enjoyed in the mystery of creation."[26] This loss has great consequences because such a right "had its foundation in man's innermost [being], in the fact that he himself participated in the divine vision of the world, and of his own humanity, which gave him a deep peace and joy in living the truth and value of his body in all its simplicity, transmitted to him by the Creator."[27]

21. TOB 27:1; emphasis added.
22. See *ST* II–II, q. 144, a. 2, c.
23. See ibid., q. 144, a. 3, c.
24. See TOB 27:4.
25. See *ST* II–II, q. 162, a. 3, ad 1.
26. TOB 27:4.
27. Ibid. Adam and Eve's knowledge in the Creator, as described by John Paul II, resembles Aquinas's position regarding their knowledge before the fall, especially when one considers that John Paul has spoken of a degree of unity between body and soul, and a receptivity to grace unknown to us. Thus, both authors seem to propose that by means of reason and grace and usually through intelligible effects of God, the human person knew the Creator more clearly than we know him now. See TOB 18:2; *ST* I, q. 94, a. 1, c.

The loss of one's certainty of God's image in the human body transpires in Genesis 3:10: "I heard the sound of thee in the garden, and I was afraid, because I was naked; and I hid myself." This verse expresses man's awareness of being defenseless and insecure about his own somatic structure. This resistance foretells man's toil and suffering. Ultimately, it foretells his death.[28] Consequently, the human person experiences a sort of *"cosmic shame."* Instead of being aware of his superiority and mission to subdue the earth, he experiences being subjected to the earth. This situation parallels in the world, at a cosmic level, man's rebellion against God, wherein what is inferior attempts to subdue what is superior. Moreover, Gen 3:10 also points to an experience of *immanent and sexual shame*. It manifests man's internal disorder in his relationship to others. Immanent sexual shame compels Adam and Eve to cover their nakedness. Thus, Genesis 3:10 reveals "a certain constitutive *fracture in the human person's interior*, a breakup, as it were, of man's original spiritual and somatic unity. He realizes for the first time that *his body has ceased drawing on the power of the spirit*, which raised him to the level of the image of God. Its shame bears within itself the signs of a specific *humiliation* mediated by the body."[29]

John Paul II, like Aquinas, will see in this humiliation a sort of pedagogy, whereby the human person is challenged to struggle for unity or integration between the exterior and the interior man with the aid of supernatural grace. The pope links it to the experience described by Paul in Romans 7:22–23. This immanent shame preannounces the unrest of conscience connected with concupiscence, as well as the loss of the unity between body and soul, which was present in the state of original justice. "The body is not subject to the spirit as in the state of original innocence, but carries within itself *a constant hotbed of resistance against the spirit* and threatens in some way man's unity as a person, that is, the unity of the moral nature that plunges its roots firmly into the very constitution of the person."[30] The very integration, self-possession, and self-dominion of the human person is being threatened. Since one cannot give what he does not possess, the human person's capacity to give himself is at risk as well.

To fully capture John Paul's commentary on Gen 3:10, one needs to go back to his analysis of sexual shame in LR and read it in light of Thomas Aquinas, Max Scheler, and the pope's conclusions in TOB. According to Wojtyła, sexual shame should be understood as "a tendency, uniquely characteristic of the human person, to conceal sexual values sufficiently *to prevent them from obscuring the value of the person as such*."[31] The sphere of sexuality seems to manifest very clearly that imbalance between body and spirit just mentioned. Aquinas also agrees with this statement. He explains that all the powers of the soul have been affected by original sin. Yet, the powers that

28. See TOB 27:4; Gen 3:17–19.
29. TOB 28:2; emphasis added.
30. Ibid., 28:3; emphasis added.
31. LR, 187; emphasis added.

concur in the transmission of this sin in the act of generation—that is, the generative power and the concupiscible appetite—are especially infected.[32] Genesis 3:10 testifies to such an imbalance. It offers a witness to the birth of human concupiscence as a fracture of the personal integrity of one's body. At the same time, immanent and sexual shame is a relative phenomenon, something that involves others.

Eating from the tree of the knowledge of good and evil has caused in man "a specific *fracture of the personal integrity of his own body*, particularly in that which determines its sexuality and which is directly linked with the call to that unity in which man and woman will be one flesh."[33] This fracture in the unity, with which form conquers matter, explains shame's relative character.[34] "It is shame of one's own sexuality in relation to another human being. It is in this way that shame is shown in the account of Genesis 3, and so we are in some sense witnesses of *the birth of human concupiscence.*"[35] Shame's birth reveals the moment in which the inner man or the heart closes itself to what comes from the Father and opens itself to what comes from the world (concupiscence). His shame is motivated not by the body but by concupiscence, namely, by that "state of the human spirit distanced from original simplicity and from the fullness of values that man and the world possess in the dimension of God."[36]

John Paul II's Thomistic foundations are further manifested when one adds the following considerations. Aquinas explains that unchecked concupiscence is most slavish or disgraceful for man. It goes directly against his dignity as a rational creature. This kind of concupiscence makes the human person resemble an irrational animal. It subordinates what is higher in man to what is lower in him. As a result, unchecked concupiscence is most repugnant to man's beauty, for it dims the light of reason wherefrom the beauty of virtue arises.[37] Shame makes one recoil from the disgrace of unchecked concupiscence. For this reason, in man's historical state, together with honesty, shame can be considered as an integral part of temperance—a condition necessary for temperance to exist.[38] In this context, shame is the fear of something base or disgraceful, which is considered as possible and difficult to avoid.[39] The experience of original nakedness and its contrast with original shame can be explained by means of a historical *a posteriori*, by noting Aquinas's insistence on the fact that a virtuous man does not experience shame. The virtuous person considers the disgrace of intemper-

---

32. See *ST* I–II, q. 83, a. 4, c.

33. TOB 28:4. See Gen 2:24.

34. For the Thomistic understanding of form conquering matter, see *ScG* II. 68; De Finance, *Persona e valore*, 111.

35. TOB 28:4; emphasis added.

36. Ibid., 28:5.

37. See *ST* II–II, q. 142, a. 4, c.

38. See ibid., q. 143, a. 1, c.

39. See ibid., q. 144, a. 1, c.

ance, for example, as impossible for him or as something very easily avoidable.[40] But this is exactly what changes in man after original sin. The sexual shame experienced by Adam and Eve had to do with their own perception of unchecked concupiscence's disgrace as a real threat that was both possible and difficult to avoid.

These Thomistic premises seem to be subjacent to Wojtyła's fine analysis of immanent and relative sexual shame. Our author explains that the human person is "ashamed above all *of the way in which he reacts* to the sexual value of persons of the other sex."[41] From this relative shame, there extends another immanent shame which has to do with the sexual values connected with one's body. This second form of shame, however, is probably the result of the first. Indeed, the human person "is ashamed of his body *because* he is ashamed of the reaction to the value body which he encounters in himself."[42] Consequently, "shame is not only a response to someone else's sensual and sexual reaction to the body as an object of use—a reaction to a reaction—it is also, and *above all, an immanent need to prevent such reactions to the body in oneself*, because they are incompatible with the value of the person."[43] In a similar vein, Scheler explains that shame seems to include a sort of "disharmony in man between the senses and the claim of spiritual personhood and embodied needs."[44] Ultimately, Scheler says, "man feels ashamed of himself and feels shame before God in him."[45] Shame conceals, like a defensive reflex, the sexual values of the human being, because it opposes the use and abuse of the person that denigrates his dignity. Thus, it reveals the supra-utilitarian character of the person. Consequently, shame is not a flight from love but an opening towards it. Shame longs to inspire love as a reaction to the value of the person. In the woman, this sexual shame is expressed in the following manner: "You must not touch me, not even in your secret carnal thoughts."[46] Instead, in the man, it is expressed like this: "I must not touch her, not even with a deeply hidden wish to enjoy her, for she cannot be an object for use."[47]

For this reason, John Paul II explains in TOB that this kind of shame is a reaction of man's heart that indicates the threat to the value of the person, while at the same time, it preserves this same value in an interior way. Since man's heart reacts with shame in order to protect the value denigrated by concupiscence, it makes sense

40. See ibid., q. 144, a. 4, c.
41. LR, 177; emphasis added.
42. Ibid.; emphasis added.
43. Ibid.; emphasis added.
44. Scheler, "Shame," 5. Although Scheler's words could be inserted within an integral vision of man, within his own vision of the human person, they are highly incompatible with Christian anthropology. Scheler's view of man, even that corresponding to his most Catholic period, presents a radical dualism within the human person between that which is spiritual and that which is merely psychophysical. I have explained this problem in depth in my *De la experiencia*, 69–134.
45. Scheler, "Shame," 6.
46. LR, 180.
47. Ibid.

that Christ appeals to the same heart in order to protect these same values. Shame not only reveals the moment of concupiscence; concomitantly, it also makes the human person aware of the spousal meaning of the body. It makes one aware of one's dignity as a creature created for its own sake and of one's vocation to the gift of self. Therefore, shame provides ahead of time some weapons against the consequences of the threefold concupiscence. It allows the human person to protect the body from concupiscence and to defend its vocation to interpersonal communion.[48]

Insatiability of the Union and the Utilitarian Attitude

The following experience analyzed by John Paul II is that of the insatiability of the union. Just like original shame, the experience of the insatiability of the union arises as a result of the irruption of concupiscence in the human heart. It is described in Gen 3:16, where God says to Eve: "[Y]our desire shall be for your husband and he shall rule over you." These words are in clear contrast with Gen 2:24 and the experience of original unity explained above. Gen 3:16 shows that the communion of persons between Adam and Eve has now disappeared. They continue to be human persons who share in a conjugal union. But their union has taken another direction from the one intended at the beginning. It is now possible for them to fail "to satisfy the aspiration to realize in the conjugal union of the body the reciprocal communion of persons."[49] Their conjugal union is not directed by the characteristic way in which the spousal meaning of the body is fulfilled in the exercise of conjugal charity. Instead, original sin "confers on *the realization of this union another direction that was to be the one proper to the man of concupiscence*."[50] Concupiscence "brings with it an almost constitutive difficulty in identifying oneself with one's own body, not only in the sphere of one's own subjectivity, but even more so in regard to the subjectivity of the other human being, of woman for man and man for woman."[51]

Within this new direction, there is a sort of second rediscovery of sexuality. It is very different from the one described in Gen 2:24. Under the new light of concupiscence, sexuality is rediscovered as an *obstacle* to the communion of persons. "It is as if the personal profile of masculinity and femininity, which before has highlighted the meaning of the body for a full communion of persons, had given up its place to the mere sensation of sexuality with regard to the other human being. *It is as if sexuality became an 'obstacle' in man's personal relationship with woman*."[52] The temptation, in

---

48. See TOB 28:6; 31:1.
49. Ibid., 30:5.
50. Ibid.; emphasis added.
51. Ibid., 29:4.
52. Ibid., 29:3; emphasis added.

this new rediscovery, is to blame the human body as the cause of such an obstacle. However, in reality, concupiscence should be blamed, not the body nor sex.[53]

Genesis 3:16 identifies two clear threats to the fulfillment of the spousal meaning of the body characteristic in conjugal charity: domination and desire. John Paul interprets "he shall rule over you" as a prophecy concerning the common utilitarian attitude found in men towards women, that is to say, the tendency to reduce women to sheer instruments of pleasure. Adam's responsibility and that of all of his sons is clear. When women experience this kind of use and abuse, there arises in them an insatiable desire for a different kind of union. If the male's attitude persists, however, it is very common that this same utilitarian approach is also adopted by women, who now desire as well to use and abuse men in this same regard. For this reason, the pope explains that "if a man relates to a woman in such a way that he considers her only as an object to appropriate and not as a gift, he condemns himself at the same time to become, on his part too, only an object of appropriation for her and not a gift."[54] Not in vain, Adam had an original and special responsibility in receiving femininity as a gift, a responsibility of being "the guardian of the reciprocity of the gift and its true balance."[55]

Corruption of the Spousal Meaning of the Body

The corruption of the spousal meaning of the body is intimately related with the experiences of original shame and the insatiability of the union. It results from them as a conclusion. The corruption of the spousal meaning of the body refers to the subjective experience of how original sin, materially understood as concupiscence, has obscured the measure of God's image and charity. Turning away from God, the human person is unable to esteem himself aright. As a result, he neither loves himself orderly, nor can he love others as he should love himself.[56] After the fall, the threefold concupiscence "brings with it a *limitation* of the spousal meaning of the body."[57]

The word "corruption" should be properly understood here as a *limitation* in the human person's awareness of his supernatural vocation. Man has a limited awareness

---

53. See *In IV Sent.*, d. 26, q. 1, a. 3, ad 3, 4, 6.

54. TOB 33:1.

55. Ibid., 33:2. See Gen 2:23-25. Nevertheless, John Paul II also notes that, at times, these desires from the woman "precede the man's desire or even attempt to arouse it and give it impetus" (ibid., 31:3). As the pope also says: "Although maintaining the balance of the gift seems to be something entrusted to both, the man has a special responsibility, as if it depended more on him whether the balance is kept or violated or even—if it has already been violated—reestablished" (ibid., 33:2).

56. See *ST* I-II, q. 99, a. 1, ad 2 and ad 3; *ST* II-II, q. 25, a. 7, c; AP, 315n74.

57. TOB 31:5; emphasis added. Waldstein's English edition, which incorporates the subtitles from the Polish manuscript, uses the word corruption. Instead, the Italian edition uses the expression "*la triplice concupiscenza limita il significato sponsale del corpo.*" See UD, 138. Both expressions belong to John Paul II and should be understood as I just explained.

of his supernatural end. Before the fall, the body was clearly perceived as the expression of the spirit. The spousal meaning of the body was clearly seen as a call and task to exist in the communion of persons in God's image, acting according to the measure of the image of God and the inner man. Instead, concupiscence limits and deforms this objective mode of existing of the human body. However, the objective call to love and communion remains. "The spousal meaning of the body has *not become totally foreign to that heart*: it has not been totally suffocated in it by concupiscence, but only habitually threatened."[58] For this reason, as Thomas teaches, "there was need for man to receive a precept about loving God and his neighbor, because in this respect *the natural law had become obscured on account of sin*."[59] As Hall explains, with the old law, "we must learn (or relearn) the natural law because sin obscures our understanding of it and of our end."[60]

Even if original sin has not managed to make the spousal meaning of the body totally foreign to the consciousness of the human person, his heart now becomes the battlefield for a war between authentic love and disordered concupiscence. The more concupiscence possesses the human heart, the less awareness of the spousal meaning of the body the human person experiences. As concupiscence conquers the human heart in original sin, the communion of persons is substituted by a mutual appropriation and exploitation, which directly contradicts personal dignity and the freedom of the gift.[61] Concupiscence casts a doubt on the fact that the human person is a creature willed by the Creator for his own sake, a creature who finds meaning in life in the gift of self. This doubt directs the human person to find fulfillment, instead, in egoistical enjoyment. Concupiscence "pushes man toward the possession of the other as an object [as a nonspiritual or merely material thing], pushes him towards enjoyment, which carries with it *the negation of the spousal meaning of the body*. In its essence, the disinterested gift is excluded by egoistical enjoyment."[62]

This redirection of the human heart has great implications for the conjugal experience of man and woman, and for their view of sexuality. For this reason, "the human body in its masculinity and femininity has *almost lost the power of expressing this love in which the human person becomes a gift*, in conformity with the deepest structure and finality of his or her personal existence."[63] As the pope also explains, "concupiscence signifies, so to speak, that the personal relations of man and woman are *one-sidedly and reductively tied to the body and to sex*, in the sense that these relations become almost incapable of welcoming the reciprocal gift of the person. They neither contain nor treat femininity and masculinity according to the full dimension

58. TOB 32:3.
59. *ST* I–II, q. 100, a. 5, ad 1; emphasis added.
60. Hall, *Narrative*, 48.
61. See TOB 32:3; *ST* I–II, q. 98, a. 6, ad 1.
62. TOB 33:4.
63. Ibid., 32:3.

of personal subjectivity; they do not constitute the expression of communion, but remain one-sidedly determined by sex."[64] As a result, Adam and Eve lose the reciprocal belonging inherent in love and mutual self-gift that fulfills the spousal meaning of the body and comes from the Father—"My beloved is mine and I am his" (Song 2:16). Instead, "the threefold concupiscence, and in particular the concupiscence of the flesh, deprives the reciprocal belonging of man and woman of the dimension proper to the personal analogy."[65] Hence, what comes from the world reduces the human person to a thing that can be possessed, used, and exploited.

The Old and New Ethos

The "primary antithesis" contained in Matthew 5:27–28 deals with the sixth commandment: "You have heard that it was said, 'You shall not commit adultery'. But I say to you that every one who looks at a woman lustfully has already committed adultery with her in his heart."[66] With these words, Jesus radicalizes the content of God's commandment while retaining its full truth, thereby expressing the authentic will of God as legislator. Conversely, the "secondary antithesis" found in Matthew 5:31–32 regarding the bill of divorce is of a different nature: "It was also said, 'Whoever divorces his wife, let him give her a certificate of divorce.' But I say to you that every one who divorces his wife, except on the ground of *porneia*, makes her an adulteress; and whoever marries a divorced woman commits adultery." In the first text, the sixth commandment remains completely intact. Instead, the bill of divorce is abolished by Christ except in the case of *porneia*.[67] Christ's judgment in this second case is interpreted by John Paul II in parallel with Matthew 19:8. It was *because of the hardness of their heart* that Moses allowed for that bill of divorce. This hardness of heart indicates that which, "according to the *ethos* of the people of the Old Testament, had given rise to the situation contrary to the original design of God-Yahweh according to Genesis 2:24."[68]

John Paul's use of the concept of ethos needs some explanation in light of his main sources. Scheler distinguishes the objective moral order from its subjective appropriation present in a people or nation. This subjective appropriation, which can

---

64. Ibid., 32:5.

65. Ibid., 33:4.

66. See Estrada, "L'importanza delle antitesi." For a more general Scriptural study, see Ognibeni, *Il matrimonio*.

67. See Lambrecht, *The Sermon*, 103. For an explanation of the *porneia* exception as illicit sexual relationships due to affinity, see Schnackenburg, *The Moral Teaching of the New Testament*, 132–43.

68. TOB 34:1. Aquinas thinks that this bill of divorce was not just divorce, absolutely speaking (*ST* I-II, q. 105, a. 4, ad 8). Moses *allowed* for the bill of divorce so that a greater evil would not occur, namely, so that the Jews would not kill their wives: "we oppose the custom of those who put away their wives, though this was permitted to the Jews in the old law, by reason of the hardness of their hearts; that is, because they were ready to kill their wives. So, the lesser evil was permitted them in order to prevent a greater evil." *ScG* III.123. See Matt 19:18; *In III Sent.*, d. 37, q. 1, a. 6, ad 1; d. 33, q. 2, a. 2, qc.1; *ST* I-II, q. 107, a. 2, ad 2.

vary and be more or less perfect with respect to the immutable moral order, he named "ethos."[69] A similar distinction can be found in Aquinas, who explains that, "the state of mankind may change according as man stands in relation to one and the same law more or less perfectly."[70] For this reason, he continues to explain that "the state of the old law underwent frequent changes, since at times the laws were very well kept, and at other times were altogether unheeded."[71] John Paul II also distinguishes between the law given by God in the Old Testament, and its subjective appropriation by the people. What is contrary to God's original design is the hardness of their hearts. The "corruption" of the spousal meaning of the body and concupiscence's "irruption" in the human heart lead to an imperfect subjective appropriation of the old law, which contradicts the very intention of God as legislator. Thus, Christ "speaks about a *human interpretation of the law that cancels and does away with the right meaning of good and evil specifically* willed by the Divine Legislator."[72] His correction was needed because the law as understood and appropriated by the people of the OT, "while *combating sin, at the same time* contained in itself *the social structures of sin*; in fact, it *protected* and legalized them."[73]

In Matthew 19:8, Jesus does not accept the Pharisees's *casuistic* interpretation of the law because they have subjected its authentic content to their own *defective* ethos. But Jesus does not want to abolish the law in Matt 5:31–32.[74] Rather, assuming God's divine authority as legislator, he intends a transformation of ethos that retains everything that was correctly understood by the people of the Old Testament. At the same time, Christ invites the human person to a new ethos, linked to the original intention of "the beginning." Not only does he bring a correct understanding of the content of the Law and of the sixth commandment, he also offers to the human heart the transformative and redemptive power of his grace. Thus, just as the powerless old law prepared the way to the new as a teacher,[75] despite its imperfections, the ethos of the people of the Old Testament also prepared for the ethos of the New Testament or the ethos of redemption.

---

69. See Scheler, *Formalism*, 299, note 73 and pages 301–306; Wojtyła, *Max Scheler*, 25–27.
70. *ST* I–II, q. 106, a. 4, c.
71. Ibid.
72. TOB 35:1; emphasis added.
73. Ibid., 36:1.
74. That would be directly contrary to Matt 5:17. In the case of the woman caught in adultery, he clearly identified adultery with sin (John 8:11). However, it is significant that Christ appealed to the consciences of those who wanted to stone her. Such an appeal manifests that "the discernment of good and evil inscribed in human conscience can turn out to be deeper and more correct than the content of a legal form" (TOB 35:5).
75. See Rom 8:3–4; Gal 3:24.

A Pedagogical Approach

Thomas Aquinas teaches that the Divine Law's end is "to constitute the friendship of man with God."[76] As we know, this friendship between God and man is exactly the fulfillment of the spousal meaning of the body. The old law aimed at this very end, not at once, but little by little, as a good *pedagogue*. Thus, it prepared Christ's coming by shedding light into the darkness of people's consciences, and by teaching them to be *humble* in acknowledging their need for God's grace.[77] But the effects of original sin had a great impact in the conscience of the human person. Even precepts which belong to the natural law were darkened. Proof of this darkness is that, as John Paul notes, the history of the people in the OT is "the theater of the systematic defection from monogamy."[78]

God's pedagogical approach begins with the patriarchs. For them, procreation was so evidently the essential end of marriage that wives who loved their husbands, but were unable to give them children, asked their husbands to receive children from other women.[79] The commandment concerning adultery did not manage to change this mentality. On the contrary, the exceptional circumstances under which it was permitted were expanded. And so, David and Solomon each practiced polygamy "undoubtedly for reasons of concupiscence."[80] They thought that the commandment not to commit adultery did not prescribe monogamy, but only not taking a woman who was the possession of another man.[81] The laws prescribed in Lev 20:10 and Dt 22:22 were defectively appropriated to mean "the violation of the man's property right regarding every woman who was his legal wife (usually one among many); adultery is not understood, by contrast, as it appears from the point of view of the monogamy established by the Creator."[82]

Although the ethos of the people of the OT opposed sexual deviations such as homosexuality, bestiality, or onanism, it was marked by a certain compromise with the concupiscence of the body. This compromise transpires in the way in which the sexual is conceived as shameful or impure. Yet, "this certainly does not cancel the truths we know from Genesis, nor can one accuse the Old Testament—and, among others, also the legislative books—of being a sort of precursor of Manichaeism."[83] The Old Testament was concerned first and foremost with the order of the social life as a whole, and not so much with the order of man's heart. As a result, "the judgment about

---

76. *ST* I–II, q. 99, a. 2, c.
77. See ibid., I–II, q. 98, a. 2, ad 3; q. 98, a. 6, c.
78. TOB 35:2.
79. See Gen 16:2; 30:3; TOB 35:2; 36:2.
80. TOB 35:3.
81. See 2 Sam 11:2–27.
82. TOB 35:4.
83. Ibid., 36:3.

the body and sex expressed in it is not primarily *negative* or even severe, but rather *marked by an objectivism* motivated by the intention of setting this area of human life in order. It is not concerned directly with the order of the heart but with *the order of social life as a whole*, at basis of which stands, as always, marriage and the family."[84]

The time of the prophets represents a substantial growth and preparation for the new law. They speak more about "the analogy of adultery" than about adultery itself. This analogy reminds God's chosen people of the great sin of abandoning the one and true God in favor of idols. Thus, "while Isaiah emphasizes in his texts above all the love of Yahweh, the Bridegroom, who in all circumstances goes to meet the Bride, overlooking all her infidelities, Hosea and Ezekiel abound in comparisons that show above all the ugliness and moral evil of the adultery committed by the Bride, Israel."[85] These comparisons offer another avenue to understand in a deeper way God's commandment within the context of the covenant.[86] Adultery is not understood anymore as the mere violation of property rights. One's legal wife is not considered anymore as one among many. Indeed, "the prophets reveal a different meaning of adultery than the legislative tradition gives it. Adultery is sin because it is the breaking of the personal covenant between the man and the woman."[87]

Moreover, from the viewpoint of the prophetic tradition and in congruity with Genesis 2:24, "*monogamy seems to be the only right analogy of monotheism* understood in the categories of the covenant."[88] Adultery, in turn, is the antithesis. Thus, monogamous marriage "actualizes in itself the interpersonal covenant of man and woman and it realizes the covenant that is born from love and welcomed by both parties as a marriage (and recognized as such by society)."[89] Therefore, the prophets draw us closer to understand the spouses' bodily union as a bilateral "right" and, above all, as the regular sign of the conjugal communion of persons. Accordingly, adultery is seen as the violation of this right that belongs exclusively to the other spouse. Above all, adultery is seen—and this will be very important later on—as a sin of the body that implies "*a radical falsification of the sign*,"[90] an "*antithesis to the moral good of conjugal faithfulness*."[91] Since adultery indicates the act whereby a man and a woman who are not husband and wife in a monogamous marriage become one flesh, in order to judge the morality of this act's objective content, one has to evaluate "whether this

---

84. Ibid.; emphasis added. See *ST* I–II, q. 108, a. 1, ad 1.
85. Ibid., 36:6.
86. See TOB 36:5; 37:1; Hos 1:2; 2: 4–5, 15, 18, 21–22; 3:1; Ezek 16:5-8, 12–15, 30–32; TOB 37:2.
87. Ibid., 37:4.
88. Ibid.; emphasis added.
89. Ibid.
90. Ibid.; emphasis added.
91. Ibid., 37:5; emphasis added.

relationship makes such a unity of the body true and whether or not it gives to that unity the character of a truthful sign."[92]

The wisdom literature is primarily of a pedagogical nature. Excelling in the knowledge of the human heart, it points to experience and to God's law in order to teach virtue. However, unlike Christ, these texts remain within the ethos that prevailed in their historical period. There are eulogies about the woman who is the perfect companion of her husband.[93] Yet, there is also a frequent warning against the beauty and charm of a woman who is not one's wife and who is, therefore, an occasion for adultery.[94] Thus, just like the prophetic tradition, the wisdom literature prepared the people to understand Christ's words concerning the concupiscent look or "adultery in the heart."[95] Sirach 23:17-22 offers a clear example of that preparation. In this passage, the biblical author analyzes the inner state of the man of concupiscence. He offers some elements that have become classical in the description of this phenomenon. He compares the concupiscence of the flesh with a fire. On the one hand, this fire takes possession of man's "heart" to the point of suffocating conscience's voice and the sense of responsibility before God. On the other hand, this fire of passion brings a restlessness of the body and of the senses characteristic of the outer or exterior man. "Once the inner man has been reduced to silence and passion has, as it were, gained freedom of action, passion manifests itself as an insistent tendency toward satisfying the senses and the body."[96]

The New Ethos and the Way of Temperance

Christ's appeal to the heart contains a new ethos of the body. Inspired by Romans 8:20-23, John Paul II calls this new ethos of the new law the "ethos of redemption" or the "ethos of the redemption of the body." In this text, Paul contrasts the slavery of corruption, which results from the sin of our first parents, with a desire for the redemption of our bodies and the insertion into the freedom of God's children. This redemption will not be completed until the resurrection. To be sure, there is a connection and a continuity between the Redemption of the body and the mystery of Creation. However, "Christ does not invite man to return to the state of original innocence, because humanity has left it *irrevocably* behind."[97] The human person is called to find the perennial meaning of what is human, the living form of the "new

---

92. Ibid., 37:6.
93. See Prov 31:10; Sir 26:15-18.
94. See Prov 6:25; Sir 9:1-9.
95. TOB 38:6.
96. Ibid., 39:2. Besides the obvious yet implicit reference to Thomas's understanding of the interior and the exterior man, this particular description of John Paul II is very similar to that of John of the Cross in 1 *Subida* 6.1.
97. TOB 49:4; emphasis added.

man," which God had intended from the beginning. "Christ shows that the way to attain this goal must be *the way of temperance* and of mastery of desires."[98] For John Paul, generic self-mastery is another name for integration *in* the person. In the area of sexuality, this integration entails the virtues of temperance, chastity, and purity as they relate with other virtues and gifts of the Holy Spirit.

Despite the experience of beginners, who have to fight against contrary habits that resulted from yielding to the concupiscence of the flesh, temperance and self-mastery are not purely negative enterprises suspended in the void. Rather, both are oriented towards a concrete good, a definite positive value, namely, the spousal meaning of the body or man's vocation as created in the image of God. "The value in question is that of the body's spousal meaning, the value of a transparent sign by which the Creator . . . has written into the heart of both [man and woman] the gift of communion, that is, the mysterious reality of his image and likeness."[99] In view of his future commentary on HV, John Paul II confers an important role in the ethos of redemption to the virtue of temperance as perfected by charity. Of course, this is a very Thomistic position, for Aquinas explains that charity is what makes any true virtue become perfect virtue.[100] Thus, true temperance is made perfect by charity because the latter orients temperance to the love of God. In this sense, temperance can be understood, as Augustine says, as "love giving itself entirely to that which is loved," as "love keeping itself entire and incorrupt for God."[101] This is exactly the way of temperance within the new ethos of the redemption of the body. This is the way of understanding temperance within the perspective of charity, as directed towards the fulfillment of the spousal meaning of the body.

Without abandoning *the perspective of charity*, John Paul II notes that Christ pointed to purity as something that should inform *all* reciprocal relations between man and woman, inside and outside of marriage.[102] Broadly understood, moral purity is not restricted to the area of sexuality. In this broad sense, moral purity contrasts with *every* moral evil understood metaphorically as "being dirty." Strictly speaking, though, purity is a virtue that makes reference to temperance and the area of sexuality. Thus, the beatitude concerning the pure of heart who will see God can be understood in a twofold manner. The purity of one's heart can be understood either in a broad sense, or in a more specific sense, parallel to the one present in Matthew 5:27–28. This teaching seems to run parallel to Thomas's understanding of purity as *munditia* or cleanliness, and as *pudicitia*. On the one hand, *munditia* is a disposition of the appetite to see God whereby one is cleansed of inordinate affections.[103] On the other hand,

---

98. Ibid.; emphasis added.
99. Ibid., 49:5.
100. See *ST* II–II, q. 23, a. 7, c.
101. Augustine, *De Moribus Ecclesiae*, cap. 15, 25.
102. See Knapp, "Purity."
103. See *ST* II–II, q. 8, a. 7, c.

purity (*pudicitia*) has to do with shame (*pudor*). Broadly speaking, *pudicitia* is a virtue that regulates all that is shameful, that is, everything which has to do with inordinate concupiscence. However, strictly speaking, it has to do with temperance, especially in the area of sexuality. Hence, *pudicitia* is closely related to the virtue of chastity.[104]

Lust and the Spousal Meaning of the Body

Christ goes beyond the polemics concerning the meaning of adultery on the level of legislation and casuistry. Jesus shifts the center of gravity of the argument. Thereby, he lays the foundations for a new ethos that, in this case, calls for a life of purity fully realized in the Spirit. His words must have reminded most of his immediate listeners about many precepts and admonitions against the concupiscence of the body found in the wisdom literature. Perhaps, for this reason, Christ does not provide an analysis of concupiscence of the flesh as Sirach does. His words refer to an interior act of the heart. They point to a desire not yet transformed into an exterior act of the body. The cognitive act of looking, when mixed with concupiscence, could mean either the cognitive act of looking used by man in desiring concupiscibly, or the cognitive act wherefrom concupiscent desire is born. In both cases, one is dealing with an *interior* act hidden in the heart, an act standing at the threshold of the look, which intentionally diminishes or reduces the dignity of the woman. Since *operari sequitur esse*, this interior act of the heart is revealed by the look, which in turn becomes the threshold of the interior truth: *intueri sequitur esse*. Jesus shows that within the orbit of lustful desire, the experience of the person is far from the dignity and vocation of the human person contained in the spousal meaning of the body.

Pay close attention now to the way in which the spousal meaning of the body becomes relevant in the moral analysis of this lustful desire. The following text merits to be quoted in full:

> [Lustful] desire has the effect that in the interior, in the "heart," in man and woman's interior horizon, *the meaning of the body proper to the person itself is obscured*. In this way, femininity ceases to be above all a subject for masculinity; it ceases to be a specific language of the spirit; it loses its character as a sign. It ceases, I would say, to bear on itself *the stupendous spousal meaning of the body*. It ceases to be located in the context of the *consciousness and experience of this meaning*. The desire born precisely from concupiscence of the flesh, from the first moment of its existence in the man's interior—of its existence in the "heart"—bypasses this context in some way (to use an image, one could say *it tramples on the ruins of the spousal meaning of the body and of all its subjective components*), and, in virtue of its own axiological intentionality, it

---

104. See *ST* II-II, q. 151, a. 4, ad 2.

aims directly toward one and only one end as its precise object: to satisfy only the body's sexual urge.[105]

This lustful desire "indicates an experience of the value of the body *in which its spousal meaning ceases to be spousal precisely because of concupiscence.*"[106] The reason why there is no spousal character here is simple: there is neither gift of self nor charity. Lust corrupts love in a way that it cannot be any more a "love giving itself entirely to that which is loved," a "love keeping itself entire and incorrupt for God."[107] In John Paul II's theology, *conjugal* charity and the gift of self inherent in it are like the root where the procreative meaning of the body springs forth. Thus, he clarifies that, within the orbit of lust, "what also ceases is its [the human body's] procreative meaning (we have spoken about this meaning above), which—when it concerns the conjugal union of man and woman—is *rooted in the spousal meaning of the body and comes forth organically, as it were, from it.*"[108] Concupiscence effects a reduction of charity's perennial call, always present yet obscured by sin, in the heart of man. In Matt 5:27–28, "Christ wanted to emphasize to his listeners the detachment from the spousal meaning of the body experienced by man (in this case by the male) when he gives in to the concupiscence of the flesh with an interior act of desire."[109] Within the orbit of lust and concupiscence, there is an opposition to charity and to the personal dignity of the other. "The detachment from the spousal meaning of the body at the same time brings with it a conflict with its dignity as a person: an authentic conflict of conscience."[110] Lust and concupiscence oppose charity because they are "the deception of the human heart with regard to the perennial call of man and woman to communion through reciprocal gift."[111]

Healing the Human Heart

As John Paul continues his extended commentary on Matthew 5:27–28, he makes an important distinction. One thing is the perennial reciprocal attraction of man to femininity and of woman to masculinity. Another thing is the concupiscence of the flesh and its inherent reduction of the human person to a sheer means for pleasure.[112] The pope is very far from considering the sexual urge, an objective dimension of human nature, as morally evil. The question of morality implies the relationship between

---

105. TOB 40:4; emphasis added.
106. Ibid., 39:5.
107. Augustine, *De Moribus Ecclesiae*, cap. 15, 25.
108. TOB 39:5; emphasis added.
109. Ibid., 40:1.
110. Ibid.
111. Ibid.
112. See TOB 40:3.

human freedom and this urge, a relationship in which man and woman experience themselves as "co-authors of their history."[113]

According to Wojtyła's anthropology of love, the sexual urge can be the material out of which results either the conjugal communion of persons, or the utilitarian violation of the other's dignity. Remember that our author envisions integration or one's growth in virtue by establishing a relationship between person and nature in second act, that is to say, a relationship between the human being as free author or creator of his action (man-author-agent; *człowiek-twórca*), and his own dynamism as the material which is informed by this action (man-matter-patient; *człowiek-tworzywo*).[114] Thus, the integration between person and nature consists in the free affirmation of our own rational nature in bringing to fulfillment the direction of integration of our natural inclinations.[115] When this political government and affirmation are missing, there is a sort of disintegration or lack of integration. Then, desire gains mastery over one's heart, and man is dominated by and abandoned to the ethos of concupiscence.[116] Thus, the human person loses the freedom of the gift connatural to the spousal meaning of the body, when his will reduces the woman to a sheer object for the possible satisfaction of the sexual urge. This reduction neither corresponds to the supernatural vocation of the human person, nor to his natural dignity as a being created in God's image. It is against the very nature or intelligible structure of human sexual attraction. It is against natural and divine law. For this reason, John Paul explains that lust consists in a reduction of the "the rich content of reciprocal and perennial attraction among human persons in their masculinity and femininity."[117] This reduction "does not correspond to the nature of the attraction in question."[118] Moreover, it directs the sexual drive away from the communion of persons and towards "utilitarian dimensions, in whose sphere of influence one human being makes use of another human being, *using her* only to satisfy his own urges."[119]

Rediscovering the values lost in the general understanding of his interlocutors, Christ intends to build a *new* ethos. He intends to *heal* the human heart. The key phrase of the entire passage is "adultery *in the heart*." This phrase reveals the passage's ethical meaning as well as the essential values of the new ethos of the Sermon on the Mount. Obviously, adultery "in the flesh" is adultery, properly speaking. When Christ speaks of the object of the act of looking with concupiscent desire, he simply refers to a woman, without stressing that she is another's wife. This fact manifests that, "adultery committed in the heart is not circumscribed by the limits of the interpersonal relation

---

113. TOB 44:3.
114. See AP, 69–70.
115. See AP, 116; *In IV Sent.*, d. 26, q. 1, a. 1, c; *ST* I–II, q. 94, a. 3, c.
116. See Sir 23:17–22.
117. TOB 41:5.
118. Ibid.
119. Ibid.

that allows one to identify adultery committed in the flesh."[120] What is decisive in adultery in the heart is *the internal utilitarian attitude in man, as a detachment from the spousal meaning of the body and personal dignity*. For this reason, the pope argues that it is possible to commit such "adultery" even with one's wife.[121]

In consequence, purity of heart is the fulfillment of Christ's commandment. Christ came to heal us. He came to fulfill the law in himself and to make possible its fulfillment in the human heart. Thus, this same heart must be *exposed* and *healed* but *not condemned*.[122] Jesus's words address two extremes that are wrong. Often the human person "passes from the pole of pessimism to the pole of optimism, from puritanical strictness to present-day permissiveness."[123] Thus, "the accusation of the moral evil that the desire born from carnal intemperate concupiscence contains within itself is at the same time a call to overcome this evil."[124] This overcoming should not imply a transfer of the moral negativity inherent in the consented carnal and intemperate concupiscible desire to the human body, to women, or to sexuality. Such a transfer would imply the acceptance of the Manichean anti-value.[125] Instead of a real victory over the evil inherent in the act, one would be tempted to justify the act to the detriment of the human body, women, and sexuality—like the Manicheans ended up doing.

Christ accuses the human heart of concupiscence to appeal to that same heart so as to *heal* it, and *avoid* such a transfer. Jesus confronts the human heart in order to heal it, and to give to it the purity of the beatitudes.[126] Thus, there is a foundational difference between the masters of suspicion and Christ. Jesus's words "do not allow us to turn such concupiscence into the absolute principle of anthropology and ethics or into the very nucleus of the hermeneutics of man."[127] The Lord's words are an appeal to the human heart based on the mystery of the Redemption of the body and its new ethos. For this reason, "man must feel himself called *to rediscover, or even better, to realize, the spousal meaning of the body and to express in this way the interior freedom of the gift, that is, the freedom of that spiritual stage and power that derive from mastery over the concupiscence of the flesh*."[128] This call is not purely extrinsic to man. It corresponds to his original vocation and to the grace given to him in order to bring it to fulfillment. In this sense, Christ's appeal "concerns the very nature, the very substrate of the humanity of the person, the deepest impulses of the heart . . . It always signi-

---

120. Ibid., 43:2.

121. See TOB 43:3. John Paul II does offer here a reflection on whether or not such an "adultery in the heart" is a mortal or a venial sin. As we will see, Aquinas also accepts that such an attitude may occur between spouses. See *In IV Sent.*, d. 31, q. 2, a. 3, c, and also ad 1 and ad 3 of this same article.

122. See TOB 44:1; Matt 5:17.

123. TOB 44:4.

124. Ibid., 45:4.

125. See *In IV Sent.*, d. 26, q. 1, a. 3, c.

126. See Matt 5:8; TOB 43:5.

127. TOB 46:2.

128. Ibid., 46:4.

fies—even if only in the dimension of the act to which it refers—the *rediscovery of the meaning of the whole of existence, of the meaning of life, which includes also the meaning of the body that we have called spousal here.*"[129]

Consequently, Christ's appeal to the heart is a call to purity that *integrates eros in the new ethos*. If eros is not reduced to a sensible desire but is seen, above all, as the power that impulses man to pass from the sensible to the spiritual, then Christ's appeal to the heart is an appeal to integrate one's desires in the truth about the good. The fullness of human eros is found in what is true, good, and beautiful. To reach this fullness, one needs to transform what has been affected by the threefold concupiscence. Such a transformation is an ethical task which, in Wojtyła's anthropology of love, is called *integration*. "It is, therefore, indispensable that ethos becomes the constitutive form of eros."[130] Within the contours of this integration, there is no ultimate opposition between ethos and spontaneity. The virtuous man who makes ethos the form of eros spontaneously loves, enjoys, and finds pleasure in that which is truly good.

John Paul II explains this integration or maturation, appealing to the Thomistic notion of the integration of the exterior man into the interior man, which we discussed before. "The inner man is the specific subject of the ethos of the body, and it is with this [ethos] that the Christ wants to impregnate the consciousness and will of his audience and disciples."[131] He argues that the human person "should *succeed in being really an interior man*, able to obey right conscience, able to be authentic master of his own innermost impulses, like a watchman who watches over a hidden spring, and finally able to draw from all these impulses what is fitting for purity of the heart by building with consciousness and consistency the personal sense of the spousal meaning of the body, which opens the interior space of the freedom of the gift."[132] Such integration of the exterior man into the interior man brings with it the deeper and more mature spontaneity of virtue that pertains to purity of heart.

The Flesh and the Spirit

John Paul II expands on Christ's call to purity by looking at the writings of Saint Paul, wherein one finds a parallel teaching to that of the threefold concupiscence: the opposition and tension between the flesh and the Holy Spirit.[133] The connection is clear: the lustful desire spoken of in Matthew 5:27–28 corresponds to the life in the flesh, whereas the purity and the way of temperance indirectly alluded to by our Lord corresponds to the life "according to the Spirit." The tension between the flesh and the Spirit does not refer to the distinction and opposition between body and soul. Rather,

129. Ibid., 46:5–6; emphasis added.
130. Ibid., 48:1.
131. Ibid., 49:1. See AP, 315, note 74; *ST* II–II, q. 25, a. 7, c.
132. TOB 48:3; emphasis added.
133. See Gal 5:16–17; Rom 8:5; Durkin, *Feast of Love*, 203–34.

it signifies concupiscence as the quasi-material dimension of original sin. This tension points to the disposition of man's faculties wounded by original sin. Such wounds result in a subjection of the inner man to the outer man. They result in a sort of encapsulation of the human person into the sphere of sensitive goods. The flesh opposes the Spirit because the human person, wounded by original sin and living in this subjection, opposes what the Holy Spirit wants.[134] Thus, Paul's teaching on life according to the flesh and the Spirit offers a revered anthropological synthesis. Moreover, it also provides a *transformative moral program*. At its core, one finds the doctrine on justification, that is to say, Paul's teaching on Christ's power working in the human person through the Holy Spirit, so that justice may abound in him in the measure God wills and expects.[135]

The opposition between the flesh and the Spirit is not only an interior tension within the human person; it is also manifested outwardly in his external works or actions. These are the works of the flesh. In them, one follows what John calls the threefold concupiscence to the point of experiencing moral death and the exclusion from God's Kingdom.[136] Among these works, in Galatians 5:11–21, Paul lists not only sins of the flesh (like fornication, impurity, licentiousness, orgies, etc.), but also other sins which are not of a carnal nature (like idolatry, jealousy, anger, envy, etc.) and that, according to our standards, could be said to be of the human spirit, springing from the concupiscence of the eyes or the pride of life. All of them are called works of the flesh, because of the opposition or antithesis between the Holy Spirit who works in the human person's soul and these sins. Paralleling Matthew 15:2–10 and in accordance with Thomas, the pope finds in Paul a broad understanding of impurity, and a more specific one. The works of the flesh may refer, either to *any sin* as an inordinate affection or, more specifically, to *sins of a sensual or sexual character*. Conversely, there are the fruits of the Spirit. They are works of man but above all, "a fruit of the human spirit permeated by the Spirit of God, which manifests in choosing the good," which springs from the so-called ethos of redemption and its mastery over concupiscence.[137]

Closely related with the aspect of *integration*, one of these fruits of the Spirit is *self-mastery* (*enkrateia*). According to Wojtyła's philosophical premises, self-mastery and self-possession are structures which belong to self-determination as innate freedom. This kind of freedom finds its fulfillment in the integration of the human person, when he acts in accordance with the truth about the good. Indeed, "human freedom is not fulfilled by subordinating truth to itself but *by subordinating itself to the truth.*"[138]

134. See Gal 5:17; Rom 7:19; *Super Ga.*, cap. 5, lect. 4; *Super Rom.*, cap. 5, lect. 5; cap. 7, lect. 4; cap. 8, lect. 1.

135. See TOB 50:5; 51:1; Rom 8:5–10; Matt 5:20.

136. See Gal 5:21; Eph 5:5; TOB 52:4.

137. TOB 51:6. See *ST* I–II, q. 70, a. 1, c.

138. AP, 154; emphasis added and translation altered. See OC, 370. Let us remember that one should read this teaching in light of John of Cross, for whom perfected or true freedom consists in being able to love God with all of one's strengths, namely, with all of one's faculties or powers (*potentiae*).

Thereby, the human person becomes an authentic collaborator with the Creator by freely obeying him. Such an obedience entails the very fulfillment of freedom in choosing the true good as opposed to the merely apparent one. This is exactly what a human person does with proper love of self as friendship with one's higher or interior man. Instead of being encapsulated into the sphere of sensible goods, he wants for himself what is best, what brings him salvation. In so doing, he masters concupiscence and subordinates his intellect and will to the truth about the good.[139]

Following John of the Cross and Thomas, John Paul II explains at this point that Romans 8:12–13 introduces an ethical dimension in the sphere of the meanings of the terms "body" and "spirit." This ethical dimension corresponds to Christ's appeal to man's heart. To put to death the deeds of the body with the help of the Spirit is to master concupiscence.[140] Paul sees this mortification as a mastery over concupiscence. It leads to that freedom for which Christ has set us free, namely, perfected or acquired freedom. Such a fulfillment of our innate freedom consists in subordinating to the truth about the good in one peculiar way. One is to use his innate freedom not as an instrument to live according to the flesh, but rather as an instrument for the gift of self inherent in the fulfillment of the commandment to love.[141] Thus, John Paul II considers evangelical purity (or purity of the heart) according to the measure of that freedom for love, which relies on the ethos of the Gospel.[142] He looks at purity from the perspective of the restoration of the spousal meaning of the body and the freedom of the gift.

Within this larger context, the pope also relates purity and self-mastery to the virtue of temperance: "One can recognize this mastery as a virtue that concerns continence in the area of all desires of the senses, above all in the sexual sphere, and thus in antithesis to fornication, impurity, licentiousness and also to drunkenness and orgies."[143] Self-mastery and purity are virtues concerned with "the right way of treating the sexual sphere, depending on one's personal state of life (and not necessarily absolute abstinence from sexual life)."[144] Hence, John Paul acknowledges that his correlation inserts us into "the well-known system of virtues that later theology, especially Scholasticism, in some way borrows from Aristotle's ethics."[145] The reference to Scholasticism is of no little importance. It is valuable in order to understand the internal logic of the proposal. Under his notion of self-mastery, one is to locate the three fruits of the Spirit that, according to Aquinas, regulate the relationship of the interior with the exterior man, namely, modesty, continence, and chastity. While

---

See *Cántico* B 28.5; *Noche* II.11.4–5; *Subida* I.4.6.

139. See *ST* II–II, q. 25, a. 7, c.
140. See TOB 52:4.
141. See Gal 5:1, 13–14.
142. TOB 53:1.
143. Ibid. 53:5.
144. Ibid.
145. Ibid.

continence and chastity regulate internal desires, modesty regards external actions (words and deeds) so that they observe the "mode."[146] This last fruit of the Spirit will play a particular role in TOB. Relating modesty with chastity and continence, John Paul II will draw an analogy between human language and human acts, the so-called language of the body. We will talk about this analogy in chapters 11–12.

Little Known Guiding Thread

According to 1 Thessalonians 4:3–8, purity is a manifestation of the life in the Spirit. It consists in abstaining from unchastity and in knowing how to keep one's body with holiness and reverence.[147] Saint Paul explains that "whoever disregards this, disregards not man but God, who gives his Holy Spirit."[148] He is reasoning within the framework of the ecclesiological analogy of the church as the body of Christ. In light of this analogy, 1 Cor 12:18–27 teaches that the human body deserves reverence and respect.[149] This last text mentions unrepresentable members and the members of the human body that seem to be weaker and less honorable. However, body members are not experienced as unrepresentable or less honorable because of their somatic nature. Rather, they are so because of shame as a feeling that springs from the "disunion within the body" or "disharmony of the heart," which results from original sin and its wounds.

Commenting on this same text, John Paul contrasts the experiences of original unity and original shame. Just as there is a harmony among the different members of the body, so there is a harmony of the heart, that is, a harmony of the interior faculties of the human person. "This harmony, or precisely purity of heart, allowed man and woman in the state of original innocence to experience in a simple way (in a way that made both of them originally happy) the unitive power of their bodies that was, so to speak, the unsuspectable substratum of their personal union or *communio personarum*."[150] *By contrast, original sin and concupiscence have effected a disharmony of the heart healed by the new law as the Holy Spirit and God's grace.* Since Paul argues that "those members of the body that we think less honorable we clothe with greater reverence,"[151] John Paul II concludes that shame points to the road of purity as the way that leads to the gradual victory over the body's lack of integration or unity.[152]

As we already know, purity is a moral virtue centered on the dignity of the human body and the human person. It is an ability whereby the human heart is detached from the concupiscence of the flesh and abstains from unchastity. Yet, purity also has a

---

146. See *ST* I–II, q. 70, a. 3, c.
147. See TOB 54:2; Shivanandan, "Conjugal Spirituality."
148. 1 Thess 4:8.
149. See TOB 54:4–6.
150. TOB 55:6; 1 Cor 12:25.
151. 1 Cor 12:23.
152. See TOB 55:7.

charismatic dimension inasmuch as it is a fruit of the life in the Holy Spirit, whose temple is the human body. By means of this fruit, one avoids the sins of the flesh, that is, the sins against the body that profane this sacred temple.[153] This last dimension of purity evidences a new theological source for the dignity of the human body, a theological argument that is complementary to the more philosophical consideration of the human body's being the result of matter informed by a spiritual soul. This new theological source is rooted in the mystery of the Incarnation and in its consequent supernatural elevation of the human body. Thus, theologically, the dignity of the human body is also founded on "the supernatural reality of the indwelling and continuous presence of the Holy Spirit in man—in his soul and in his body—as the fruit of the redemption accomplished by Christ."[154] As the pope explains, "through redemption, every human being has received himself and his own body anew, as it were, from God. Christ inscribed in the human body—in the body of every man and of every woman—a new dignity, because he himself has taken up the human body together with the soul into union with the person of the Son-Word."[155]

A moral theology of the human body must explain an "administration" or use of the body worthy of its dignity and role in the life of the human person. Such administration is, in reality, what Wojtyła means by his teaching on integration. This administration or integration, especially when dealing with sexual morality, should take into account that the body is for the Lord and that the Lord is for the body. This theological argument is clearly rooted both in scripture and in Thomas Aquinas: "As the Apostle says in speaking against lust, 'You are bought with a great price: glorify and bear God in your body'. Wherefore, by inordinately using the body through lust, a man wrongs God who is the supreme Lord of our body. Hence, Augustine says: 'God who thus governs his servants for their good, not for his, made this order and commandment, lest unlawful pleasures should destroy his temple which thou hast begun to be.'"[156] Indeed, as John Paul explains, "the redemption of the body brings with it the establishment in Christ and for Christ of *a new measure of the holiness of the body*."[157] The Holy Spirit as gift, paid at the great price of Christ's Redemption, becomes the source for the moral duty that springs from such a dignity and commits Christians to purity: the duty not to commit unchastity and to keep one's body with holiness and reverence.[158]

The mystery of Redemption bears fruit in man in a charismatic way, thanks to the gifts of the Holy Spirit. Among them, John Paul II gives a place of preference to the gift of piety (*eusebia; donum pietatis*) in relationship to purity: "If purity disposes man to 'keep his own body with holiness and reverence' . . . piety as a gift of the Holy

---

153. See 1 Cor 6:18–19; TOB 56:2.
154. Ibid., 56:3.
155. Ibid., 56:4; 1Cor 6:18, 20.
156. *ST* II-II, q. 153, a. 3, ad 2; 1 Cor 6:20.
157. TOB 56:4; emphasis added.
158. See 1 Cor 6:20; 1 Thess 4:4. TOB 56:4.

Spirit seems to serve purity in a particular way by making the human subject sensitive to the dignity that belongs to the human body in virtue of the mystery of creation and of redemption."[159] This correlation echoes LR's emphasis on the connection between conjugal chastity and the virtue of religion as justice towards the other spouse, and towards the Creator.[160] However, in this theological realm, the gift of piety surpasses the virtue of religion inasmuch as the former moves us to have a filial affection towards God, paying duty and worship to him as our Father.

Once again, John Paul II's reasoning is grounded in Thomas's theology. Aquinas sees in the gift of piety the perfection of the virtue of justice. Moreover, he also argues that by means of the gift of piety, we pay duty and worship to God as our Father. In piety, we glorify God because we manifest his goodness through our good works. Thus, Jesus himself commands in Matt 5:16: "Let your light so shine before men, that they may see your good works and give glory to your Father who is in heaven." However, the gift of piety also entails actions towards human beings. "As by the virtue of piety man pays duty and worship not only to his father in the flesh, but also to all his kindred on account of their being related to his father so by the gift of piety he pays worship and duty *not only to God, but also to all men on account of their relationship to God.*"[161] Tacitly based on these premises, John Paul brings up again our vocation to charity as contained in the spousal meaning of the body. To love oneself and to love others on account of their relationship to God belongs intimately to the logic of charity. In charity, one is to love oneself and others in the Lord and because of him. Thus, the gift of piety opens a *"fuller access to the experience of the spousal meaning of the body and of the freedom of the gift connected with it,* in which the deep face of purity and its organic link with love reveals itself."[162]

We can see now why John Paul made such an emphasis on the two dimensions of original unity. In the first and most foundational dimension, Adam and Eve were united in their common dignity of being brother and sister. Acknowledging and affirming their common dignity as human persons implied acknowledging their common relationship to God, their being created in his image and likeness. The second dimension of original unity inserted into the first dimension the values of conjugality, sexuality, and procreation. But, in the beginning, the second meaning of original unity was based upon the first. Adam and Eve's spousal meaning of their bodies found a concrete fulfillment in their marriage because they loved each other in the Lord and because of the Lord, not only as husband and wife, but most foundationally, as brother and sister in God. Similarly, in the life in the Spirit, sexual purity is also based on piety. Christian spouses are to love each other in God and because of God, as their

---

159. See TOB 57:2.

160. See LR, 211–264.

161. *ST* II–II, q. 121, a. 1, ad 3; emphasis added. For a good study of piety as a virtue, see Senovilla García, *La virtud de la piedad*.

162. TOB 57:2.

bodies are temples of the Holy Spirit, and because they share the common dignity of being brothers and sisters in Christ. Thus, there is a foundational connection between sexual purity, love, and piety. John Paul II explains that this connection offers a fuller access to the spousal meaning of the body as it is fulfilled in the vocation to marriage.

This fuller access to the spousal meaning of the body has a theological orientation in view of 1 Cor 6:20. Purity allied with piety "causes the body such a fullness of dignity in interpersonal relations that God himself is thereby glorified. Purity is the glory of the human body before God. It is the glory of God in the human body, through which masculinity and femininity are manifested."[163] In quite implicit agreement with Aquinas, John Paul II argues that from purity, as a virtue in the province of temperance, emerges a certain splendor of beauty of the human body.[164] Moreover, looking at Christ's words together with Paul's teaching, we can say that they prescribe purity in its relation to piety. Purity is here understood not only as the abstinence from unchastity, but also as the discovery of the theological dignity of the human body. In this manner, temperance as abstinence from unchastity "matures in the heart of the human being who cultivates it and who *seeks to discover and affirm the spousal meaning of the body in its integral truth.*"[165] Precisely for this reason, abstinence from unchastity within the life of grace leads to a vision of purity, which unveils the theological dignity of the human body. In fact, the enjoyment of the fruits of the victory over concupiscence, in keeping one's body with holiness and reverence, thanks to the gift of piety, reveals the human body as the temple of the Holy Spirit. Thus, Christ's appeal to the heart directs the human person towards the joy found in the augmentation of self-possession and, consequently, in the gift of self.[166] Augustine's understanding of temperance as "love giving itself entirely to that which is loved," as "love keeping itself entire and incorrupt for God,"[167] finds here a fuller theological justification.

John Paul II notes that this link between purity, temperance, love, and piety is "a *little known* guiding thread of the theology of the body."[168] This guiding thread is little known for one simple reason: it has been *forgotten* by the modern attitude which promotes the search for originality and novelty to the detriment of the value of tradition. Thus, some of the proponents of contraception postulated an *autonomous* conjugal morality without anything specifically Christian about it. They have *forgotten and made little known* this guiding thread to the theology of the body. In my opinion, the pope is reminding them about the intimate link between purity, charity, and the gift of piety. He is correcting their claim according to which, conjugal morality is completely autonomous from revelation and the magisterium. The pope is correct-

---

163. Ibid., 57:3. See Bellafiore, "Paul on the Human Body."
164. See *ST* II–II, q. 180, a. 2, ad 3; II–II, q. 141, a. 2, ad 3; TOB 57:3.
165. Ibid., 58:6; emphasis added.
166. See ibid., 58:7.
167. Augustine, *De Moribus Ecclesiae*, cap. 15, 25.
168. TOB 57:3; emphasis added. He will continue this topic in TOB 89 and 131–132.

Humble Realism

There is still an important clarification to be made regarding that false optimism that Wojtyła noted as present in the advocates of contraception's proposals.[169] Even within the ethos of redemption, the virtues of temperance or chastity do not have the power to alter all of our passions or emotions, *charging them with a sort of virtuous spontaneity of their own*. Were this the case, the activity of reason would be needed only while our passions are in training, so to speak.[170] Once again, we need to distinguish between *antecedent* and *consequent* passions.[171] Aquinas makes a very important observation regarding antecedent passions and the morality of an action. Often, these passions obscure the judgment of reason. They can do so by leading one astray from what is good. But they can also affect our *mode* of acting. What is done may be right. However, the way in which it is done may not be the most appropriate for a human person. For instance, one may be taken by the feeling of pity for someone. Moved by this feeling, one may do a good deed for him. In this case, the goodness of the act is actually *diminished*.

Indeed, "the passions of the soul may stand in a twofold relation to the judgment of reason. First, antecedently, and thus, since they obscure the judgment of reason, on which the goodness of the moral act depends, *they diminish the goodness of the act; for it is more praiseworthy to do a work of charity from the judgment of reason than from the mere passion of pity.*"[172] We are not falling into a sort of Kantian position here. Thomas is not saying that one should always act against our inclinations in order to carry out a morally good action; he is only saying that a morally good action is always better the more *human* it is. And a human act is a free and voluntary act of reason and will. For this reason, it is more praiseworthy to do a work of charity from reason (and will) than just from *antecedent* passion. The distinction is very important, because a *consequent* passion would actually increase the goodness or merit of the act. Aquinas explains the contrast in another place: "A good passion *consequent* to the judgment of reason *increases merit*; but if it *precede*, so that a man is moved to do well, rather by his passion than by the judgment of his reason, such a passion *diminishes the goodness and praiseworthiness of his action.*"[173]

---

169. See KD, 335. Although I am not primarily concerned with this other topic, I think that indirectly these clarifications will also contribute to the debate between West, Schindler, Alice von Hildebrand, and Smith. See Smith, "The Need to Read Carefully." Delaney and Smith, "Concupiscence." See also Eden, *Towards a "Climate of Chastity*," 30–32, 38–45.

170. For an excellent, sharp, and persuasive study of this peculiar topic which successfully refutes this "spontaneity view of temperance," see Butera, "On Reason's Control of the Passions."

171. See *ST* I–II, q. 24, a. 3, ad 1.

172. Ibid.; emphasis added.

173. Ibid., I–II, q. 77, a. 6, ad 2; emphasis added.

A consequent passion may result from the intensity of the will in doing what is good. The will is moved so intensely to do something good that the lower appetites "reverberate," as it were, in the movement to follow the will.[174] It may also happen that one may consent to be affected by a passion in order to do something morally good. This passion is not antecedent anymore; it is now consequent. It aids the morally good act being commanded by reason. In this case, passion also increases the goodness of the act. The point is not that one needs to deliberate for a long time in order to make better moral choices. For the virtuous, there is a need for rational discernment but not for a long deliberation. The whole point is that passions should not interfere with the rational judgment of the discernment. And this is the danger of *antecedent* passions. Consequent passions help more than they hurt. They usually make the virtuous man into a cheerful person in doing what is good. Pay close attention to this other text:

> Both choice and execution are necessary in a virtuous deed. Discernment is required for choice. For the execution of what has been decided upon, alacrity [cheerfulness in acting] is required. It is not, however, highly necessary that a man actually engaged in the execution of the deed deliberate very much about the deed. This would rather stand in the way than be of help, as Avicenna points out. Take the case of a lute player, who would be greatly handicapped if he had to give thought to each touch of the strings; or that of a penman if he had to stop and think in the formation of each letter. This is why *a passion which precedes choice hinders the act of virtue by hampering the judgment of reason necessary in choosing*. But after the choice has already been made *purely* by a rational judgment, *a passion that follows helps more than it hurts*, because even if it should disturb rational judgment somewhat, it does make for alacrity in execution.[175]

Hence, Thomas Aquinas thinks that the virtues in the province of temperance perfect our passions in a different way, depending on whether they are antecedent or consequent. One's action is not more meritorious because he is inclined to it by *antecedent* passion. Thomas thinks quite the contrary. But a virtue is to make our actions more meritorious. Hence, the perfection that temperance effects in our passions cannot consist in decreasing the merit of our actions by intensifying antecedent passions.

As Butera explains, what Aquinas proposes is that the virtue of temperance "disposes the concupiscible appetite to remain more or less still in the absence of any command from reason to move, thus preventing vehement spontaneous passions of any sort, ordinate or inordinate, from arising in the concupiscible appetite prior to reason's immediate command."[176] Moreover, temperance "also disposes the concupiscible appetite to obey reason's command so that a person may incite, increase, decrease, or

---

174. See ibid., I–II, q. 24, a. 3, ad 1.
175. *De Veritate*, q. 26, a. 7, ad 3.
176. Butera, "On Reason's Control," 133.

curb a passion as needed."[177] Hence, what Aquinas seems to deny is that temperance effects an affective spontaneity on antecedent passions, making them virtuous. Such a position would really contradict Thomas's teaching on the need for prudence in order to be virtuous. For example, someone may be inclined to eat a certain kind or amount of breakfast in the morning before he makes a choice or judgment about it. But that inclination can hardly be considered as virtuous when the circumstances change and he is required to eat substantially more. That particular day, he may have to do a great amount of physical exercise. Affective spontaneity cannot replace right reason. Butera's interpretation is solidly supported by Thomas's view of Adam before the fall and the blessed in heaven.[178] Before the fall, Adam experienced only *consequent* passions.[179] In the fallen state, temperance disposes our concupiscible appetite not to move vehemently antecedent to reason's command. It can certainly move not so vehemently, especially if one considers the *fomes*. Moreover, temperance disposes the concupiscible appetite to move consequent to reason's command.

Now, based on this brief Thomistic explanation, we can approach John Paul's understanding of the growth into the virtue of chastity as a process which has to begin from these *realistic* premises. Certainly, we are in need of integrating our sensuality and affectivity. Such a need is greater ever since original sin. "The truth of original sin explains a very basic and very widespread evil—that a human being encountering a person of the other sex does not simply and spontaneously experience love, but a feeling muddied by the longing to enjoy, which often overshadows loving kindness and robs love of its true nature, leaving only the outward appearance intact."[180] We do not experience the preternatural gift of integrity that our first parents enjoyed before the fall and that accounted for their original unity, their interpersonal communion, and the absence of shame. This is not our situation anymore and make no mistake, it never will be *on this earth*.[181] Not even baptism takes away the wound of concupiscence.[182] This is the traditional teaching of the Council of Trent.[183] And Trent's teaching is also that of John Paul II and Karol Wojtyła. Our continuous wrestling with concupiscence permeates our earthly existence, even after baptism. Occasions of sin *should be avoided* for this very reason. We are not neutral with respect to evil. We cannot be naïve. We are *already inclined to sin from the get go*. For this reason, we should pay attention to the following advice from Wojtyła:

> *No-one can demand of himself* either that he should experience *no sensual reactions at all*, or *that they should immediately yield* just because the will does

---

177. Ibid., 134.
178. See *De Veritate*, q. 26, a. 8, c.
179. See *ST* I, q. 95, a. 2, c.
180. LR, 161.
181. See TOB 49:4.
182. See *CCC* 1264.
183. See DS 1515.

> not consent, or even because it declares itself definitely against. This is a point of *great importance* to those who seek to practice continence. There is a difference between not wanting and not feeling, not experiencing.[184]

Hence, according to Wojtyła, temperance and chastity cannot charge our appetites with a sort of virtuous spontaneity of their own that would allow one to demand of himself not to experience antecedent passions. As our author points out, one may not want to experience or to feel a sensual reaction. One can certainly make that free choice. However, no one can demand of himself not to experience or not to feel. Moreover, no one can demand of himself that once one makes the free decision of not wanting to experience or feel, one's passions yield immediately and without opposition. One cannot demand any of this *after the fall*. As John Paul explains, "the fact that the energies of the spirit succeed in mastering the forces of the body does *not take away the possibility of their reciprocal opposition*."[185] This realism was certainly lacking in the advocates of contraception. It really opposes their false optimism. Even within the context of the redemption of man's heart, the development of the virtue of chastity has to humbly take into account the wound of concupiscence (*fomes peccati*). As Trent says, we can bravely resist by the grace of Jesus Christ.[186] But it would be very imprudent to attempt to develop virtue as if original sin would not have wounded our nature.

John Paul offers a way to overcome the latent pessimism in the proposal of the contraception advocates. He explains that the doctrine of justification is "the expression of faith in *the anthropological and ethical realism of the redemption brought about by Christ*, which Paul, in a context already known to us, also calls redemption of the body."[187] This justification "is essential for the inner man and is intended precisely for that 'heart' to which Christ appealed when he spoke about 'purity' and 'impurity' in the moral sense."[188] Based on this realism, the pope invites us to learn the lesson from the old law and cling to God's help in this endeavor. As Thomas would say in his realism as well, instead of presuming on our own powers, let us have recourse to the help of grace.[189] After all, in the theology of the spousal meaning of the body, the omnipotent God is one's friend. And "what we can do through our friends, we can do in some way through ourselves."[190]

---

184. LR, 162; emphasis added.
185. TOB 67:2; emphasis added.
186. See DS 1515.
187. TOB 52:1.
188. Ibid., 51:4.
189. See *ST* I–II, q. 98, a. 2, ad. 3; q. 106, a. 3, c.
190. Ibid., I–II, q. 5, a. 5, ad 1. Translation altered.

9

Fulfillment and Eschatological Anticipation

The Fullest Sense of the Spousal Meaning of the Body

John Paul's theology of the spousal meaning of the body reaches its apex in his detailed commentary on Matthew 22:24–30, Mark 12:18–27, and Luke 20:35–36. These passages recount the Sadducees's controversy with Jesus on the question of the resurrection. Even if the Sadducees's argument is based on Deuteronomy 25:5–10, according to the Lord, their argument is fallacious. They know neither the scriptures nor the power of God. In the future resurrection, human beings regain their bodies in their masculinity and femininity.[1] However, at that moment, they will take neither wife nor husband, for marriage between man and woman "belongs exclusively to this world."[2] In man's definitive and eternal fatherland, there is a new state of human life later confirmed by Christ's Resurrection.[3] After the resurrection, the meaning of being male and female will be constituted and understood in a different way. It will not be exactly the same as in the second sense of original unity. There will be no procreation in heaven.[4] Even if there will be the most intimate communion among the saints, there will be no marriage. Moreover, in the biblical passages John Paul is commenting on, Jesus offers an additional argument in favor of the resurrection, based on Ex 3:2–6,14. He appeals to God's mighty power when he reminds his interlocutors that God is the God of Abraham, Isaac, and Jacob. Since he is not the God of the dead but of the living, there must be a resurrection. What is more, "the God whom the Sadducees deprive of this power, is no longer the true God of their Fathers, but *the God of their hypothesis and interpretations*."[5]

Christ's appeal to the resurrection allows "us in some way to reread in a new way—that is, *in all its depth*—the whole revealed meaning of the body."[6] The pope speaks of the spousal meaning of the body *in all its depth*, that is, in its fullest sense.

---

1. See TOB 66:2; *ScG* IV. 88.
2. TOB 66:2.
3. See Rom 6:5–11; Phil 3:20.
4. See TOB 66:2; *ScG* IV.83.
5. TOB 65:7; emphasis added.
6. Ibid., 69:8; emphasis added.

As it was explained in chapter 7, in the spousal analogy, the *primum analogatum* is not the conjugal love between husband and wife, but Christ's spousal love for the church. Thus, the eschatological fulfillment of the spousal meaning of the body is of axial importance to understand both marriage and celibacy. These two ways of fulfilling the spousal meaning of the body on this earth are illuminated by the eschatological fulfillment of Christ's love for the church. Thus, "these reflections have a *fundamental significance for the whole theology of the body, for understanding both marriage and celibacy for the Kingdom of heaven.*"[7] In the encounter with the Sadducees, we find the revelation of the *ultimate fulfillment of the spousal meaning of the body* as the human person's vocation to charity, a fulfillment marked by two important factors: the spiritualization and the divinization of the human body.

Spiritualization of the Body as Ultimate Integration

Luke 20:27–40 speaks of "a spiritualization of man according to a dimension that is different from that of earthly life (and even different from that of the very beginning)."[8] The spiritualization of the body cannot mean that we will become an angelic person. The resurrection implies that we will keep our bodylines.[9] Angels are pure spirits, intellectual beings who are naturally incorporeal. For this reason, Christ's comparison with the angels does not signify a dis-incarnation of the human person. Rather, it refers to a spiritualization of our somatic nature. It points to a further and inexperienced degree of integration in man. As Thomas teaches, "the body of the risen will be spiritual, indeed, but not because it is a spirit."[10] Instead, "it will be spiritual because it will be entirely subject to the spirit."[11] John Paul II describes this same idea in Thomistic terms. He characterizes such spiritualization as an unprecedented "new submission of the body to the spirit,"[12] or as a "perfect system of powers in the reciprocal relations between what is spiritual and what is bodily in man."[13] Indeed, Aquinas also taught that the resurrected body "will be entirely subject to the soul—the divine power will achieve this—not only in regard to its being, but also in regard to action, passion, movements, and bodily qualities."[14] Thanks to this spiritualization of the human body or new degree of integration, "man will no longer experience the opposition between what is spiritual and what is bodily in him."[15]

7. Ibid., 72:7; emphasis added.
8. Ibid., 66:5.
9. See John 5:25, 28; *ScG* IV.79, 84.
10. *ScG* IV.86.
11. Ibid.
12. TOB 66:5.
13. Ibid., 67:1.
14. *ScG* IV.86.
15. Ibid.

To explain the spiritualization of the body, the pope explicitly appeals to Thomas Aquinas's *hylomorphism*. Thomas's reflection about the resurrection led him "to abandon Plato's philosophical conception on the relation between the soul and the body and to draw near to Aristotle's view."[16] In Aquinas's time, the common opinion was exactly the other way around. Influenced by the Latin Averroists, it was thought that Aristotle's anthropology jeopardized the immortality of the soul and personal identity after death. Thus, in light of that historical context, John Paul II commends Thomas. The Angelic Doctor realized that the resurrection attests that the human body "is not, contrary to Plato, only temporarily linked with the soul (as its earthly prison, as Plato maintained), but that together with the soul it constitutes the unity and integrity of the human being."[17] Furthermore, the resurrection shows that "*man's eschatological perfection and happiness* cannot be understood as a state of the soul alone, separated (according to Plato, liberated) from the body, but *must be understood as the definitively and perfectly integrated state of man* brought about by such a union of the soul with the body that it definitively qualifies and assures this perfect integrity."[18] Consequently, the spiritualization of the body should *not* be understood as the definitive victory of the spirit *against the body*. Rather, it is the final victory *against concupiscence* as a law that opposes the spirit. In the final victory of the resurrection, "the possibility of another law at war with the law of my mind is *completely* eliminated."[19]

Similarly, Paul's anthropology of the resurrection concentrates on the inner structure of the human person. The resurrected body will be imperishable, glorious, full of power, and spiritual. There is a clear contrast between the interrelationship between the faculties in man before and after the resurrection. Paul's literary style often uses antithesis in order to bring closer together what is being contrasted. He uses one of those antitheses in order to illustrate the change brought about by the resurrection in the inner structure of the human person, in his faculties or powers. Thus, by means of an antithetical metaphor, 1 Corinthians 15:42–43 compares the body sown in weakness, and the spiritual body raised full of power. The human body that rises from the earthly seed seems weak because it is perishable, subject to death, and because it is *psychikon*.[20] This last Greek adjective signifies what is here meant by the term "carnal," as opposed to spiritual. It is an adjective directly linked with concupiscence.[21] As a result, the expression a *psychikon* body signifies "sensuality as

---

16. TOB 66:6.

17. Ibid. See, for instance, Aquinas's explanations on the individuality and personal identity of the separated soul in *ScG* IV.81.

18. TOB 66:6; emphasis added. See *ScG* IV.79; *ST* I, q. 89, a. 1, c.

19. TOB 67:2. See Matt 22:30; Mark 12:25; Luke 20:35-36; Rom 7:23.

20. This pejorative adjective is often translated as "natural." Paul uses it not only in 1 Cor 15:44 but also in 2:14, and 15:46.

21. See 2 Cor 1:12; 10:4.

the force that often determines man inasmuch as, by living in the knowledge of good and evil, he is often urged or pushed, as it were, toward evil."[22]

By contrast, the resurrected body will overcome this carnal weakness and become powerful and immortal, because of its spiritualization. The spiritualization of the resurrected body entails that "the spirit will gain a just supremacy over the body, spirituality over sensuality."[23] Again, what is meant here is not a sort of Platonic liberation from the senses and all that is sensual. The contrast is not between matter and soul. Rather, the contrast is between the whole human person affected by sin and opposed to the Spirit, and the whole human person under the influence of Christ's life-giving Spirit. Thus, the resurrection of the body implies that the human person will remain a bodily creature. Consequently, the spiritualization of the resurrected body is far from a Platonic opposition between body and soul. Instead, it "should signify precisely the *perfect sensitivity of the senses*, their *perfect harmonization* with the activity of the human spirit in truth and in freedom."[24]

Once again, John Paul's interpretation is grounded in the theology of Thomas Aquinas. The Angelic Doctor speaks about the *agility* of the resurrected body in very similar terms: "[T]he soul which will enjoy the divine vision, united to its ultimate end, will in all matters experience the fulfillment of desire. And since it is out of the soul's desire that the body is moved, the consequence will be the body's utter obedience to the spirit's slightest wish. Hence, the bodies of the blessed when they rise are going to have agility."[25] Aquinas adds a little bit later the following consideration: "[J]ust as the soul which enjoys God will have its desire fulfilled in the achievement of every good, so also will its desire be filled in the removal of every evil, for with the highest good no evil has a place."[26] Now, keeping in mind Wojtyła's anthropology of love, one could say that the spiritualization of the resurrected body is *the ultimate integration*, an integration that surpasses even that of our first parents before the fall. John Paul hints at that same idea, manifesting his realistic optimism: "St. Paul sees the future resurrection as a certain *restitutio in integrum*, that is, as the reintegration and at the same time as the attainment of the fullness of humanity."[27] Such reintegration is not a mere coming back to the beginning, to the state of original justice, but "an introduction to a new fullness."[28]

22. TOB 72:4.
23. Ibid.
24. Ibid.; emphasis added.
25. *ScG* IV.86.
26. Ibid.
27. TOB 72:3.
28. Ibid.

Divinization of the Body

Luke 20:27–40 also makes a reference to the "sons of God." This reference shows that the human person's state after the resurrection will not only be one of spiritualization, but also one of divinization. Indeed, "the degree of spiritualization proper to eschatological man will have its source in the degree of his divinization, incomparably superior to what can be reached in earthly life."[29] The totality of the human person, body and soul, will participate in this divinization as the fruit of grace. As the pope puts it, the entire human person will partake "of God's self-communication in his very divinity."[30] To take neither wife nor husband is explained "by the 'eschatological authenticity' of the response to that 'self-communication' of the Divine Subject that will constitute the beatifying experience of God's gift of self."[31]

The human person's gift of self as the requisite answer to God's gift of himself *excludes* marriage between man and woman. *It exalts the virginal state of the body as the fulfillment of its spousal meaning.* This is the fulfillment of the spiritual marriage that both Aquinas and John of the Cross talked about. In heaven, people will see God in different levels of depth. Charity will be the determining factor of this hierarchy. The more charity one has, the more perfectly he or she will see God, because he or she will be more apt for a fuller participation in the light of glory: "[T]he intellect which has more of the light of glory will see God the more perfectly; and he will have a fuller participation of the light of glory who has more charity."[32] The reason is this, that he who has more charity has a greater desire. Such a desire makes the desiring person more receptive. Thus, "he who possesses the more charity, will see God the more perfectly, and will be the more beatified."[33] As John Paul would say, he who has greater charity will find a greater fulfillment of the spousal meaning of the body.

Moreover, "in this reciprocal gift of self by man, a gift that will become completely and definitively beatifying as the response worthy of a personal subject to God's gift of himself, the virginity or rather the virginal state of the body will manifest itself completely *as the eschatological fulfillment of the spousal meaning of the body*, as the specific sign and authentic expression of personal subjectivity as a whole."[34] The ultimate fulfillment of the spousal meaning of the body excludes marriage between man and woman not only because there will no procreation but also because "a love of such depth and power of concentration on God himself will be born in the person that it completely absorbs the person's whole psychosomatic subjectivity."[35]

---

29. Ibid., 67:3.
30. Ibid.
31. Ibid., 68:2.
32. *ST* I, q. 12, a. 6, c.
33. Ibid.
34. TOB 68:3; emphasis added.
35. Ibid.

Obviously, John Paul does not believe that in heaven there is an alienation from other human beings. Sharing the inner life of God implies a rediscovery of oneself and a perfect intersubjectivity as well. There will be a deep relationship of communion with the rest of the blessed, in God. Thus, "we profess faith in the communion of saints (*communio sanctorum*) and profess it in organic connection with faith in the resurrection of the body."[36] That communion of charity with God and others "means the true and definitive fulfillment of human subjectivity and, on this basis, *the definitive fulfillment of the 'spousal' meaning of the body.*"[37] Therefore, there is a perennial or constant element present in the beginning, in the historical experience, and in the eschatological fulfillment: man is created as a person in the image and likeness of God, and is called to charity, to a life in the communion of persons. This is exactly the very essence of the spousal meaning of the body.

These considerations should put things in their proper place. They exclude any trace of sexualization of the Christian vocation. According to John Paul II, "marriage and procreation *do not definitively determine the original and fundamental meaning of being a body nor of being, as a body, male and female.*"[38] What determines this spousal meaning definitively, instead, is the vision of God and the communion of saints. In this way, "the spousal meaning of the body in the resurrection to the future life will perfectly correspond both to the fact that man as male-female is a person, created in the image and likeness of God, and to the fact that this image is realized in the communion of persons."[39] We are clearly talking about charity in the image of glory. Such charity is both personal and communitarian. It manifests the perfected freedom of the gift in the communion with God and all the saints.

In 1 Cor 15:27, Paul uses another antithesis in order to bring closer together what is being contrasted. He compares the first man, Adam, with Christ as the second Adam. Paul explains that just as we have borne the image of the man of earth, we will bear the image of the heavenly man, or the man of the resurrection, whose prototype is Christ.[40] There is no real opposition between the man of the earth and that of the resurrection. Instead, the man of the resurrection, modeled after the second Adam, should be viewed as the fulfillment and confirmation of the man taken from the earth. The latter carries within himself a "desire for glory," that is, "a tendency and capacity to become glorious in the image of the risen Christ," or put differently, "a particular potentiality (which is capacity and readiness) for receiving all that the second Adam became, namely, Christ: what he became in his resurrection."[41] Consequently, what the man of the resurrection fulfills and confirms "corresponds to the psychosomatic

---

36. Ibid., 68:4.
37. Ibid.; emphasis added.
38. Ibid., 69:4; emphasis added.
39. Ibid.
40. See 1 Cor 15:49.
41. TOB 71:3.

constitution of humanity in the realm of eternal destiny, that is, in the thought and plan of the one who created man from the beginning in his image and likeness."[42] There is a universality to be underlined here: "[E]veryone bears in himself the image of Adam, and everyone is also called to bear in himself the image of Christ, the image of the Risen One."[43]

Continence for the Kingdom and the Spousal Meaning of the Body

John Paul II proceeds to explain the spousal meaning of the body as it is fulfilled on this earth by those who are continent for the sake of the Kingdom.[44] Again, his treatment of this question is not comprehensive but quite selective. His goal is to analyze the complementary relationship between marriage and continence for the sake of the Kingdom, so as to provide some additional theological foundations to his future commentary on HV. Indeed, these two ways of fulfilling on this earth the spousal meaning of the body illuminate each other: "[M]arriage helps us to understand continence for the Kingdom of heaven, but also that continence itself throws a particular light on marriage viewed in the mystery of creation and redemption."[45] John Paul's main interests lies in this second aspect of that mutual enlightenment, on how continence illumines marriage in the mystery of Creation and Redemption. He offers two main arguments that relate celibacy or virginity with the fulfillment of the spousal meaning of the body. On the one hand, celibacy or virginity is a sign of that ultimate fulfillment in the state of glory which we explained previously; it is *an eschatological anticipation*. On the other hand, celibacy or virginity is also *one way of fulfilling on this earth the spousal meaning of the body*. Continence for the Kingdom is a gift of self to Christ, *the Bridegroom of souls*.[46]

Eschatological Anticipation

The pope concentrates his analysis on Matthew 19:11–12 and 1 Corinthians 7. The call to continence finds an echo in the human soul living in the conditions of temporality. This echo is based on an *eschatological anticipation*. The human person called to continence for the sake of the Kingdom "seems to *anticipate*, already in these conditions of temporality, what man will share in *the future resurrection*."[47] Christ's words concerning virginity are found in the context of his appeal to the beginning, in the dis-

---

42. Ibid.
43. Ibid., 71:4.
44. See McDermott, "Virginity." Tettamanzi, *La verginità*. For a broader study, see Selin, *Priestly Celibacy*.
45. TOB 76:6.
46. See *In IV Sent.*, d. 27, q. 1, a. 2, qc. 3, ad 3; a. 3, qc. 1, ad 3.
47. TOB 73:1; emphasis added.

pute with the Pharisees concerning marriage's indissolubility. Having listened to these words, the disciples claim that if this is the condition of man in relation to woman, it is *not advantageous* to marry.[48] Christ's answer takes no position about their statement. He does not follow their rather utilitarian line of reasoning. Continence for the Kingdom is not based on an opposition to marriage or on a deficient appreciation of its value. Christ chose to link it with his teaching on marriage to indicate that continence for the sake of Kingdom is an exception to marriage, the latter being the general rule of life for the human person on this earth. Thus, Jesus appeals to another principle, to another rule for understanding his words: not everyone can understand them. Such a state of life is both a choice and a vocation. It is to be undertaken in view of both these things, considered in their own value. Christ's words "do not express a commandment that is binding for all, but a counsel that regards only some persons."[49] This is an exception, a charismatic choice, and an orientation toward that eschatological state of the glorified body, wherein human beings will take neither husband nor wife. Thus, there is a distinction between continence *in* the Kingdom or in the Triumphant Church and continence *for* the Kingdom in the Pilgrim Church. Without confusing one with the other, continence *for* the Kingdom should be viewed as an anticipation and sign of the state of glory.

For Christ's audience, marriage was so common that only physical impotence could justify an exception. What Jesus is about to teach concerning the meaning of the body is a turning point. It is something new and difficult to understand, even for the disciples. Appealing to the mentality of his audience, Jesus takes as a point of departure for his explanation three categories of "eunuchs."[50] The first two categories appeal to the non-voluntary inborn or acquired physical defects whereby the procreative power of marriage is impossible. Instead, the third category refers to those who make themselves eunuchs voluntarily, and for the sake of the supernatural finality of the Kingdom. Continence, therefore, is a choice connected in this earthly life with renunciation and with a spiritual effort.[51] It also is intrinsically related to the fact that in the Kingdom, human persons take neither husband nor wife because God will be all in all.[52] Thus, to live in continence in the earthly situation is *a charismatic sign of the absolute fulfillment of the spousal meaning of the body in the eschatological virginity of the risen man.*

The *primum analogatum* for spousal love and for the spousal meaning of the body is not marriage between man and woman, but Christ and the church: "This way of existing as a human being (male and female) *points out the eschatological virginity of the risen man, in which*, I would say, *the absolute and eternal spousal meaning of the*

---

48. See Matt 19:10.
49. TOB 73:4. See LG 42.
50. See Matt 19:10-12.
51. See TOB 74:5.
52. See 1 Cor 15:28.

glorified body will be revealed in union with God himself, by seeing him face to face, glorified moreover through the union of a perfect intersubjectivity that will unite all the sharers in the other world, men and women, in the mystery of the communion of saints. Earthly continence for the Kingdom of God is without doubt *a sign that indicates this truth and this reality.*"[53] Continence for the Kingdom becomes *a sign that the body tends towards glorification.* Against the pessimism of the advocates of contraception, it shows the power of the redemption of the body. Moreover, since Christ himself made this choice for the Kingdom of heaven, this kind of continence "carries above all the imprint of likeness to Christ."[54]

The expression "for the Kingdom of heaven" indicates motivation. Compared with the tradition of the Old Testament, Christ gave to celibacy and virginity an unprecedented privileged place of honor of the utmost relevance for the ethos and theology of the body, but *not at the cost of the value of marriage*. Moving beyond the utilitarianism inherent in the disciples's words in Matthew 19:10, Christ has appealed to the beginning, indicating indirectly that marriage possesses a fundamental, universal, and ordinary value for the kingdom. Likewise, chosen for supernatural reasons, continence possesses a particular and exceptional value for this same Kingdom. For those called to continence, the Kingdom is both an objective supernatural finality or end, and a subjective purpose or motivation. The person choosing continence needs to be aware of its end in the power of a deep faith, which enables one to believe in the future fulfillment of the Kingdom and allows him to identify with the truth and the reality of this same kingdom.

Christ does not "hide the travail that such a decision and its long-lasting consequences can have for man, for the normal (and also noble) inclinations of his nature."[55] It implies a conscious and voluntary renunciation and self-sacrifice. The person called to this vocation, with full awareness and without diminishing its value, has to break away from "that within man which, by the will of the Creator himself, leads to marriage and to go toward continence."[56] As John Paul II says a bit later, "The one who renounces marriage also renounces generation as the foundation of the community of the family composed of parents and children."[57] Such travail, though, must be lived as a participation in the mystery of the Redemption of the body: "[T]he one who consciously chooses such continence chooses in some sense a particular participation in the mystery of the redemption (of the body); he wishes to complete it in a particular way in his own flesh."[58] Yet, this participation does not lead to frustration but to personal fulfillment and happiness.

53. TOB 75:1; emphasis added.
54. Ibid.
55. Ibid., 76:5.
56. Ibid., 77:1.
57. Ibid., 77:3.
58. Ibid., 76:3. See 1 Cor 1:24.

The person called to continence has to *enlarge his view up to the resurrection of the body*. To do so does not eliminate the natural condition of historical man. For this reason, whoever answers a call to a vocation in this state of life "must make this decision by subordinating the sinfulness of his own humanity to the powers that flow from the mystery of the redemption of the body."[59] The sincere gift of self is fulfilled in celibacy or virginity in accordance with the fulfillment of the spousal meaning of the body. From the viewpoint of motivation, continence for the Kingdom *lies in between renunciation and love*. As is known, the Kingdom of heaven is God's Kingdom, the same one Christ preached both in its temporal realization and its eschatological fulfillment. The temporal establishment of the Kingdom is both its beginning and the preparation for its ultimate fulfillment. Hence, when God calls some to continence, "he calls them to participate uniquely in the establishment of the Kingdom of God on earth, through which the definitive stage of the Kingdom of heaven is begun and prepared."[60] This dimension of celibacy or virginity underlines a *renunciation*. It speaks about the denying of oneself, the taking up of one's cross, and the following of Christ in giving up marriage and a family of one's own in order to "contribute more to the realization of the kingdom of God in its earthly dimension with the prospect of the eschatological fulfillment."[61] But the motivating factor for those who are continent for the Kingdom is *love*. Their continence is a vivid sign of their love for God and the church. And just as those called to marriage, the ones God calls to celibacy and virginity are called *to integration and purity of heart*. They also "need to keep watch over the concupiscence of the body."[62] Since the same power of the redemption of the body is at work here, their very presence is a living sign of hope for married people, who also need to be transformed by Christ's grace so as to attain integration and purity. John Paul II is laying the groundwork here to overcome the advocates of contraception's pessimism.

Spousal Dimension

Continence and marriage are both vocations of historical man. They bring about his self-fulfillment in different ways. Continence implies an invitation to a certain solitude for God. But this solitude does *not* imply a denial of the human person's social nature. In continence for the Kingdom, the human person reaches self-fulfillment preserving "the integral truth of his humanity, without losing along the way any of the essential elements of the vocation of the person created in the image and likeness of God."[63] As a result, this solitude does not entail a renunciation to *all* friendships

59. TOB 77:4.
60. Ibid., 79:2.
61. Ibid., 79:3. See Luke 9:23.
62. TOB 77:4.
63. Ibid., 77:1.

or communions of persons. It only means renunciation to conjugal friendship and to physical paternity or maternity. Even so, this initial renunciation is transformed by a certain abundance in other friendships, in other forms of the communion of persons, even in other forms of paternity and maternity. The person who lives celibacy or virginity is able to discover in his solitude for God "a new and *even fuller form of intersubjective communion with others*."[64] He "has the awareness that in this way he can realize himself differently, and in some sense *more than in marriage*, by becoming a sincere gift for others."[65] Thus, solitude for God ends up meaning a *fuller* way of being in communion with other human persons, an even greater fulfillment of the human person's vocation to the gift of self for others.

Since one's call to celibacy or virginity lies in between renunciation and love, in order to make a mature choice, a person called to continence for the Kingdom needs an authentic consciousness of the value of the disposition of masculinity and femininity for marriage. One would not know what he chooses, if he does not know what he is renouncing. For this reason, "this renunciation is at the same time *a particular form of affirmation* of the value from which the unmarried person consistently abstains by following the evangelical counsel."[66] Such a renunciation entails a recognition of the particular way in which the same spousal meaning of the body which grounds celibacy or virginity is also fulfilled in marriage. Thus, one's renunciation to marriage becomes "indispensable for the clearer recognition of the *same* spousal meaning of the body in the whole ethos of human life and above all in the ethos of conjugal and family life."[67] This is made more evident when one recalls that the key to understanding "the sacramentality of marriage is the spousal love of Christ for the Church (see Eph 5:22–23), of Christ who was son of the Virgin, who himself was a virgin, that is, a eunuch for the Kingdom of heaven in the most perfect sense of the term."[68]

At the same time, the difficult demands of celibacy or virginity are accepted *in the name of love*. Indeed, the spousal meaning of the body is also the foundation of Christ's call to continence. The Kingdom "is the fullness of good that the human heart desires beyond the limits of all that can be its portion in earthly life; it is the greatest fullness of God endowing man with the gift of grace."[69] Despite the severity, seriousness, and responsibility of this vocation, "what shines and gleams is love: *love as the readiness to make the exclusive gift of self for the kingdom of God.*"[70] This gift of self, understood as a renunciation but realized out of love, is directed to Christ as *the* Bridegroom of souls. Thus, celibacy or virginity fulfills the spousal meaning of

64. Ibid., 77:2; emphasis added.
65. Ibid.; emphasis added.
66. Ibid., 81:3; emphasis added.
67. Ibid.; emphasis added.
68. Ibid., 81:4.
69. Ibid., 79:7.
70. Ibid., 79:8; emphasis added.

the body: "It is precisely in relation to this concept, *to this truth about the spousal meaning of the human body, that one must reread and understand the words of Christ about continence*."[71] Indeed, John Paul explains that "in this call to continence 'for the kingdom of heaven,' first the disciples and then the whole living Tradition of the Church quickly *discovered the love for Christ himself as the Bridegroom of the Church, Bridegroom of souls, to whom he has given himself to the end in the mystery of his Passover and of the Eucharist*."[72] We already know that both Thomas Aquinas and John of the Cross inserted themselves into that same tradition which the pope mentions here. Grounded in it, the pope conceives celibacy or virginity as "*the act of a particular response to the love of the Divine Bridegroom*, and therefore *acquired the meaning of an act of spousal love*, that is, of *spousal gift of self with the end of answering in a particular way the Redeemer's spousal love*; a gift of self understood as a renunciation, but realized above all out of love."[73]

In relation to the spousal meaning of the body, the call to voluntary continence finds a full guarantee and motivation. In Genesis 2:23–25, the human person's call to love and communion manifested that the spousal meaning of the body is the foundation for one's vocation to marriage. Indeed, "the choice of marriage as it was instituted by the Creator 'from the beginning' presupposes *the consciousness and inner acceptance of the spousal meaning of the body*."[74] In Matthew 19:11–12, Christ also grounds virginity or celibacy in the human person's call to love and communion, in the spousal meaning of the body. He does so when he clarifies that it is *for the Kingdom*. If the human person chooses continence for the Kingdom, he renounces freely the gift of marriage in order to give himself totally to Christ as *the* Bridegroom. Thus, celibacy or virginity "is made *on the basis of the full consciousness of the spousal meaning, which masculinity and femininity contain in themselves*."[75]

The spousal character of virginity is marked by a certain fruitfulness in the Spirit, by spiritual fatherhood and motherhood. Just as conjugal love matures by procreation and parenthood, so the spousal love of those who live continence for the Kingdom matures in spiritual fatherhood or motherhood: "[S]pousal love that finds its expression in continence 'for the kingdom of heaven' must lead in its normal development to 'fatherhood' or 'motherhood' in the spiritual sense ..., in a way analogous to conjugal love, which *matures in physical fatherhood and motherhood* and is confirmed in them precisely as spousal love."[76] In turn, physical generation is not the whole story about human procreation within conjugal love. Those who live celibacy or virginity can be a sign in this regard for those who are married. They can help them realize that "physical

71. Ibid., 80:5; emphasis added.
72. Ibid., 79:9; emphasis added. See John 13:1; 19:30.
73. TOB 79:9; emphasis added.
74. Ibid., 80:6; emphasis added.
75. Ibid., 80:7; emphasis added.
76. Ibid., 78:5.

generation also fully corresponds to its meaning *only if it is completed by fatherhood and motherhood in the spirit,* whose expression and fruit is the whole educational work of the parents in regard to the children born of their bodily conjugal union."[77] We will come back to this affirmation, when we analyze John Paul's understanding of human procreation within his adequate anthropology.

Virginity and Marriage

Virginity and marriage are both vocations grounded in the spousal meaning of the body. They are two ways of exercising charity on this earth. They illuminate each other. They do so, not only with respect to procreation, as was just suggested. Additionally, those who live celibacy and virginity make evident for those who are married that human or natural conjugal love reaches its perfection in supernatural conjugal charity. Using the famous words of Fulton Sheen, it takes three to get married: God and the spouses.[78] Jesus Christ must be at the center of one's marriage. Thus, "perfect *conjugal* love must be marked by the faithfulness and the gift *to the one and only Bridegroom* (and also by the faithfulness and gift of the Bridegroom to the one and only Bride) *on which religious profession and priestly celibacy are based.*"[79] In this sense, both marriage and virginity are two ways of living out the spousal meaning of the body as one's supernatural vocation to charity. As John Paul says, "the nature of the one as well as the other love is spousal, that is, expressed through the complete gift of self. The one as well as the other love tends to express that spousal meaning of the body, which has been inscribed from the beginning in the personal structure of man and woman."[80]

Christ implicitly points to the superiority of continence for the Kingdom of heaven with respect to marriage. Paul makes it explicit in 1 Corinthians 7:38. However, this superiority "*never* means, in the authentic tradition of the Church, *a disparagement of marriage or a belittling of its essential value.*"[81] It is based neither in any implicit or explicit Manichean position nor in the fact that celibates or virgins abstain from the conjugal act. Instead, "the evangelical and genuinely Christian superiority of virginity, of continence, is thus *dictated by the motive of the Kingdom of heaven.*"[82] Celibacy and marriage do not oppose two classes of Christians, those who are perfect on the mere basis of continence, and those who are imperfect. Tradition, based on Matthew 19:21, speaks about the *status perfectionis* in view of one's life informed by the evangelical counsels of poverty, chastity, and obedience. And, indeed, "the *evangelical counsels*

---

77. Ibid.
78. See Sheen, *Three to Get Married.*
79. TOB 78:4; emphasis added.
80. Ibid.
81. Ibid., 77:5; emphasis added.
82. Ibid., 77:6; emphasis added.

undoubtedly help one to reach a fuller love."[83] Nevertheless, *perfection is measured by charity*. One thing is the objective superiority of a state of life, inasmuch as it *helps* one to reach a fuller love. Another thing is the subjective growth one actually acquires in his or her corresponding objective state of life. Someone who is married may love more and, consequently, be more perfect than another person who, for instance, is part of a religious order: "[A] person who does not live in the state of perfection (that is, in an institution that bases its plan of life on the vows of poverty, chastity, and obedience) or in a religious institute, but in the world, can *de facto* reach a higher degree of perfection—the measure of which is love—than a person who lives in the state of perfection with a lesser degree of love."[84]

1 Corinthians 7:25–38 is a *magisterial* text in the measure in which it teaches the doctrine that Christ *the* Teacher handed down to the apostles. Moreover, it is also a *pastoral* text, for it is marked by a certain emphasis due to the concrete situation of the community of Corinth. Just like Jesus, Paul underlines in 1 Corinthians 7:25 that virginity or continence flows from a counsel and not from a commandment. Paul adds personal advice or counsel. He says that the one who voluntarily refrains from marriage in order to be like him (a virgin for the Kingdom) does even better.[85] Yet, "the Apostle clearly realized that, when he encouraged abstinence from marriage, he had to highlight, at the same time, a way of understanding marriage that would be in agreement with the whole evangelical order of values."[86] Aquinas agrees with this interpretation and, for this reason, he comments on this text by pointing out that some Christians filled with zeal but lacking in wisdom went so far as to condemn marriage.[87] Consequently, as the pope clarifies, "it is not a question of discernment between good and evil, but only between good and better."[88] Paul's argumentation to justify his advice appeals to his own experience of the practice of the evangelical counsel of celibacy.

Paul would like to spare the Corinthians from the "troubles of the flesh" inherent to the married life.[89] Conjugal love is a *difficult* love. This is a very *realistic* observation. As John Paul comments, in this Pauline expression, "one should see a justified warning for those who think—as at times young people do—that conjugal union and life should bring them only happiness and joy."[90] Moreover, in order to prepare the ground for his teaching on continence, Paul points out the transitory character of the temporal world. Thereby, he is advising those who have wives to live as though they

---

83. Ibid., 78:3; emphasis added.
84. Ibid., 78:3. This agrees with *ST* II–II, q. 152, a. 4, ad 2.
85. See 1 Cor 7:7, 36–38.
86. TOB 84:6.
87. See 1Tim 4:2–3; *Super I Cor.*, cap. 7, lect. 1, n. 313.
88. TOB 82:6.
89. See 1 Cor 7:28.
90. TOB 83:3.

had none.[91] The Apostle renders the content of Christ's expression "for the Kingdom" by stating that the unmarried person (the virgin or celibate) is anxious about what is the Lord's, about how to please him.[92] Appealing to Luke as a disciple of Paul, "being anxious" must be understood as seeking the Kingdom, the better part: the one thing that is necessary.[93] Paul uses this expression in the same sense. With it, he describes his being anxious for all the churches and his seeking Christ through solicitude for the problems of the brothers as members of the body of Christ.[94] Hence, the unmarried, being anxious about what is the Lord's, should be understood as seeking God's Kingdom. In one sense, since the entire earth and everything in it belongs to the Lord, this solicitude is universal.[95] Yet, in another sense, what is the Lord's corresponds to what is Jesus's in his body, that is, the church.[96]

What does Paul mean by "pleasing the Lord"? This expression echoes Deuteronomy 13:19. It refers to the life in God's grace of the one who behaves according to God's will in order to please him, like Christ who did not seek to please himself.[97] It also denotes the holiness of one who is not closed within one's self, but that *loves in order to please God*. In this way, "the spousal character of continence for the Kingdom of God becomes in some way apparent here."[98] Additionally, connected with the biblical notion of holiness, Paul explains that while the married person finds himself divided because of his family duties, the unmarried "should be characterized by an inner integration, by a unification that would allow him to devote himself completely to the service of the kingdom of God in all its dimensions."[99] The biblical conception of holiness refers both to an ontological character of separation of that which is offered to God from what is profane, and to a moral character marked with purity which presupposes a way of acting without spot or wrinkle.[100] Considering the importance given to "pleasing the Lord", and "being anxious about what is the Lord's," the conclusion from the argumentation is based on Paul's theology of a great expectation. This theology underlines that *man's eternal destiny is not this world, but the kingdom of God*. Consequently, the human person should not be too much attached to the goods of this transitory world. Marriage counts amongst these goods. Hence, one should love God above one's marriage. One should love one's husband and wife in God, and because of him. The vocation to marriage should be lived with one's eyes raised to heaven. Thus,

---

91. See ibid., 83:5; 1 Cor 7:29, 31; *In IV Sent.*, d. 26, q. 1, a. 3, ad 1.
92. See TOB 83:6; 1 Cor 7:32.
93. See Luke 10:41; 12:31.
94. See TOB 83:7; Phil 2:20–21; 1 Cor 12:25; 2 Cor 11:28.
95. See 1 Cor 10:26; Ps 24:1.
96. See TOB 83:8; Col 1:18.
97. See Rom 15:3.
98. TOB 84:1.
99. Ibid., 84:2. See 1 Cor 7:34.
100. See TOB 84:5; Eph 5:27.

the pope interprets Paul as making room here for conjugal charity: "[T]he Christian must live marriage from the point of view of his definitive vocation."[101]

According to Paul, the only reason why one who chooses continence does better is because "while marriage is tied to the stage of this world, which is passing, and thus imposes in some way the necessity of closing oneself in this transitoriness, abstaining from marriage, one could say by contrast, liberates from such a necessity."[102] This is key to understanding how celibates teach and complement married people in their state of life: married people should live their vocation from the viewpoint of their definitive vocation in heaven. Instead, the Corinthians seemed to have understood marriage as a way of "using the world." Paul conforms his words to this kind of mentality, when he explains that it is better to marry than to be aflame, or that because of the danger of incontinence, each man should have his own wife and each woman her own husband.[103] This way of speaking could lead someone to understand Paul's words concerning marriage under a reductive view of the theological category of *remedium concupiscentiae*. However, Paul's teaching is unambiguous: "[W]e do not find any foundation for considering those who live in marriage carnal and those, by contrast, who for religious reasons choose continence spiritual."[104] To both married and celibates (or virgins) belongs a particular gift from God.[105] Also those who are married, like the ones called to virginity for the sake of the Kingdom, receive a particular grace that corresponds to their vocation or state of life.[106]

Charity and the Spousal Meaning of the Body

As we conclude the second part of this book, it is important to highlight that our analyses have demonstrated that, according to John Paul II, the expression "the spousal meaning of the body" signifies one's supernatural vocation to charity. Moreover, we have also demonstrated that this notion is rooted in the theology of Thomas Aquinas, and in the Second Vatican Council, as interpreted by Karol Wojtyła. It is really difficult to overestimate the role that the spousal meaning of the body plays in TOB. It signifies the way in which the human person's being created in God's image and likeness is perfected. The spousal meaning of the body is initially discovered by our first parents as a result of the understanding originated by the original experiences before the fall. However, even if the first discovery of the spousal meaning of the body took place in the context of Adam and Eve's conjugal union, its *primum analogatum* is found in Christ's love for the church.

101. TOB 85:2.
102. Ibid.
103. See 1 Cor 7:1–2, 8–9.
104. TOB 85:4.
105. See 1 Cor 7:7.
106. See *In IV Sent.*, d. 26, q. 2, a. 3, ad 4.

This notion of the spousal meaning of the body helps John Paul overcome the proponents of contraception's claim for an autonomous morality, wherein neither revelation or the magisterium would have a say regarding conjugal ethics. The spousal meaning of the body underlines the fact that, in charity, the gratuitous initiative in the total gift of self is always God's, while ours is the responsibility. Appealing to the spousal meaning of the body, John Paul manages to place the new ethos of redemption, and every virtue therein contained under its proper perspective, the perspective of charity. Thus, the pope manages to overcome with this notion the pessimistic and false optimism inherent in the advocates of contraception's moral theology. Moreover, the spousal meaning of the body is the common ground which allows for a mutual enrichment and illumination between the vocation to celibacy or virginity, and the vocation to marriage. Both are seen as two distinct but complementary ways of living out the one vocation to charity. Additionally, the spousal meaning of the body gives God his due place of honor in conjugal love. God must be "at the center," as it were, of one's marriage.

This Thomistic and personalistic understanding of the human vocation at large finds very specific traits within marriage. What makes generic charity into *conjugal* charity? We already know that, in the beginning, procreation was the common good that specified Adam and Eve's friendship in charity and truth. Their common union in view of procreation, as their common good and end, gave their friendship in the Lord the specific character of conjugality. It is time now to deepen that affirmation. What does John Paul II understand by procreation? What is its role as the conjugal common good? What is the role of procreation within the sphere of the sacramentality of marriage? How does the spousal meaning of the body and procreation relate with each in other in John Paul's commentary on HV? Does John Paul's answer to these questions constitute a Thomistic argument grounded in Vatican II?

Part III: Procreation

10

Conjugal Common Good

The Ends of Marriage and the Perspective of Charity

Karol Wojtyła's philosophy and theology of procreation has as its immediate context a heated debate in Catholic theology concerning the ends of marriage. In general terms, this debate opposed traditional doctrine to some new personalistic approaches.[1] As Petri notes, in part, this opposition was due to "the physicalist methodology that so dominated Catholic moral theology at the beginning of the twentieth century, which tended toward a moral evaluation based on the physical structure of human action and an identification of the purposes of nature with biophysical processes."[2] Our author is quite emphatic in teaching that, "the expressions the order of nature and the biological order must not be confused or regarded as identical, the biological order does indeed mean the same as the order of nature but only in so far as this is accessible to the methods of empirical and descriptive natural science, and not as *a specific order of existence with an obvious relationship to the First Cause, to God the Creator.*"[3] Wojtyła inserts himself into this question. He does so initially by means of LR's Thomistic personalism. Secondly, grounded in his mature philosophical anthropology, he contributes to this question by means of TOB's theological approach. Herein is offered a very succinct sketch of the controversy, in which will be emphasized what I deem most important in order to fully appreciate John Paul's views on procreation and the spousal meaning of the body.

As is known, the 1917 Code of Canon Law expressed a long standing tradition when it taught that "the primary end of marriage is the procreation and education of offspring; the secondary is the mutual aid and remedy of concupiscence."[4] The former code did not imply that licit and valid marriages are only those in which the

---

1. See Petri, *Aquinas*, 45–91. For a classic work on the history of the theology of contraception, see Noonan, *Contraception*.

2. Petri, *Aquinas*, 63.

3. LR, 56–57; emphasis added.

4. *Codex Juris Canonici*, n. 1013. For a good summary of the patristic and medieval sources on this topic, see Carney, *The Purposes of Christian Marriage*. Thomas Aquinas also affirms that procreation is the primary end of marriage. See, for instance, *In IV Sent.*, d. 26, q. 1, a. 1, c; d. 31, q. 1, a. 2, ad 1; d. 33, q. 1, a. 1, c; q. 2, a. 1, ad 4; d. 40, q. 1, a. 3, c; *ST* III, q. 29, a. 2, c.

spouses actually intend procreation and education of offspring as the primary motive for their getting married. A licit and valid marriage could take place for other primary personal motives, as long as marriage's objective ends are not willfully excluded. As was later clarified by the Roman Rota, the canon does not speak of a primacy of procreation from the subjective viewpoint of the spouses as agents, and of their purposes for getting married (*finis operantis*). Instead, the canon emphasizes a primacy in the *objective* order of marriage (*finis operis*), that is to say, in the order of marriage as an institution established by God himself.[5]

This doctrine was not well received by some theologians, such as Herbert Doms. He conceded that procreation is the *biological* purpose of matrimony.[6] Yet, Doms postulated that "the constitution of marriage, the union of two persons, *does not consist in their subservience to a purpose outside themselves*, for which they marry. It consists in *the constant vital ordination of husband and wife to each other until they become one*."[7] Doms knew full well that he was challenging the teaching of the magisterium. Additionally, he also was thought to be opposing the Angelic Doctor. Thus, he argued that "there can no longer be sufficient reason, from this standpoint, for speaking of procreation as the primary purpose (in the sense in which St. Thomas used the phrase) and for dividing off the other purposes as secondary."[8] Doms suggested, consequently, that "it would be best if in the future we gave up using such terms as primary and secondary in speaking of the purposes of marriage."[9]

Doms's proposal was seen by many as heterodox, for few years earlier, in 1930, Pius XI had confirmed and cited the above mentioned canon from the 1917 Code of Canon Law in *Casti Connubi*.[10] Additionally, without undermining that doctrine, Pius XI also offered an important consideration: "[M]atrimonial faith [the *bonum fidei*] demands that husband and wife be *joined in an especially holy and pure love*, not as adulterers love each other, but *as Christ loved the Church*."[11] Conjugal charity, the pope continues, is a common good of the spouses which brings about their mutual perfection. Hence, Pius XI explains, regarding conjugal charity, that it can "be said to be the primary cause and reason for matrimony [*primaria matrimonii causa et ratio dici potest*], provided matrimony be looked at not in the restricted sense as instituted for the proper conception and education of the child, but more widely as the blending of life as a whole and the mutual interchange and sharing thereof."[12]

5. See AAS 36 (1944), 179–200. De Broglie makes the same point with respect to Aquinas's theology. See "La conception Thomiste," 10–11.

6. See Doms, *The Meaning of Marriage*, 85.

7. Ibid., 87; emphasis added.

8. Ibid.

9. Ibid., 88.

10. See *Casti Connubi*, 17. For a more detailed analysis, see García de Haro, *Marriage and the Family*, 107–45.

11. *Casti Connubi*, 23; emphasis added.

12. Ibid., 24. Translation altered.

Note well the difference between Pius XI's and Doms's position. Unlike Doms, Pius XI affirms the primacy of procreation as an *objective* end of marriage. Moreover, unlike Doms's, Pius XI's perspective of charity sees the cause and reason/meaning (*ratio*) of marriage as something that *is subservient to a purpose outside the spouses*. Pius XI thinks that this cause and *ratio* for marriage can be found in God as the object of a peculiar kind of charity. That is the whole point of seeing in *conjugal* charity the primary cause and *ratio* for marriage. Conjugal charity is one specific kind of charity, inasmuch as the objective primary end of marriage determines the specific form of this kind of love. Something similar happens for priests with *priestly pastoral* charity. The latter is specified by the end of priestly pastoral activity: what priests are to do in order to lead souls to salvation. Pastoral charity *permeates* and *coordinates* the whole of priestly pastoral life, because it *directs* all priestly pastoral activities to God and to his infinite goodness. Likewise, conjugal charity permeates the whole of married life. It directs all activities characteristic of the married vocation to God and to his infinite goodness. Indeed, *conjugal* charity is a supernatural love that is *in* God and *because of God*, a love that *leads the spouses outside of themselves towards* union with God, thanks to their charity for each other as husband and wife.

Commenting on *Casti Connubi*, García de Haro has rightly understood that "with respect to the good of fidelity, the most original contribution of the encyclical is the way in which it develops the perfecting of the love between the spouses through conjugal charity."[13] Hence, according to Pius XI, the "conjugal love—which establishes and must *inform the entire community of life between the spouses and whose end is the work of generating and educating children*—cannot be other than a faithful love."[14] Pius XI lists *conjugal* love in the second place because "metaphysically, *the end determines the form*: the ordination to the generation and education of human life *defines the requirements and unique characteristics of conjugal love*."[15] However, conjugal love must pervade the entirety of married life, including the fulfillment of its primary end: the good of children. Thus, "the encyclical links itself to the line of the Augustinian-Thomistic tradition, which gave to love the role of being the vital principle of marriage, informing it, giving it its dynamic."[16]

With this kind of argumentation, Pius XI is appealing to an effect of the very sacrament of marriage. Thus, he explicitly teaches that Christ, "by raising the matrimony of His faithful to the dignity of a true sacrament of the new law, made it *a sign and source of that peculiar internal grace* by which it *perfects natural love*, it confirms an indissoluble union, and sanctifies both man and wife."[17] Note the twofold dimension pointed out by Pius XI: the sacrament of matrimony as a *sign* and as a source or *cause*

---

13. García de Haro, *Marriage and the Family*, 123.
14. Ibid.; emphasis added.
15. Ibid.; emphasis added.
16. Ibid.
17. *Casti Connunbi*, 38; emphasis added.

of grace. This will be the exact perspective adopted in TOB by John Paul II, as we will see in chapter 11. Moreover, it is also important to underline how *Casti Connubi* views the specific and distinct grace conferred by the sacrament of matrimony. Like any other sacrament, matrimony certainly increases sanctifying grace. But it does so with specific and distinct gifts that assist spouses in knowing and putting into practice what belongs to the married state.[18] One could say that the spouses receive the specific grace to fulfill their marriage promises.[19] As will be shown, this doctrine is the foundation for John Paul's argument based on the language of the body.

On April 1, 1944, what we know today as the Congregation for the Doctrine of the Faith—at that time, the so-called Holy Office—clarified the same teaching contained in the 1917 Code of Canon Law. The decree issued was entitled *De Finibus Matrimonii*.[20] However, the perspective of charity mentioned by Pius XI in *Casti Connubi* is not mentioned in this document. In the period that spans from 1944 until the Second Vatican Council, we find Wojtyła's LR, published in 1960. We will look closely at LR in this chapter. However, let it be noted that one can already see the influence of *Casti Connubi* on this rather philosophical book. Wojtyła explains therein that the ends of marriage cannot be understood apart from love. He argues that to do so would simply be unchristian.[21] Vatican II also adopts Pius XI's perspective of charity. During the Council, there was an explicit petition to insert the primacy of procreation into GS.[22] However, the petition to insert that exact language was dismissed. The Council fathers refused to use that language, not because the doctrine was deemed as erroneous, but simply because of the pastoral and nontheological nature of the document.[23] Nevertheless, GS 50 asserts, with different terminology, the same idea by incorporating Pius XI's perspective of charity as well.[24]

GS 50 explains that God's plan has ordained conjugal love to the procreation and education of children. Thus, the family *perfects* marriage: "[M]arriage and conjugal love are by their nature ordained toward the begetting and educating of children. Children are really the supreme gift of marriage and they maximally contribute to the good of their own parents [*ad ipsorum parentum bonum maxime conferunt*]."[25] The Council teaches that this affirmation does not "neglect the other ends of matrimony [*non posthabitis ceteris matrimonii finibus*]."[26] To be sure, they also retain their own

---

18. See García de Haro, *Marriage and the Family*, 128.
19. See Sarmiento, *El Matrimonio*, 257–70.
20. See AAS 36 (1944), 103.
21. See LR 66.
22. See Petri, *Aquinas*, 68–70.
23. See De Broglie, "La conception Thomiste," 4–6.
24. See also FC 14's interpretation of GS 50.
25. GS 50. Translation altered; emphasis added. The English Vatican translator has rendered *bonum* as "welfare" and *maxime* as "substantially," thereby obscuring the emphasis of the passage.
26. Ibid. Translation altered.

worth or value. However, their having their own internal value in and of themselves does not take away the fact that, from a certain perspective, the good of offspring *maximally* perfects the conjugal union between husband and wife. Obviously, the notion of procreation in this text is not purely biological. And that certain perspective is none other than that of conjugal charity. Thus, the text continues, explaining that the true practice of conjugal love and the whole meaning of the family aim [*tendunt*] to the following end: "[T]hat the couple be ready with courageous spirit [*forti animo*] to *cooperate* with the *love of the Creator* and that *of the Savior* [*cooperandum cum amore Creatoris atque Salvatoris*], who through them will enlarge and enrich his own family day by day."[27]

Thus, GS 50 offers some valuable coordinates. First, procreation is seen as a cooperation with the Creator in the transmission and education of human life, which perfects the communion of persons established in matrimony by contributing maximally to the good of the parents. Second, procreation is infixed within the perspective of charity. Within this orbit, procreation maximally perfects one's marriage because it is a *conjugal* kind of cooperation with the Creator's and with Jesus's love (*cooperandum cum amore Creatoris atque Salvatoris*), that is to say, it is a kind of cooperation in charity. Finally, such cooperation with divine love or charity also assumes into its orbit the virtue of courage or fortitude, whereby one is able to withstand difficulties for the sake of doing what is truly good.

In TOB, John Paul II adopts a position very similar to that of Pius XI and to the one found in GS 50. While upholding the primacy of procreation, John Paul explains that the ends of marriage are *coordinated by love*: "According to the traditional language, love, as a *superior power, coordinates the acts of the persons*, of the husband and wife, in the area of the ends of marriage."[28] The pope alludes here to the Thomistic teaching according to which charity is the mover, the end, the form, and the mother of the virtues.[29] Thus, without charity there is no true or perfect virtue that leads to salvation. This is what we should understand in John Paul's text by the "power of love." The pope is really talking about charity as a *theological* virtue that comes from God, and is about God. Furthermore, he refers to that charity as an effect of the sacrament of marriage. Thus, the power of love does not signify sheer *human* love among spouses. Rather, it signifies that human love as *elevated to the supernatural level of conjugal charity* by the specific grace of matrimony. All of these qualifications are made clear from the way in which the text continues: "As a higher power that man and woman *receive from God* together with the *particular consecration of the sacrament of Marriage*, love involves a right coordination of the ends according to which—in the Church's traditional teaching—the moral (or rather the theologal and moral) order

---

27. Ibid.

28. TOB 127:3; emphasis added.

29. See *In III Sent.*, d. 27, q. 2, a. 4, qc. 3, c; *ST* II–II, q. 23, a. 8, c; *De Veritate*, q. 14, a. 5, c; *De Malo*, q. 8, a. 2, c.

of the life of the spouses is constituted."[30] Consequently, just like Pius XI and like GS 50, John Paul II is appealing to *conjugal charity* as an effect of the sacrament of matrimony. This kind of charity *involves* a right coordination of the objective ends of marriage. Obviously, the ends of marriage to which John Paul makes reference in the text are the ones listed in the 1917 Code of Canon law: procreation and education of offspring, mutual help, and remedy for concupiscence.

It is of the utmost importance for the topic of this book to emphasize that John Paul II declares that the perspective of conjugal charity, that is, *the perspective of how the spousal meaning of the body is fulfilled within marriage*, is the key to understanding Paul VI's teaching in HV as grounded in Vatican II. Pay close attention to how the text I am commenting on unfolds: "The teaching of *Gaudium et Spes* as well as that of *Humanae Vitae* clarifies the *same moral order* [of the objective ends of marriage] *in reference to love, understood as a superior power* that *gives adequate content and value to conjugal acts* according to the truth of the two meanings, the unitive and the procreative, in reverence to their *inseparability*."[31] Consequently, John Paul II teaches magisterially that there is strict continuity between the perspectives found in *Casti Connubi*, GS, and HV. He thinks that adopting this exact perspective of charity helps to better understand the primacy of procreation. It is like a renewed orientation that avoids naturalistic physicalism and transports this whole question to the realm of virtue. Therefore, John Paul says about GS and HV: "In this renewed orientation, *the traditional teaching on the ends of marriage (and on their hierarchy) is confirmed and at the same time deepened* from the point of view of the interior life of the spouses, of conjugal and familial spirituality."[32] To fully comprehend these texts just quoted from TOB constitutes the goal of this entire third part of the book, for they already establish the main coordinates for the relationship between procreation and the spousal meaning of the body. In reality, I believe that they are rather programmatic for John Paul II's commentary on HV.

Reductionistic and Utilitarian Views

Our next step consists in understanding the philosophical substratum for John Paul's teaching in TOB concerning procreation and the spousal meaning of the body. Such philosophical substratum is found in LR. Therein, our author explains what he understands by procreation. He also argues that love coordinates the hierarchy of marriage's ends. Thereby, he distinguishes his position from a reductionistic and utilitarian interpretation of that same hierarchy and adopts the perspective of virtue. Wojtyła's main philosophical thesis in LR concerning our topic is that love coordinates the ends of marriage in such a way that it offers a foundation for the inseparability between two

30. TOB 127:3; emphasis added.
31. Ibid.; emphasis added.
32. Ibid.; emphasis added.

responsibilities: the responsibility for procreation, and the responsibility for the integration of the love between the spouses into virtuous conjugal friendship.

Our author begins by recalling the traditional teaching just mentioned. He points out that the church "teaches, and has always taught, that the primary end of marriage is *procreatio,* but that it has a secondary end, defined in Latin terminology as *mutuum adiutorium*. Apart from these a tertiary aim is mentioned—*remedium concupiscentiae*. Marriage, *objectively considered*, must provide first of all the means of continuing existence, secondly a conjugal life for man and woman, and thirdly a legitimate orientation for desire."[33] Wojtyła's presentation seems to be aware of the distinction between *finis operis* and *finis operantis*. Thus, he speaks in the text about marriage as "objectively considered." Moreover, our author continues explaining that the way in which the hierarchical ends of marriage are listed has led some authors to believe "that procreation as the primary end is something distinct from love, as also is the tertiary end, *remedium concupiscentiae*."[34] Within this view, procreation as the primary end of marriage could be fully accomplished without love. Conjugal love would compete with procreation in terms of importance in such a way that, to hold the latter as primary, would mean to reduce the former to a sheer useful good, with no importance in-and-of-itself. There would be no virtues inherent to procreation. It would be just a biological fact. Wojtyła certainly knows that Max Scheler had rightly protested against this exact view, which reduces marriage to a sheer means to perpetuate the species or to secure one's patrimony. Scheler had explained that, in such a view, conjugal "acts preserve the species as human fodder for business, industry, war and the like. But they merely re-produce, whereas love creates."[35] Wojtyła suggests a similar but more precise critique: "A man and woman become father and mother only in consequence of the marital act: it *must be an act of love*, an act of unification of persons, and *not merely the instrument or means of procreation*."[36]

In turn, detached from love, marriage as a remedy for concupiscence would be reduced to a sort of "safe haven" for "lawful" incontinence. Again, the perspective of virtue would be abandoned in favor of the ethos of concupiscence. For this reason, Wojtyła concludes that "if any one of the above-mentioned purposes of marriage is considered without reference to the personalistic norm—that is to say, without taking account of the fact that man and woman are persons—this is bound to lead to some form of utilitarianism."[37] Here we see a sort of philosophical application of the perspective of charity. Love coordinates the ends of marriage without denying their hierarchical order. Without love coordinating these ends, they lose their very meaning. They are reduced to something else. For instance, when procreation is viewed in

33. LR 66; emphasis added. See also Gil Hellín, *El matrimonio*, 59–87.
34. LR, 68; emphasis added.
35. Scheler, *Nature of Sympathy*, 233–34.
36. LR, 234; emphasis added.
37. Ibid., 67.

a naturalistic or physicalist way—that is, purely from the biological perspective—, it is seen as sheer animal reproduction attainable without virtuous love. At that point, one can fall into the rigorist trap that conceives sexual pleasure as the necessary and tolerated evil in favor of reproduction. The goodness of the sexual union would reside exclusively in being an effective instrumental means for the generation of another human being.[38] On the other hand, this same biologistic and physicalist way of separating procreation from love could also lead to the other extreme: the Freudian libidinistic interpretation. This other interpretation reduces procreation to something marginal, to something which does not touch the meaning and purpose of sexual interpersonal relations. Such meaning and purpose would be reduced, instead, to the attainment of pleasure. Pleasure would be *the* end of human sexuality, an end in itself. Instead, procreation would only be an end *per accidens*, something that could be, and at times should be, avoided in order to maximize the attainment of pleasure. The ethos of concupiscence would triumph over virtue and the ethos of redemption.

These two examples clearly manifest the truth inherent in Wojtyła's thesis. Love coordinates the ends of marriage. Without altering their objective hierarchy, love allows their essence or true meaning to shine forth. Once love is taken out of the equation, the very essence of the ends of marriage is falsified or extremely obscured. Moreover, when love is not viewed in its role of coordinating the ends of marriage, one falls into a harsh separation between the human person and the world of nature. This separation ends up hindering the same human person from "understanding his role in creation in relation to the Creator, as a form of *participation in the work of creation.*"[39] (We can already see in this last affirmation a sort of anticipation of GS 50.) Wojtyła also appeals to mutual help in his main thesis. Thus, he explains that, for different reasons, in both errors just described—puritanical rigorism and the Freudian libidinistic interpretation—the mutual help of the spouses, instead of corresponding to true spousal love, is falsified and reduced to a "utilitarian pact" in which there is nothing more than a union of egoisms.[40] Against these distortions and the physicalism inherent in them, Wojtyła defends that "conjugal morality consists of a stable and mature *synthesis of nature's purpose with the personalistic norm.*"[41] As the Author of nature and as the Author of matrimony, God never could have intended a realization of the purposes of marriage apart from the commandment of love, a commandment which also belongs to the natural law.[42] Hence, the Polish philosopher notes the great theological incongruence in the error that he is combating: "[T]he idea that the purposes of marriage could be realized on some basis other than the personalistic norm

---

38. See LR, 57–61.
39. Ibid., 62; emphasis added.
40. See ibid., 34–40.
41. Ibid., 67.
42. See DA, 142; *ST*, I-II, q. 100, a. 3, ad 1.

would be utterly un-Christian, because it would not conform to the fundamental ethical postulate of the Gospels."[43]

We need to understand well this synthesis between nature's purposes and the personalistic norm. Reading more popular presentations and even some scholarly commentaries, this is always a tricky hermeneutical point.[44] Once again, the modern search for originality and novelty to the detriment of the value of tradition can be a serious obstacle in understanding the true mind of John Paul II. He is certainly not attempting to "go beyond" Thomas Aquinas by providing a more "personalistic" philosophy, as if Thomism was not personalistic enough for Wojtyła.[45] As was noted, the personalistic norm is not excluded from the realm of the natural law. Wojtyła's use of the word "synthesis" rests on very Thomistic foundations: Aquinas's different meanings for the term nature, and his distinction between first and second act. Just like marriage or any of the virtues, the personalistic norm does not flow necessarily from the natural principles of the human person. In this peculiar sense, the personalistic norm is not natural but free or personal. Yet, the personalistic norm is natural in another sense, inasmuch as the human being is inclined to it by his rational nature and is called to freely affirm such an inclination with his freedom. In this last case, there is a responsible synthesis or integration at the level of second act, between what merely happens in man and what man freely does, that is to say, a synthesis between what is natural and what is personal. Consequently, this synthesis or integration between nature and person has nothing to do with complementing Thomas's allegedly insufficient personalism. If anything, this distinction is directly rooted in the teachings of the Angelic Doctor that were already explained in chapter 4.[46]

Generically Animal But Specifically Rational

In order to overcome these reductionistic and utilitarian views, we need to go beyond the naturalistic physicalism or biologistic way of understanding procreation. Additionally, as Wojtyła insisted during Vatican II's preparatory *vota et consilia*, we also need to distinguish the Christian view of the human person from other personalisms incompatible with the faith. A Christian personalism cannot be a spiritualistic Cartesian personalism, like the one promoted by the advocates of contraception. Rather, it has to account for man's substantial unity, for the spirituality and immortality

---

43. LR, 67.

44. See Heaney, *The Concept of the Unity of the Person*. This author sees in this passage and in others in which Wojtyła speaks about this synthesis a *novelty* with respect to Thomas Aquinas, a novelty *incompatible* with the human person's substantial unity. I have explained Heaney's objection in my *De la experiencia*, 23–26. For an explanation of Wojtyła's Thomistic foundations for this distinction, see ibid., 201–58. For the *total compatibility* between Wojtyła's position and the human person's substantial unity, see ibid., 301–6, 360–63, 399–408.

45. See PC, 165–76.

46. See *In IV Sent.*, d. 26, q. 1, a. 1, c.

of his soul, and for his place of honor within the created cosmos by virtue of his rational mode of being (*esse*). To a great extent, GS 12–22 satisfied Wojtyła's concerns. However, these same issues surfaced again in the philosophical and theological discussions before and after HV. Thus, Wojtyła's interpretation of HV reiterated the importance of an integral view of the human person in order to understand the phenomenon of procreation in its full human character.[47] That goal could only be accomplished, Wojtyła insisted again, by keeping in mind a correct understanding of man's substantial unity.[48]

Only if the human person's substantial unity is well understood can procreation be conceived as a generically animal but specifically rational phenomenon. Of course, the distinction between genus and species is not a real but a *logical distinction*. In truth, there is not one real part in man that is purely animal and another that is purely rational. Even our sensitivity and sensuality are rational inasmuch as they find their origin in our one rational soul. Moreover, they also have real aptitudes or potentialities absent in the sensitivity and sensuality of other animals. What interests me most in appealing to this logical expression is to emphasize an essential point for this study. Based on Thomistic anthropology, Wojtyła offers in LR a precise description of procreation in its human character, which foretells GS 50, and informs TOB. Precisely because of man's substantial unity, *human procreation is not only animal but also personal and spiritual*. It is something that cannot be simply equated with the reproduction of irrational animals. Human procreation can certainly be compared with their reproduction by means of a logical distinction. Thus, at a very generic level, one could compare how rabbits and human persons reproduce and find some minimal commonalities. But this logical level of comparison will always fall short in understanding the full reality of human procreation. The differences will always be greater.

For this reason, Aquinas adopts the same logical distinction I referred to, acknowledging that "the nature of man inclines to something in two ways. In one way, because it befits the nature of his genus: and this is common to all animals. In another way, because it befits the nature of the difference by which the human species exceeds

---

47. See Wojtyła, "Anthropological Vision," 735.

48. For this reason, I do not think that John Paul II would fully endorse Petri's idea according to which the unitive dimension of the conjugal act stands for what is immaterial or formal, while the procreative dimension stands for what is material. In this manner, Petri argues for their inseparability, believing to ground his argument on the hylomorphic unity of the human person: "The material and the immaterial cannot be separated in this life, nor can the procreative and the unitive aspects of the conjugal act" (Petri, *Aquinas*, 308). However, in my opinion, Wojtyła grounds his views on procreation and conjugal love on man's substantial unity for a very different reason, namely, because *both* phenomena are distinctively human as *generically animal but specifically rational*. Thus, John Paul so emphasizes that according to the Scriptures, the human person created in the image and likeness of God cannot be confused with an irrational animal; he "cannot be qualified in a fundamental way as an animal as well, but as an animal *rationale*" (TOB 80:4). Rhonheimer has also pointed out the need to go beyond the dangerous reduction of procreation to its material dimensions. See Rhonheimer, *Natural Law and Practical Reason*, 96–101, 123–26.

its genus, inasmuch as man is rational . . . And thus the nature of the genus, although it is one among all animals, yet it is not in all in the same way."[49] In reality, we do not reproduce like rabbits but like *rational* animals, like human persons. Thus, procreation is a distinctively human phenomenon.

Gathering Theological Insights

Before explaining the philosophical differences between animal reproduction and human procreation, it is important to briefly gather TOB's dispersed theological insights around this very topic. The first account of creation relates man's *esse* to the phenomenon of procreation as a sign of man's contingency. Moreover, the correct understanding of procreation was intimately linked with our being created in God's image and likeness.[50] In the second account of creation, John Paul explained the *specific* way in which Adam and Eve formed a *we*, a married couple in their one-flesh union. He appealed to the specifying role of the common good for the community. What is more final is also more formal. The final cause is the cause of the causality in the formal cause of the community. Thus, their procreative *munus* specified their communion of persons as conjugal. In the second meaning of original unity, Adam and Eve experienced themselves in the new dimension opened by procreation as their common conjugal good. In a sense, they rediscovered their own identity in light of this common good. Within the sphere of their conjugal *we*, the unitive meaning of the body as a generic capacity for communion acquired a conjugal dimension closely linked with the parenting *munus* expressed in the *mandatum*. Remember that this unitive meaning of the body, even within the sphere of conjugality, is not to be simply identified with the unitive meaning of the conjugal act.[51] As was said, the conjugal act is *one more* act within conjugal life but not the only one.

Moreover, Gen 4:1 already manifested that human procreation requires *the help of the Lord*. Adam and Eve *procreated* in collaboration with the Creator as God's partners, who can be the free cause of their obedience to the *mandatum*. In this way, the beginning to which Christ directed us already points to the fact that God must always be present in the conjugal union of the spouses. Conjugal charity, therefore, entails a love between husband and wife that is in God and because of God, a love which collaborates with the Creator in the procreative *munus*, thereby placing one's "whole humanity *under* the blessing of fruitfulness."[52] For this reason, John Paul II already said that the procreative meaning is "*rooted* in the spousal meaning of the body and *comes forth organically*, as it were, from it."[53] Thus, conjugal charity is like the mover, the end,

49. See *In IV Sent.*, d. 26, q. 1, a. 1, ad 1.
50. See TOB 2:5.
51. See TOB 29:3.
52. Ibid., 10:2; emphasis added.
53. Ibid., 39:5; emphasis added.

the form, and the mother of the virtuous exercise of the entire parental *munus*. As a result, when the spouses place their humanity under the blessing of fruitfulness in charity—that is, out of love for God and in a mutual love that is in God—they actualize more fully their self-fulfillment as husband and wife. By contrast, the conjugal act is *vitiated* by the ethos of concupiscence as an ethos that is diametrically opposed to the virtues, especially to conjugal charity and to the spousal meaning of the body.

The conjugal act cannot be separated from the personalistic norm, and the affirmation of the common dignity shared by husband and wife as brother and sister in the Lord. For the conjugal act to be *truly unitive*, one should take upon oneself all the truths about personal identity and dignity as discovered in original solitude. These same truths are to be reciprocally acknowledged, and freely affirmed among the spouses. This reciprocal acknowledgement and free affirmation was at the heart of the pope's visualization of Adam and Eve's marriage before the fall. Commenting on their communion as it had been intended by the same God who is loved above all things and persons in charity, the pope clarifies that their communion "had been *intended* to make man and woman mutually happy through the search of a simple and pure *union in humanity*, through a reciprocal offering of themselves, that is, through the experience of the gift of the person *expressed with soul and body*, with *masculinity* and *femininity*—"flesh of my flesh" (Gen 2:23)—and finally through the *subordination* of such a union to the *blessing of fruitfulness with procreation*."[54] Once again, love coordinates the ends of marriage. According to the pope, the fulfillment of the spousal meaning of the body in conjugal charity leads to the subordination of Adam and Eve's one-flesh union to procreation as a collaboration with the Creator in the transmission and education of human life.

Philosophy of Procreation

These theological insights find a robust philosophical substratum in Wojtyła's philosophy of procreation as developed in LR. He explains that human procreation is not just a matter of sheer biology, or the numerical increase of the human race. Rather, it marks the beginning of a person's existence, as well as the future task of his education. For this reason, procreation "is more appropriate here than reproduction, which tends to have *a purely biological meaning*. We are speaking of course, not merely of the beginning of life in a purely biological sense but of the beginning of a person's existence, and so it is *better to use the term procreation*."[55] Going beyond naturalistic physicalism implies the recognition that "in the animal world there is only reproduction, which is achieved by way of instinct."[56] In this animal world, there is only instinctual reproduction without elective love. The reason is simple. Therein, "there are no persons, hence

54. Ibid., 30:3. See McCarthy, "El amor esponsal."
55. LR, 226; emphasis added.
56. Ibid.

there is no personalistic norm to proclaim the principle of love."[57] The animality of the human person is very different. It is not governed by instincts. The human person has a great deal of inclinations, impulses, or drives with the real aptitude or potential to be informed by freedom and virtue. These natural inclinations certainly head in one definitive direction. However, they are not instinctively fixed but open to, and in need of, personal integration. For this reason, Wojtyła notes a big difference between the animality found in the world of the brutes, and in the world of persons. "In the world of persons on the other hand instinct alone decides nothing, and the sexual urge passes, so to speak, through the gates of the consciousness and the will thus furnishing *not merely the conditions of fertility but also the raw material of love*."[58]

Hence, at a very natural level, one finds an intimate connection between procreation and love. This natural level is none other than the human or personal level, provided we go beyond biologistic physicalism. For this reason, Wojtyła explains: "At a truly human, truly personal level the problems of procreation and of love cannot be resolved separately. Both procreation and love are based on the conscious choice of persons."[59] It is precisely this connection with human conjugal love that sheds light onto another specifically human trait of procreation. Out of the reproduction of irrational animals flows a relatively brief period of nourishment and physical care for the offspring, which is accomplished by instinct. In the case of the human person, procreation also includes, as its extension, the care for the offspring. However, although this care includes nourishment and physical sustenance, it also entails the very distinctive human phenomenon of education, understood as the "full spiritual development of a human person."[60] As Wojtyła explains, "education is a creative activity with persons as its only possible object—only a person can be educated, an animal can only be trained—and also one which uses entirely human material; all that is by nature present in the human being to be educated is material for the educators, material which their love must find and mold."[61]

As we can already see, among human persons, procreation elevates all of the generic traits of animal reproduction just mentioned to a rational or personal level: "[P]aternity and maternity in the world of persons are certainly *not limited to the biological function of transmitting life*."[62] That would be the limitation imposed by naturalistic physicalism. Instead, we need to remember that "the transmitter of life, father or mother, is a person."[63] This fact opens our eyes to the spiritual realm. "Paternity

57. Ibid.

58. Ibid.; emphasis added. As I already explained in chapter 4 commenting on "człowiek-tworzywo," I do not think *raw* material is the best choice for an English translation.

59. LR, 226–27.

60. Ibid., 55.

61. Ibid., 56.

62. Ibid., 260; emphasis added. See also ibid., 227.

63. Ibid.

and maternity in the world of persons are the mark of *a certain spiritual perfection, the capacity for procreation in the spiritual sense, the forming of souls.*"[64] It is of the outmost importance to realize that spiritual parenthood is not restricted to those who live celibacy or virginity. It also belongs to those who are married. Thus, "a father and mother who have given their children life in the merely biological sense must then *supplement physical parenthood by spiritual parenthood*, taking whatever pains are necessary for their *education.*"[65] By education, Wojtyła means the full spiritual development of a human person, that is, his formation in virtue. Therefore, he is implicitly referring to Thomas's classic definition of education as "the [human person's] development and promotion to the perfect state of man inasmuch as he is man, that is, the state of virtue."[66] As a result, parenthood entails a process of education, wherein children reach their own integration by acquiring a state of virtue through which they may freely choose to love virtuously. Thus, their education is geared towards the attainment of their final end.

Human procreation is fully attained in *responsible* parenthood. Parents need to respond to God. Since spouses are persons, God rules them in his providence, not by way of instinct, but rather by asking them to freely and virtuously collaborate with the Creator.[67] This constitutes another specifically rational mark of the essence of human procreation, unveiled by the intrinsic presence of virtuous love. "When a man and a woman consciously and of their own free will choose to marry and have relations they choose at the same time the possibility of procreation, they choose to *participate in creation* (for that is the proper meaning of the word procreation). And it is only when they do so that they put their sexual relationship within the framework of marriage *on a truly personal level.*"[68]

For such collaboration or participation with the Creator to take place, there are two dimensions of interpersonal communion which need to grow within marriage. First, there is an interpersonal dimension which directly involves the relationship between husband and wife. For the sake of clarity, I am going to call it the "horizontal dimension of procreation." The second dimension presupposes this first one. In order to collaborate with the Creator, spouses need to be united as in a common subject. They need to be in communion by their sharing in their common parental *munus*. Again, for the sake of clarity, I am going to call this second dimension "the vertical dimension of procreation." As we will see, these two dimensions of procreation effect a certain perfection of conjugal love.

---

64. Ibid.; emphasis added.

65. Ibid.; emphasis added.

66. "Traductionem, et promotionem usque ad perfectum statum hominis, inquantum homo est, qui est virtutis status." *In IV Sent.*, d. 26, q. 1, a. 1, c. See Millán-Puelles, *La formación de la personalidad humana*.

67. See *ScG* III.113; GS 24, 50.

68. LR, 227; emphasis added.

Vertical Dimension

The vertical dimension of procreation unveils ulterior religious and metaphysical traits of this rich phenomenon. Since God directly creates man's spiritual soul *ex nihilo*, what husband and wife "provide for" in their collaboration with the Creator is the adequate "matter" for the reception of that spiritual soul. In that sense, their collaboration with the Creator is material, so to speak.[69] However, in this other sense, their collaboration with the Creator is also formal. They decide in right and informed conscience to adhere to God's will. They want to find out whether or not God wants them to have another baby. This intimate discernment and adherence to God's will is possible when the decision is based on a self-sacrificial and loving evaluation of the true good of the family, that of other children (if any), that of the spouses, society, and the church.

These religious and metaphysical marks of human procreation reveal that the participation with God extends beyond the generation of human offspring. The Creator also participates in the educational process by sustaining the child in his being, by loving him, by acting in his providential care, by giving him sanctifying grace, virtues, gifts, etc. As Wojtyła said, education has certain materials. They include not only human inclinations, passions, or faculties but also "that which God gives, by supernatural dispensation of his Grace."[70] This an important aspect of the vertical dimension of procreation. God "does not leave the work of education, which may in a certain sense be called the continuous creation of personality, wholly and entirely to the parents but Himself takes part in it, in His own person."[71]

However, only God is *the* Creator. Human parents collaborate with him but their collaboration does not imply that they are equal to God. They are not on a par. Thus, although the love of parents should be present at procreation, we cannot forget about the love of the Creator. Indeed, "something more than the love of parents was present at the origin of a new person—they were only co-creators; the love of the Creator decided that a new person would come into existence in the mother's womb."[72] That divine love finds its continuation in the work of supernatural grace. Thus, "God Himself takes the supreme part in the creation of a human person in the spiritual, moral, strictly supernatural sphere."[73] Parents, instead, have their proper role in this supernatural dimension as well, but always as co-creators *subordinated* to the Creator.

---

69. See ibid., 55.
70. Ibid., 56.
71. Ibid.
72. Ibid.
73. Ibid.

PART III: PROCREATION

Horizontal Dimension

The horizontal dimension of human procreation unveils its specifying role as the common end or good that determines the friendship between husband and wife to be conjugal. Wojtyła seems to follow herein both human experience and Thomas's lead. As is known, the imposition of names often provides a direct contact with what is most evident in the human experience of a given phenomenon. Thus, the Scholastics used to begin their studies with a nominal definition of the reality under scrutiny. Thomas offers some interesting insights in this regard. He identifies five different possibilities for the etymology of the word marriage (*matrimonium*). First, Thomas notes that *matrimonium* could be derived from *matris* + *munus*, thereby indicating the *officium* of the wife in the education of children.[74] Thus, a woman should marry a man because she loves him in such a way that she wants to become a mother with him as the father of her children. Second, *matrimonium* could be derived from *matrem* + *muniens* (from the verb, *munio*, to protect or fortify), thereby indicating that marriage provides for the mother a support and protector for her *officium* in the person of her husband. Third, *matrimonium* could be derived from *matrem* + *monens* (from the verb, *moneo*, to admonish), thereby indicating that marriage admonishes a mother in view of her *officium* not to leave her husband for another man. Fourth, *matrimonium* could be derived from *materia* + *unius*, thereby indicating that husband and wife come together in marriage, providing the matter—God provides the form or the soul—for the generation of offspring. Fifth, *matrimonium* could be derived from *matre* + *nato* (from the adjective *natus*, born, designed, intended or even destined), thereby indicating that marriage brings the woman to fulfillment in that for which she was made, in that for which she was born: to become a mother.

This etymological array is important only to underline that parenthood and procreation is something evidently known by human beings as intimately related to marriage. A more philosophical and essential consideration sees marriage as *conjugal friendship*, that is, as a union of persons of the opposite sex specified by the common good of procreation. Unlike the unity that exists among Divine Persons in the Trinity, union among human persons is always an accidental union based on a common origin or a common end. We have already analyzed in detail this point when dealing with the experience of original unity. I will not repeat here all the considerations already made in chapter 6. Instead, I will only note their presence in LR.

In this book, Wojtyła describes what happens as two people freely share the same end when viewed as their common good. "If this happens, a special bond is established between me and this other person: the bond of a *common good* and of a common aim. This special bond does not mean merely that we both seek a common good, it *also unites the persons involved internally and so constitutes the essential core around which any love must grow*. In any case, love between two people is quite

---

74. Wojtyła mentions the same etymology in ibid., 221 and 259.

unthinkable without some common good to bind them together."[75] The love that pertains to conjugal friendship, although being generically benevolent and beneficent, deserves a more specific qualification. This benevolent love, whereby one unites his destiny and existence to that of another person becoming, as it were, one subject, must essentially be between persons of the opposite sex, and disposed to procreation. Not every union of persons in friendship or *communio* can be conjugal or marital. For a friendship to be conjugal, it must be affected by the parenting *munus*, that is, by the possibility of procreation: "[T]he *marital relationship* is therefore not just a union of persons, a reciprocal relationship between a man and a woman, but *is essentially a union of persons affected by the possibility of procreation.*"[76]

Wojtyła envisions procreation as that common end or good which specifies the very nature of the characteristic union and friendship between husband and wife.[77] Pursuing such a common good conditions and implies, at the same time, the continual ripening or maturation of the love between spouses. His reasoning begins by reminding us that love "is conditioned by the common attitude of people towards the same good, which they choose as their aim, and to which they *subordinate* themselves."[78] Human persons that are part of this *we* are *subordinated* to their common good. "Marriage is one of the most important areas where this principle is put into practice."[79]

The importance underlined here by Wojtyła has to do with a very peculiar phenomenon disclosed by the following question: "How is it possible to ensure that one person does not then become for the other—the woman for the man and the man for the woman—nothing more than a means to an end—that is, an object used exclusively for a selfish end?"[80] In marriage, procreation is not only the common good that specifies the friendship; it is also the common good that *perfects and ripens* it. If procreation is understood beyond naturalistic physicalism as a characteristic human phenomenon, as the virtuous collaboration with the Creator in the transmission and education of human life, then, procreation is the common good and end which excludes the possibility mentioned by Wojtyła's question. Thus, he says about spouses that "to exclude this possibility, they must share the same end. Such an end, where marriage is concerned, is procreation, the future generation, a family, and, at the same time, the continual ripening of the relationship between two people, in all the areas of activity which conjugal life includes."[81] Wojtyła is already emphasizing something

---

75. LR, 28; emphasis added.
76. Ibid., 226; emphasis added.
77. See ibid., 228.
78. Ibid., 30; emphasis added.
79. Ibid.; emphasis added.
80. Ibid.; emphasis added.
81. Ibid. A development of this same doctrine can be found in John Paul II, *Letter to the Families*, 10. Waldstein has seen the congruity of Wojtyła's and John Paul II's teaching with *In IV Sent.*, d. 33, q. 2, a. 1, ad 4. See Waldstein, "Children," 708.

quite important in this text: aiming at procreation is *at the same time* to aim at the maturation of conjugal union. Viewed beyond the limits of naturalistic physicalism as free collaboration with the Creator in the transmission and education of human life, procreation *includes* such a ripening within its own essence or meaning.

Procreation and Virtuous Conjugal Love

Primary and Secondary

Wojtyła just claimed that the love between husband and wife is freed from the threat of utilitarianism and is ripened when the spouses aim at procreation as their common good or end. This is where one can see the primacy of procreation amongst the ends listed above.[82] Procreation is the objective primary end of marriage because it objectively specifies the very essence of marriage and because it objectively presupposes the other ends for its fulfillment. Thus, responsibility for procreation includes, in itself, responsibility for the integration of love between the spouses. To understand this view, one must be freed from prejudice against the term "secondary end." Here is a way of understanding it in consonance with Wojtyła's position: "In each genus of causes one has to consider what is primary and what is secondary. Indeed, the primary end is the final end, while the secondary end is the good that is [ordered] to the end."[83] But then, how is it that one may intend the secondary end when intending the primary one?

To answer this question, an analogy could be offered from the experience of movement.[84] When one wants to travel from city A to city C, one surely intends to go to C. But, at the same time, one is also intending to go to the unavoidable intermediary destinations of the trip. Similarly, provided procreation is understood in the way described above, virtuous conjugal friendship is unavoidably or objectively included in it. The maturation of conjugal love is like a necessary intermediary destination in order to reach the goal of collaborating with the Creator in the transmission and education of human life. Intending procreation, thus understood, is to intend the maturation of conjugal love as well. Virtuous conjugal friendship is ordered to procreation with this kind of hypothetical necessity. This hypothetical necessity is not to be confused with the way in which Kant understands it. Rather, it should be conceived in a Thomistic way as a *ligans* that is already *ligatum*, that is, as something binding because of its objective and not arbitrary dependency with the end. The *responsibility* for the integration of love within marriage is a *ligans* that is objectively *ligatum* with hypothetical

---

82. Aquinas also explains that procreation effects the characteristic union among spouses in *In IV Sent.*, d. 33, q. 2, a. 1. See also Waldstein, "Children," 701.

83. *ST* II–II, q. 17, a. 4, c. See in this light, *In IV Sent.*, d. 31 , q. 1, a. 2, ad 1.

84. See *ST* I–II, q. 12, a. 2, c; *ST* I–II, q. 12, a. 3, ad 2.

necessity by procreation as the common good of marriage.⁸⁵ Thus, intending human procreation *necessarily* means to intend the virtuous character of conjugal friendship.

To be sure, animal reproduction and a minimal upbringing at a physical level could be attained even if the friendship between the spouses is based only on utility and/or pleasure. However, there cannot be *authentic participation* with the Creator in the generation and education of children to the state of virtue unless the love between the spouses has matured to a correct *ordo amoris*. After all, education in moral matters is achieved not only by word, but above all, by example. Hence, besides the acquisition of virtues implied in aiming to have the number of children God wants, aiming at their education in virtue also entails to teach them those virtues not only by word, but also by example. The first example must be that of love. Being a loving husband and a loving wife is the best first step in being a good father and a good mother. It is the first needed example when teaching virtue to children. And as Thomas explains, "when we are dealing with the conduct of people, example has more influence than words. A person chooses and does what seems good to him, and so what one chooses is a better indication of what is good than what one teaches should be chosen. This is why when someone says one thing and does another, what he does has more influence on others than what he has taught. Thus it is especially necessary to give example by one's actions."⁸⁶ Leading children to the perfect state of virtue entails welcoming them into a family that is a true school of love.

Conjugal Love as *Bonum Honestum*

The view just explained gives rise to an important question concerning the value of conjugal love. Can conjugal love retain its intrinsic worth and objective importance within the view just described? Someone could be lead to think that the real value at hand, or *bonum honestum*, is only procreation. Is conjugal love in this view a sheer *bonum utile*? Dietrich von Hildebrand has expressed a similar concern. If conjugal love is something ordered by its very nature or form to an ulterior end, this kind of love would lose its objective importance. It would not be a meaningful good loved for its own sake, but only an instrument used for the sake of something else. In order to solve this quandary and still remain faithful to magisterial teaching, Hildebrand distinguished between conjugal or spousal love as the *meaning* of marriage, and procreation as marriage's primary end. He connected both of them through his notion of superabundant finality. His main distinction between instrumental and superabundant finality is this, that "in instrumental finality the being which is considered as a means is in its meaning and value completely dependent upon the end."⁸⁷ It seems then that to be a useful good excludes being an honest good. Thus, instrumental finality excludes

---

85. See *ST* I–II, q. 99, a. 1, c; Millán-Puelles, *La libre afirmación*, 292.
86. *Super Io.,* cap. 13, lect. 3, n. 1781.
87. Hildebrand, *The Encyclical "Humanae Vitae,"* 30.

an importance or value that is *independent* from the end. Instead, "in superabundant finality, it [the good in question] has a meaning and value independently of the end to which it leads. In the instrumental finality the *causa finalis* determines the *causa formalis*; in the superabundant the *causa formalis* differs from the *causa finalis*."[88]

Unfortunately, we are not before a mere difference in terminology. Hildebrand's position does not seem to account for the intimate relationship between spousal love and procreation as explained in original unity. More concretely, it does not seem to concede to procreation the specifying role given to it by Wojtyła. Hildebrand's superabundant finality suggests that the *causa formalis* of marriage is not determined by its *causa finalis*. Instead, for John Paul II and for Thomas Aquinas, procreation is the objective primary end of marriage, which specifies it as one peculiar kind of friendship distinct from others. In my opinion, at the heart of the matter, there is a misunderstanding on the nature of the *bonum honestum*. Hildebrand's position does not seem to account for the fact that the distinction between an honest, a useful, and a pleasurable good is not always a distinction about two or three opposed real things. Rather, these are three different *rationes* or notions.[89] A real thing that is honest or beautiful will always be delightful. Instead, not all delightful things are honest. Some are against the order of reason and, hence, against Beauty (*decor*). An honest thing, in turn, may be useful for the attainment of one's happiness.[90] Honesty and usefulness are always exclusively opposed only when considered in themselves, namely, when taken in their definition. However, this is not always the case when one looks at concrete existing realities. In fact, Ambrose of Milan already noted that something which is *truly* useful for the human person must also be honest or good in itself.[91]

Since Aquinas thinks that the distinction between *honestum*, *utile*, and *delectabilis* is best seen in human goods,[92] I think that Hildebrand's position finds an important phenomenological difficulty in the *experience* of morality. Virtues have a value in and of themselves. They are ends for our actions. At the same time, virtues are pleasurable realities for the virtuous. A virtuous person enjoys acting out of his good habits. Moreover, virtues are, at the same time, useful goods. Indeed, they are very useful in order to be happy and to reach salvation. Nevertheless, they are ends and goods that have worth in themselves, that are pleasurable, and that are useful. Thus, in this particular case, we can see that "the honest concurs in the same subject [*in idem subjectum*] with the useful and the pleasant, but it differs from them in notion [*a quibus tamen differt ratione*]."[93] To be sure, virtues are not the final end but they

---

88. Ibid.

89. Thomas clarifies that "this division is not by opposite things; but by opposite notions [*per oppositas rationes*]." *ST* I, q. 5, a. 6, ad 2.

90. See *ST* II–II, q. 145, a. 3, c.

91. See ibid., II–II, q. 145, a. 3, ad 3.

92. See ibid., I, q. 5, a. 6, c.

93. *ST* II–II, q. 145, a. 3, c. Yet, I think that Hildebrand would not agree with Thomas based on

certainly are *intermediary* ends; they are *secondary* ends.[94] For this reason, there is no contradiction in affirming that conjugal love has meaning and value in and of itself and, at the same time, that it is ordered by its own nature to procreation. Procreation can be the common good that specifies and perfects conjugal love without diminishing a bit the objective importance and value of the latter. Provided that love coordinates the ends of marriage, their objective hierarchy does not entail an obliteration of their intrinsic value.

Furthermore, inspired by the distinction between meaning and end, some theologians find it problematic to speak of conjugal love as an *end* of marriage. Instead, they argue that conjugal love cannot be an end of marriage because it is something that belongs to the very essence of matrimony.[95] This position reflects the mentality of married couples who would readily say, "You are my spouse, because I love you." Yet, they would hesitate more to say, "I love you, because you are my spouse." However, in my opinion, Wojtyła would never grant this point without distinctions. He would not admit for the love between spouses to be reduced to a sheer fact confirmed by matrimony. Additionally, such a love is also a *responsibility* in which one ought to mature within marriage. Indeed, one thing is the metaphysical essence of marriage—that without which marriage does not exist. Another thing is its second perfection—that which makes an already existing marriage, a better marriage.[96] No one would deny that marriage would be more perfect when conjugal love has matured in virtue and is integrated. Yet, such accomplished integration is not a requirement without which one cannot get married. Marriage is like a "school of love" in which both children and parents are educated. Certainly, the incipient beginnings of love are spontaneous, emotional, and also ephemeral. But in this "school," one may be admitted with only those incipient beginnings, provided one commits to mature in

---

Scheler's rejection on eudemonism (see Scheler, *Formalism*, 5–44, 239–369). For Scheler, to be happy is never the end of a good act, because in the very moment in which happiness is the end of a good action, such an action becomes bad. In Scheler's lapidary axiom: the surest way of not attaining happiness is to will it. I have offered a detailed analysis of this view in my *De la experiencia*, 69–134. Scheler's claim is based on a very deficient understanding of the will as rational appetite and its relationship with the good as that which all things desire. In fact, the Aristotelian definition does not mean to say that things are good because they are desired, but rather the contrary, because they are good they are desired. See *In I Ethic.*, lect. 1, n. 9; *In XII Meta.*, lect. 7, n. 2522; Aersten, *Medieval Philosophy and the Trascendentals*, 300; Waldstein, "Dietrich von Hildebrand and St. Thomas."

94. A similar point could be made from the theology of charity. In charity, one loves another in God and because of God. But this kind of love does not violate the dignity of the human person. Wojtyła knows this position well because, in LR, he appeals to Augustine's distinction between *uti* and *frui* (see LR, 44). As is known, Augustine differentiates between a correct and an incorrect use. The first respects the natural order of the eternal law and the end for which creatures have been ordered. The second, instead, does not. Only in the first case is there proper *frui*: "[A] man is just when he seeks to use things only for the end for which God appointed them, and to enjoy God as the end of all, while he enjoys himself and his friend in God and for God. For to love in a friend the love of God is to love the friend for God" (Augustine, *Contra Faustum*, XXII.78).

95. See Gil Hellín, "Los 'bona matrimonii,'" 160.

96. See García López, *Individuo*, 151.

virtuous conjugal love, and to take upon oneself its specific *munus*. Parenting brings in a special way this incipient and imperfect love to the state of mature and virtuous conjugal friendship.

Coming back to the distinction between meaning and end, it seems to me that in Wojtyła's mind, there is a way in which conjugal love could be viewed as part of the meaning of marriage. One would have to concede exactly what Hildebrand denies regarding the *causa finalis* and the *causa formalis*. For Wojtyła, "meaning" is always related to a nature and to its end. It signifies the intellectual apprehension of the nature of something as oriented towards its end. Conjugal love is part of the meaning of marriage because it is part of its nature as conjugal friendship. But conjugal friendship receives its specific difference because of its objective and intrinsic orientation to procreation. Moreover, it is also perfected in the family as it was explained before. However, none of the things explained so far hinder spousal love between a man and a woman to have meaning and value in and of itself and, at the same time, be ordered to something else, such as parenthood. This is why Wojtyła thinks that a marriage does not cease to be such, nor does it lose its value when it cannot fulfill its primary end, due to infertility. This point shows how our author fully agrees with the Thomistic clarifications made previously regarding the nature of the *bonum honestum*.

Looking at the relationship between marriage and the family and explaining the specific case just mentioned, Wojtyła explicitly denies that marriage is a sheer *bonum utile* with no honesty or value in and of itself. The fact that marriage naturally leads to a family does not make marriage itself to be "absorbed by and lost in the family."[97] Indeed, that marriage leads to the family being thus perfected by the latter "does not mean that marriage should be regarded as solely a means to an end—the end being the family."[98] Just like any virtue, despite its being useful, marriage is a *bonum honestum* with an inherent value and meaning of its own. Thus, "the inner and essential *raison d'être* of marriage is not simply eventual transformation into a family but above all *the creation of a lasting personal union between a man and a woman based on love*."[99] That lasting union based on love is objectively ordered to procreation, even if subjectively this end cannot be attained. But even if it cannot be attained, conjugal love is something good on its own accord *independently* from the end towards which it objectively leads. Thus, "a marriage which, through no fault of the spouses, is childless retains its full value as an institution."[100] As Wojtyła clarifies, "a marriage which cannot fulfill that purpose does not lose its significance as an institution of an interpersonal character."[101] In this case, the secondary end of marriage becomes, as it were, primary. But it does so because of a certain imperfection in marriage (arguably amended by adoption).

97. LR, 217.
98. Ibid.
99. Ibid., 218.
100. Ibid.
101. Ibid.

No one would deny that not being able to have children is a certain imperfection in conjugal love. For this reason, Wojtyła says that there is "no doubt, *a marriage serves love more fully when it serves the cause of existence, and develops into a family.* This is how we should understand the statement that "procreation is the principal end of marriage."[102] Hence, there is no doubt that our author understands procreation to be the primary end of marriage because it includes all of the others. It is the conjugal common good that specifies and perfects the union in love between husband and wife. Thus, he continues saying that the "*realization of the principal purpose of marriage demands that its inter-personal character be realized to the full, so that the love of the spouses may be fully mature* and creative. It should be added that if their love is already more or less ripe *procreation will ripen it still further.*"[103] Consequently, that conjugal friendship is objectively ordered by nature to procreation in such a way that procreation is the conjugal common good that species this union and brings it to maturation does not take away the honesty, intrinsic worth, importance, or value of conjugal love. On the contrary, such a subordination makes the value of conjugal love shine even more. Procreation highlights the splendor of the truth of the *bonum honestum* of conjugal love, making it an obligation, a responsibility.

Responsibility for the Integration of Love

LR's very title points to the requirements of marriage as a "school of love." These same requirements are the ones made manifest by and included in procreation as its objective primary end. Wojtyła's central goal in the book is to promote the spouses' responsibility for the integration of their love. Thus, reaching that very topic, he explains that "nowhere else in the whole book, perhaps, is its title, *Love and Responsibility*, more to the point than it is here. There exists in love a particular responsibility—the responsibility for a person who is drawn into the closest possible partnership in the life and activity of another, and becomes in a sense the property of whoever benefits from this gift of self."[104] Note that Wojtyła agrees completely with Aquinas in saying that marriage is the closest possible partnership or as Thomas would say "the greatest friendship [*maxima amicitia*]."[105] Such a partnership is so close and intimate that both Thomas and Wojtyła agree that there are *philosophical* grounds to argue for its indissolubility.[106] This greatest of unions carries with it a responsibility for one's love for the

102. Ibid.; emphasis added.
103. Ibid.; emphasis added.
104. Ibid., 130.
105. *ScG* III.123.

106. I am taking the opportunity to dissipate the alleged contrast between Wojtyła's personalistic considerations on marriage's indissolubility and Thomas's traditional arguments based on natural law theory. Koterski, for example, thinks that Aquinas's arguments in favor of marriage's indissolubility are *not* based on love. Explicitly, he affirms that Thomas's view, although not incompatible with Wojtyła's, is substantially different in this regard. See Koterski, "Aquinas on the Sacrament of Marriage," 108–9.

other. Thus, spouses should ask about their love: "[I]s it mature and complete enough to justify the enormous trust of another person, the hope that giving oneself will not mean losing one's own soul, but on the contrary enlarging one's existence—or will it all end in disillusionment?"[107] Wojtyła's conclusion is as powerful as it is true: "Love divorced from a feeling of responsibility for the person is a negation of itself, is always and necessarily egoism. *The greater the feeling of responsibility for the person the more true love there is.*"[108]

Wojtyła describes such a responsibility, thanks to an analogy with art, already present in his anthropology of love. The human being is author or *creator* of his action (człowiek-*twórca*). He creates or shapes his own moral identity by using some materials already constituted in their nature, such as one's faculties, passions, or feelings. Thus, the same human being can be seen as the man-material that is informed by his action (człowiek-*tworzywo*). It is not really a raw material. One's faculties or passions are not raw; they already have their own nature. They are the apt or adequate materials for some specific virtuous behaviors and they are ready to become so from their very origin in the one rational soul. They owe to the same soul their reciprocal configuration and aptness for each other. Thus, the integration between person and nature at the level of second act consists in the free affirmation of our own nature by bringing to fulfillment the direction of integration of our natural inclinations.[109]

In LR, this is exactly the perspective under which our author explains the spouses' responsibility to integrate their love. The *ars amandi* uses and shapes the material offered by that which merely happens in man. Thereby, this material is conformed to mature conjugal love. It is integrated so as to become an ally for the gift of self among the spouses, a gift that is simultaneously inseparable from their love for the Creator

---

However, I do not think that this position is sustainable taking a closer look at *ScG* III.123–24 and to LR, 185, 214, and 253. Looking at these texts, one concludes that both Aquinas and Wojtyła argue that the foundation for monogamy, and for the indissolubility of marriage, is found in the interpersonal character of conjugal love, a kind of interpersonal love affected by the possibility of procreation, prescribed by the commandment of love or the personalistic norm, and whose habitual state is called conjugal friendship. The more intense friendship is, the more lasting and firm. Since the kind of friendship or habitual love that is to be found between husband and wife is of maximum intensity, precisely because of the characteristic common good they share in parenthood, it should be more lasting and firm than any other friendship or habitual form of love. Moreover, if marriage were not indissoluble, the wife would suffer a great injustice. Her husband would enjoy her company as long as she was young, beautiful, and fertile. Once these qualities were gone, she would be abandoned, thereby manifesting that there never was true conjugal friendship among persons of equal dignity, but only servitude and utility. In anticipation of Wojtyła's arguments, Thomas would say that in that case, the woman would not be treated in justice as a human person worthy of love for its own sake. Her husband would have not taken upon himself the responsibility of maturing his love in order to integrate his concupiscible love for all of her qualities and virtues, into a love of benevolence informed by liberality and equality in dignity.

107. LR, 130.
108. Ibid., 131; emphasis added.
109. See AP, 116.

and their participation with God in procreation.[110] What happens in man as a natural inclination, a sensible passion, or a spiritual affection, constitutes the material out of which one has to build artistically, as it were, virtuous conjugal love. Virtuous love orders and informs that which happens in husband and wife, so that together, they may attain their common end or good in parenting children into the state of virtue. And it does so, by bringing to fulfillment the natural purpose inscribed by the Author of nature as a "directive" or "instruction," that is, the direction inherent in human sexuality towards its integration in the truth about the good.

The Sexual Impulse, Chastity, and Religion

In the human person, the sexual impulse is a natural inclination, in itself good but open to a morally good or bad use.[111] It is not the fixed instinct of irrational animals but a vector of aspiration potentially apt to be finalized by free and conscious activity. In the human person, due to his substantial form, this inclination is generically animal but specifically rational. It is an inclination to human procreation. It is an inclination that points to a human good, wherefrom derives a precept or obligation experienced in conscience as a responsibility to obtain such a good according to right reason (*recta ratio*), that is, according to the proper order found in virtue.[112] According to this same order, the sexual urge is not only directed towards the *qualities* of the person of the opposite sex, but above all towards his or her *person*. Thus, conjugal love meets, assumes, and elevates the sexual impulse.

In LR, Wojtyła chooses to look at how the virtues of chastity and justice towards the Creator established that due order according to right reason. This choice seems to be intimately connected with the two dimensions of procreation mentioned before. Chastity is a virtue that perfects the horizontal dimension, not only at the level of integration *in* the person but also at the level of integration *between* persons, at the level of the *I-thou* community of the spouses. Justice towards the Creator, instead, seems to concentrate on the vertical dimension of procreation. It concentrates on the *we* formed by the spouses as it relates to God, the Creator. Aquinas himself seems to suggest this very perspective when offering some examples in which the conjugal act is a meritorious act. He argues that "if a virtue leads one to the martial act, whether justice, in order to render the debt, *or religion, in order to procreate children for the worship of God, it is meritorious.*"[113] However, note well that the vertical dimension presupposes the horizontal, just like procreation includes the ripening and perfection of the spouses' love. Procreation includes the union of the spouses in mature and

---

110. See LR, 93.
111. See ibid., 286–87, 46–47.
112. See *ST* I-II, q. 94, aa. 2–3.
113. *In IV Sent.*, d. 26, q. 1, a. 4, c; emphasis added.

virtuous love. Spouses cannot give God what is his due when collaborating with the Creator in procreation unless they are perfected by the virtue of chastity.

From the viewpoint of the horizontal dimension of procreation, one can distinguish chastity's role at the level of *integration in the person* and *integration between persons*. At the first level, through the virtue of chastity, what is inferior in the human person remains subordinated to what is superior. His sensible faculties are subordinated to his rational ones, while the latter are subordinated in their turn to the intelligible order derived from the Creator. Thus, there is a peculiar integration of one's sexual impulse in the truth about the good, in which the sexual urge is perfected in the individual according to right reason (*recta ratio*).[114] However, this perfection of the individual also affects the *I–thou* dimension of the conjugal community. It dispels the ethos of concupiscence and allows for the acknowledgement and affirmation of the personal dignity of the other, for lust affects each of the main acts of the human person's spiritual faculties.[115]

Indeed, lust is a great obstacle for speculative knowledge and its perfection in wisdom, and for practical knowledge and its perfection in prudence. It blinds the mind (or perverts the heart) by hindering the simple act of apprehension, whereby the end is understood as good. It also hinders one's counsel about the means to attain a good end. Lust rushes one into decisions without sufficient deliberation and counsel.[116] It causes thoughtlessness, by hindering one's judgment about what is to be done.[117] It engenders inconstancy and places an obstacle to the act of *imperium* (command) about what is to be done. On the part of the will, lust makes the rational appetite to desire inordinate pleasures (false self-love), and to hate God for their being prohibited.[118] Moreover, it directs the will to love this world and to hate the world to come, finding displeasure in spiritual things. For all these Thomistic reasons, inasmuch as chastity opposes lust, Wojtyła argues that at the level of *integration between persons*, chastity is a virtue that contributes to revealing the complementarity between male and female, as well as the contingency of the human person as a being in need of perfection.[119] Most importantly, in this dimension, chastity becomes the best defense against two great enemies of virtuous love: carnal concupiscence, and the more "spiritual" emotional egoism.[120]

In turn, from the viewpoint of the vertical dimension of procreation, the virtue of religion subsumes or redimensions what is accomplished by chastity. The virtue of

---

114. See LR 165–69; CCC, 2337.
115. See *ST* II–II, q. 153, a. 6, c.
116. See ibid., II–II, q. 53, a. 3.
117. See Dan 13:9.
118. See *ST* II–II, q. 153, a. 5, ad 3.
119. See LR, 146.
120. See ibid., 152, 158.

justice has the capacity to redimension any other virtue for the common good.[121] Religion, as a virtue within the province of justice, does so but in relationship with God. It is justice towards the Creator. Thus, the connection between chastity and religion orders the spouses to participate rationally with God in the transmission and education of human offspring to the state of virtue. Thereby, it focuses the entire sexual life of the spouses in giving back to God what is his due. "If I want to be completely just to God the Creator, I must offer Him all that is in me, my whole being, for He has first claim on all of it."[122] At the natural level, justice towards the Creator takes the place of charity in the sense that it commands a complete gift of self to God. The spouses' love for God becomes a matter of justice. Even the mutual love between spouses is redimensioned and elevated here by this transcendent common good.

The personalistic norm expresses the natural aspect of the commandment of love as the first precept of natural law. It is also a matter of justice. Hence, Wojtyła links procreation and justice towards the Creator with the personalistic norm. Not in vain, "the personalistic norm may be said to have its fullest justification and its ultimate origin in the relationship between God and man."[123] Thus, virtuous conjugal friendship is really the only way to attain procreation in a truly human way. This is the direction of integration that belongs to the human sexual urge. This urge is like matter apt and already oriented to be informed by these virtues. It was made for this kind of integration in free, benevolent, and responsible love for the other. As a result, a correct interpretation of the sexual urge must see its existential and religious dimension when considering the primary end of marriage. All of these considerations will become extremely important in order to understand the evil of contraception in chapter 12.

Beyond Physicalism and Towards Priestly Participation

Wojtyła's emphasis on the virtue of justice, and particularly on religion, was already present in TOB's adequate anthropology. Remember his emphasis on reverence and the gift of piety. In my opinion, there are different reasons for this "coincidence." Obviously, this perspective remains permanent because of Wojtyła's constant view of marriage from the twofold perspective of the *I–thou* and the *we* dimension. However, I would like to point out two other less evident reasons for this constant perspective. First, this perspective is one of the ways in which our author fights against naturalistic physicalism. Second, this same perspective is the philosophical correlate of that moral attitude identified in Wojtyła's interpretation of Vatican II: participation in Christ's priestly *munus*.

The perspective of religion as justice towards the Creator allows Wojtyła to reorient what Scheler and some contraception proponents call the biological or

---

121. See *ST* II–II, q. 58, a. 12, c.
122. LR, 249–50.
123. Ibid., 245–46.

psychophysical order, ruled by the laws of nature as opposed to the laws of the spirit. Wojtyła has taken that necessary distance from such phenomenological notions of nature so as to not fall into Kant's radical distinction between the laws of nature and the laws of practical reason or freedom.[124] In so doing, he has referred back to the Creator the intelligible order found in nature. He has come back to the order of nature "*as a specific order of existence with an obvious relationship to the First Cause, to God the Creator.*"[125] Thus, in the human person, the sexual urge is not something merely biological, but rather something that is also metaphysical and religious. It is the result of the impression of the eternal law in man's rational nature.

The order of existence is the work of the Creator. Its laws find their foundation in God. He is *the* Author of nature. He has intelligently disposed that, in the human person, the sexual urge is naturally oriented like a vector in a direction of integration. Although this order is apprehended by human reason, it is not constituted by it but by the Creator's intellect. The conjugal act cannot be measured solely from the biological viewpoint of the empirical sciences. There needs to be a metaphysical and even a religious approach to the question. Only this last approach can serve as grounds to the more anthropological and ethical considerations in which we are about to enter. Within these metaphysical (religious), anthropological, and ethical considerations, the perspective of justice towards the Creator has a special relevance. It envisions conjugal and sexual life under the prism of love and responsibility. Wojtyła argues that this perspective "makes possible a correct attitude to the whole of the real world, in all its component parts and elements. This attitude is a specific form of love and not merely love of the world, but also *love of the Creator.*"[126]

To respect the intelligible order of nature, ontologically constituted by God's infinite and eternal ordering of created reality, but apprehended by human reason in his own moral adventure, is not only an act of justice but also, an act of love for the Creator. "True, the love of the Creator is only indirectly present in it, but it is nonetheless real. The man who has a correct attitude to the whole of created reality thereby adopts, if only indirectly, a correct attitude to the Creator, and is essentially just to Him."[127] Especially, any violation of the personalistic norm as part of this natural order is also a violation of the order of justice established by the Creator. Thus, "there can be no justice towards the Creator where a correct attitude to his creatures, and in particular to other human beings, is lacking. This brings us back to the personalistic norm. Man can only be just to God the Creator if he loves his fellows."[128] As we will see, God has given to the conjugal act a definitive rational nature oriented to virtue, which the human person intellectually understands.

124. See Kant, *Foundations of the Metaphysics of Morals*, 3–4.
125. LR, 57; emphasis added.
126. Ibid., 247; emphasis added.
127. Ibid.
128. Ibid.

Moreover, the perspective of justice towards the Creator is also the direct offshoot of Wojtyła's views on responsibility and moral obligations. Indeed, Wojtyła affirms that the impact on one's conscience by the truth about the good "is best formulated in St. Paul, in his demand of *rationabile obsequium,* which is the *personalistic synonym of obligation*."[129] Hence, the perspective of justice towards the Creator refers back to God the intelligible order found in human nature as oriented to virtue, an order understood by reason, which leads to the formulation and knowledge of the natural law. Thus, the fulfillment of moral responsibility is seen as a *rationabilem obsequium*, as a matter of religion or justice towards the Creator.

As is known, on the day of their wedding, spouses made promises *to each other*. However, from the perspective in which we are right now, these promises also involve God. He is the Author of marriage and the ultimate source of the experience of moral obligation. And spouses also promise to accept lovingly children from God. Additionally, there is a Thomistic sense in which the marital promises could be considered as vows.[130] Hence, granted that marriage promises are vows under a certain aspect (*secundum quid*), Wojtyła's perspective acquires an unsuspected force. The Angelic Doctor explains that *any virtue* can fall under the orbit of a vow. Conjugal chastity could also be a part of this sphere. That being the case, acts of conjugal chastity would be even better and more meritorious. They would belong not only to the virtue of chastity; additionally, these same acts would also "belong to the divine worship, being like sacrifices to God [*pertinent ad divinum cultum, quasi quaedam Dei sacrificia*]."[131]

Within this perspective, acts of conjugal chastity and procreation would be done with that kind of *sacrificial* spirit, which John Paul II has already spoken about. Moreover, this same perspective of justice towards the Creator does not only correspond exactly to moral obligation as a *rationabilem obsequium*, it also offers a philosophical correlate to Wojtyła's theological explanation of one's participation in Christ's priestly *munus*. Our author considered this attitude as the heart of Vatican II.[132] It referred to "the simplest and most complete attitude," the attitude that "expresses the vocation of the person in its existential nucleus."[133] This is the same attitude whereby the human person gives himself and offers the world to God in the manner of a sacrifice that is true spiritual worship (*rationabilem obsequium*).[134] At a more supernatural level, by partaking of this attitude, one fulfills the gift of self or self-offering inherent in the obedience of faith and expressed as the ethical conclusion of the christocentric anthropology of man created in the image of God explained in GS 24. Furthermore,

---

129. AP, 166; emphasis added. See Rom 12:1.
130. See Sommers, "Marriage Vows."
131. *ST* II–II, q. 88, a. 6, c.
132. See SR, 225.
133. Ibid., 224.
134. See Rom 12:1; PO 2; SR, 223.

participation in this priestly attitude unifies the virtues and the sacraments.[135] For married people, this attitude envisions the sacramentality of matrimony from the twofold perspective of cause of grace and sign, which was pointed out by Pius XI and which will be the direct object of our next chapter.[136]

---

135. SR, 237.
136. See LG 11; SR, 239; SC 59.

11

In the Sphere of Marriage's Sacramentality

Marriage as the Foundation of the Sacramental Order?

Grounded in Vatican II and in Thomas Aquinas, John Paul II's theology of procreation proposes that the fulfillment of the spousal meaning of the body in conjugal charity coordinates the objective ends of marriage. This same structural thesis animates TOB's second part. Once again, the pope does not offer either a comprehensive sacramental theology or an exhaustive view of the theology of matrimony. Rather, he makes a selection of topics in view of his future commentary on HV. In my opinion, his strategy consists in looking at how conjugal charity, as an effect of the sacrament of matrimony, coordinates the *bonum prolis* and the *bonum fidei*.[1] In so doing, John Paul is bringing "out of his treasure what is new and what is old."[2] Indeed, as García de Haro noted, the scheme of the *tria bona* had traditionally been used to understand the dynamics of conjugal morality, because the goods of marriage lay the foundation for its moral precepts. Traditionally, "*the ends [of marriage] established by God are, precisely, the goods promised by him*; and he has *established his laws in their service*, as the active intimate principle and external guide for the successful attainment of those very ends."[3] However, as usual, the pope looks at this traditional doctrine with his philosophical and theological depth and in light of new historical circumstances, enacting thereby a sort of renewal in the sources of tradition.

The Council of Trent dogmatically declared the sacramentality of marriage, emphasizing Eph 5:25–32 as its scriptural basis.[4] John Paul II concentrates his analyses on this same text. His precise goal is to establish the sacramentality of matrimony as

---

1. John Paul does not explicitly declare this strategy in TOB's text. There was an indirect hint in PC, 302, which I explained in chapter 3. However, John Paul's strategy becomes more apparent when one reads TOB not only as a book by Karol Wojtyła but also as part of the church's magisterium. Under this other light, one should read it following Wojtyła's principle of integration. Thus, TOB should be read in continuity with *Casti Connubi*, GS, HV, and FC. If one applies Wojtyła's principle, we should rediscover and reread TOB's magisterium in these other magisterial documents. Conversely, we should rediscover and reread *Casti Connubi*, GS, HV, and FC in TOB. See SR, 40–41.

2. Matt 13:52.

3. García de Haro, *Marriage and the Family*, 118–19; emphasis added.

4. See DS 1797; 1800.

a source of grace and of responsibility, from which to envision not only the goods of offspring and fidelity, but also the moral norms founded upon them. Now, to analyze the pope's proposal in some depth, I would like to begin by addressing a potential misunderstanding. As a prelude to his explanation about the "The Great Spousal Analogy," West offers a bold claim: "[M]arriage is not just one of the seven sacraments. Insofar as marriage points us from the beginning to the infinitely greater mystery of Christ's union with the Church, *John Paul teaches that marriage 'is the foundation of the whole sacramental order.'"*[5] I believe that West is referring to the following text:

> The mystery hidden from all ages in God, that is, the Invisible, became visible first of all in the historical event of Christ. The relationship of Christ with the Church, which is defined in Ephesians as "*mysterium magnum*, the great mystery," constitutes the fulfillment and concretization of the visibility of the same mystery . . . One can say that the visible sign of marriage "in the beginning," inasmuch as it is linked to the visible sign of Christ and the Church on the summit of God's saving economy, transposes the eternal plan of love into the "historical" dimension and makes *it* the foundation of the whole sacramental order.[6]

West is not just citing John Paul's text. He has made an important choice for his reader by deciding that the italicized *it* in the text stands for the sacrament of marriage. His choice can easily lead someone to think that John Paul II is teaching something here beyond the commonly upheld position, by Church Fathers and tradition, that marriage is a sacrament of creation or the *primordial* sacrament because it is the first visible sign of God's hidden *mysterium*.[7] Without a doubt, temporally speaking, marriage is that *first* and most ancient visible sign of God's eternal plan of love, as it is fulfilled in Christ's union with the Church. That affirmation is entirely correct and beyond dispute. If West only means to say that marriage is a special sacrament because it points to the "infinitely greater mystery of Christ's union with the Church,"[8] I would agree with him, even if I still do not think that John Paul's text refers to marriage as the foundation of the sacraments. However, what mainly concerns me is that West's choice to substitute the italicized *it* in John Paul's text for the sacrament of marriage could lead some to think that marriage is the foundation of the whole sacramental order as its *ontological origin and cause*. Hence, my main goal now is to answer this precise question: is John Paul II claiming in his interpretation of the great spousal analogy in Eph 5:21–33 that marriage is that kind of ontological foundation for the sacramental order?

---

5. West, *Theology of the Body Explained*, 23; emphasis added.
6. TOB 95b:7; emphasis added.
7. See Sarmiento, *El Matrimonio*, 127.
8. West, *Theology of the Body Explained*, 23; emphasis added.

Were the pope to uphold this position, he would be directly contradicting Thomas Aquinas and a very long tradition, which sees such a foundation not in the sacrament of matrimony, but in Christ's *redemptive Incarnation*. Moreover, how could marriage be *part* of the sacramental order and, at the same time, be the *foundation* of the *whole* sacramental order? Is that even possible? The italicized *it* holds the key to unlock this quandary. Does it stand for the visible sign of marriage? Does it substitute, instead, the eternal plan of love, fully manifested and brought about in the redemptive Incarnation of the Lord and in his gift of self for the church? As far as I can tell, from the grammatical viewpoint, there is no conclusive argument. It seems that this text could be read either way, even in the original Italian.[9] Hence, the only way to properly answer this question is to look closely at other texts in TOB. In so doing, we will have the opportunity to understand Paul's spousal analogy in Eph 5:21–33 in the measure that is needed in order to follow John Paul's precise argumentation in the rest of the book.

The Great Spousal Analogy

Following Trent's lead and relying on the church's *lex orandi*, John Paul II elaborates an in-depth analysis of Eph 5:21–33 in order to understand the sacramentality of marriage. The pope offers some methodological parameters. This text crowns his previous anthropological considerations regarding the spousal meaning of the body in the beginning, in the redemption of the human heart, and in its fulfillment in glory. Conversely, Eph 5:21–33 should be interpreted in light of the same theology of the spousal meaning of the body previously outlined. Finally, this passage's teachings on conjugal morality should be read in light of the context of the whole letter, especially in light of God's eternal plan of love and salvation in Christ, out of which flows the entirety of the Christian moral life as a vocation.[10] Under this light, it is easier to understand Paul's identification of the measure and exemplar of married love. From the epistemological viewpoint, marriage uncovers God's eternal plan of love fulfilled in Christ's spousal love for the church as his bride and body. However, marriage is not the ontological measure and exemplar of Christ's love for the church. Marriage images Christ's love for the church, not the other way around. Thus, "the reciprocal relationship between the spouses, husband and wife, should be understood by Christians according to the

---

9. The original Italian reads: "Il mistero da secoli nascosto in Dio—ossia invisibile—è divenuto visibile prima di tutto *nello stesso evento storico di Cristo*. E il raporto di Cristo con la Chiesa che nella Lettera agli Efesini viene definito *mysterium magnum*, costituisce l'adempimento e la concretizzazione della visibilità dello stesso mistero [. . .]. Si può dire che il segno visibile del matrimonio in principio, in quanto collegato al segno visibile di Cristo e della Chiesa al vertice dell'economia salvifica di Dio, *traspone l'eterno piano di amore nella dimensione storica e ne fa il fondamento di tutto l'ordine sacramentale*." UD, 501–2; emphasis added.

10. See TOB 88:1; Eph 1:3–7, 10; 4:25–32; 5:1–2.

image of the relationship between Christ and the Church."[11] As the pope also says, by quoting Genesis 2:24, Paul wants "not so much to recall the unity of the spouses . . . but to present the mystery of Christ with the Church, from which the author deduces the truth about the unity of the spouses."[12]

John Paul II identifies four distinct yet interrelated elements in Paul's great spousal analogy. First, we have *God's eternal plan of love*.[13] This eternal plan is the foundation of the whole of salvation history and it aims to make the human person a son in the Son, thereby fulfilling the spousal meaning of the body: "[M]an carried in his soul the fruit of eternal election in Christ, the eternal Son of the Father. Through the grace of this election, man, male and female, was holy and immaculate before God."[14] Second, we have *Adam and Eve's marriage* as a "sacrament of creation," or as the primordial sacrament. That first marriage was a visible sign of God's plan, for it made manifest one possible way of fulfilling on this earth the spousal meaning of the body, or man's supernatural call to charity. Additionally, that first marriage was also a way of conferring grace.[15] Before original sin, procreation was the channel to transmit to the human race the *imago Dei*, both in the natural and in the supernatural order.[16]

Third, we have *Christ's spousal love for the church*, his bride and body, as the ultimate fulfillment and revelation of God's eternal plan of love.[17] Christ's redemptive love gives birth to the church: "[T]hrough a total gift that springs from love, he formed the Church as his body and continually builds her, thus becoming her head."[18] The pope sees a very important christological and ecclesiological connection here: "As head and Savior of the Church, he is also Bridegroom of his Bride."[19] At the same time, the church continues the mission of the Redeemer, in union with Christ as her bridegroom. She draws from such a union her spiritual fruitfulness and motherhood.[20] Right here, the sacraments find their proper ecclesiological *locus*. Fourth, we have *marriage as a sacrament of the new law* that is both a cause of grace and a sign. After original sin, marriage was wounded. The sacrament of matrimony in the new law assumes, heals, and elevates matrimony as a sacrament of creation.[21] This elevation

---

11. TOB 89:8.
12. Ibid., 93:1.
13. See LG 2; SR, 45.
14. TOB 96:4. See GS 2; SR, 47.
15. See TOB 96:7.
16. See ibid., 19:3; 96:1.
17. See ibid., 97:2,5.
18. Ibid., 90:5.
19. Ibid.
20. See 1 Pet 1:23.
21. See TOB 97:3; Rom 5:20.

consists in being a visible sign of Christ's love for his bride and body, the church. Additionally, it consists in being a cause of grace in the new creation in Christ.

It is important to distinguish each of these four elements, and to understand with precision their role in Paul's great spousal analogy. Additionally, we need to distinguish between two directions in Paul's analogy. The first direction of the analogy is more epistemological in nature. It concentrates especially on how marriage gnoseologically makes visible or known God's eternal plan of salvation as fulfilled in Christ's spousal union with the church. In turn, the second direction of Paul's spousal analogy is more ontological in nature. It focuses on Christ's spousal love for the church as the exemplar for the sacramentality of marriage. In order to explain why marriage is not the foundation of the sacramental order, we need to begin with the first direction of this analogy.

Within this first direction, we encounter the place of marriage as a *primordial sacrament*. Since Eph 5:31 refers to Gen 2:25, the first direction of Paul's analogy includes how marriage as a sacrament of creation in the Old Testament is the first and most ancient sign that foreshadowed, with biblical typology, that very union between Christ and the church. Moreover, in this order of knowledge, marriage is a *figure used in human language* to describe Christ's spousal gracing of his church. Insofar as marriage is used in this way to describe such a foundational gracing for the church in her extension of the mission of the Redeemer, John Paul calls marriage a *prototype for all the sacraments of the new law*. Thus, he argues that "if we reflect deeply on this dimension, we have to conclude that *all the sacraments of the New Covenant find their prototype in some way in marriage as the primordial sacrament*."[22]

Marriage is not a prototype because it is the ontological source or foundation. We are in the first direction of the analogy, not in the second. Marriage is that prototype only because it is the *preferred* human reality used in God's revelation to speak analogically of a *different reality* other than marriage. We already know why marriage is that preferred human reality to signify Christ's spousal gracing of his church by means of an analogy. As the highest form of human friendship, the analogy with marriage underlines the whole order of created grace as God's radical and irrevocable gift of self in Christ and to man. As the pope said, this gift is total inasmuch as "it is in some sense all that God could give of himself to man, considering the limited faculties of man as a creature. In this way, the analogy of spousal love indicates the radical character of grace: of the whole order of created grace."[23] However, the order of knowledge and the order of being should not be confused. This other reality *signified by marriage* is the *real* foundation of the whole sacramental order. As a result, such an ontological foundation is Christ's redemptive Incarnation, perfected in his spousal gift of self to the church as his body and bride. It really corresponds with the third element identified in Paul's analogy. Let us look at some texts from TOB which confirm this position.

22. TOB 98:2.
23. Ibid., 95b:4.

Referring to this third element as contained in Paul's text, John Paul argues that Ephesians 5:21–33, "speaks *about the bases of the sacramentality of the whole Christian life and in particular about the bases of the sacramentality of marriage.*"[24] But note that the pope clearly teaches that marriage is *part* and not foundation *of the sacramental order*. The entire sacramental order draws its *origin from the sacrament of Redemption*: "Christ not only confirms the existence of marriage from the beginning by the Creator, but he declares also that it is an integral *part of the new sacramental economy*, of the new order of salvific signs that *draws its origin from the sacrament of redemption*, just as the original economy emerged from the sacrament of creation."[25] Redemption is called a sacrament here, inasmuch as it visibly discloses and fulfills God's eternal plan of love. But it clearly refers to Christ's redemptive Incarnation as perfected in his gift of self for the church. In this manner, John Paul II explains the central role of Christ's humanity for the sacramental order, especially for the sacramentality of marriage. "The Incarnation—and the redemption that flows from it—has also become *the definitive source of the sacramentality of marriage.*"[26] As the pope plainly says, within the supernatural order, "marriage is a visible and efficacious sign. Having originated in the mystery of creation, *it draws its new origin [as one of the sacraments of the Church] from the mystery of redemption* in order to serve the union of the sons of God in truth and love."[27] Thus, the body finds a central role in theology. "The fact that theology also includes the body should not astonish or surprise anyone who is conscious of *the mystery and reality of the Incarnation*. Through the fact that the Word of God became flesh, the body entered theology—that is, the science that has divinity for its object—I would say, through the main door."[28] Consequently, John Paul's theology of the body emphasizes the role of Christ's body in the sacrament of Redemption, that is, in the visible manifestation and fulfillment of God's eternal plan of love in Jesus's gift of self for the church in his passion. John Paul's emphasis squares perfectly with the traditional view of Christ's humanity as a conjoined instrument of our salvation, and the sacraments as the separated instruments that cause grace, while signifying those salvific actions of Jesus's life.

Thomistic Ways of Being Grounded in Vatican II

The previous clarifications further unveil John Paul II's remarks on sacramental theology as Thomistic and grounded in Vatican II. The pope's identification of Christ's spousal gift of self to the church as the ontological source for the sacraments corresponds exactly with Aquinas's teachings: "[T]he institution and the power of the

24. Ibid., 93:4; emphasis added.
25. Ibid., 98:2.
26. Ibid., 23:4.
27. Ibid., 103:7; emphasis added.
28. Ibid.

sacraments has its beginning in Christ. For the Apostle says of Him: 'Christ loved the Church and gave Himself up for it: that he might sanctify it, cleansing it by the laver of water in the word of life.'"[29] Hence, both John Paul II and Thomas find the origin of the sacramental order in Christ; they both point to the same text (Eph 5:25–26) as the foundation for the sacramental order.

Moreover, the pope's emphasis on the Incarnation and on the role of the body corresponds to Vatican II's and to Thomas Aquinas's sacramental theology founded upon Christ as *the* Way. As was said, SC 5 identifies the humanity of Christ united to the Person of the Word—that same spousal union between Christ and humanity of which both Aquinas and John of the Cross spoke about—as the instrument of our salvation.[30] Likewise, Thomas explains that Jesus says in John 14:6 that "he is the way by reason of his human nature, and the destination because of his divinity. Therefore, as human, he says, I am the way; as God, he adds, and the truth, and the life."[31] The sacraments are founded upon Jesus's priestly actions "represented" in their actual power by him, through the sacraments and their proper ministers.[32] The theandric human acts of the Son of God have saved mankind and in them, Christ's humanity is a conjoined instrument of our salvation.[33] The sacraments, in turn, are the separated instruments that cause grace while signifying those salvific actions of Jesus's life. They lead us to the truth and the life—that is, to salvation—through the way of Christ's humanity.[34]

Furthermore, Wojtyła's emphasis on our participation in Christ's priesthood as maximally expressed in Eph 5:25 corresponds to Thomas's view, according to which Jesus's passion is his greatest priestly action. According to Aquinas, Christ's priesthood and kingship were principally consummated in his passion.[35] There were other actions in Jesus's earthly life that were priestly. However, he grew in wisdom and grace inasmuch as he did ever wiser and greater works.[36] Consequently, Jesus's sacrificial gift of self on the cross is the salvific action which perfectly fulfills the *ratio sacerdotalis*.[37] Christ's passion is, therefore, at the heart and root of the sacraments as signs of

---

29. *ScG* IV.74; Eph. 5:25–26. For a brief historical exposition of Aquinas's doctrine of marriage in light of his main sources, see Carpin, *Il sacramento del matrimonio*.

30. See SC 5; SR, 68.

31. *In Ioan.*, cap. 14, lect. 2, n. 1868.

32. See Weinandy, "The Human Acts of Christ," 150–68; LG 11; SC 2.7.

33. See *ST* III, q. 19, a. 1, ad 1, 5; III, q. 13, a. 2, c.

34. See ibid., III, q. 60, prologue.

35. See SR, 237; *ST* III, q. 35, a. 7, ad 1.

36. This is how Thomas explains the testimony of Scripture according to which Jesus grew in wisdom and grace (see Luke 2:52; Heb 2:10; 5:9; 7:18; *ST* III, q. 7, a. 12, ad 3). One should add that Christ's sacrificial gift of self, being the wisest and greatest work of Christ, perfected him, as the Letter to Hebrews says, in the sense that it made Jesus's humanity pass from the state of passibility to that of impassibility (see *Super Heb.*, cap. 5, lect. 9).

37. See *ST* III, q. 22, a. 2; q. 26, a. 2, c, ad 3.

a holy thing that make men holy. As a result, this same passion and gift of self is at the heart and root of the sacrament of marriage.

Additionally, Wojtyła's interpretation of Vatican II and his remarks on sacramental theology in TOB also correspond with Aquinas's realism concerning our participation in the sacraments. Thus, both John Paul II and Thomas Aquinas understand the sacraments in general, and matrimony in particular, to offer a real participation in Christ's paschal mystery. Both argue for a certain *conformity* with Christ, which has ontological as well as moral dimensions.[38] Hence, the fulfillment of the attitude of participation, as it was condensed in the participation of Christ's priesthood, entailed the perfecting of God's image in man through conformity with Christ. As a result, Wojtyła claimed that, in the teaching on Christ's priesthood and in our participation therein, the heart of the entire Second Vatican Council is contained.[39]

Since Christ's priesthood is eternal, his sacrificial and salvific gift of self lasts forever in its effects.[40] The sacraments in general, and matrimony in particular, offer a real participation in this central event. They are perfecting instrumental efficient causes, they contain within themselves the power to cause grace, in the manner proper to a separated instrument.[41] God is the principal cause of grace, because no one except him could cause such an effect. Christ's humanity is used by God as the *conjoined* instrument through which grace is caused in man. The sacraments are the *separated* instrument through which Christ's passion is applied to men in the life of the church. Consequently, since the sacraments participate in both the cause and the effect, they offer a real participation in the efficacy of past historical events, and a real contact with the power of Christ's priestly saving actions. That real contact and participation, offered by the sacraments, takes place in their dimension of sign, and in their dimension of being efficient secondary and instrumental causes of grace, exactly the two dimensions treated by John Paul II in his study of the sacramentality of marriage in TOB.

One should not oppose John Paul II's scriptural explanation of the sacramentality of marriage and Thomas's metaphysical view of the sacraments. Aquinas's sacramental theology is metaphysical, but also scriptural.[42] Metaphysical categories are only an instrument to explain our connection with the salvific events. For instance, Christ "was put to death for our trespasses and raised to our justification."[43] As a result, "all of us who have been baptized into Christ Jesus were baptized into his death."[44] And

---

38. See Gal 4:19; LG 7, 11; SR, 85–87.
39. See SR, 225.
40. See *ST* III, q. 22, a. 5, ad 1.
41. See ibid., III, q. 62, a. 4, c, ad 3.
42. See Blankenhorn, "The Place of Romans 6."
43. Rom 4:25.
44. Rom 6:3.

thus, "as many of you were baptized into Christ have put on Christ."[45] Jesus's passion is a universal cause of salvation that needs to be applied to each individual.[46] The notion of being *conformed* with Christ, for example, is the metaphysical explanation of "putting on Christ" as that application.[47] This conformity implies both a certain moral similitude whereby one resembles the Lord and an ontological conformation to Christ himself, through the justifying power of his death. Both dimensions, moral and ontological, enable John Paul II to make the connection between sacraments and the ethos of redemption.

Moreover, Wojtyła's emphasis on partaking in Christ's priestly *munus* has further justification in Thomas's theology of the sacramental character. Since some passive power is needed to receive divine gifts, and some active power is also needed to bestow them on others, there are sacraments that impart a character, namely, a certain spiritual power ordained to things pertaining to divine worship.[48] The active power given by a sacramental character empowers the recipient to be a *minister* through which divine gifts are bestowed. The passive power given by the sacramental character grants the capacity to *receive* divine gifts. Since this sacramental character is the character of Christ to whom the faithful are likened, sacramental characters are a certain participation in Christ's priesthood, which flow from Christ himself and are ordained to priestly actions.[49] For this reason, Weinandy argues that, "the sacramental character empowers the soul of the Christian to perform actions in a manner keeping with its Christian nature, that is, to perform actions in conformity with Christ the priest."[50] And Thomas clearly holds that Christ's sacrificial and spousal gift of self on the cross is the exemplar of how to offer oneself in sacrificial charity.[51] For this reason, Wojtyła explained the attitude of participation in Christ's priesthood as the perfecting of the image of God in man, through conformity with Christ.[52] This will be true, as we will shortly see, for those who live the sacrament of matrimony.

Furthermore, both Thomas and John Paul II would understand conjugal morality under the new law, or under the ethos of redemption, as flowing from the specific graces received in the sacraments, especially that of matrimony.[53] The sacraments make this reality possible, thanks to the application of the passion in us. But this application brings with it a certain ethos or subjective appropriation of the new law. Indeed, "Christ's passion attains its effect in those to whom it is applied through faith

---

45. Gal 3:27.
46. See *ST* III, q. 49, a. 1, ad 4.
47. See *Super Rom.*, cap. 4, lect. 3.
48. See *ST* III, q. 63, a. 2.
49. See ibid., III, q. 63, a. 3.
50. Weinandy, "The Human Acts," 165. See *ST* III, q. 63, a. 5, c.
51. See *In Eph.*, cap. 5, lect. 1, n. 270.
52. See SR, 225.
53. See LG 11; SR, 97.

and charity and by means of the sacraments of faith."[54] The sacramental life of the church is then the foundation for a "new" moral order in which each Christian, by his participation in the *munus sacerdotalis* of Christ, is called to bear the marks of Jesus in his own body.[55] And the sacraments are the means whereby we receive the power to live in the true freedom that characterizes those who reign by serving Christ and his Kingdom, the children of God.[56] For this very reason, Wojtyła argued, when explaining the meaning of the liturgy by means of LG 11, that "the attitude which results from sharing in the priesthood of Christ is manifested and confirmed not only by the testimony of liturgical life but also by the whole of Christian morality and the aspiration to holiness."[57] This is exactly what the sacraments, as causes and signs, make possible.[58] This is where the sacraments connect with the fulfillment of the *imago Dei* and the spousal meaning of the body in the ethos of redemption, inasmuch as they procure conformity with Christ, image of the invisible God. Therefore, "although Ephesians does not speak directly and immediately about marriage as one of the sacraments of the Church, it nevertheless particularly confirms and deeply explains the sacramentality of marriage. *In the great sacrament of Christ and the Church, Christian spouses are called to shape their life and vocation on the sacramental foundation.*"[59]

Conformity to Christ's Spousal Charity

GS 48 directs our attention to Pius XI's *Casti Connubi* in order to understand the sacramentality of matrimony. This pope had already explained that the good of the sacrament denotes both the indissolubility of the matrimonial bond, and the consecration whereby Christ elevated this contract to the rank of a sign that is a cause of grace. Thus, the Lord made matrimony "a sign and source of that *peculiar internal grace* by which it perfects natural love, it confirms an indissoluble union, and sanctifies both man and wife."[60] Pius XI recalls that the sacrament of matrimony "*increases sanctifying grace*, the permanent principle of the supernatural life, in those who, as the expression is, place no obstacle (*obex*) in its way."[61] There are also particular graces. The grace of the sacrament of matrimony "adds *particular* gifts, dispositions, seeds of grace, by elevating and perfecting the natural powers."[62] Through these particular graces of the sacrament of matrimony, spouses "are assisted not only in understand-

---

54. *ST* III, q. 49, a. 3, ad 1.
55. See Gal 6:17; LG 11.
56. See *Super Rom.*, cap. 6, lect. 4; LG 36; SR, 96–98.
57. SR, 231.
58. See *ST* III, q. 61, a. 1, ad 3; KD, 342n50.
59. TOB 99:3; emphasis added.
60. Pius XI, *Casti Connubi*, 38; emphasis added. See GS 48.
61. *Casti Connubi*, 40; emphasis added.
62. Ibid.; emphasis added.

ing, but in knowing intimately, in adhering to firmly, in willing effectively, and in successfully putting into practice, those things which pertain to the marriage state, its aims and duties, giving them in fine right to the actual assistance of grace, whensoever they need it for fulfilling the duties of their state."[63] In LG, Vatican II proposes the same teaching but focalizing the source of matrimonial grace in Christ's spousal charity as it influences conjugal love and procreation. "Christian spouses, in virtue of the sacrament of matrimony, whereby *they signify and partake of the mystery of that unity and fruitful love which exists between Christ and His Church*, help each other to attain to holiness in their conjugal life and in the rearing and education of their children."[64]

Grounded in that same teaching, John Paul II explains that marriage is one of the seven sacraments of the church.[65] Reading Ephesians 5:21–23 with the whole sacramental economy in view, one realizes that, in the great analogy, marriage is presupposed and, at the same time, rediscovered. It is presupposed as a sacrament of creation. But it is rediscovered as a sacrament of the new economy, created anew as the fruit of Christ's spousal and redemptive love for the church.[66] Christ's revelation of the truth about marriage "reaches its definitive fullness in the gift of love which the Word of God makes to humanity in assuming a human nature, and in the sacrifice which Jesus Christ makes of Himself on the Cross for His bride, the Church."[67] The sacrament of matrimony gives a specific grace. Based on 1 Corinthians 7:7 and LG 11, John Paul II speaks of a gift of their own.[68] The pope appeals to the grace of the sacrament, which "renders man and woman capable of *loving one another as Christ has loved us*."[69] In continuity with Pius XI and Vatican II, John Paul II teaches that in this manner "conjugal love reaches that fullness to which it is interiorly ordained, *conjugal charity*, which is *the proper and specific way in which the spouses participate in and are called to live the very charity of Christ who gave Himself on the Cross*."[70] The sacramentality of marriage assumes and elevates this natural institution. The pope speaks of an assumption and elevation "into the *spousal charity of Christ*."[71]

John Paul views the sacrament of marriage as organically linked with the ethos of redemption that should characterize the life of Christians. The sacramental economy of the new law is directed to the human person in the state of sinfulness (*status naturae lapasae*), and wounded by the threefold concupiscence.[72] Thus, the redemption of the

63. Ibid.
64. LG 11; emphasis added.
65. See TOB 98:7; Collins, "Marriage," 252.
66. See TOB 102:1.
67. FC 13.
68. See TOB 103:6.
69. FC 13; emphasis added.
70. Ibid.; emphasis added.
71. Ibid.; emphasis added.
72. See TOB 98:3–5.

body accomplished in Christ helps "to overcome the consequences of sin and to build the unity of man and woman according to the Creator's eternal plan."[73] Redemption is a grace or God-given gift to man in the new covenant in Christ. Yet, it requires a personal and moral response to that gift. As a result, marriage is not only a sacrament, but also *a moral exhortation* to share consciously in the redemption of the body. The human person receives "in marriage the sacrament of redemption as grace and sign of the covenant with God—and it is assigned to him as an ethos."[74] John Paul envisions the sacrament of marriage in the sphere of Christian responsibility by emphasizing its being a memorial, an actuation, and a prophecy. Inasmuch as the sacrament of marriage is a memorial, it gives spouses "*the grace and duty* of commemorating the great works of God and of bearing witness to them before their children. As actuation, it gives them *the grace and duty of putting into practice in the present*, towards each other and their children, the demands of a love which forgives and redeems. As prophecy, it gives them *the grace and duty* of living and bearing witness to the hope of the future encounter with Christ."[75]

This whole argument is grounded in Wojtyła's interpretation of Vatican II. Conferring a specific grace, the sacrament of marriage consecrates the spouses to a particular exercise of the priestly mission. Its fulfillment implies a Christian witness that is informed by the theological virtues, a witness to which spouses have been predestined and called in Christ. Thus, the *mission* and the *testimony* of the spouses is based on their *participation* in the mission of Christ. Their mutual and fruitful love is elevated into the realm of charity and Christian responsibility. Due to the sacramentality of marriage as a cause of grace and as a sign, spouses are to make present in a visible manner Christ's spousal charity for the church. They are to do so by being just and faithful to their conjugal love, and by being sacrificially generous in their fruitfulness. This is the prophetic testimony (*martiria*) that results from their participation in Christ's priestly *munus* "through the sacraments and the exercise of virtues."[76] In turn, this participation implies the true freedom of those who reign with Christ by serving the Lord, living out the precepts of charity.[77] Therefore, TOB adopts this same emphasis on the spouses' responsibility to participate in Christ's sacrificial and fruitful spousal gift of self for the church.

Metaphysical and Christological Basis

Moreover, John Paul II's position is also founded upon the theology of the Angelic Doctor. Thomas opposes those who reduce marriage to a sheer sign of grace without

73. Ibid., 100:2.
74. Ibid., 100:7.
75. FC 13; emphasis added.
76. See LG 11; SR, 97.
77. See LG 36; SR, 97–98.

accounting for its causality as a sacrament of the new law. He teaches, instead, that marriage is one of the seven sacraments of the church and that, like any of them, matrimony carries within it a "remedy of holiness for man against sin."[78] However, matrimony's grace should not be identified with the excusing from sin when having sex within the boundaries of the goods of marriage. Thomas argues for much more. He says that "marriage, inasmuch as it is contracted in the faith of Christ, is able to confer *a grace helping those things to be done which are required in marriage*."[79] Thus, the *bonum sacramenti* is not only the indivisibility of the spousal union between husband and wife, but also everything that results from marriage being a sign of Christ's union with the church.[80] Within this last dimension, Aquinas explains matrimony's specific grace by saying that "the external acts and words expressing consent directly effect a bond of obligation."[81] Marriage is a source of grace, but also of responsibility. Thomas identifies this bond with the *res et sacramentum* effected by the words of consent as the *sacramentum tantum*.[82] Aquinas compares the bond to the sacramental character of baptism. As a result, he explains that "a bond of this kind operates dispositively for grace by the power of divine institution."[83] In perfect consonance with Vatican II and with John Paul II, Thomas teaches that the special grace given by matrimony consists in a special conformation with Christ's passion, with Christ's spousal charity. To be sure, "marriage does not conform to the passion of Christ in suffering, yet it *conforms* to the same passion *in the charity* by which he suffered for the Church in order that she might be joined to him *as bride* [*conformat tamen ei quantum ad caritatem per quam pro Ecclesia sibi in sponsam conjungenda passus est*]."[84] Such a conformity directly impacts the goods of offspring and fidelity: "[S]ince in marriage a man is given by divine institution the faculty of enjoying [*uti*] his wife for the procreation of children, *grace is also given without which he could not do this fittingly*."[85]

For instance, the conformation of the spouses to Christ's spousal charity remedies concupiscence.[86] Like any other sacrament of the new economy, marriage offers healing to the human person wounded by the threefold concupiscence.[87] Already at the level of a natural institution, marriage remedied concupiscence inasmuch as it called for a virtuous integration of one's sexual desire into the order of right reason.[88]

---

78. *In IV Sent.*, d. 26, q. 2, a. 1, c.
79. Ibid., d. 26, q. 2, a. 3, c; emphasis added.
80. See ibid., d. 31 , q. 1, a. 2, ad 4; *Super I Cor.*, cap. 7, lect. 1.
81. *In IV Sent.*, d. 26, q. 2, a. 3, ad 2. See also d. 27, q. 1, a. 1, qc. 1, ad 2.
82. See ibid., d. 26, q. 2, a. 1, ad 5; a. 3, ad 2; d. 27, q. 1, a. 1, qc. 1, ad 2.
83. Ibid., d. 26, q. 2, a. 3, ad 2.
84. Ibid., d. 26, q. 2, a. 1, ad 3. See also TOB 131:1.
85. *In IV Sent.*, d. 26, q. 2, a. 3, c; emphasis added.
86. See ibid., d. 26, q. 2, a. 3, ad 4.
87. See TOB 98:3–5.
88. *Super I Cor.*, cap. 7, lect. 1. See *In IV Sent.*, d. 26, q. 2, a. 3, c.

However, as a sacrament of the new law, matrimony does much more. It empowers spouses to live up to that call to integrate their conjugal love. The sacrament of matrimony confers a specific grace with the power to conform and elevate human conjugal love to Christ's spousal charity. Since concupiscence is a great threat to the fulfillment of any of the Christian responsibilities of marriage, the grace given by the sacrament of marriage must be a remedy to such a threat.[89]

Consequently, marriage is not a remedy for concupiscence because it gives lust, as it were, "lawful citizenship." On the contrary, the grace of the sacrament of marriage is a remedy for concupiscence because it helps to integrate sexual desires into the conjugal act, the latter being ordered by right reason and conjugal charity to the goods of marriage, especially those of *proles* and *fides*.[90] Evoking Wojtyła's law of the absorption of shame into love, Aquinas even teaches that the very grace of the sacrament elicits shame when the conjugal act is not in view of these goods. Instead, it takes shame away (at least partially), when the conjugal act is ordered to them.[91] Thus, the goodness of the conjugal act shines through the grace of the sacrament, because its utility and pleasure are integrated into its honesty. One could say that it is integrated into real goodness, or the truth about its goodness. For this reason, it is better to marry than to be aflame! Again, not because marriage is a safe haven for lust, but because the order of one's passions in view of the truth about the good is better than the disorder of passions that enslave reason to the service of selfish desire.[92]

Let us pause to better understand this conformity with Christ's spousal charity effected by the sacrament of matrimony. We need to do so within the parameters of Aquinas's metaphysical realism in sacramental theology. Hence, such conformity has *moral* and *ontological* dimensions.[93] Christ is *the* way towards salvation. He is the moral and ontological example for spouses in matrimony. Indeed, the sacrament of marriage is Christ-conforming. Its grace becomes a sort of education, a leading-by-the-hand (*manducatio*) towards eternal salvation.[94] The moral aspect of Christ's exemplarity in marriage focuses on the spouses' imitation of Christ in their collaboration with God and the sacrament of matrimony in its dimension of sign. Such collaboration is christocentric because Christ is the living pattern of evangelical virtues and of the human effort to collaborate with God.[95] However, Christ's moral exemplarity differs radically from that of other virtuous men. Unlike the example of a human person, Christ's is theandric. It is the example of the God-Man. It transcends all times and situations.[96]

89. See *In IV Sent.*, d. 26, q. 2, a. 3, c.
90. See *Super I Cor.*, cap. 7, lect. 1.
91. See *In IV Sent.*, d. 26, q. 2, a. 3, ad 4.
92. See TOB 101:3. Crosby, "John Paul II's Vision," 58; Gondreau, "The Redemption," 407–8.
93. See Torrell, *Christ and the Spirituality*, 74–125.
94. See *ST* III, q. 7, a. 9.
95. See *Super Io.*, cap. 13, lect. 3, n. 1781.
96. See *ST* III, q. 40, a. 2, ad 1; III, q. 40, a. 1, ad 3.

As a result, Jesus is the example of conjugal charity always, everywhere, and under every circumstance. Nothing that the Incarnate Word experienced is without meaning for salvation. Each and every act performed in his humanity did bear, and continues to bear, salvific efficacy, thanks to the sacraments.[97] Among those salvific events, Christ's passion is foundational for the sacrament of marriage. At the celebration of this sacrament, the spouses are in a real "contact" with Christ's spousal gift of self on the cross for the church. This particular event configures the spouses to the Son by the Holy Spirit, so that their will is rendered capable of imitating Christ's willful self-gift in obedience to the Father.[98] Thus, the spouses are empowered with the grace to will in their marriage what God wills, and as God wills it.

Hence, the ontological aspect of Christ's exemplarity is intrinsically tied into the moral aspect. Christ is not only the *Exemplum* but also the *Exemplar* of Creation and of the new creation (justification) as well.[99] The ontological dimension of the spouses' conformation to Christ's spousal charity centers on how their collaboration with God is *rooted and made possible* by the sacrament of matrimony as an instrumental cause of grace mediated by Christ's humanity. The sacramental grace given in matrimony has a christic character; it conforms to the Son as *the* image of the invisible God.[100] Christ's humanity is an instrumental cause of his divinity, such that it modifies, as it were, God's action as the principal cause of grace. Whence, the final result bears the stamp of both the principal agent and the instrument. And since every agent produces its like, Christ's salvific actions produce in us a likeness, first, to Jesus, then, through him, to God.[101] In this manner, thanks to the grace of the sacrament of matrimony, the spouses' being in God's image is perfected with regard to likeness or, as it were, a second *conformitas*.[102] With their collaboration in responsibility, God, as a craftsman, repairs and perfects them according to Christ, *the* Exemplar, in whom the whole truth about man is revealed and brought to fulfillment.[103] This second conformation, effected in its own way by the sacrament of matrimony and the Christian responsibility of the spouses, perfects the *imago Dei* by bringing to fulfillment the spousal meaning of their bodies.[104]

Consequently, Aquinas's metaphysical and christological views on sacramental theology are, in reality, the structural guiding principle for John Paul's second part of TOB, which looks at marriage as *a cause of grace* and in its *dimension of sign*. The

---

97. See *ST* III, q. 48, a. 6; *Super Rom.*, cap. 6, lect. 2, n. 490.

98. See *Super Mt.*, cap. 24, lect. 4, n. 2003.

99. See *ST* III, q. 46, a. 3, c; 1 Pet 2:21.

100. See Col 1:15.

101. See *ST* I, q. 93, a. 5, ad 4. Obviously, to speak of conformity here does not mean equality but only imitation (see *ST* I–II, q. 19, a. 9, ad 1).

102. See *De Veritatae*, q. 22, a. 6, ad 2.

103. See *Super Io.*, cap. 1, lect. 6, n. 149; GS 22.

104. See TOB 102:4.

pope is considering first the ontological dimensions of the spouses' conformity with Christ's spousal charity. Second, John Paul concentrates on the moral dimensions of the spouses' conformity with Christ's spousal charity, especially as they are expressed in the words of consent, in the marriage promises. Moreover, TOB's second part seems to be directly rooted in Wojtyła's interpretation of Vatican II, in his view of marriage within the sphere of Christian responsibility. This is why John Paul II repeats that, in the sacrament, both grace and duty come together. The grace conferred by matrimony is also an aid, to fulfill in justice and truth, all of the obligations contracted in the marriage promises, and expressed materially by the words and actions of the marriage ceremony. This same grace, contained in the *bonum sacramenti*, redimensions the relationship between spouses. Their ontological conformation to Christ's spousal charity establishes the spouses' friendship with God as the foundation of their supernaturally elevated mutual love and conjugal friendship. As a result, spouses are inserted into the ethos of redemption of the new law. They acquire the Christian responsibility to cooperate with God's grace in order to attain a conformity that perfects the spousal meaning of their bodies.

Parenting for Heaven

John Paul II reasserts the generically animal but specifically rational nature of human procreation. Although similar to the sexual instinct of irrational animals, man's sexual drive is elevated to the "level of image of God and to the level of the person and communion among persons."[105] The philosophical distinction between animal reproduction and human procreation studied previously is not foreign to the scriptures. They connect "the perspective of procreation with the fundamental characteristic of human existence in the personal sense."[106] Thus, Genesis establishes a correlation between knowledge (*yadah*) and procreation. In fact, we need to distinguish two different ways of knowing. On the one hand, by knowing, Adam named the irrational animals and distinguished himself from them as a personal being. Conversely, when he knows Eve, Adam does not experience such a distinction. She is a neighbor, another human person. Moreover, their union is not simply that of two human persons. It is *specified as conjugal* inasmuch as it is affected by the possibility and *munus* of procreation. As a result, Adam experiences in this knowledge that Eve is his wife. As her name indicates, she is known as the mother of all the living.[107]

Adam's knowledge of irrational beings implied a possession whereby he subdued and dominated the earth. In turn, interpersonal knowledge fulfills the other part of the *mandatum*, namely, that of being fruitful and multiplying.[108] Thus, scriptures tes-

---

105. Ibid., 14:6.
106. Ibid.
107. See Gen 3:20.
108. See Gen 1:28.

tify to the first awareness of a meaning of the human body bound to parenthood: "[K]nowledge in the biblical sense signifies that man's biological determination, on the part of his body and his sex, is no longer something passive but reaches a level and content specific to self-conscious and self-determining persons; therefore, it brings with it a particular consciousness of the meaning of the human body bound to fatherhood and motherhood."[109] This meaning bound to fatherhood and motherhood is clearly the *procreative meaning of the body*. It is best expressed by Eve's words, "I have acquired a man *from the Lord*."[110] The new human being is also flesh of their flesh, a being in the image and likeness of God. For this reason, Gen 5:3 emphasizes that Seth is in the image and likeness of Adam. Additionally, Gen 4:1 also reveals that procreation implies a certain participation or collaboration with the Creator. His role is of fundamental importance in order to understand human parenthood. Together with Adam and Eve's free cooperation, the Creator calls the new human being to existence. And this call or vocation is united to a mission, a predestination to God's work.[111] Hence, God is the Creator and *the* Educator, "God is the one who not only *calls to existence*, but *sustains* and *develops* life from the first moment of conception."[112] Consequently, as an end of marriage, the scriptures envision the good of offspring as the participation or free collaboration with God in the transmission and education of children.[113]

The good of the sacrament adds a healing and elevating power to procreation as the common good of conjugal friendship. It empowers spouses to carry out in conjugal charity a parenting for heaven. *Casti Connubi* offers an important consideration in this regard. It really stands in the background of John Paul II's Thomistic understanding of procreation from the viewpoint of the sacramentality of marriage. Pius XI explained that "God wishes men to be born not only that they should live and fill the earth, but much more that they may be *worshippers of God*, that they may know Him and love Him and finally enjoy Him for ever in heaven."[114] God's intent clearly manifests the greatness of the *bonum prolis*. In light of these considerations, "it is easily seen how great a gift of divine goodness and how remarkable a fruit of marriage are children born by the omnipotent power of God through the *cooperation* of those bound in wedlock."[115] As a result, Christian parents are to raise their eyes to heaven. Indeed, "they are destined not only to *propagate and preserve the human race on earth*, indeed not only to *educate* any kind of worshippers of the true God, but children who are to become *members of the Church* of Christ, to raise up *fellow-citizens of the Saints*,

---

109. TOB 21:4.
110. Gen 4:1; emphasis added.
111. See Jer 1:5; Isa 44:1, 49:1,5.
112. TOB 21:6, note 34. See Pss 22:10; 139:13–15.
113. See *Super I Cor.*, cap. 7, lect. 1.
114. Pius XI, *Casti Connubi*, 12; emphasis added.
115. Ibid.; emphasis added.

and members of God's household, that the worshippers of God and Our Savior may daily increase."[116]

In continuity with *Casti Connubi*, LG relates the good of the sacrament with that of offspring as the good that abbreviates, as it were, the perfection to which conjugal friendship is ordered. The elevation that the good of the sacrament effects in the good of offspring is the basis upon which the Council relies in order to speak of the family as if it were (*velut*) a "domestic Church." As we know, LG envisions spouses signifying and partaking of Christ's spousal charity. As a result, they help each other out of love for God, and by means of God's love, "to attain to holiness in their conjugal life and in the rearing and education of their children."[117] Their procreative *munus* is thus elevated in view of the supernatural realm. Through it, "new citizens of human society are born, who by the grace of the Holy Spirit received in baptism are made children of God, thus perpetuating the people of God through the centuries."[118] For this reason, the family is like a domestic church. Within this context, spouses exercise their parenting for heaven. Parents "should, by their word and example, be the first preachers of the faith to their children; they should encourage them in the vocation which is proper to each of them, fostering with special care vocation to a sacred state."[119]

Thomas explains this same reality saying that, matrimony "consists in the union of a husband and wife purposing to *generate and educate offspring for the worship of God.*"[120] Later on, underlining that children are a gift from the Creator, Aquinas explains that the *bonum prolis* consists in that "offspring be *accepted* and *educated* for the *worship of God.*"[121] Consequently, there is a clear connection between the spousal meaning of the body as fulfilled in the triumphant church that worships God in glory for all eternity, and the good of offspring as parenting for heaven. Although there will be neither procreation nor marriage in glory, the human citizens of the heavenly Jerusalem remain linked to the reality of marriage, and that of procreation.[122] For this reason, while explaining that marriage comes from the Father, and not from sin or the "world," John Paul II clarifies that although the children of the resurrection take neither husband nor wife, the same children of the resurrection "owe their origin in the visible temporal world to the marriage and procreation of man and woman."[123] As a result, marriage "performs an *irreplaceable service with regard to man's extra-temporal future*, with regard to the mystery of the redemption of the body in the dimension of

---

116. Ibid., 13.
117. LG 11.
118. Ibid.
119. Ibid.
120. *ScG* IV. 78; emphasis added.
121. Ibid.; emphasis added.
122. See TOB 69:4; 101:10.
123. TOB 102:11.

eschatological hope."[124] Therefore, "man's origin in the world is linked with marriage *as a sacrament*, and his coming to be is inscribed in marriage, not only in the historical but *also in the eschatological dimension*."[125]

The good of offspring also includes a union or fellowship (*consortio*) of the personalities of husband and wife, made possible by a communion of works (*communio operum*).[126] That communion of works becomes like a common good, which renders possible and demands an *intensification* of the union of the spouses. For this reason, human friendship finds in marriage its maximum expression. Not in vain is man willing to leave father and mother and become one flesh with his wife, one life, one existence.[127] In this manner at the natural level, there is a *mutual inclusion and inseparability* between the good of offspring, and the union of the spouses contained in the good of fidelity. Wojtyła explained the communion of the spouses as being made possible by, and subordinated to, procreation as their conjugal common good. And now, John Paul II takes this same line of reflection in TOB. Commenting on Genesis 2:24; 1:28; and 2:25, he speaks about the life of the spouses being subordinated to or "*under the blessing of fruitfulness, that is, of procreation.*"[128] As he explicitly says later, Adam and Eve's conjugal communion of persons was ordered to attain happiness "through *the subordination of such a union to the blessing of fruitfulness with procreation.*[129]

Subjacent here is Wojtyła's view on how procreation or the good of offspring requires the integration of concupiscent love into a love of benevolence that is proper only among persons, thereby safeguarding and perfecting conjugal communion. But in the ethos of redemption, and thanks to the sacramental economy of the new law, the union of the spouses subordinated to procreation is also elevated, as we know, by the reality of grace. This common union is now elevated by conjugal charity to partake of the communion inherent in Christ's gift of self for the church. Hence, to an elevation of the common good of marriage as parenting for heaven belongs an elevation in the communion or union of the spouses, who act together and are perfected by this common good with the aid of the grace afforded by the sacrament. Thus, marriage is a participation in God's creative love because of the spouses' call to communion, and because of their communion being ordered to procreation. Marriage is "the sacrament in which man and woman, called to become one flesh *share in the creative love of God himself*. They share in it both by the fact that, created in the image of God, they have been called in virtue of this image to a particular union (*communio personarum*,

---

124. Ibid.; emphasis added.
125. TOB 101:7; emphasis added.
126. See *In IV Sent.*, d. 31, q. 1, a. 2, ad 1.
127. See *ScG* III.123; Gen 2:24.
128. TOB 14:6; see Gen 1:28.
129. TOB 30:3.

the communion of persons), and because this union has itself been blessed from the beginning with the blessings of fruitfulness."[130]

Marriage is "a word of the Spirit exhorting man and woman to shape their whole life together by drawing strength from the mystery of the redemption of the body."[131] The Holy Spirit exhorts them to chastity in the hope that they reach integration, as a mastery over the concupiscence of the flesh, a mastery that results in a conjugal communion of persons. He exhorts and enables them to lead a "new" life in the Spirit, in the grace received by the sacrament of marriage, in order "to find the true freedom of the gift together with the awareness of the spousal meaning of the body in its masculinity and femininity."[132] This new life in the Spirit expresses itself when the spouses "*submit their femininity and masculinity to the blessing of procreation.*"[133] Through procreation, the spouses discover their parenthood as a gratuitous gift with a deep awareness of the holiness of the life to which they cooperate to give rise; a new life that increases "the hope of the revelation of the sons of God, a hope of which every newborn who comes into the world carries a spark with himself."[134]

Faithfulness to the Divine Plan

Thomas Aquinas envisions the good of fidelity (*fides*) as directly related to the virtues of justice and veracity. For this reason, he explains that "*fides* is not taken here as the theological virtue of faith, but as *part of justice*, according to which it is named fidelity from the fact that *things said are done in the observation of promises.*"[135] These promises refer obviously to the words of consent as they express the divine plan for human love within marriage. These are the same promises spouses make to each other until death dissolves the marriage bond. To fulfill them is a matter of justice towards each other and, in a sense, towards the Creator as the Author of marriage. Thus, in fidelity, spouses are truthful to their marriage promises by conforming their deeds during their married life to their words at the moment of consent. From this same perspective, *Casti Connubi* describes the good of fidelity, explaining that it "consists in the mutual fidelity of the spouses in fulfilling the marriage contract."[136] Pius XI includes in it "unity, chastity, charity, and honorable noble obedience."[137]

John Paul II concentrates on the *bonum fidei*, when reflecting on how the specific grace of matrimony is given to the spouses as ethos. He does so especially when

130. Ibid., 102:2; emphasis added.
131. Ibid., 101:4.
132. Ibid., 101:5.
133. Ibid., 101:6; emphasis added.
134. Ibid.
135. *In IV Sent.*, d. 31, q. 1, a. 2, ad 2; emphasis added. See also *In IV Sent.*, d. 31, q. 1, a. 2, ad 5.
136. Pius XI, *Casti Connubi*, 19.
137. Ibid., 30.

dealing with matrimony in the dimension of sign and when explaining the most central notion for his second chapter on the sacrament: the language of the body. Indeed, according to the pope, to reread the language of the body in the truth consists in the spouses *being truthful to their wedding promises* by *conforming their daily actions to the words of consent*. In this manner, they are faithful to God's plan for human love within marriage. Thus, they are truthful to their particular way of fulfilling the spousal meaning of their bodies. In this way, they fulfill the *bonum fidei*. Once again, the pope's treatment of this matter is quite selective. His commentary on HV is now imminent; it belongs to the next chapter of his book. Hence, John Paul's goal is to complete his grounding for the mutual inclusion and inseparability of the goods of fidelity and offspring.

Now, if one takes a broader look at John Paul's treatment of the sacrament of matrimony with the intent of elucidating its Thomistic foundations, one could add two other points from TOB which belong to the *bonum fidei*. The pope also speaks in this second part of his book about the unity of the spouses as a characteristic communion of persons marked by a reciprocal belonging. Additionally, he explains quite well the mutual subjection of spouses in piety towards God as their common Father. Since these two points are part of the wedding promises and as I am interested in showing John Paul's Thomistic foundations, I will explain them before I analyze the language of the body.

Reciprocal Belonging

GS 48 opens by characterizing the intimate communion of life inherent in conjugal love. The spouses' *consent* entails a mutual gift of self. It implies that they "mutually bestow and accept each other" [*coniuges sese mutuo tradunt atque accipiunt*]. Consequently, as part of the wedding promises, this reciprocal belonging pertains to the *bonum fidei*. As we know, the mutual gift of self, inherent in marriage, includes a way of possessing the other, which does not violate his or her personal dignity. We are not speaking here from the *metaphysical* perspective. Therein, the human person possesses and governs himself, and is *alteri incomunicabilis*. Rather, we are focusing on the moral perspective. Therein, one freely decides to surrender his own free will to another out of charity. He gives the other a certain power over oneself by making a gift of what one loves most within himself, namely, his own will.[138] This is exactly one important way in which the *bonum fidei* appears in TOB, in the characteristic communion of persons in marriage animated by the grace of the sacrament in the form of conjugal charity and resulting in what John Paul II calls "reciprocal belonging." This is why the bride says, "my beloved is mine and I am his."[139] Marriage constitutes a unity

138. See LR, 96; Wojtyła, "On the Meaning of Spousal Love," 279; *De perfectione*, cap. 10; TOB 31:3; 110:8.

139. Song 2:16. See Song 6:3; TOB 110:8.

among spouses in which the body of the other should be loved as one's own.[140] In this way, within marriage, "love not only unites the two subjects, but it allows them to penetrate each other so mutually, thereby *belonging spiritually to each other.*"[141]

The Thomistic foundations for this personalistic reciprocal belonging between spouses are found in Aquinas's theology of the power (*potestas*) given by matrimonial consent and consummation. In the gift of this *potestas*, one imitates Christ and freely becomes, as it were, a servant of the other. Strictly speaking, man belongs to God, the Creator. Thus, appealing to Ps 100:3, "He made us, we belong to Him," Thomas interprets Paul's expression in Phil 2:7, "taking the form of a servant," meaning that the Son took human nature, thereby espousing humanity.[142] Aquinas seems to have this in mind when he argues against the opinion that a father could force his own son into marriage. Thus, "since marriage is like *a certain perpetual servitude*, a father cannot compel his child to marry by his command, since the child is of a free condition."[143] Thomas believes that this "servitude" applies to both men and women. Moreover, this "servitude" should be freely accepted. We see here that moral perspective which Wojtyła mentioned when explaining the mutual belonging of spouses. Thomas reasserts this same idea when he explains that consent is the efficient cause of marriage: "[O]ne person does not receive power over what is freely another's except by his consent. But in marriage both spouses receive power over each other's bodies, as is evident from 1 Corinthians 7, since beforehand each would have had free power over his own body."[144]

Matrimonial consent makes a free gift of one's body. However, one should understand well this gift of one's body. It is not opposed to John Paul's affirmation that spouses belong *spiritually* to each other. In Aquinas's view, since marriage is a good of mortals, matrimonial consent makes a gift of one's body because it offers one's self in one's corporeal and earthly existence.[145] This gift of one's body should not be viewed either from the utilitarian or from the materialistic perspective. Rather, in Aquinas's theology of marriage, it takes place within the context of a relationship of friendship, in which both husband and wife share in the same dignity, and partake of a reciprocal love.[146] This equal dignity and reciprocity are conditions without which there could not be friendship at all. Without them, there could not be true union among spouses. For this very reason, Thomas explains that matrimonial consent should not be compelled: "[A]lthough an act of a lover can pass to someone who does not love, never-

---

140. See Eph 5:28.
141. See TOB 117:4; emphasis added.
142. See *Super Philip.*, cap. 2, lect. 2.
143. *In IV Sent.*, d. 29, q. 1, a. 4, c.
144. *In IV Sent.*, d. 27, q. 1, a. 2, qc. 1, s. c. 2.
145. See *In IV Sent.*, d. 31, q. 1, a. 3, ad 3.
146. For this reason, I fully agree with Petri in finding incipient elements of a theology of the gift of self in Aquinas's understanding of the marriage debt. See Petri, *Aquinas*, 299–307.

theless, *the union between them cannot be unless there is mutual loving*. And thus the Philosopher says in Book 8 of the Ethics, that friendship, which consists in a certain union, requires love in return."[147] Generically speaking, mutual belonging in marriage is like the spiritual union found in any friendship, in which the one loves the other as another *I*. However, marriage is not any union of persons, but a conjugal friendship. As a result, the specific difference of this reciprocal belonging is determined by their conjugal common good. As was noted, this same common good intensifies the union of the spouses, transforming it into the maximum expression of human friendship.[148] Thus, since it implies parenthood and procreation, this conjugal mutual belonging of spouses is something deeply spiritual and, at the same time, deeply corporeal. It entails the gift of one's corporeal existence here on earth, in which there is a substantial unity of body and soul.

However, in Aquinas's theology, it is the consummation of marriage and not just consent that seals the deepest union between human persons in this conjugal reciprocal belonging. Thomas makes this evident when answering a question that might sound bizarre to our contemporary ears. Could a man who has consummated his marriage enter into the religious state without the consent of his wife? In Thomas's theology, the husband's gift of self in the consummation of marriage is so radical that, in a certain sense, one could say that he is not his own any more. From the moral viewpoint, he is to himself, as it were, a sort of *res aliena*. "No one can make an offering to God from what belongs to another. Consequently, since in a consummated marriage the body of the man has already become his wife's, he cannot offer himself to God by a vow of continence without her consent."[149] What interests me most in this text is not the entering into the religious state, but the fact that no one can make an oblation to God of what is not his. As a result, Thomas explains that a husband is not his own anymore after consummating his marriage. His entire corporeal existence until death is tied to the will of his wife. The same applies to the wife in relation to her husband. The consummation of marriage effects this mutual submission, whereby one belongs to the other.

Aquinas compares and contrasts the unity of spouses before and after such consummation by means of an analogy. Such unity relates to the union that exists between Christ and the soul, and Christ and the church respectively. The union of a newly wedded couple, who have not consummated their marriage, is only a spiritual union which signifies the union in grace between Christ and the soul. Instead, the union of a couple, who have already consummated in the flesh what they consented to with their words, brings that spiritual union to a carnal level, thereby signifying

---

147. *In IV Sent.*, d. 29, q. 1, a. 3, qc. 2, ad 1; emphasis added. I will not deal in this book with Thomas's assimilation of Aristotle's views on women and its relationship with TOB. For this important topic, I refer the reader to Petri, *Aquinas*, 275–279.

148. See *ScG* III.123.

149. *In IV Sent.*, d. 27, q. 1, a. 3, qc. 1, c.

the union between Christ and his church.[150] Unlike the first union, this last one is indissoluble until death, for it was effected in the Son's redemptive Incarnation which united human nature to the Person of the Word.[151] For this reason, Thomas offers another surprising advice to a contemporary audience: couples would do well to wait *two months after consent before the consummation of marriage.*

> Before carnal intimacy, the body of one has not been transferred to the power of the other absolutely, but under the condition that if meanwhile the other spouse should not aspire to the fruits of a better life: but by carnal intimacy this transfer is said to be completed, for then each person enters into bodily possession of the power handed over to each other. Therefore, even before carnal intercourse someone is not bound to render the debt immediately after the marriage is contracted in terms of the present. But the time *of two months is given to him*, for three reasons. First, so that in meantime he might deliberate about entering religious life. Secondly, so that the necessary things may be prepared for the *solemnization* of the wedding. Thirdly, lest the husband should hold cheap a wife whom he did not have to pine in wait for.[152]

Again, I am not interested in all the details of this rather fascinating text. Instead, I just want to concentrate on some important points which further unveil John Paul's Thomistic foundations. Thomas clearly teaches that spouses should not take the consummation of their marriage as an automatism, as something of little worth which could just be given away. Rather, it is a *solemnity* in which there is a reciprocal gift of self (body and soul) unto death that should not be taken lightly. Additionally, the wait is also explained so that the young husband may aspire to that delayed union, not considering it as something of little value, but as a gift. These reflections help to eradicate a false "myth" one often hears in popular talks on TOB. According to this "myth," spousal love was not appreciated by the so-called "dark ages," during which, medieval theology would have developed. We had to wait until John Paul II came, the myth continues, for the appreciation of its true value. However, a closer look reveals that, in the Middle Ages, spousal love was considered as the soul of marriage.

Indeed, Parmisano has convincingly shown that medieval liturgies point to spousal love as the soul of marriage.[153] Of particular interest is the Hereford ritual of marriage. It begins the marriage celebration stating what is called the law of marriage. This law provides "that husband and wife be two in one flesh, subject to each other, and inseparable."[154] In the same ritual, the marital consent contains a promise to love each other, and to grow in that love. This love and growth is clearly seen as the result of

---

150. See *In IV Sent.*, d. 27, q. 1, a. 3, qc. 2, c.

151. See *In IV Sent.*, d. 27, q. 1, a. 3, qc. 2, ad 1.

152. *In IV Sent.*, d. 27, q. 1, a. 3, qc. 2, ad 2; emphasis added. I am grateful to Rev. Prof. Robert Wielockx for the time he spent helping me to better understand this text.

153. See Parmisano, "Spousal Love."

154. Ibid., 802.

a choice. It is not reduced to something that merely happens in man. This last point is even more evident in the liturgy of York. Therein, the priest prays over the spouses in the following manner: "All powerful and eternal God, who by his power created Adam and Eve, sanctified them by his blessing, and joined them in a community of love [*societatem amoris copulavit*]; may He sanctify and bless your hearts and bodies and join them in truest love [*amorem verae dilectionis*]."[155] Parmisano also offers concrete examples on how medieval disciples of Thomas Aquinas had an immense appreciation for the sacrament of marriage. This author refers to the Dominicans Jacques de Vitry and to William Peraldus. (The latter is the true author of *De eruditione principium*. His work is so faithful to Thomas Aquinas that, for a long time, it was attributed to the Angelic Doctor). Now, both De Vitry and Peraldus speak in their sermons about the dignity of marriage. They list some reasons as to why, under a certain aspect (*secundum quid sed non simpliciter*), marriage may be viewed as a higher state of life than that of a religious. Some of the reasons adduced are the following. Unlike religious orders who were founded by a man and not long ago, marriage was founded by God himself and it exists since the creation of Adam and Eve as a natural institution, even before original sin. Moreover, the Blessed Virgin Mary was married. Furthermore, Jesus worked a great miracle at Cana to demonstrate the power of marriage: "God changed vile water into precious wine, thus showing how the sexual act [*opus carnale*] without marriage is vile but within marriage is precious."[156] The fact that, *simpliciter*, the religious state is higher than marriage, does not change what is being argued. And what is more relevant: *after this kind of preaching, no one can take seriously the claim that marriage was for the medievals a poor substitute for a nobler Christian calling.*

Mutual Subjection

According to John Paul II, Eph 5:21's invitation to "be subject to one another in the fear of Christ," concerns a relationship that is, at the same time, reciprocal and communitarian. Its reciprocal dimension signifies the mutual relationship between the spouses themselves. In turn, its communitarian dimension involves the common relationship of the spouses with Christ. Moreover, the communitarian dimension of this relationship, based on the fear of Christ, is the basis for the reciprocal one. Much in line with the Old Testament, such fear denotes not a defensive fright in the face of a perceived evil, but piety.[157] One can see here an emphasis on justice, as perfected by piety, which is consonant with LR, with the little-known guiding thread studied previously, and with the very nature of the good of fidelity as part of justice. The mystery of God's election for them to become his adoptive sons should enkindle in the heart of the spouses the holy fear of Christ, as piety. And this common piety towards God and reverence for holiness

---

155. Ibid., 789.
156. Ibid., 800.
157. See TOB 89:1; Ps 103:11; Prov 1:7, 23:17; Sir 1:11–16.

should be what leads them towards their mutual submission.¹⁵⁸ In this exact sense, Eph 5:21's communitarian dimension is the basis for the reciprocal one.

Consequently, John Paul II combats a wrong interpretation of Ephesians 5:22. Paul explains there that wives are told to be submissive to their husbands. However, the pope clarifies that this text cannot be interpreted as if marriage were "a contract of domination by the husband over the wife."¹⁵⁹ Instead, reading this verse in light of Ephesians 5:21, John Paul II reasserts the validity of his foundational principle: the communitarian dimension of husband's and wife's submission to God, in charity and in piety, is the basis for their mutual subjection. Indeed, "the source of this reciprocal submission lies in Christian *pietas* and its expression is love."¹⁶⁰ As he explains, "love makes the husband simultaneously subject to the wife, and subject in this to the Lord himself, as the wife is to the husband."¹⁶¹ In this way, "reciprocal submission in the fear of Christ—a submission born on the foundation of Christian *pietas*—always forms the deep and firm supporting structure of the community of spouses, in which the true communion of persons is realized."¹⁶²

Moreover, according to Paul's presentation, the husband is he who loves. In turn, the wife is the one being loved. As a result, it seems that "one might even venture the idea that the wife's submission to the husband . . . means above all the experiencing of love. This is all the more so, because this 'submission' refers to the image of the submission of the Church to Christ, which certainly consists in experiencing love."¹⁶³ One should recall here Adam's responsibility in being the guardian of the gift of self. As the new Adam, Christ has perfectly fulfilled that responsibility towards the church as the new Eve. These are the foundations for the moral exhortation in Ephesians 5:28 to become morally one, belonging spiritually one to the other, in the same kind of love Christ has for the church. Thus, Paul "presents the love of Christ for the Church—the love that makes the Church the body of Christ, whose head he is—as the model of the love of the spouses and as the model of the wedding feast of bridegroom and bride."¹⁶⁴ Clarifying the meaning of the one-flesh union, Ephesians 5:29–30 shows that its unitive dimension consists in more than sheer physiology. The human body of husband and wife truly become one flesh, when this union is informed by spousal love, namely, by the kind of love that implies a total gift of self. Then, the "I" becomes—in a moral sense—the "you" and the "you" the "I."¹⁶⁵

---

158. See TOB 89:2.
159. TOB 89:3.
160. Ibid.
161. Ibid., 89:4.
162. Ibid., 89:6.
163. Ibid., 92:6.
164. Ibid., 92:4.
165. See TOB 92:7.

The Thomistic foundations of this interpretation are found in Thomas's mature theology of marriage as conjugal friendship. We have already seen how this theology is rather personalistic. It rejects polygamy based on the dignity of women. It views marriage as the greatest friendship. In short, it clearly emphasizes the common dignity of husband and wife. Moreover, we have also seen an echo of this same mature theology of marriage when Aquinas explained that "the woman was *not formed from the feet of the man as a servant*, nor from the head as lording it over her husband, *but from the side as a companion*, as it says in Genesis."[166] Furthermore, Thomas's understanding of the common good and of procreation as the primary end of marriage highlights a very similar distinction to the one used here by John Paul II. In chapter 10, I used a different terminology. I referred to the vertical and horizontal dimensions of procreation. John Paul, instead, speaks here about the communitarian dimension to signify the couple as a common subject being subordinated to God. This dimension I called vertical because of its reference to the Creator. However, one could easily see here a similar structure. The same Thomistic understanding of the virtues and the little-known guiding thread fits perfectly in this new context. Thus, it seems that for both Thomas Aquinas and John Paul II, marriage is called to be a form of virtuous friendship founded on the equality in dignity of the spouses, a friendship in which *both* husband and wife are subordinated to and elevated by their common good, namely, the fulfillment of the spousal meaning of their bodies in their characteristic *munus* of parenting for heaven. Their mutual subjection is founded upon their subjection to their common mission in charity and in truth. It is a submission in which God's will is always *the* determinant factor.

However, once again, it is important to dispel the "myth" according to which medievals could have never fathomed the idea of a mutual subjection among spouses. Parmisano's study of medieval liturgy, as informed by the Thomistic theology of marriage, shows that the wife's obedience to the husband "is *not to be in response to any show of the husband's superiority and control but rather his love and concern*: If she is to obey him, it is because he loves, cherishes, and cares for her."[167] According to Parmisano, the medieval liturgies show that such an obedience "is also qualified by the more persistent explicit insistence on *spousal equality*."[168] Moreover, in these liturgies, "bride and groom are together, side by side throughout the nuptial ceremony, and if at one or two moments the bride expresses her submission to her spouse, it is she who, as in weddings today, receives the greater honor and attention from groom and priest and therefore, presumably, from congregation."[169] Furthermore, the Hereford rite explicitly prays "that the obedience be *mutual*—husband and wife are to be *subject to one another*, and in another that *each prefer the other to oneself* and that they

---

166. *Super I Cor.*, cap. 7, lect. 1, n. 321; emphasis added. See Gen 2:21.
167. Parmisano, "Spousal Love," 804; emphasis added.
168. Ibid.; emphasis added.
169. Ibid.

be united in the marriage partnership (*consortium*) with *equal* effect, like mind, and mutual charity."[170]

Objective and Subjective Language of the Body

The language of the body is a philosophical and theological notion of vast proportions in TOB. Waldstein has rightly noted that the Italian term *linguaggio* transcribes the Polish *mowa*, which signifies *words* that are actually spoken.[171] The pope is appealing here to a brilliant image, which very graphically harmonizes a great number of philosophical and theological points in order to lay the immediate foundation to his commentary on HV. John Paul II distinguishes two senses of the language of the body. He speaks about an objective and about a subjective sense.[172] The *objective* sense of the language of the body refers to *what has been said about the human body* in the book of nature (*liber naturae*) and in revelation. Properly speaking, God is its author. He has "spoken" its "words." He is the origin of its *logos*, that is, of its intellectual structure. Thus, the pope talks about "the perennial language of the body to which God himself gave its beginning by *creating* man male and female: a language that was *renewed by Christ*."[173] In this objective sense, "the language of the body was *spoken by* the word of the living *God*, from the beginning in Genesis through the prophets of the Old Covenant all the way to the author of Ephesians."[174] The language of the body manifests both who the human person *is* and who he *ought* to be. It traces back both nature and revelation to the divine intellect as exemplar for moral action. In classical terms, it points to the eternal law as the root of both the natural and the revealed law.[175]

John Paul emphasizes the divine origin of the language of the body by connecting it to another brilliant image: the prophetism of the body. This other image has a definitive anti-Kantian flavor. Moreover, it also overcomes the naturalistic physicalism which confuses the biological with the natural order.[176] As we know, the latter consists in "a specific order of existence with an *obvious relationship to the First Cause, to God the Creator*."[177] The prophetism of the body evidences quite graphically this very idea because, by definition, a prophet is "one who expresses with human words the truth that *comes from God*, one who speaks this truth *in the place of God*, in his name and in some sense *with his authority*."[178] As a result, the prophetism of the body moves

---

170. Ibid., 804–5; emphasis added.
171. See TOB, p. 682.
172. See ibid., 104:4.
173. Ibid., 105:4; emphasis added.
174. Ibid.; emphasis added.
175. See *ST* I-II, q. 93, a. 3, c.
176. See SR, 50.
177. LR, 56–57; emphasis added.
178. TOB 105:3; emphasis added.

beyond Kantian autonomy. It patently shows that human "conscience is no lawmaker; it does not itself create norms; rather it discovers them, as it were, in the objective order of morality or law."[179] Additionally, the prophetism of the body also goes beyond physicalism and biologism by pointing to a certain *metaphysical transparency* in human nature. Indeed, the phenomenon of language presupposes interpersonal, reciprocal, and communicated intelligibility. Thus, this transparency results from God's eternal law being intimated at the creation of the rational creature, as a being who participates in the divine intellect, a being capable of understanding the intelligible structure of his own nature as a human person, and of recognizing God's authorship as well as his authority.[180] Consequently, the pope clearly explains that, in this objective sense, "*the human body speaks a language of which it is not the author in the proper sense of the term.*"[181]

Moreover, the objective language of the body allows John Paul II to harmonize these metaphysical considerations on the natural law with his christocentric biblical theology. As a result, the pope lays the groundwork to overcome the greatest limitation in the advocates of contraception's moral theology: their incapacity to harmonize the biblical and metaphysical foundations of a christocentric moral theory, which is compatible with the natural law and is grounded on the substantial unity of man as a being created in the image of God. Indeed, the objective language of the body also refers to what God has said in revelation about the human person. Especially, it signifies how the human person is fully manifested in the mystery of the Incarnate Word, and everything in revelation that we have studied about the spousal meaning of the body and the sacrament of matrimony. For this reason, in the sphere of conjugal morality, the objective language of the body finds its abbreviation in the words of consent, whereby spouses enter into marriage.

At the same time, since spouses are the ministers of the sacrament of matrimony, these words also become *their* language. Through them, they subjectively appropriate and express the objective language of the body. Thus, the *subjective* sense of the language of the body refers to a "language" spoken by the human person by means of words and moral actions. It signifies our conscious apprehension of its objective meaning, as well as the intentional conformity (or lack thereof) between our actions, and the objective word concerning the human person, and marriage made known by God in the book of nature and in revelation.[182] As a result, there is a subjective and conscious way in which man is the author of the language of the body. He is so, inas-

---

179. AP, 165.

180. Thomas explains that the natural law is "nothing other than the light of the intellect planted in us by God, by which we know what should be done and what should be avoided. God gave this light and this law in creation." *In Duo Praecepta*, prologus, 1. See also VS 42, 44.

181. TOB 105:5.

182. See TOB 103:5. For some illuminating remarks on the *liber naturae* and revelation in Christ, see Benedict XVI, *Verbum Domini*, 7.

much as he faithfully rereads in the objective orders of nature and of God's revelation about the spousal meaning of the body and the sacrament of matrimony. The pope already spoke in his intepretation of Vatican II about the importance of fidelity and subordination to God in this realm.[183] In this subjective and conscious sense, "the author is man—male and female—who rereads the true sense of that language, thereby bringing to light again the spousal meaning of the body as integrally *inscribed in the very structure* of the masculinity and femininity of the personal subject."[184] Moral actions are one special way of carrying out this "rereading." They can be true or false, depending upon if there is conformity (*adequatio*), or not, with the divine exemplar manifested in the objective language of the body. To be sure, the human person is neither the author of his nature nor of revelation. Yet, as participant in the eternal law through his rationality, he is capable of apprehending their *meanings* through reason and faith, and of acting in conformity with them, or not.

The human person "is a conscious subject capable of self-determination. Only on this basis can he be the author of the language of the body, can he also be the author (co-author) of marriage as a sign: a sign of the divine creation and redemption of the body."[185] Spouses "reread" the language of the body in the truth by means of their words when, in the wedding ceremony, they exchange consent through their promises. These same promises bind them to reread in the truth the language of the body not only with their words, but also with their actions, each and every day of their lives, united together in marriage.[186] Thus, the sacrament of matrimony in the dimension of sign connects with the same sacrament as a cause of grace and with conjugal morality. The spouses' conformation with Christ's spousal charity offers them the grace to live according to the spousal meaning of the body. Thereby, they overcome the ethos of concupiscence that falsifies the truth about man as expressed in the objective sense of the language of the body.[187] Thus, "the essential truth of the sign will remain organically linked with the ethos of conjugal conduct."[188]

At the same time, the image of the language of the body allows John Paul II to harmonize HV's emphasis on the *meanings* of the conjugal act with the *objective nature* of this same act. He is able to do so by means of his Thomistic understanding of consciousness, and its "realistic semantics."[189] As I explained, consciousness is not intentional in the sense that it does not have the intentionality of the intellect. It is neither the full actualization of a power of the soul, nor does it have the capacity of the intellect to penetrate into the essences of things, conferring to them *intentional* or

---

183. See SR, 50.
184. TOB 105:5; emphasis added.
185. Ibid., 107:5.
186. See ibid., 106:5; 105:9; 106:2; 107:3.
187. See TOB 108:3; 107:3.
188. Ibid., 105:6.
189. See my "Karol Wojtyła's Thomistic Understanding of Consciousness."

mental being. Hence, the conscious conceptual meanings of the conjugal act are like formal signs that signify the conjugal act as it is in its real nature. Since the human intellect is not the measure of reality, but rather is measured by reality, the source of those meanings is neither consciousness nor the will, but the very nature of the conjugal act. The meanings of the conjugal act are not restricted to phenomena given as objects of consciousness. They attain the real and extra-mental realities signified by those mental meanings as realities in their *esse reale in rerum naturae*, that is, as they are *independently* of one's knowledge and one's awareness of them. Thus, the objective moral order is safeguarded when through his efficacy, the human person "is the causal origin of actions *that have through themselves (per se) clear-cut meanings*. He is thus the causal origin of actions and at the same time the author of their meanings."[190]

For this reason, John Paul explains that "if man, male and female, is the author of that language, he is so above all inasmuch as *he wants to give, and effectively does give, to his behavior and to his actions the meaning in conformity with the reread eloquence of the truth of masculinity and femininity in the reciprocal conjugal relationship*."[191] Spouses are to conform the meaning of their actions to the meanings contained in the words of consent. They express the objective nature of conjugal morality. "The sum of these meanings constitutes in some sense the whole of the language of the body with which the spouses decide to speak to each other as ministers of the sacrament."[192] Aquinas already explained that "the external acts and words expressing consent directly effect *a bond of obligation*."[193] John Paul II argues now very similarly: "The sign they bring into being with the words of the conjugal consent is not merely an immediate and fleeting sign, but a sign that looks toward the future and produces a lasting effect, namely, the conjugal bond, one and indissoluble."[194] This bond is not only the source of grace but also of *obligation and responsibility*. Thus, spouses "*must* fill that sign with the manifold contents offered by the conjugal and familial communion of persons, and also with the content that springs from the language of the body and is continually reread in the truth."[195]

Furthermore, John Paul's rich theology of the language of the body has another subjacent Thomistic notion, intimately related with Wojtyła's philosophical considerations on exemplarity as the metaphysical foundation for the moral norm.[196] According to Aquinas, the virtue of truth refers to "a certain kind of truth according to which man shows himself in deed and words as he really is. Particularly, *the truth*

---

190. TOB 105:6; emphasis added.
191. Ibid., 105:5; emphasis added.
192. Ibid., 105:6.
193. *In IV Sent.*, d. 26, q. 2, a. 3, ad 2; emphasis added. See also *In IV Sent.*, d. 27, q. 1, a. 1, qc. 1, ad 2.
194. TOB 105:6.
195. Ibid.; emphasis added.
196. See PC, 73–94.

of life refers to man as he fulfills in his life that to which he is ordained by the divine intellect."[197] Thus, the Thomistic notion of the truth of life points back to the pope's christocentrism, to GS 22. Christ is *the* Truth, Exemplar, and *exemplum* of the moral life. The entire Christian vocation is a conformity with Christ, a conformity brought about by the sacraments of the new law, and by their unfolding in the virtues and gifts within the sphere of responsibility in the ethos of redemption. In this way, the truth of life, as conformity with the divine mind, applies to the human person within marriage when, through the use of the body, "the body tells the truth through faithfulness and conjugal love."[198] One conforms to the truth about life when he "agrees with the spousal meaning that corresponds to the human body (because of its masculinity and femininity) in the integral structure of the person; in the second case [when one commits falsehood or lies], by contrast, the same subject finds itself in contradiction against, and in collision with, that meaning."[199]

These realistic premises also safeguard the objective *mutual inclusion and inseparability* between the goods of fidelity and offspring. Indeed, from the perspective of the good of fidelity, spouses are to be faithful to the promise to lovingly cooperate with the Creator in conjugal charity in the transmission and education of human life. "Into this truth of the sign, and consequently into the ethos of conjugal conduct, there is inserted, in a future-related perspective, the procreative meaning of the body, that is, fatherhood and motherhood, which we discussed earlier. To the question, *Are you ready to accept children lovingly from God and bring them up according to the Law of Christ and his Church?* the man and the woman answer, Yes."[200] Consequently, the words of consent contain the sacrament of matrimony from the dimension of sign and responsibility. They "constitute this sign because the spousal meaning of the body in its masculinity and femininity finds expression in them . . . In addition, these words confirm the essential truth of the language of the body and (at least indirectly, implicitly) they also exclude the essential untruth, the falseness of the language of the body."[201] Spouses are to adopt in their actions the meanings given by God to the institution of marriage as a sacrament. This conscious adoption makes them act in such a way that their actions speak in God's name. As a result, they are *true* prophets.[202] They are so by sharing in the conciliar attitude of testimony, namely, by "proclaiming the language of the body reread in the truth as the content and principle of their new life in Christ and the Church."[203]

---

197. *ST* I, q. 16, a. 4, ad 3; emphasis added. See also *ST* II–II, q. 109, a. 2, ad 3; SR, 15 and 420.
198. TOB 104:8.
199. Ibid., 104:9.
200. Ibid.; emphasis added.
201. Ibid., 105:1.
202. See ibid., 106:4.
203. Ibid., 105:3.

Note that the language of the body is not restricted, in John Paul II's mind, to the conjugal act. It also encompasses all areas of the mutual life of spouses as they relate to the *bonum fide*, to fidelity to their wedding promises as the abbreviation of the divine plan for human love within marriage. "If the human being—male and female—*in marriage (and indirectly also in all spheres of mutual life together)* gives to his behavior a meaning in conformity with the fundamental truth of the language of the body, then he too is *in the truth*. In the opposite case, he commits lies and falsifies the language of the body."[204] All of these considerations have provided all the needed elements to understand the interrelationship between procreation and the spousal meaning of the body in the inseparability of the meanings of the conjugal act.

---

204. Ibid.,106:3.

12

The Inseparable Connection: In Defense of Conjugal Love

Rereading HV in Light of TOB

John Paul II intends to comment on HV in light of the conclusions previously reached concerning procreation and the spousal meaning of the body.[1] The pope's commentary concentrates on "the passage of the encyclical that deals with the two *meanings* of the conjugal act and their inseparable connection."[2] This single passage directly connects with his reflections on the sacrament of marriage in the dimension of sign, and with the rereading of the language of the body in the truth, as an "indispensable condition for *acting in the truth* or for behaving *in conformity with the value and the moral norm.*"[3] Wojtyła also appeals to his *realistic semantics* in order to distinguish the ontological dimension corresponding to the nature of the conjugal act from the subjective and psychological dimension of the conscious meanings. Thus, he says that Paul VI looks for "the foundation of the norm determining the morality of the actions of man and woman in the conjugal act, in the *nature of this act* itself and more deeply still in the *nature of the acting subjects themselves.*"[4]

Neither the spouses' nature nor that of the conjugal act should be identified with sheer naturalistic biology. Since we are dealing with an ethical question within the *genus moris*, the nature of the conjugal act refers here to the generically animal but specifically rational inclination to the union of the sexes and to procreation, as integrated into a human act (*actus humanus*) in accordance with right reason (*recta ratio*). The nature of the spouses refers to the *rational* nature of each one of them as human persons. This exact view of the nature of the conjugal act and of the spouses is the proper metaphysical and anthropological basis for the "*reading and discovery of the meanings* that must be carried over into the *consciousness* and the *decisions of the acting persons*. It also constitutes the necessary basis for grasping the adequate

---

1. See TOB 118:1.
2. Ibid., 118:3.
3. Ibid., 118:4. See also ibid., 119:2.
4. Ibid., 118:5; emphasis added.

relationship of these meanings, namely, their *inseparability*."[5] Pius XII had already pointed out a similar viewpoint to that of John Paul II: "[T]he marital act within its *natural* context is *a personal action*, a simultaneous and immediate *cooperation* of the spouses, something *in accordance with the essence of those doing the action and with the nature of the act itself*, an *expression of mutual self-giving* that effects the becoming one flesh as the words of Scripture state."[6] Pius XII continues clarifying that "this is much more than the joining of two gametes, which could also take place by artificial methods, and without the marital act of the spouses. The marital act, as nature has ordained it, is a *personal cooperation*, to which the spouses have given each other the *right* with their marriage *promises*."[7]

According to John Paul II, the inseparability of the meanings of the conjugal act belongs to the *natural law* because "it conforms *to reason as such*."[8] Moreover, this same teaching has solid foundations in biblical anthropology. It also belongs to divine *revealed law* and to the ethos of the redemption of the body.[9] Furthermore, Paul VI's teachings on the inseparability of the meanings of the conjugal act are grounded in Vatican II. The basic text is GS 51, according to which, "the question of *harmonizing conjugal love with the responsible transmission of life* ... must be determined by objective standards" which are "*based on the nature of the human person and his acts*," and "preserve the full sense of mutual self-giving and human procreation in the context of true love." Therefore, divine laws concerning procreation and true conjugal love are never opposed to each other.[10] Against contraception's proponents, John Paul argues that this teaching is fully *pastoral*. Dispelling their pessimistic and false optimism and appealing to his humble realism, the pope explains that this teaching is truly doable in light of the aid of the supernatural grace inherent in Christ's redemption of the human heart. Again, we can see that this teaching is not about biology or about methods in their artificiality. Rather, it is *all about preserving the integrity of conjugal love in its proper natural and supernatural virtues, all of them animated by charity and the gift of self*.[11] Indeed, "pastoral concern means seeking the *true* good of man, *promoting* the *values* impressed by God in the human person; that is, it signifies applying the rule of understanding, which aims at the ever clearer discovery of God's plan for human

---

5. Ibid., 118:6; emphasis added.
6. AAS (1951): 850; emphasis added.
7. Ibid.; emphasis added.
8. TOB 119:3; emphasis added.
9. See ibid., 119:5.
10. See ibid., 120:2.

11. Smith has rightly underlined that self-mastery and gift of self are at the heart of John Paul's proposal. See Smith, *Humanae Vitae*, 230–65. I would add two considerations to Smith's fine treatment. First, that generic self-mastery is another name for integration *in* the person. In this instance, this is the precise connection between TOB and Wojtyła's anthropology of love. Second, that John Paul's proposal shines better by considering the gift of self as an act of the virtue of charity as it relates to the other virtues he talks about from the perspective of the spousal meaning of the body.

love, in the *certainty* that the *one and only true* good of the human person consists in putting this divine plan *into practice*."[12] Responsible parenthood is to be exercised in conformity with the objective divine plan for marriage, manifested in the nature of the conjugal act and in the inseparable connection between its two meanings.[13]

The Virtuous Conjugal Act and the Goods of Marriage

John Paul II's personalistic understanding of the *bonum prolis* as parenting for heaven and of the good of fidelity as faithfulness to the divine plan already points to a mutual inclusion and inseparability between these two goods. According to his own premises, procreation presupposes conjugal love. In fact, procreation assumes and matures conjugal love into a virtuous state, which is needed for the education of children that is carried out, not only by words, but above all with one's example. In turn, conjugal love is procreative by nature. It is specified as conjugal in its essence and perfected as virtuous in a very special way when inserted into the common good of procreation. Thus, the rereading of the language of the body in the truth is John Paul's personalistic way of showing how the good of fidelity also brings conjugal love to maturation in virtue, this time within the context of justice, chastity, and in close connection with procreation. Spouses promise to lovingly accept children from the Creator. They promise to perfect the nature of their conjugal love in their procreative *munus*. This mutual inclusion of these two goods also seems to entail a certain inseparability. Intending the *bonum prolis* in actuality entails to intend at least habitually the *bonum fidei*. Conversely, actually intending the *bonum fidei* entails to intend at least habitually the *bonum prolis*. As a result, no marital act which is a true expression of conjugal love can be against the *bonum prolis*. On the other hand, no truly procreative marital act can take place outside the context of virtuous conjugal love inherent in the *bonum fidei*.

For these reasons, John Paul argues that the conjugal act is upright or morally good when there is a rereading of the language of the body *in the truth*. In this manner, the pope constructs quite a unique theological argument for conjugal morality. *Conformity* between the conjugal act and the objective language of the body means responsibility and fidelity to one's wedding promises as the abbreviation of God's exemplary plan for marriage. This is the way to ensure the goodness of the conjugal act, or its moral truthfulness, as it were. Consequently, the subjective rereading of the objective language of the body in the truth is not without its originality, in the best sense of the word. It places, within a personalitic framework, Paul VI's teaching on the inseparability of the procreative and unitive meanings of the conjugal act, and it does so by establishing a direct line of continuity, which runs from Pius XI's teaching on the goods of marriage to GS 48, GS 51, and HV 12. Moreover, the pope's position seems to also have a clear Thomistic foundation in Aquinas's discussion of the morality of

12. TOB 120:6; emphasis added.
13. See ibid., 121:6.

the conjugal act and the goods of marriage. The Angelic Doctor explains that "just as the goods of marriage, in accordance with the fact that they are in a habit, make marriage upright [*honestum*] and holy, so also do they make the act of marriage upright [*honestum*], in accordance with the fact that they are in an actual intention [*actuali intentione*]."[14] The goods which need to be in the actual intention of the spouses, an intention for which they come together in the marital embrace, are the *bonum prolis* and/or the *bonum fidei*. Thus, "when the spouses come together specifically for the purpose of procreating or to render their due to one another, which belongs to fidelity, they are totally [*totaliter*] excused from sin."[15]

In Thomas's view, the goods of marriage justify the conjugal act by making it morally upright or good as a true human act.[16] They make the marital embrace the bearer of *the goodness of virtue*, by ordering it in accordance with right reason, and by placing it in the mean between extremes.[17] As a result, these goods of marriage do not deny a certain spontaneity to the marital act. On the contrary, they actually build such spontaneity in a virtuous way, in those whose conjugal love is perfected by them. Thus, the good of offspring and fidelity make conjugal love virtuous by bringing it to its full or total maturation. This is the same perspective found in John Paul II's defense of the inseparability of the meanings of the conjugal act, the perspective that we cannot abandon to make full sense of our author's commentary on HV, the perspective of the integrity and virtuous character of conjugal love, the perspective of integration, and the perspective of virtue.

Let us come back to Aquinas's argument. To follow it through, we need to remember that Thomas does not reduce the *bonum prolis* to physical generation. In the text, he identifies procreation with the *bonum prolis*, but this is because at other times, he explains procreation as including the acceptance of children from God as well as their education, oriented to the Lord's worship both on this earth and in the life to come.[18] When this good is in the actual intention of the spouses performing the conjugal act, Aquinas argues that this act is *totally* upright, or *always* morally good. As I will shortly explain, the Angelic Doctor considers it possible to sin venially or even mortally, as when moved by concupiscence, spouses do not willfully impede generation but actually intend the sheer attainment of pleasure. Hence, it is quite a statement to say that intending the *bonum prolis* makes the conjugal act morally good in every respect and always. Thomas cannot mean here only the fact of not voluntarily impeding generation. That being included, the Angelic Doctor has in mind a richer notion of the *bonum prolis* which frees conjugal love from the threat of the ethos of concupiscence.

14. *In IV Sent.*, d. 31, q. 2, a. 2, c.
15. Ibid.
16. See *In IV Sent.*, d. 31, q. 2, a. 1, c.
17. See ibid.
18. See *ScG* IV.78; *In IV Sent.*, d. 31, q. 2, a. 2, ad 1; *Super I Cor.*, cap. 7, lect. 1.

In this case, spouses intend to collaborate with God in the transmission and education of human life by perfecting their conjugal love with virtues such as conjugal chastity, justice, piety (religion), or conjugal charity. These virtues are needed for the fostering of the common good of the family, which is at the heart of the *bonum prolis*. Thomas himself explains that to have intercourse in a way that allows generation to occur, but that impedes the kind of *education* due to the human person, is also against right reason and, hence, against the good of man, human nature, and the Creator as its author: "It is also against the good for man [*contra bonum hominis esse*] if the semen be emitted under conditions such that generation could result but that *proper education may be impeded* [*conveniens educatio impediatur*]."[19] Remember the richness of Aquinas's understanding of education; it is not just sending the kids to school. Thomas mentions proper or convenient education (*conveniens educatio*) of the offspring, that is to say, "the [human person's] development and promotion to the perfect state of man inasmuch as he is man, that is, the state of virtue."[20] Hence, Thomas's moral principle is *directly* applicable to premarital and extramarital relations, which may result in generation outside the very institution that establishes the conditions of possibility for proper education in virtue to occur. However, in my opinion, one could *indirectly* extend Aquinas's moral principle a bit further. A married couple could use it in order to argue, on the basis of justice and the common good of the family, for the need to have more children, as they often contribute to the education of their brothers and sisters and to the growth in charity of their parents. Conversely, this same principle could be the moral base to find *just* and serious reasons to limit the use of the marital act to the infertile periods. Even then, one would be acting with the *bonum prolis* in his or her actual intention, especially from the perspective of justice.

Be that as it may, note that by intending the *bonum prolis*, understood as collaboration with the Creator in the transmission and education of human life, spouses also exclude vices directly opposed to conjugal love, such as lust, or vices opposed to the spouses' collaboration with the Creator in justice and fidelity. These vices are against the nature of their conjugal love and against the example parents need to give in order to properly educate their children in virtue. Consequently, intending the *bonum prolis*, they are intending at least habitually to love each other and God virtuously, and to collaborate with him as they promised in their wedding vows. Thus, they are intending the *bonum fidei* as well. They are intending at least habitually the maturation of their conjugal love into its proper and due virtues.

Let us turn now to the other scenario, the one in which the couple intends in actuality the *bonum fidei*. Thomas's precise point is that one could have in the *actual* intention *either* good, because he knows well that married couples do not always have sex actually intending to have a baby. Without excluding what they promised at their wedding concerning procreation, but keeping it as a habitual intention, married

---

19. *ScG* III.122.
20. *In IV Sent.*, d. 26, q. 1, a. 1, c.

couples often have intercourse intending their mutual conjugal love, also promised at their wedding day. Thus, both Aquinas and Wojtyła understand that one cannot "demand of the spouses that they must positively desire to procreate on every occasion when they have intercourse. To say that intercourse is permissible and justified only on condition that the partners hope to have a child as a result of it would be an exaggeratedly strict ethical position."[21] Precisely for this reason, Thomas is granting that the *bonum fidei* can be in the actual intention of the spouses; the *bonum prolis* would not be positively excluded. At least, it would be habitually intended.

Thomas thinks that the *bonum fidei* is a matter of justice and veracity. Spouses act with this good in their actual intention when they are truthful to their wedding promises. Spouses promise to love each other and to give themselves to each other as husband and wife. The Angelic Doctor mentions the marital debt in the text and in this precise context. Thus, his language should not throw anyone off, nor should it be interpreted in a dry and legalistic sense which violates the dignity of the human person. In fact, the marital debt and the conjugal gift of self are intimately connected as two sides of the same coin. Remember our previous clarifications regarding reciprocal belonging in chapter 11. Spouses belong to each other because of the spiritual and bodily conjugal gift of self inherent in married love and the gift of self promised at their wedding. The marital debt is a direct consequence, within the virtue of justice's sphere, of the conjugal gift of self inherent in matrimonial consent. They offer their own self to each other because of their conjugal and reciprocal gift of self. Now, what is most important here is to understand why Thomas also grants that when spouses intend the *bonum fidei* in performing the conjugal act, their act is *totally* sinless or morally good. It is so because by actually intending fidelity to their promises, they are intending the maturation of conjugal love in virtue, especially as this maturation takes place in the loving acceptance of children from God and their education unto heaven. This particular maturation is intended at least habitually.

What about having sex with one's wife *only because it is pleasurable*? Thomas answers this question, defending the integrity of conjugal love and making several distinctions. These distinctions further clarify what it means to have in the actual intention of either the good of offspring or the good of fidelity. Of course, if one is actually intending the conjugal love inherent in the good of fidelity or the parenting for heaven included in the *bonum prolis*, the experience of pleasure in the marriage act is a good thing in itself; it is *never* sinful: "[F]or the delectation of a good operation is good, and a bad operation carries bad delectation."[22] Hence, intending either parenting for heaven or the conjugal love contained in the good of fidelity as reciprocal belonging makes the marital act a good operation and its delectation a good thing. The problem is when pleasure is intended for its own sake and in isolation, separated from the goods just mentioned. Then, the conjugal act is not morally good in every

21. LR, 233.
22. *In IV Sent.*, d. 31, q. 2, a. 3, c.

way. Its true nature is falsified. It could be deformed into a mortal or a venial sin. Indeed, outside the sphere of these goods, conjugal love is threatened in its integrity and virtuous character.

Consider the following scenario, for it clearly shows that fidelity is not only the material fact of not having sex with anyone except one's spouse. Thomas explains that "if pleasure should be sought outside the dignity of marriage, such that, for example, someone should not turn to his wife because she is his wife, but only because she is a woman, prepared to do the same with her as if she were not his wife, that is a *mortal* sin."[23] This man's "ardor is borne outside the goods of marriage."[24] His disordered passions have led him outside the boundaries of the love required by justice towards his wife. Quite strongly, Aquinas affirms that "a man seeks a harlot's pleasures in his own wife whenever he sees nothing else in her than what he might look for in a prostitute."[25] As was noted in chapter 8, John Paul II makes a similar point when he explains the possibility of committing adultery in the heart, even with one's wife.[26] The Angelic Doctor also provides for the scenario in which husband and wife were to make a sort of utilitarian pact, whereby they use each other beyond the boundaries of the goods of marriage. That willful consent would not diminish the fact that this behavior amounts to mortal sin.[27] On the other hand, if the actual intention of sexual pleasure is sought "within the limits of marriage, so that namely such delectation were not sought in any woman but in one's wife, then it would be a *venial* sin."[28] By contrast, these different scenarios show the depth and richness of Aquinas's understanding of the goods of marriage. Their sinful character is *entirely* avoided by actually willing either *fides* or *proles*. By doing so, none of those two sinful scenarios would ever happen.

With respect to the good of the sacrament, Aquinas clarifies that it does not belong to the moral use of marriage in the conjugal act, but rather to the very essence of matrimony. Thus, the good of the sacrament "makes marriage itself upright [*honestum*] but not its act."[29] Indeed, the conjugal act as an executed human or moral act is not made morally good *just because one is sacramentally married*. One could sin, even mortally, while having sex with one's lawful wife. Nevertheless, considered in itself, Thomas explains that the conjugal act receives its very *holiness* from the good of the sacrament: "[B]y the goodness of the sacrament, the conjugal act is *not only called good but also holy*; and the marital act has this goodness from the indissolubility

---

23. Ibid.; emphasis added.
24. Ibid.
25. Ibid., d. 31, q. 2, a. 3, ad 1.
26. See TOB 43:3.
27. See *In IV Sent.*, d. 31, q. 2, a. 3, ad 2.
28. Ibid., d. 31, q. 2, a. 3, ad 1.
29. Ibid., d. 31, q. 2, a. 2, c.

of the union, according to which it designates the union of Christ and his Church."[30] Consequently, Thomas Aquinas's moral theology of the conjugal act provides an important foundation for John Paul's commentary on HV. What clearly transpires in the Angelic Doctor's theology is not only the mutual inclusion of the goods of fidelity and offspring, but above all *their role in defending, protecting, and perfecting conjugal love by leading it to its virtuous state of maturation or integration*. They do so not only as goods which belong to marriage as a natural institution, but also as goods elevated by the grace of the sacrament, by that conformity to Christ's spousal love for the Church.

The Good Use of Periodic Continence

John Paul's commentary on HV is best revealed by presenting first the good use of periodic continence. In light of this good action, we can appreciate the evil of contraception as a *privation*. Only then should that exact evil be distinguished from the bad use of periodic continence. Now, different moral scenarios could be considered in the analysis of John Paul's commentaries. First, one could speak about a married couple who abandons their procreative responsibility to "chance," thinking that God's providential care will determine the whole matter. Second, a married couple may use periodic continence for serious and just reasons. Third, a married couple may use periodic continence for non-serious and unjust reasons. Fourth, a married couple may use contraception for serious and just reasons. Fifth, a married couple may use contraception for non-serious and unjust reasons. This is the worse, and unfortunately, most common case of contraception. It is usually accompanied by a selfish and materialistic life-project, oriented to comfort and well-being and against the difficulties of raising the children God wants the couple to have. However, in alignment with HV 16, my analysis of John Paul's commentary on HV will mostly deal with scenarios two and four. Comparing and contrasting them best elucidates the evil of contraception. Following the pope's text, I will briefly address the evil intention in the fifth scenario, together with the third scenario.

The Primacy of Virtue and the Morally Natural Character of Periodic Continence

The central message in John Paul II's commentary on the good use of periodic continence is *"the primacy of virtue."* This is the very title given by the pope to the section where he contrasts the evil of contraception with the good use of periodic continence.[31] The virtues inherent to this upright use of periodic continence make it *morally natural*, insofar as it conforms to the natural law as an *order of reason and*

---

30. Ibid., d. 31, q. 2, a. 1, c; emphasis added.
31. See TOB 124:1.

virtues. TOB explains the moral goodness of periodic continence, commenting on HV 21. Following GS 51, the pope especially emphasizes the role of conjugal chastity, perfected by charity and by the other virtues and gifts, as contained in his previous reflections on purity, in the life according to the Spirit (self-mastery or integration in the person, the virtues of justice and religion, the gift of piety, and added now, the fear of the Lord). John Paul argues that the primacy of virtue is the correct perspective which unlocks the key moral distinction between the good use of periodic continence and contraception. Thus, one can explain why periodic continence is *not* catholic contraception.

The doctrine of conjugal chastity, as perfected by charity and the other virtues previously mentioned, "remains, in fact, *the true reason in terms of which* Paul VI's teaching defines the ethically upright regulation of births and *responsible fatherhood and motherhood*."[32] As a result, "in the case of a morally right regulation of fertility brought about by periodic continence, *the point is clearly to practice conjugal chastity*."[33] The reason why HV calls it natural is not because of sheer biology, but because of its "conformity with the natural law."[34] The pope goes on to define exactly what he means: "By natural law we understand here the order of nature in the field of procreation *as it is understood by right reason*: this order is the expression of the Creator's plan for the human person."[35] The relevant point here is that periodic continence is *morally natural*: it is in accordance with the human person's rational nature, and with the nature of the conjugal act, insofar as both are perfected by the human person's *proper operation*—conscious and rational activity—in the practice of the virtues.

Karol Wojtyła made very similar points in LR. Therein, he spoke about the *personalistic* value of periodic continence. This value shines "in the fact that *in the wills* of the persons concerned *it must be grounded in a sufficiently mature virtue*."[36] By contrast, the utilitarian attitude deprives periodic continence from its morally natural character, as it falsifies "the true character of what we call the natural method, which is that *it is based on continence as a virtue and this is very closely connected with love of the person*."[37] Similarly, in TOB, John Paul II explains that "the qualifier "natural" ... is also to be explained by the fact that the way of behaving in question *corresponds to the truth of the person* and thus to the person's dignity: a dignity that belongs "by nature" to man *as a rational and free being*."[38]

---

32. TOB 124:4.
33. Ibid., 124:6; emphasis added.
34. Ibid. This is also the best reading of LR, 235, which envisions the morally relevant natural order as referred to the eternal law.
35. TOB 124:6; emphasis added.
36. LR, 241; emphasis added.
37. Ibid.; emphasis added.
38. TOB 125:1.

Procreative and Unitive Meanings

The good use of periodic continence implies that it is both unitive and procreative. Now, when John Paul speaks about periodic continence, he is not referring to the means employed to determine a woman's fertility cycle. Those means are not per se part of the pope's moral analyses. Moreover, as is known, "responsible parenthood contains the disposition, not only to avoid a new birth, but also to increase the family according to the criteria of prudence."[39] However, for clarity's sake, it is best to concentrate now on the married couple, who judging with prudence or discernment the circumstances in their family, collaborate with the Creator in matters concerning the transmission of life. They judge in right conscience, for just and serious reasons, that it is not God's will for the moment to have another baby. Then, the type of human action, willed in the good use of periodic continence, is *to abstain from marital intimacy during the fertile period*, with the added intention to collaborate with the Creator's will in the transmission and education of human life.

This good use of periodic continence is a unitive act of love. As we know from chapters 2 and 9, to abstain from the marital act can be an even greater sign of love than having sexual intercourse. Those who live in celibacy and virginity manifest this very point with their lives. Moreover, the good use of periodic continence *promotes virtues which perfect conjugal love*. According to Wojtyła's anthropology of love, the good use of periodic continence promotes integration *in* the person and *between* persons. It promotes virtues which combat the ethos of concupiscence. "Inherent in the essential character of continence as a virtue is the conviction that the love of man and woman loses nothing as a result of temporary abstention from erotic experiences, but on the contrary gains: *the personal union takes deeper root*, grounded as it is above all in affirmation of the value of the person and not just in sexual attachment."[40] In light of HV 21 and TOB, we can certainly conclude that the good use of periodic continence fosters the way of temperance characteristic of the redemption of the human heart as well as the little-known guiding thread, which envisions chastity and purity under the sphere of the virtue of religion and the gift of piety. Even more importantly, the good use of periodic continence promotes conjugal charity, that is, the married couples's particular way of fulfilling the spousal meaning of the body. It promotes that view of temperance as animated by charity, which Augustine described as "love giving itself entirely to that which is loved," as "love keeping itself entire and incorrupt for God."[41]

As we know, "the spousal meaning of the body has been deformed almost at its very roots by concupiscence."[42] The virtue of continence is an aid in this regard. Informed by charity, that is to say, "in its mature form, the virtue of continence gradu-

---

39. Ibid., 121:5.
40. LR, 241; emphasis added.
41. Augustine, *De Moribus Ecclesiae*, cap. 15, 25.
42. TOB 130:5.

ally reveals the pure aspect of the spousal meaning of the body."[43] Indeed, within the realm of the conjugal act, continence "plays an essential role in *maintaining the inner equilibrium between the two meanings, the unitive and the procreative in view of truly responsible fatherhood and motherhood.*"[44] No one can give what he does not have. The virtue of continence helps to acquire the necessary self-possession to be able to make a gift of oneself in true or perfected freedom. After all, "this freedom presupposes that one is able to direct sensual and emotive reactions in order to allow the gift of self to the other *I* on the basis of the mature possession of one's own 'I' in its bodily and emotive subjectivity."[45] The point here is not sheer technique but "to practice conjugal chastity."[46] Additionally, one "should keep in mind the whole teaching about purity understood as life according to the Spirit."[47] Within the ethos of redemption, the interior man is aided by the Holy Spirit to lead an integrated life in that same chastity. As a result, the good use of periodic continence promotes the maturation of conjugal love. For this reason, HV 16 distinguishes it from contraception by saying that the good use of periodic continence is a "testimony of a truly and completely upright love [*vere et omnino recti amoris testimonium*]." Indeed, the good use of periodic continence inserts conjugal love into the sphere of the conjugal common good and makes it grow with virtues. As chapter 10 explained, responsibility for procreation includes and effects the responsibility for the integration of the love between the spouses into virtuous conjugal friendship.

On the other hand, *the good use of periodic continence is also a procreative act*. The truth of this last statement could be challenged by a misinterpretation of HV 11. Since this text says that each and every conjugal act should be opened to the transmission of life, it would seem that marital intercourse should be limited exclusively to the *fertile* periods. This objection loses sight of the precise perspective adopted by HV. It is not merely biological, but rather moral. John Paul calls attention to this perspective by commenting on HV 11, underlining the role of the term *meaning*. The spouses' conscious awareness of the conjugal act's nature emphasizes the role of reason in directing this same action *as a moral and voluntary action*.[48] Thus, Wojtyła clarified that "the man and the woman are aware of the meaning of the conjugal act. Moreover, in performing this act, *they can and should intend by it precisely what it means essentially*. It means both a special union of persons and, at the same time, the possibility (not the necessity!) of fecundity, of procreation. If, in acting jointly, this is precisely what *they intend to signify by their activity*, then the activity is intrinsically true and free of

---

43. Ibid.
44. Ibid., 130:3; emphasis added.
45. Ibid., 130:4.
46. Ibid., 124:6.
47. TOB 124:4.
48. See ibid., 119:1.

falsification."⁴⁹ In classical terms, the conjugal act is considered here as an *actus humanus*, as an intentional and voluntary action. As a result, the openness to the transmission of life signified by HV 11 is not merely biological, but intentional in nature.

Hence, each and every conjugal act, inasmuch as it is a human act, should be "per se oriented [*per se destinatus*] toward the transmission of life"; it should be oriented to the collaboration with the Creator in the transmission and education of human life. However, not every conjugal act has to be physiologically or biologically generative. For instance, pathological or age-conditioned sterile married couples do not sin because of the non-generative nature of their conjugal acts. Their *unwilled* infertility is very different from the contraceptive *will to disconnect sexual activity from its procreative dimension*. Consequently, HV 11 is not closing the door to the good use of periodic continence; it is not condemning all non-generative conjugal acts. It is only pointing at the way in which the conjugal act must be *chosen*. It must be *chosen* as an act per se, oriented to the transmission of life, as a procreative act.

However, can a conjugal act be at the same time procreative and non-generative, or should we conclude that infertile conjugal acts do not have a procreative meaning at all? I think that John Paul II would say that if procreation is understood as the free collaboration with the Creator in the transmission and education of human life, there can be procreative acts that are non-generative.⁵⁰ The pope insists that "the couple must conform their activity to the creative intention of God."⁵¹ Hence, their activity is not deprived of procreative meaning. As Rhonheimer has pointed out, without granting this point, it would be very difficult to make sense of HV's teachings on the two meanings of the conjugal act and their inseparability in each and every conjugal act that is morally upright.⁵² To be sure, periodic continence, understood as abstaining from marital intimacy during the fertile period, is non-generative. However, the just reasons which animate this abstention make it an act of procreative responsibility. There can be no authentic collaboration with the Creator without faithfulness to him. And as John Paul II says, the good use of periodic continence in accordance with the natural law is all about "*faithfulness . . . to the personal Creator,* the source and Lord of

---

49. PC, 308.

50. Similarly, Thomas Aquinas grants that Mary and Joseph had a perfect marriage with respect to the *bonum prolis* (see See *ST* III, q. 29, a. 2, c). Their marriage was certainly non-generative. However, they collaborated with God in the transmission of human life inasmuch as they never had sexual intercourse *only because they were doing God's will*. Their marriage was validly contracted precisely because they would have done otherwise, provided that is what God wanted. Hence, in my opinion, their marriage could be seen as non-generative but certainly as procreative in this exact measure: they collaborated with God in doing his will with respect to the transmission of human life, and they collaborated with God in educating Jesus.

51. TOB 121:5.

52. In his disputes with the advocates of contraception, Rhonheimer distinguishes meaning and function: "Only a *fertile* sexual act can have a procreative function; an *infertile* act, by definition, will never have a procreative function, but it may have a procreative meaning if it is intentionally open to procreation." Rhonheimer, *Ethics of Procreation*, 78. See also Anscombe, *You Can Have Sex*, 85.

the order that is shown in this law."⁵³ We see again in this text Wojtyła's nexus between moral obligation and the *rationabilem obsequiuum* to God. Consequently, a conjugal act in the good use of periodic continence can be at the same time non-generative but procreative, insofar as it takes place within the context of responsible parenthood, collaborating with the Creator and his laws, and in view of the goods of fidelity and offspring.

This procreative dimension of the good use of periodic continence contributes to the maturation of conjugal love with a set of virtues and gifts, which perfect the spouses as a common subject in their relationship with God. The procreative dimension of the good use of periodic continence is a collaboration in accordance with the natural law and with the dignity of the human person as a temple of God. Within this theological context, the gift of piety informs the spouses' collaboration with God as their common Father. Thus, the Christian responsibility of spouses is fulfilled in their fidelity to their promises, in which they accepted to receive children lovingly from God and to educate them according to the law of Christ and his church. In this way, spouses are to be mutually subordinated to their conjugal common good in the fear of Christ. John Paul II combines his reflections on the gift of piety, which perfects the virtue of justice and stands behind Paul's teaching on the spouses' mutual subjection to one another and to God as their common Father, with the gift of fear of the Lord, which perfects the virtue of temperance. This fear "indicates the gift of the fear of God (a gift of the Holy Spirit), which accompanies the virtue of continence. This is very important for an adequate understanding of the virtue of continence and, in particular, of so-called periodic continence discussed by *Humanae Vitae*."⁵⁴

Piety and fear of the Lord connect in that the latter is a *filial* fear of committing a fault and offending *the Father*.⁵⁵ It is a kind of fear whereby "we revere God and avoid separating ourselves from Him."⁵⁶ It is a fear which springs from charity, in this case, from *conjugal* charity. As a human passion, fear is all about the possible loss of a good that is *loved*. Filial or chaste fear of the Lord consists in a kind of supernatural love which destroys every other fear, except the fear of not being with God, as the beloved loved above all things, and above all persons. This kind of filial or chaste fear is said to be the beginning of wisdom, inasmuch as it is the first effect of wisdom. And, "since the regulation of human conduct by the Divine law belongs to wisdom, in order to make a beginning, man must first of all fear God and submit himself to Him: for the result will be that in all things he will be ruled by God."⁵⁷ From this perspective, we can better understand why "the concept of a morally right regulation of fertility is nothing other than rereading the language of the body in the truth. The same natural

---

53. TOB 124:6.
54. Ibid., 128:1. He explicitly names Aristotle and Aquinas in 130:1.
55. See *ST* II–II, q. 19, a. 2, c; II–II, q. 19, a. 9, c.
56. *ST* II–II, q. 19, a. 9, c.
57. *ST* II–II, q. 19, a. 7, c.

rhythms immanent in the generative functions belong to the objective truth of this language, which the persons involved should reread in its full objective content."[58] In this manner, "the gifts of the Holy Spirit, and in particular the gift of reverence for what is sacred, seem to have a fundamental meaning here."[59] According to the pope, this gift "sustains and develops in the spouses a singular sensibility for all that in their vocation and shared life carries the sign of the mystery of creation and redemption: for all that is a created reflection of God's wisdom and love."[60] Consequently, John Paul II explains, "this gift seems to initiate man and woman particularly deeply *into reverence for the two inseparable meanings of the conjugal act*."[61]

Piety, reverence, and filial fear increase when *charity* increases.[62] Hence, the more spouses love God, and each other in God, with conjugal charity, the more they fear to offend him and the more they want to avoid sinning sexually in their use of marriage. This is where John Paul connects all the virtues and gifts seen thus far with charity as the fulfillment of the spousal meaning of the body. The gifts of piety and fear of the Lord "united with love and chastity, helps one to identify, in the whole of conjugal shared life, the act in which, at least potentially, the spousal meaning of the body is linked with the procreative meaning."[63] Let us go back to the virtue of continence as a virtue in the province of temperance and perfected by the fear of the Lord. To be sure, the virtue of continence directly opposes the concupiscence of the flesh. But this virtue is to be seen within the *nexus virtutum*. From this other perspective, the virtue of continence, "through this resistance also opens itself to the deeper and more mature values that are part of the spousal meaning of the body in its femininity and masculinity, as well as to the authentic freedom of the gift in the reciprocal relationship of persons . . . In this way, the essential character of conjugal chastity also becomes clear in its organic link with *the "power" of love*, which is poured out in the hearts of the spouses together with the consecration of the sacrament of marriage."[64] Again, this power of love, which relates the spousal meaning of the body with procreation, corresponds to the traditional teaching about charity as the form of all virtues. More specifically, it corresponds to the grace of the sacrament of matrimony as conformity with Christ's spousal charity for the church.

In conclusion, the good use of periodic continence is not a birth control method but a virtuous conjugal lifestyle, which fosters integration, responsibility, virtue, and communion between spouses, and between spouses and God. The spousal meaning of the body is central for the good use of periodic continence. Conjugal charity, as

58. TOB 125:1.
59. Ibid., 131:5.
60. Ibid.
61. Ibid.; emphasis added.
62. See *ST* II–II, q. 19, a. 10, c.
63. TOB 132:2.
64. Ibid., 128:2–3.

conformed to Christ's spousal love for the church, animates the married couple's discernment process of God's will. It prompts their obedience to his intelligible order as well as their sacrificial generosity and spirit of fortitude in having a numerous family. Spouses are to take their decisions regarding procreation out of love for God, out of the love they have for each other and their children in God, and because of God.

The Essential Evil of the Contraceptive Act

Paul VI defines contraception in HV 14 as "every action which, either in anticipation of the conjugal act, or in its accomplishment, or in the development of its natural consequences, propose, whether as an end or as a means to render procreation impossible." Its moral evil resides neither in a sheer biological fact nor in its articificiality.[65] Sheer biological facts, like the sterility of a couple, do not render the conjugal act contraceptive, and a contraceptive behavior such as *coitus interruptus* is "natural," as opposed to artificial. Since the *natural* character of the good use of periodic continence consists in its accordance with man's rational nature, the evil of contraception is really a privation of such an accordance; it is a matter of being *against* man's rational nature, a matter of being *against* the order of right reason and the virtues. Thus, FC 32 explains that contraception and the good use of periodic continence are based on two *mutually exclusive* anthropologies. Contraception is based on a spiritualistic Cartesian personalism. By opposing consciousness—identified with the human person—to the human body, everything corporeal is reduced to the sheer somatic level that can be manipulated at will, to a raw material belonging to a pre-moral order. Instead, the good use of periodic continence is based on an *integral view of the human person*, which accounts for his substantial unity and his being created in God's image and likeness. In John Paul's case, the good use of periodic continence is based on the theology of the body and of its spousal meaning. While the good use of periodic continence promotes the virtues that perfect conjugal love or communion in fulfillment of Christian responsibility, contraception irresponsibly deprives this same conjugal love or communion of all those virtues, thereby abandoning it to the ethos of concupiscence. Hence, contraception is neither procreative nor unitive.

When a married couple chooses contraception, they implicitly *reject the alternative*. They choose contraception *over* the difficult demands of periodic continence. Hence, contraceptive intercourse entails a (false) liberation of the conjugal act from the virtuous demands of periodic continence. Thereby, it abandons conjugal love to *a principle of disintegration*, to the tendency of one's sensible appetite wounded by sin not to follow the order of right reason but seek, instead, disordered self-love and gratification. These are very fragile grounds for conjugal love. They are not in accordance

---

65. Rhonheimer has rightfully drawn attention to these two points. He speaks of an *ignoratio elenchi* or *mutatio enlenchi*, that is, an ignorance or change of the point of dispute. Such ignorance and change have caused much confusion. See Rhonheimer, *Practical Reason and Natural Law*, 135.

with the enormous responsibility inherent to conjugal love, "the responsibility for a person who is drawn into the closest possible partnership in the life and activity of another, and becomes in a sense the property of whoever benefits from this gift of self."[66] Remember, Wojtyła invites married couples to ask themselves the following question about their conjugal love: "[I]s it mature and complete enough to justify the enormous trust of another person, the hope that giving oneself will not mean losing one's own soul, but on the contrary enlarging one's existence—or will it all end in disillusionment?"[67]

Thus, John Paul's interpretation of the inseparability of the unitive and procreative meanings is, in reality, *a defense of conjugal love*. "Love divorced from a feeling of responsibility for the person is a negation of itself, is always and necessarily egoism. *The greater the feeling of responsibility for the person the more true love there is*."[68] Consequently, we better understand the importance of Wojtyła's interpretation of the theology of marriage in Vatican II *within the sphere of Christian responsibility* as developed in chapter 1. It is one of the key foundations of John Paul's Thomistic argument against contraception, an argument also grounded in Vatican II. Contraception entails precisely a negation of responsibility for the integrity of conjugal love and its maturation in virtue. Contraceptive intercourse is not just biologically non-generative but, above all, intentionally anti-procreative. It deprives the conjugal act and the married couple from being perfected by their collaboration with the Creator in the transmission and education of human life. Contraceptive intercourse circumvents and opts not to grow in the virtues inherent in the good use of periodic continence. Thereby, it promotes the contrary vices. While the good use of periodic continence is both procreative and unitive, contraception is neither procreative nor unitive.

At first, it could *seem* that contraceptive intercourse could be chosen with the intention of doing God's will. Could a couple choose contraceptive intercourse out of procreative responsibility? The object of choice would be evil, but the intention would be good. However, in reality, the contraceptive choice is *incompatible and contradictory* as a "means" to that intention, as something which actually leads to that end. Contraception *eliminates responsibility*. Consequently, it eliminates authentic cooperation in justice and obedience to the Creator and to the rational moral order. Since it is an action against the procreative conjugal common good, which specifies conjugal love and intensifies the union among spouses, it is an action which directly corrodes their unity. It erodes their common union in collaboration with the Creator. It can never be procreative or unitive. It is an action against the spousal meaning of the body, against conjugal charity.

Contraceptive intercourse destroys the loving union of the spouses, even if this destruction is *not subjectively experienced all at once* by the couple. Indeed, it promotes

---

66. LR, 130.
67. Ibid.
68. Ibid., 131; emphasis added.

vices that lead to a self-gratifying and isolating dynamic, thereby eroding virtuous conjugal friendship by the promotion of unchastity and the violation of the personalistic norm.[69] Contraceptive intercourse is no longer procreatively responsible love, informed by conjugal charity and the freedom of the gift of self. Thus, Wojtyła was totally right eight years before HV when he explained: "An outright conflict with that purpose [procreation] *will also perturb and undermine love between persons*. People sometimes find this purpose a nuisance and try to circumvent it by artificial means. Such means must however have *a damaging effect of love between persons*, which in this context is most intimately involved in the use of the sexual urge."[70] All along, Wojtyła's argument is clear: contraception damages conjugal love because of the inseparable connection. The damage consists in clear moral evil: the privation of its due integration in virtue and procreative responsibility. As he also said, contraception is wrong because "the active undermining of the *meaning and purpose that corresponds to the plan of the Creator* must work *against* the 'intimate union' of the spouses. One could say, as a way of interpreting this thought, that *the conjugal act then lacks the value of a true union of persons*."[71]

In TOB, all of these elements are integrated into the following theological argumentation: contraception attacks the conjugal communion of persons, because of its lack of conformity with the objective language of the body spoken by the Creator in the creation of the rational creature, and in revelation. Hence, "one can say that in the case of an artificial separation of these two meanings in the conjugal act, a real bodily union is brought about, but it does not correspond to the inner truth and dignity of personal communion."[72] The reason why there is no correspondence or conformity is, because "if this truth is lacking, one can speak neither of the truth of the reciprocal gift of self nor of the reciprocal acceptance of oneself by the person. Such a violation of the inner order of conjugal communion, a communion that plunges its roots into the very order of the person, *constitutes the essential evil of the contraceptive act*."[73] By means of this philosophical and theological argument constructed under the category of the language of the body, John Paul II adopts the perspective of the order of reason and the order of virtue, and within them, the perspective of charity. For this reason, the pope has spoken about conjugal spirituality as a life of married virtues centrally animated by conjugal charity. That is the way of promoting *conjugal communion*. This is the whole point of looking at HV from the perspective of the spousal meaning of the body. From this perspective, the real question is not what can one get away with, but rather what leads to a happy marriage here on earth and to heaven in the life to come. In HV, we have one of the laws in the law of life as our inheritance. Contra-

69. See HV 17; Rhonheimer, *Ethics of Procreation*, 37.
70. LR, 53; emphasis added.
71. PC, 311.
72. TOB 123:7.
73. Ibid.

ceptive intercourse leads neither to a happy marriage nor to eternal life. It opposes conjugal charity, conjugal chastity, temperance, justice, religion, the gift of piety, the gift of the fear of the Lord, and the other virtues inherent in responsible procreation. Although chastity is not the greatest of the virtues, unchastity or lust is certainly one quick way to destroy charity and, consequently, to frustrate the peculiar fulfillment of the spousal meaning of the body that belongs to marriage. Contraceptive sex at low cost avoids sacrificial love, conjugal charity, and the gift of self inherent in virtuous conjugal friendship. It promotes the opposite values.

In light of what John Paul II has identified in TOB as *the essential evil of the contraceptive act*, let us turn now to another *locus classicus* in the pope's teachings against contraception in order to offer some needed clarifications:

> When couples, by means of recourse to contraception, separate these two meanings that God the Creator *has inscribed in the being of man and woman and in the dynamism of their sexual communion*, they act as arbiters of the divine plan and they manipulate and *degrade human sexuality*—and with it themselves and their married partner—by altering its value of total self-giving. Thus the innate language that expresses the total reciprocal self-giving of husband and wife is overlaid, through contraception, by an objectively contradictory language, namely, *that of not giving oneself totally to the other*. This leads not only to a positive refusal to be open to life but also to *a falsification of the inner truth of conjugal love*, which is called upon to give itself in personal totality.[74]

The *falsification* or untruth John Paul mentions consists in a lack of conformity between the objective language of the body spoken by God in the creation of the rational creature and in revelation, and the rereading of this language by spouses when using contraception. There is no conformity or *adequatio* between one and the other. That is the heart of the argument. Contraception goes against the total gift of self, because it undermines the very virtues that mature conjugal love and make such a gift total, the same virtues natural law and divine revelation place at the center of the objective language of the body. In so doing, contraception detaches human sexuality from the human person as created in God's image and as called to grow in virtue into a conformity with Christ. That undermining of the virtues prevents conjugal love to be truthful to its exemplar. It prevents conjugal love to mature in virtue to its full or total truth. Thereby, it amounts to the essential evil of the contraceptive act, namely, "*a violation of the inner order of conjugal communion*."[75] It is precisely this very undermining that leads to a refusal to be open to life and to the falsification of conjugal love.

I realize that this is not the most common interpretation of this text. However, I think that it is the most faithful to John Paul II. Interpreters seems to concentrate,

---

74. FC 32; emphasis added.
75. TOB 123:7.

instead, on another aspect. They tend to read into FC 32 the following syllogism. Since HV 9 clarifies that conjugal love is total, the gift of oneself in the conjugal act must be total as well. However, if one's spouse is not willing to give his or her fertility, his or her gift is not total but only partial: "If one is not willing to share one's life-giving power, one's fertility, with another, one is not giving totally of oneself: by negating the procreative meaning of sexual intercourse, one is also negating the unitive meaning of marriage, the meaning of total self-giving."[76] Without denying the elements of truth inherent to this other argument, especially the hardcore truth expressed in the last phrase of the quote, it seems to me that John Paul's is slightly different.

The pope concentrates, instead, on his basic premise according to which selfishness is "the enemy of true love."[77] The common union between husband and wife "cannot be formed and developed *in the full truth of its possibilities* on the ground of concupiscence alone."[78] Concupiscence without virtue turns conjugal love against itself by eroding it with its greatest enemy: selfishness. What makes contraception morally evil, above all, is its *depriving conjugal love from the virtues that make possible the full truth of its possibilities in the total gift of self*. Besides, we do not want to say that spouses, practicing periodic continence *for just reasons*, do not give each other totally but only *partially*. What makes the gift of self total or partial is *not* the biological fact of *fertility* or *infertility*, but rather *virtue* or its privation. For this reason, FC 32 says, exactly, that spouses do give each other *totally* even if, for just reasons, they consciously choose to have intercourse when they are *infertile*. Their conjugal gift of self may be non-generative, but it is certainly total and procreative, provided the reasons for such practice are truly just, and the virtues maturing conjugal love in accordance with the spousal meaning of the body are also present.

Finally, I would like to explain why contraceptive intercourse is also, in a special way, a sin against nature (*peccatum contra naturam*). It is so, not only because it is against the order of reason, but also because it corrodes the very foundations of this rational order. It does so by attacking the rational natural inclinations of the human person, disconnecting them from their proper end and act. Indeed, contraception contradicts the impression of the eternal law (*impressio legis aeternae*) in the human person as the basis for the ordering of right reason.[79] It especially contradicts the very foundations of two natural inclinations, which in the human person are generically animal but specifically rational: the union among the sexes in married love within the sphere of the virtue of conjugal chastity, and the cooperation with the Creator in the transmission and education of human life as it is perfected in the virtues of justice towards the Creator, the family, and the other spouse. Consequently, inasmuch as contraception is a sin against nature in this specific sense, and against the virtues that

76. Smith, *Humanae Vitae*, 256.
77. TOB 125:6.
78. Ibid., 130:5.
79. See *ST* II–II, q. 152, a. 12, c.

perfect conjugal love, we can truly define it as an *alienating behavior*. By alienation I mean exactly what Wojtyła means: "[T]he negation of participation, for it renders participation difficult or even impossible. It devastates the I—other relationship, weakens the ability to experience another human being as another I, and inhibits the possibility of friendship and the spontaneous powers of community (*communio personarum*)."[80]

The Bad Use of Periodic Continence

The bad use of periodic continence shifts the center of our discussion from the object of choice to that of intention. We move to the level which answers this precise question: *why* is periodic continence practiced by a married couple? Its bad use consists in doing something good for the wrong reason, with an evil intention. Yet, as is known, for a human action to be morally good, the object of choice, the intention, and the circumstances must all be good. In classical terms, *bonum ex integra causa malum ex quocumque defectu* (the good results from an integral cause, while evil from any defect whatsoever). Bad use of periodic continence is another attack against the integrity of conjugal love. It *falsifies periodic continence*. It reduces such a practice to a sheer technique without true virtue. This falsified version is mistakenly identified by people as Catholic contraception.

Since man is a rational being, it is consonant with his nature to act with full conscious responsibility for every conception.[81] Nevertheless, responsible parenthood should not be reduced to a sheer technique deprived from ethical rules.[82] It is all about *virtue*. Yet, sometimes "the couple who have recourse to the natural regulation of fertility can *lack the valid reasons*."[83] In this case, "the use of infertile periods in conjugal shared life can become *a source of abuses* if the couple thereby attempt to evade procreation *without just reasons*, lowering it below the morally just level of births in their family."[84] There are different potential scenarios which could explain the ulterior motivation to act without just reasons. The pope concentrates on the most common one: the utilitarian and selfish attitude that could vitiate the use of the infertile period in conjugal shared life. Since this same utilitarian and selfish intention is also present in most cases of contraceptive intercourse, this evil use of the infertile periods blurs the objective and specific distinction between periodic continence and contraception. When there is an anti-procreative intention in the use of periodic continence, then, "one no longer sees the differences between it [the recourse to the infertile periods]

---

80. PC, 206.
81. See LR, 279; KD, 336; TOB 121:2.
82. See TOB 14:4; LR, 282.
83. TOB 122:3; emphasis added.
84. Ibid., 125:3; emphasis added.

and the other methods (artificial means), and one ends up speaking about it [the recourse to the infertile periods] *as if it were just another form of contraception.*"[85]

In congruency with John Paul's thought, I have called anti-procreative the evil intention that vitiates the use of periodic continence. It is an intention which vitiates the vertical dimension of procreation explained in chapter 10, that is, the dimension of the spouses as a common subject in their relationship with the Creator. The predominant virtue which regulates this dimension, according to Wojtyła, is that of *justice*. I think that the bad use of periodic continence acts against this very virtue in matters of procreation. Inasmuch as it fosters selfishness and lack of concern for the common good, this violation of justice could also lead to unchastity and lust. In classical terms, it could lead to performing the martial act outside of the sphere of the goods of fidelity and offspring. Nevertheless, in my opinion, the bad use of periodic continence is, essentially, a question of justice. HV 16 already points to this idea when it speaks about spouses having *just* reasons [*iustae causae*] for their practice. When these just reasons are lacking, justice is being violated inasmuch as this anti-procreative intention damages the common good of the spouses' family, of their marriage, of society and of the church. Moreover, it also violates justice towards the Creator. These violations of justice often have selfishness as an ulterior motivating factor. Such disordered self-love is capable of seeing the conception of a future child as an *evil*. For this reason, I insist in calling this intention anti-procreative. I am particularly inspired by the following texts: "Those who set about regulating conception must consider this aspect of the matter before all else . . . A determination on the part of husband and wife to have as few children as possible, to make their own lives easy, is bound to inflict moral *damage both on their family and on society at large*. Limitation of the number of conceptions must in any case not be another name for renunciation of parenthood. From the point of view of the family, *periodic continence as a method of regulating conception is permissible in* so *far as it does not conflict with a sincere disposition to procreate.*"[86] A bit earlier in the book, Wojtyła has also explained that "if continence is to be a virtue and not just a method in the *utilitarian* sense, it must not serve to destroy *readiness for parenthood* in a husband and wife, since acceptance that 'I may become a father'/'I may become a mother' is what justifies the marital relationship and puts it on the level of a true union of persons."[87] For this reason, we cannot "speak of continence as a *virtue* where the spouses take advantage of the periods of biological infertility *exclusively for the purpose of avoiding parenthood altogether*, and have intercourse only in those periods."[88]

Consequently, the anti-procreative intention which vitiates the use of periodic continence willfully refuses to collaborate with the Creator in the transmission and

---

85. Ibid., 125:4; emphasis added.
86. LR, 243; emphasis added.
87. Ibid., 242; emphasis added.
88. Ibid.; emphasis added.

education of human life at different levels. It unjustly considers the child himself as an evil. It does not take into account in all justice the common good of the marriage, inasmuch as their conjugal love could be perfected by a more sacrificial and generous participation with God's will. It is also unjust towards the common good of the family, especially because it often befits the education of children to have more brothers and sisters, and the parental attitude perfects conjugal love as well. It is unjust towards the common good of society inasmuch as it entails a refusal of contributing more good citizens. Finally, it is also an injustice against the common good of the church, inasmuch as it refuses new members both here on earth and in the after-life. These same parameters are the ones which should effect the right discernment and intention in the good use of periodic continence. Spouses should search, above all, to do God's will by collaborating with him in justice and obedience to his moral laws. They should not view a child as an evil. With a spirit of sacrificial generosity, spouses should discern God's will based on what truly advances the common good of their family, their marriage, the church and society. These parameters can result in discerning *just* reasons for the good practice of periodic continence.

The anti-procreative intention is very different from this right discernment, which concludes, in light of the parameters just described, that the circumstances are not the right ones to have another baby. To be sure, in this last scenario, there is a non-generative intention. Spouses have discerned that their circumstances amount to just and serious reasons not to have a baby for the time being, precisely in light of the common good of their family, their marriage, the church and society. However, their discernment does not envision a future child as an evil. Instead, it is a good for which one is not prepared, due to the circumstances of one's marriage and family. Moreover, the circumstances are not judged to be the right ones in light of justice, and out of a sincere collaboration with the Creator and the fulfillment of his holy will. Thus, their prudential discernment is always subject to the moral provision, unless God wills otherwise. If God would want them to have a baby, they would lovingly welcome and accept their new offspring, as they promised on the day of their wedding. As John Paul II says, in the practice of periodic continence, "the couple must conform their activity to the creative intention of God."[89] For this very reason, Wojtyła also explains that "this acceptance of the possibility of becoming a father or a mother must be present in the mind and the will even when the spouses do not want a pregnancy, and deliberately choose to have intercourse at a period when it may be expected not to occur. This acceptance, in the context of any particular occasion of intercourse, together with a general disposition to parenthood in the broader context of the marriage as a whole, determines the moral validity of periodic continence."[90]

Consequently, the bad use of periodic continence does not promote authentic integration in the person and between persons. It certainly does not promote the virtues

---

89. TOB 121:5.
90. LR, 243.

and gifts which perfect the relationship of the couple and the Creator (justice, religion, piety). It does not even promote authentic purity, or true temperance in the form of authentic conjugal chastity. The bad use of periodic continence promotes *a certain self-restraint*. This self-restraint may have a semblance of chastity. However, in reality, such restraint is informed neither by the order of right reason and the virtues nor by conjugal charity, but by the same selfishness which informs the behavior of many who use contraception. For this very reason, it becomes difficult to distinguish them. But let us be absolutely clear: the bad use of periodic continence and contraception are *two wholly distinct types of actions*. Sometimes they may share they same intention, but their object of choice is *completely different*. Yet, both promote in *different* ways an attack on the virtues which defend conjugal love from the ethos of concupiscence. They both entail a violation of the spousal meaning of the body in matters of procreation.

Original Sources of Renewal

John Paul's commentary and interpretation of HV has centered around the category of the subjective rereading of the objective language of the body in the truth. His position is "original" in the best sense of the term. It places within a personalistic framework Paul VI's teaching on the inseparability of the procreative and unitive meanings of the conjugal act. Moreover, John Paul manages to do so in direct continuity with Pius XI's teaching on the goods of marriage, GS's teachings on conjugal love, and HV. Moreover, Wojtyła's argument is clearly Thomistic. It seems to be founded upon Thomas's theology of the conjugal act and the goods of marriage, his theology of the *imago Dei* and the virtues, the gifts of the Holy Spirit, and especially Aquinas's views on charity.

After this journey, in which we have accompanied John Paul II in his theology of procreation and the spousal meaning of the body, we can conclude that his entire theological anthropology and theology of marriage is contrary to that influence of modernity in contemporary moral theology, which exalts novelty and originality to the detriment of the value of tradition. As this book has shown, the greater part of John Paul II's contribution to TOB consists in the rediscovery of tradition in its pursuit to renew moral theology, according to the directives of Vatican II. Nevertheless, this renewal in the sources is truly "original": it goes back to the origins. It nourishes from the sources of revelation and traditional theology. Such "originality" is manifested in his understanding of procreation and its relationship with the spousal meaning of the body. Indeed, as it has been demonstrated, John Paul's understanding of these two notions, and of their interrelation, constitute *a Thomistic argument grounded in Vatican II*.

Consequently, the pope's originality is very different from Kant's *sapere aude*. John Paul II is definitely thinking with another's guidance. He is especially guided by Thomas Aquinas and by Vatican II. With his example, Saint John Paul II teaches theologians to be like that scribe, who being a son of the Kingdom, "brings out of his treasure what is new and what is old."[91] Moreover, contemporary theology can still learn another crucial point from him. The pope offers a clear path to harmonize the biblical and metaphysical foundations of a christocentric moral theology, which is compatible with the natural law and is grounded on the substantial unity of man as a being created in God's image. John Paul II accomplishes this by offering not only a theology of the body, but also a theology of love. His entire proposal has *never* abandoned the perspective of supernatural love. His theology of the body is a theology of its spousal meaning as our supernatural call to charity in its relationship with procreation as the free cooperation with the Creator in the transmission and education of human life. John Paul's theology is a "time bomb," not so much because of its reluctance to be guided by tradition, but rather *precisely* because of that humble anti-Kantian attitude, which opens the eyes of the spirit to the contemplation of truth by removing the impediment of pride and false autonomy.

For this reason, I am quite sure that John Paul would not mind if I end this book not by quoting him, but rather Aquinas's concluding remarks in his presentation of the order and division of the scriptures. These remarks invite us to look up to heaven, to the ultimate fulfillment of the spousal meaning of our bodies, to "the end of the Church, with which the whole content of Scripture concludes in the Apocalypse, with the spouse in the abode of Jesus Christ sharing the life of glory, to which Jesus Christ himself conducts, and may he be blessed for ever and ever. Amen."[92]

---

91. Matt 13:52.
92. *De Commendatione*, 1208.

Selected Bibliography

Selected Works by Karol Wojtyła/John Paul II

Wojtyła, Karol (John Paul II). *Crossing the Threshold of Hope*. London: Cape, 1994.

———. *Gift and Mystery*. New York: Doubleday, 1996.

———. *God, Father and Creator: A Catechesis on the Creed*. Boston: Pauline, 1996.

———. *Man and Woman He Created Them: A Theology of the Body*. Translated and edited by Michael Waldstein. Boston: Pauline, 2006 (Uomo e donna lo creò. Catechesi sull'amore umano. Rome: Città Nuova, 2007).

———. "Concerning the Principles of Conjugal Life." *Nova et Vetera* 10, no. 2 (2012) 321–60.

———. *El don del amor: Escritos sobre la familia*. Translated by Antonio Esquivias y Rafael Mora. Madrid: Palabra, 2001.

———. *El hombre y su destino: Ensayos de antropología*. Translated by Pilar Ferrer. Madrid: Palabra, 1998.

———. *Faith according to St. John of the Cross*. Translated by Jordon Aumann. San Francisco: Ignatius, 1981.

———. "Letter to Henri De Lubac February 1968." Translated by Anne Elizabeth Englund. In *At the Service of the Church*, by Henri de Lubac, 171–72. San Francisco: Ignatius, 1993.

———. *Love and Responsibility*. Translated by H. T. Willets. San Francisco: Ignatius, 1993.

———. *Lubliner Vorlesungen*. Translated by Anneliese Spranger y Edda Wiener. Stuttgart: Seewald, 1980.

———. *Man in the Field of Responsibility*. Translated by Kenneth W. Kemp and Zuzanna Maslanka Kieron. South Bend: St. Augustine's, 2011.

———. *Max Scheler y la ética cristiana*. Translated by Gonzalo Haya. Madrid: BAC, 1982.

———. *Mi visión del hombre: Hacia una nueva ética*. Translated by Pilar Ferrer. Madrid: Palabra, 1998.

———. "On the Meaning of Spousal Love." Translated by Grzegorz Ignatik. In *Love and Responsibility*, 275–94. Boston: Pauline, 2013.

———. *Osoba i Czyn- Persona e atto*. Edited by Tadeusz Styzcen. Rome: Bompiani, 2001.

———. *Person and Community: Selected Essays*. Translated by Theresa Sandok. New York: Lang, 1993.

———. *Rozważania o istocie człowieka*. Krakow: WAM, 2000.

———. *Sign of Contradiction*. Translated by Kenneth Kemp. New York: Seabury, 1979.

———. *Sources of Renewal: The Implementation of the Second Vatican Council*. Translated by P. S. Falla. San Francisco: Harper & Row, 1980.

———. *The Acting Person*. Translated by Andrzej Potocki. Edited by A. Tyminiecka. Boston: Reidel, 1979.

———. "The Anthropological Vision of Humanae Vitae" *Nova et Vetera* 7, no. 3 (2009) 731–50.

———. *The Collected Plays and Writings on Theater*. Translated by Bolelslaw Taborski. Berkeley: University of California Press, 1987.

———. "The Foundations of Church's Doctrine Concerning the Principles of Conjugal Life: A Memorandum Composed by a Group of Moral Theologians from Kraków" *Nova et Vetera* 10 (2012) 321–59.

———. *The Church: Mystery, Sacrament, Community. A Catechesis on the Creed*. Boston: Pauline, 1998.

———. *The Spirit, Giver of Life and Love. A Catechesis on the Creed*. Boston: Pauline, 1996.

———. *The Trinity's Embrace. God's Saving Plan. A Catechesis on Salvation History*. Boston: Pauline, 2002.

———. *Theotókos. Woman, Mother, Disciple. A Catechesis on Mary, Mother of God*. Boston: Pauline, 2000.

Other Magisterial Texts

The Sources of Catholic Dogma. Translated by Roy J. Deferrari. Edited by Henry Denzinger and Karl Rahner. St. Louis: Herder, 1954.

Acta et Documenta Concilio Oecumenico Apperando. Series I—Antepreparatoria, Vol II. Vatican City: Typis Polyglottis, 1960.

Acta Apostolicae Sedis. Commentarium Officiale. Vol. 36. Rome: Typis Polyglottis Vaticanis, 1944.

Secondary Literature on John Paul II/Karol Wojtyła

Albacete, Lorenzo. "Younger than Sin." *Communio* 22 (1995) 593–612.

Allen, Prudence. "Man-Woman Complementarity: The Catholic Inspiration." *Logos* 9, no. 3 (2006) 87–108.

———. "Integral Sex Complementarity and the Theology of Communion." *Communio* 17 (1990) 523–44.

———. "Aristotelian and Cartesian Revolutions in the Philosophy of Man and Woman." *Dialogue* 26 (1987) 263–70.

———. "Philosophy of Relation in John Paul II's New Feminism." In *Women in Christ: Towards a New Feminism*, edited by Michele M. Schumacher, 67–104. Grand Rapids: Eerdmans, 2004.

———. "Can Feminism be a Humanism?" In *Women in Christ: Towards a New Feminism*, edited by Michele M. Schumacher, 251–284. Grand Rapids: Eerdmans, 2004.

Anderson, Carl, and Granados, José. *Called to Love: Approaching John Paul II's Theology of the Body*. New York: Doubleday, 2009.

Antúnez, Horacio. *Karol Wojtyła y «Gaudium et spes». Historia de Juan Pablo II en la elaboración de la Constitución Pastoral*. Rome: Dissertatio, Pontificia Universitas Sanctae Crucis, Roma 2005.

Ashour, Monica. A. *Theology of the Body: Marriage Preparation*. Irving: TOBET, 2014.

Beigel, Gerard. "The Person Revealed in Action: A Framework for Understanding How Social Justice Is an Essential Part of the Gospel in the Teaching of John Paul II." PhD diss., Catholic University of America, 1994.

Bellafiore, Benjamin. "Paul on the Human Body and the Bodily Resurrection." In *John Paul II on The Body: Human, Eucharistic, Ecclesial*, edited by John M. McDermott and John Gavin, 297–310. Philadelphia: Saint Joseph University Press, 2006.

Bianco, María. "Giovanni Paolo II e la donna." In *Karol Wojtyła un papa venuto dall'Angelicum*, edited by Giuseppe Marco Salvati and Alberto Lo Presti, 91–102. Rome: Città Nuova, 2009.

Biffi, Inos. "Introduzione al quinto ciclo." In *Uomo e donna lo creò. Catechesi sull'amore umano*, 339–42. Rome: Città Nuova, 2007.

Bird, Phyllis. "Bone of My Bones and Flesh of My Flesh." *Theology Today* 50 (1994) 521–34.

———. "'Male and Female He Created Them': Gen 1–27b in the Context of the Priestly Account of Creation." *Harvard Theological Review* 74 (1981) 129–59.

Boniecki, Adam. *The Making of the Pope of the Millenium: Kalendarium of the Life of Karol Wojtyła*. Stockbridge, MA: Marian, 2000.

Borgonovo, Graziano. *Karol Wojtyła/Giovanni Paolo II: una passione continua per l'uomo*. Soveria, Italy: Rubbettino, 2003.

Bransfield, J. Brian. *The Human Person according to John Paul II*. Boston: Pauline, 2010.

Bosco, Domenico. "Giovanni della Croce nella lettura di Karol Wojtyła." In *Filosofia e letteratura in Karol Wojtyła*, edited by Antonio Delogu y Aldo Maria Morace, 195–230. Rome: Urbaniana University Press, 2007.

Burgos, Juan Manuel. "La antropología personalista de Persona y Acción." In *La filosofía personalista de Karol Wojtyła*, edited by Juan Manuel Burgos, 117–44. Madrid: Palabra, 2007.

Buttiglione, Rocco. *Il pensiero dell'uomo che divenne Giovanni Paolo II*. Milan: Mondadori, 1998.

———. "Introduzione al sesto ciclo." In *Uomo e donna lo creò. Catechesi sull'amore umano*. 449–52. Rome: Città Nuova, 2007.

Cafarra, Carlo. "Conscience, Truth and Magisterium in Conjugal Morality." *Anthropos* 2 (1986) 76–88.

———. "Corpore et anima unus: La rilevanza dell'unità sostanziale dell'uomo all'inizio del terzo millenio." In *Proceedings of the International Congress on Christian Humanism in the Third Millenium: The Perspective of Thomas Aquinas*, 161–72. Vatican City: Pontificia Academia Sancti Thomae Aquinatis, 2004.

———. "La trasmisione della vita nella Familiaris Consortio." *Mater et Magistra* 4 (1983) 391–99.

———. "La verdad y fecundidad del don." In *Amar el amor humano. El legado de Juan Pablo II, sobre el matrimonio y la familia*. Edited by Livio Melina y Stanisław Grygiel, 197–202. Valencia: Edicep, 2008.

———. "Introduzione al terzo ciclo." In *Uomo e donna lo creò. Catechesi sull'amore umano*. 255–56. Rome: Città Nuova, 2007.

———. "Introduzione al secondo ciclo." In *Uomo e donna lo creò. Catechesi sull'amore umano*, 111–12. Rome: Città Nuova, 2007.

Caldera, Rafael. "El don de sí" *Scripta Theologica* 20, no. 2 (1988) 667–79.

Castellano, Jesús. "La rilettura della fede in Giovanni della Croce (1948) e il magisterio odierno di Giovanni Paolo II. Continuità e novità." In *Karol Wojtyła un papa venuto dall'Angelicum*, edited by Giuseppe Marco Salvati y Alberto Lo Presti, 115–34. Rome: Città Nuova, 2009.

Castilla de Cortazar, Blanca. "Varon y Mujer en la 'Teología del Cuerpo' de Karol Wojtyła." In *La filosofía personalista de Karol Wojtyła*, edited by Juan Manuel Burgos, 277–88. Madrid: Palabra, 2007.

Chundellikat, Anthony. "Pastoral and Theological Significance of the 'Catechism on Human Love' in Indian Context." *Anthropotes* 25 (2010) 73–90.

Ciccone, Lino. *Uomo-Donna: L'amore umano nel piano divino*. Torino: Elle di Ci, 1986.

―――. "Per una corretta comprensiones della Catechesi di Giovanni Paolo II nelle udienze generali del mercoledì." *Divus Thomas* 84 (1980) 356–80.

Clavell Lluís. "L'antropologia integrale di Karol Wojtyła: un invito a unire teologia e filosofía." In *Etica e poetica in Karol Wojtyła*, edited by L. Leuzzi, 139–49. Torino: Società Editrice Internazionale, 1997.

Cokeley, Meghan. "Shame, Lust and the Human Body after the Fall: A Comparison of St. Augustine and Pope John Paul II." *Nova et Vetera* 2 (2004) 249–56.

Colosi, Peter. "The Uniqueness of Persons in the Life and Thought of Karol Wojtyła/Pope John Paul II, with Emphasis on His Indebtedness to Max Scheler." In *Karol Wojtyła's Philosophical Legacy*, edited by Nancy Mardas, Agnes B. Curry, and George F. McLean, 61–100. Washington, DC: Council of Research in Values and Philosophy, 2008.

Connor, Robert. "The One Truth of Freedom: Gift of Self." *Communio* 21 (1994) 367–71.

Collins, Christopher. "Marriage: Sacrament of Creation and in Christ." In *John Paul II on The Body: Human, Eucharistic, Ecclesial*. Edited by John M. McDermott and John Gavin, 247–54. Philadelphia: Saint Joseph University Press, 2006.

Crosby, John. "John Paul II's Vision of Sexuality and Marriage: The Mystery of 'Fair Love.'" In *The Legacy of Pope John Paul II: His Contribution to Catholic Thought*, edited by Geoffrey Gneuhs, 52–70. New York: Crossroad, 2000.

―――. "'Persona est sui juris': Reflections on the Foundations of Karol Wojtyła's Philosophy of the Person." In *Karol Wojtyła Filosofo, Teologo, Poeta*, 25–38. Città del Vaticano: Libreria Editrice Vaticana, 1984.

―――. "The Personalism of John Paul II as the Basis for his Approach to the Teaching of Humanae Vitae." In *Why Humanae Vitae Was Right: A Reader*, edited by Janet E. Smith, 195–226. San Francisco: Ignatius, 1993.

Cullen, Christopher. "Between God and Nothingness: Matter in John Paul II's Theology of the Body." In *John Paul II on The Body: Human, Eucharistic, Ecclesial*, edited by John M. McDermott and John Gavin, 65–76. Philadelphia: Saint Joseph University Press, 2006.

Curran, Charles. *The Moral Theology of Pope John Paul II*. Washington, DC: Georgetown University Press, 2005.

Dauphinais, Michael, and Matthew Levering. *John Paul II & St. Thomas Aquinas*. Naples, FL: Sapientia, 2006.

Delaney, David, and Janet E. Smith. "Concupiscence in the West-Schindler Debate." http://www.catholiceducation.org/en/marriage-and-family/sexuality/concupiscence-in-the-west-schindler-debate.html. Accessed January 16, 2017.

DeMarco, Adam. "The Body as Supernatural, Personalistic and Nuptial." *National Catholic Bioethics Quarterly* 3 (2003) 81–93.

Dinan, Stephen. "The Phenomenological Anthropology of Karol Wojtyła." *New Scholasticism* 55 (1981) 317–30.

Di Nicola, Giulia. "La mujer en el pensamiento de Juan Pablo II." In *La filosofía personalista de Karol Wojtyła*, edited by Juan Manuel Burgos, 253–76. Madrid: Palabra, 2007.

Durkin, Mary. *Feast of Love: Pope John Paul II on Human Intimacy*. Chicago: Loyola University Press, 1983.

Eden, Dawn. "Towards a 'Climate of Chastity': Bringing Catechesis on the Theology of the Body into the Hermeneutic of Continuity." PhD diss., Pontifical Faculty of the Immaculate Conception, 2010.

Fayos, Rafael. "La tendencia sexual humana." In *La filosofía personalista de Karol Wojtyła*, edited by Juan Manuel Burgos, 87–94. Madrid: Palabra, 2007.

Ferrer, Urbano. "La conversión del imperativo categórico kantiano en norma personalista." In *La filosofía personalista de Karol Wojtyła*, edited by Juan Manuel Burgos, 57–68. Madrid: Palabra, 2007.

George, Francis Cardinal, "Education in Love: The Interior Culture of the Person." *Anthropotes* 14 (1998) 179–83.

Giertych, Wojciech, "Verum Bonum in the moral teaching of John Paul II." In *Christ, Church, Mankind: The Spirit of Vatican II according to John Paul II*, edited by Zdzislaw Kijas, 70–82. New York: Paulist, 2012.

Glick, Daryl. "Recovering Morality: Personalism and Theology of the Body in John Paul II." *Faith and Reason* 12 (1986) 7–25.

Granados, José. "The Theology of the Body in the United States" *Anthropotes* 25 (2010) 101–25.

Granados Temes, José Miguel. *La ética esponsal de Juan Pablo II: Estudio de los fundamentos de la moral de la sexualidad en las catequesis sobre la teología del cuerpo*. Madrid: Publicaciones de la Facultad de Teología "San Dámaso," 2006.

———. "Creo en la Familia." *Juan Pablo II y el amor esponsal*. Murcia, Spain: UCAM, 2010.

Grygiel, Stanisław. "Introduzione al quarto ciclo." In *Uomo e donna lo creò. Catechesi sull'amore umano*, 289–92. Rome: Città Nuova, 2007.

Guerra, Rodrigo. *Volver a la persona: El método filosófico de Karol Wojtyła*. Madrid: Caparrós, 2002.

———. "La familia en la filosofía de Karol Wojtyła." In *La filosofía personalista de Karol Wojtyła*, edited by Juan Manuel Burgos, 289–302. Madrid: Palabra, 2007.

Heaney, Stephen. "The Concept of the Unity of the Person in the Thought of Karol Wojtyła (Pope John Paul II)." PhD diss., Marquette University, 1988.

Hellman, John. "John Paul II and the Personalist Movement" *Cross Currents* (1980) 409–19.

Hittinger, Russel. "Human Nature and States of Nature in John Paul II's Theological Anthropology." In *Human Nature in its Wholeness: A Roman Catholic Perspective*, 9–33. Washington, DC: Catholic University of America Press, 2006.

———. "Making Sense of the Civilization of Love: John Paul II's Contribution to Catholic Social Teaching." In *The Legacy of Pope John Paul II: His Contribution to Catholic Thought*, edited by Geoffrey Gneuhs, 71–93. New York: Crossroad, 2000.

Hogan, Richard, and John Levoir. *Covenant of Love. Pope John Paul II on Sexuality, Marriage, and Family in the Modern World: With a Commentary on Familiaris Consortio*. San Francisco: Ignatius, 1985.

Huerga, Alvaro. "Karol Wojtyła, comentador de San Juan de la Cruz." *Angelicum* 56 (1979) 348–66.

Illanes, José Luis. "Antropocentrismo y teocentrismo en la enseñanza de Juan Pablo II." *Scripta Theologica* 20 (1988) 643–65.

Johnson, Luke. "A Disembodied 'Theology of the Body': John Paul II on Love, Sex, and Pleasure." *Commonweal* 128 (2001) 11–17.
Knapp, James. "Purity in the Adequate Anthropology of John Paul II." In *John Paul II on The Body: Human, Eucharistic, Ecclesial*, edited by John M. McDermott and John Gavin, 255–76. Philadelphia: Saint Joseph University Press, 2006.
Kucharski, Paul. "Pope John Paul II and Natural Law." In *Karol Wojtyła's Philosophical Legacy*, edited by Nancy Mardas, Agnes B. Curry, and George F. McLean, 111–24. Washington, DC: Council of Research in Values and Philosophy, 2008.
Kupczak, Jaroslaw. *Gift and Communion: John Paul II's Theology of the Body*. Translated by Agata Rottkamp, Justyna Pawlak, and Orest Pawlak. Washington, DC: Catholic University of American Press, 2014.
Kurz, William. "The Scriptural Foundation of the Theology of the Body." In *John Paul II on The Body: Human, Eucharistic, Ecclesial*, edited by John M. McDermott and John Gavin, 27–46. Philadelphia: Saint Joseph University Press, 2006.
Larrú, Juan de Dios. "El significado personalista de la experiencia del pudor en K. Wojtyła." In *La filosofía personalista de Karol Wojtyła*, edited by Juan Manuel Burgos, 95–106. Madrid: Palabra, 2007.
Latkovic, Mark. "Pope John Paul II's 'Theology of the Body' and the Significance of Sexual Shame in Light of the Body's 'Nuptial Meaning': Some Implications for Bioethics and Sexual Ethics." *Nova et Vetera* 2 (2004) 305–36.
Lawler, Ronald. *The Christian Personalism of Pope John Paul II*. Chicago: Franciscan Herald, 1980.
Lio, Ermenegildo. Humanae vitae *e conscienza: L'insegnamento del Card. Wojtyła teologo e Papa*. Rome: Libreria Editrice Vaticana, 1980.
Lobato, Abelardo. "La persona en el pensamiento de Karol Wojtyła." *Angelicum* 56 (1979) 165–210.
———. "La famillia y la communio personarum." In *Educación, familia y vida. Actas del congreso internacional*, 17–38. Murcia, Spain: Universidad Católica San Antonio, 2002.
Malo, Antonio. "L'antropologia di K. Wojtyła come sintesi del pensiero classico e della modernità" *Acta Philosophica* 15, no. 1 (2006) 11–28.
———. "La coscienza dell'atto come metodo pers superare il soggettivismo e l'oggettivismo in antropologia" *Acta Philosophica* 10, no. 1 (2001) 63–72.
———. "L'originalità della filosofia di K. Wojtyła: l'antropologia come punto d'incontro di metafisica ed etica." In *Filosofia e letteratura in Karol Wojtyła*, edited by Antonio Delogu and Aldo Maria Morace, 123–44. Rome: Urbaniana, 2007.
Marengo, Gilfredo. *Giovanni Paolo II e il Concilio: Una sfida e un compito*. Siena: Cantagalli, 2011.
———. "Il contesto storico-teologico delle catechesi" *Anthropotes* 25 (2010) 19–42.
———. "La antropología adecuada en las catequesis sobre el amor humano: Líneas de reflexión." In *Amar el amor humano. El legado de Juan Pablo II sobre el matrimonio y la Familia*. 159–82. Valencia: Edicep, 2008.
Martin, Francis. "Male and Female He Created Them: A Summary of the Teaching of Genesis Chapter One." *Communio* 20 (1993) 240–65.
May, William. *Theology of the Body in Context. Genesis and Growth*. Boston: Pauline, 2010.
McCarthy, Margaret. "El amor esponsal a la luz de la 'experiencia elemental.'" In *Amar el amor humano: El legado de Juan Pablo II sobre el matrimonio y la Familia*, 139–58. Valencia: Edicep, 2008.

Melina, Livio. "A trent'anni dalla Grande Catechesi: una 'via' da percorrere" *Anthropotes* 25 (2010) 9–18.

———. "La verdad del amor: Veritatis Splendor." In *Amar el amor humano: El legado de Juan Pablo II, sobre el matrimonio y la familia*, edited by Livio Melina y Stanisław Grygiel, 241–52. Valencia: Edicep, 2008.

———. "Quale regola per l'amore?" In *L'amore e la sua regola: Karol Wojtyła e l'esperienza dell'Ambiente di Cracovia*, edited by S. Grygiel, 13–16. Siena: Cantagalli, 2009.

Mereki, Jarosław. "Sulla ricezione della teologia del corpo in Polonia" *Anthropotes* 25 (2010) 91–99.

———. "Las Fuentes de la filosofía de Karol Wojtyła." In *La filosofía personalista de Karol Wojtyła*, edited by Juan Manuel Burgos, 13–24. Madrid: Palabra, 2007.

———. "Verso l'etica empirica e normativa." In *Metafisica della persona: Tutte le opere filosofiche e saggi integrativi*, edited by Giovanni Reale y Tadeusz Styczeń, 251–62. Milan: Bompiani, 2003.

———. "El cuerpo, sacramento de la persona." In *Amar el amor humano: El legado de Juan Pablo II, sobre el matrimonio y la familia*, edited by Livio Melina y Stanisław Grygiel, 183–96. Valencia: Edicep, 2008.

———. "Presenza della metafisica di San Tommaso nel pensiero filosofico di Karol Wojtyła." In *Metafisica, persona, cristianesimo. Scritti in onore di Vittorio Possenti*, edited by Giuseppe Ludovico Goisis, Marco Ivaldo, Gaspare Mura, 71–84. Rome: Armando, 2010.

McGovern, Thomas. "The Christian Anthropology of John Paul II: An Overview." *Josephinum Journal of Theology* 8 (2001) 132–47.

Miller, Paula. "The Theology of the Body: A New Look at *Humanae Vitae*." *Theology Today* 57 (2001) 501–8.

Min, Anselm. "John Paul II's Anthropology of Concrete Totality" *Proceedings of the ACPA* (1984) 120–29.

Mitchell, Louise. "A Bibliography for the Theology of the Body." *National Catholic Bioethics Quarterly* 3 (2003) 69–77.

Modras, Ronald. "The Thomistic Personalism of Pope John Paul II." *Modern Schoolman* 59 (1982) 117–26.

Mongillo, Dalmazio. "Il magisterio morale di Giovanni Paolo II." In *Karol Wojtyła un papa venuto dall'Angelicum*, edited by Guiseppe Marco Salvati y Alberto Lo Presti, 21–38. Rome: Città Nuova, 2009.

Muller, Earl. "The Nuptial Meaning of the Body." In *Pope John Paul II on the Body. Human, Eucharistic, Ecclesial*, edited by John M. McDermott, 87–120. Philadelphia: Saint Joseph's University Press, 2007.

Nachef, Anthony. *The Mystery of the Trinity in the Theological Thought of Pope John Paul II.* New York: Lang, 1999.

Noriega, José. "La vocación al don de sí." In *Amar el amor humano: El legado de Juan Pablo II sobre el matrimonio y la Familia*. 203–14. Valencia: Edicep, 2008.

Ognibeni, Bruno. "Juan Pablo II ante la Sagrada Escritura." In *Amar el amor humano: El legado de Juan Pablo II sobre el matrimonio y la Familia*. 121–34. Valencia: Edicep, 2008.

O'Reilly, Ailbe. *Conjugal Chastity in Pope Wojtyła*. New York: Lang 2010.

Ouellet, Marc. *Divine Likeness: Toward a Trinitarian Anthropology of the Family*. Translated by Phillip Milligan and Linda M. Cicone. Grand Rapids: Eerdmans, 2006.

———. "La *communio personarum* en la familia y en la Iglesia: *Familiaris Consortio*." In *Amar el amor humano: El legado de Juan Pablo II sobre el matrimonio y la Familia*. 43–60. Valencia: Edicep, 2008.

Pérez López, Angel. *De la experiencia de la integración a la visión integral de la persona. Estudio histórico-analítico de «Persona y acción» de Karol Wojtyła*. Valencia: Edicep, 2012.

———. "Karol Wojtyła's Thomistic Understanding of Consciousness." *Thomist* 79, no. 3 (2015) 407–37.

Pérez López, Israel. "La teoría de la conciencia en Antonio Millán-Puelles y Karol Wojtyła." PhD diss., Pontifical University of the Holy Cross, 2016.

Pérez-Soba, Juan José. "El misterio del amor según Karol Wojtyła." In *La filosofía personalista de Karol Wojtyła*, edited by Juan Manuel Burgos, 69–86. Madrid: Palabra, 2007.

Petri, Thomas. *Aquinas and the Theology of the Body*. Washington, DC: Catholic University of America Press, 2016.

Pieronek, Tadeusz. "The Reception of Vatican II in the Work and Documents of the Synod of Kraków (1972–1979)." In *Christ, Church, Mankind. The Spirit of Vatican II according to John Paul II*, edited by Zdzislaw Kijas, 32–42. New York: Paulist, 2012.

Pozo, Cándido. "Juan Pablo II y el Concilio Vaticano II." *Scripta Theologica* 20 (1988) 405–37.

Prieto Solana, Juan. *Hacía una ética de la corporeidad humana: Verdad y ethos del cuerpo a la luz de las catequesis de Juan Pablo II "Hombre y mujer los creó."* Murcia, Spain: UCAM, 2004.

Ratzinger, Joseph. *John Paul II: My Beloved Predecessor*. Boston: Pauline, 2007.

Reale, Giovanni. *Karol Wojtyła: Un Pellegrino dell'Assoluto*. Milan: Bompiani, 2005.

Reimers, Adrian. "Human Suffering and John Paul II's Theology of the Body." *Nova et Vetera* 2 (2004) 445–60.

Rickert, Kevin. "Wojtyła's Personalistic Norm: A Thomistic Analysis." *Nova et Vetera* 7, no. 3 (2009) 653–78.

Rodríguez Luño, Angel. "'In mysterio Verbi Incarnati mysterium hominis vere clarescit' (Gaudium et Spes, n. 22). Riflessioni metodologiche sulla Grande Catechesi del mercoledì di Giovanni Paolo II." *Anthropotes* 8, no. 1 (1992) 11–25.

Rousseau, Mary. "Deriving Bioethical Norms from the Theology of the Body." *National Bioethics Quarterly* 3 (2003) 59–67.

Ryłko, Stanisław. "La pedagogia dell'amore di Karol Wojtyła." In *L'amore e la sua regola: Karol Wojtyła e l'esperienza dell'Ambiente di Cracovia*, edited by Stanisław Grygiel, 17–20. Siena: Edizioni Cantagalli, 2009.

Sandoval, Carlos. *El valor de la persona como fundamento del amor esponsal en el pensamiento filosófico de Karol Wojtyła*. Rome: EDUSC, 2005.

Schmitz, Kenneth. *At the Center of the Human Drama. The Philosophical Anthropology of Karol Wojtyła/Pope John Paul II*. Washington, DC: Catholic University of America Press, 1993.

Séguin, Michel. "The Biblical Foundations of the Thought of John Paul II on Human Sexuality." *Communio* 20 (1993) 266–89.

Schindler, David. "The 'Nuptial-Sacramental' Body and the Significance of World and Culture for Moral Theology." *Anthropotes* 21 (2005) 35–55.

Schu, Walter. *The Splendor of Love: John Paul II's Vision for Marriage and Family*. New Hope: New Hope, 2003.

Schumacher, Michele. "John Paul II's Theology of the Body on Trial: Responding to the Accusation of the Biological Reduction of Women." *Nova et Vetera* 10, no. 2 (2012) 463–82.

Scola, Angelo. "El misterio divino del amor en la enseñanza de Juan Pablo II." In *Amar el amor humano: El legado de Juan Pablo II sobre el matrimonio y la Familia*, 31–42. Valencia: Edicep, 2008.

———. "Gli interventi di Karol Wojtyła al Concilio Ecumenico Vaticano II. Esposizione ed interpretazione teologica." In *Karol Wojtyła, filosofo, teologo, poeta*, 289–306. Vatican City: Libreria Editrice Vaticana, 1984.

———. "Introduzione al primo ciclo." In *Uomo e donna lo creò. Catechesi sull'amore umano*. 27–30. Rome: Città Nuova, 2007.

———. "L'imago Dei nella sessualità umana. A proposito di una tesi originale della «Mulieris Dignitatem»" *Anthropotes* 8 (1992) 61–73.

———. *The Nuptial Mystery*. Translated by Michelle K. Borras. Grand Rapids: Eerdmans, 2005.

Segade, Carlos. "El amor conyugal como espacio trascendente." In *La filosofía personalista de Karol Wojtyła*, edited by Juan Manuel Burgos, 107–16. Madrid: Palabra, 2007.

Seifert, Josef. "Karol Cardinal Wojtyła (Pope John Paul II) As Philosopher of the Cracow/Lublin School of Philosophy." *Aletheia* 2 (1981) 130–99.

———. "Truth and Transcendence of the Person in the Philosophical Thought of Karol Wojtyła." In *Karol Wojtyła: filosofo, teologo, poeta*, 93–106. Città del Vaticano: Libreria Editrice Vaticana, 1984.

———. "Verdad, libertad y amor en el pensamiento ético de Karol Wojtyła." *Persona y Derecho* 10 (1983) 177–93.

Sherwin, Michael. "John Paul's Theology of Truth and Freedom: A Dissident Phenomenology in a Thomistic Anthropology." *Nova et Vetera* 3, no. 3 (2005) 543–68.

Shivanandan, Mary. "Body-Soul Unity in Light of the Nuptial Relation." In *Dialoghi sul mistero nuziale: Studi offerti al Cardinale Angelo Scola*, edited by Gilfredo Marengo and Bruno Ognibeni, 369–81. Rome: Lateran University Press, 2003.

———. "Conjugal Spirituality and the Gift of Reverence." *Nova et Vetera* 10, no. 2 (2012) 485–506.

———. *Crossing the Threshold of Love: A New Vision of Marriage in the Light of John Paul II's Anthropology*. Washington, DC: Catholic University of America Press, 2005.

———. *Original Solitude: Its Meaning in Contemporary Marriage. A Study of John Paul II's Concept of the Person in Relation to Contemporary Marriage and Family*. Ann Arbor, MI: UMI Dissertation Services, 1996.

Skrzypczak, Robert. *Karol Wojtyła al Concilio Vaticano II*. Verona: Fede & Cultura, 2011.

Smith, Janet. *Humanae Vitae. A Generation Later*. Washington, DC: Catholic University of America Press, 1991.

———. "Pope John Paul II and *Humanae Vitae*." *International Review of Natural Family Planning* 10 (1988) 1–15.

———. "The Kraków Document." *Nova et Vetera* 10, no. 2 (2012) 361–82.

———. "The Importance of the Concept of 'Munus' to Understanding 'Humanae Vitae.'" In *Humanae Vitae: 20 Anni Dopo*, 677–90. Milan: Ares, 1989.

———. "The Munus of Transmitting Human Life: A New Approach to *Humanae Vitae*." *Thomist* 54 (1990) 385–427.

———. "The Universality of Natural Law and the Irreducibility of Personalism." http://www.usccb.org/about/doctrine/intellectual-tasks/upload/intellectual-tasks-of-the-new-evangelization-smith.pdf. Accessed January 16, 2017.

———. "The Need to Read Carefully: A Response to Alice von Hildebrand's Critique of Christopher West." http://www.catholiceducation.org/en/marriage-and-family/sexuality/the-need-to-read-carefully-a-response-to-alice-von-hildebrands-critique-of-christopher-west.html. Accessed January 16, 2017.

Smith, William. "John Paul II's Seminal Contributions to Moral Theology: Foundational Issues." In *The Legacy of Pope John Paul II. His Contribution to Catholic Thought*, edited by Geoffrey Gneuhs, 38–51. New York: Crossroad, 2000.

Spinello, Richard. *The Genius of John Paul II: The Great Pope's Moral Wisdom*. New York: Sheed & Ward, 2007.

Styczeń, Tadeusz. *Comprendere L'uomo: La visione antropologica di Karol Wojtyła*. Rome: Lateran University Press, 2005.

———. "L'antropologia della Familiaris Consortio." *Anthropotes* 9 (1993) 7–42.

———. "El amor como vínculo matrimonial y familiar en la perspectiva filosófica." In *Amar el amor humano: El legado de Juan Pablo II sobre el matrimonio y la familia*, edited by Livio Melina y Stanisław Grygiel, 77–92. Valencia: Edicep, 2008.

———. "Essere se stessi è trascendere se stessi. Sull'etica di Karol Wojtyła come antropologia normativa." In *Metafisica della persona: Tutte le opere filosofiche e saggi integrativi*, edited by Giovanni Reale y Tadeusz Styczeń, 781–827. Milan: Bompiani, 2003.

———. "Karol Wojtyła: Un filosofo della morale agli occhi del suo discepolo." In *Metafisica della persona: Tutte le opere filosofiche e saggi integrativi*, edited by Giovanni Reale and Tadeusz Styczeń, cvii–cxxiv. Milan: Bompiani, 2003.

Suchocka, Hanna. "Juan Pablo II y el amor humano." In *Amar el amor humano: El legado de Juan Pablo II sobre el matrimonio y la familia*, edited by Livio Melina y Stanisław Grygiel, 27–30. Valencia: Edicep, 2008.

Tettamanzi, Dionigi. *La verginità per il Regno. Dalle Catechesi di Giovanni Paolo II*. Milan: O. R., 1982.

Vives Soto, Leopoldo. "Iluminar la verdad del amor conyugal. La teología del cuerpo en la teología de lengua española." *Anthropotes* 25 (2010) 127–50.

Waldstein, Michael. "Children as the Common Good of Marriage" *Nova et Vetera* 7, no. 3 (2009) 697–709.

———. "Introduction." In *Man and Woman He Created Them: A Theology of the Body*. Translated and edited by Michael Waldstein, 1–130. Boston: Pauline, 2006.

———. "John Paul II and St. Thomas on Love and the Trinity [I]." *Anthropotes* 18 (2002) 113–38.

———. "John Paul II and St. Thomas on Love and the Trinity: Part II." *Anthropotes* 18 (2002) 269–86.

———. "The Common Good in St. Thomas and John Paul II" *Nova et Vetera* 3 (2005) 569–78.

Weigel, George. *The End and the Beginning: Pope John Paul II ~ The Victory of Freedom, the Last Years, the Legacy*. New York: Doubleday, 2010.

———. *Witness to Hope: The Biography of Pope John Paul II (1920–2005)*. New York: Harper Perennial, 2005.

West, Christopher. *Theology of the Body Explained: A Commentary on John Paul II's Man and Woman He Created Them*. Boston: Pauline, 2007.

———. *Good News about Sex and Marriage: Answers to your Honest Questions About Catholic Teaching*. Cincinnati: Saint Anthony, 2004.

Wilder, Alfred. "Community of Persons in the Thought of Karol Wojtyła." *Angelicum* 56 (1979) 211–44.

Williams, George. *The Mind of John Paul II: Origins of his Thought and Action*. New York: Seabury, 1981.

Woznicki, Andrew. *A Christian Humanism: Karol Wojtyła's Existential Personalism*. New Britain: Mariel, 1980.

———. *The Dignity of Man as a Person: Essays on the Christian Humanism of His Holiness John Paul II*. San Francisco: Society of Christ, 1987.

Zorroza, Maria. "Exigencia de justicia: El compromiso por el otro como persona." In *La filosofía personalista de Karol Wojtyła*, edited by Juan Manuel Burgos, 183–94. Madrid: Palabra, 2007.

Other Cited Works

Abbà, Giusseppe. *Lex et Virtus: Studi Sull'evoluzione della dottrina morale di San Tommaso d'Aquino*. Rome: Libreria Ateneo Salesiano, 1983.

Aersten, Jan. *Medieval Philosophy and the Trascendentals: The Case of Thomas Aquinas*. New York: Brill, 1996.

Anscombe, Getrude E. "You Can Have Sex without Children: Christianity and the New Offer." In *The Collected Philosophical Papers of G. E. M. Anscombe*, 3:82–96. Oxford: Blackwell, 1981.

Aquila, Samuel J. "The Priest as a Man of Charity: Integrating Human and Spiritual Priestly Formation." In *Christ as the Foundation of Seminary Formation*, edited by James Keating, 35–57. Omaha: Institute of Priestly Formation, 2016.

Aquinas, Thomas. *Commentary on Aristotle's Metaphysics*. Translated by John Patrick Rowan. Notre Dame, IN: Dumb Ox, 1999.

———. *Commentary on the Nicomachean Ethics*. Translated by C. I. Lintzinger. Notre Dame, IN: Dumb Ox, 1993.

———. *Commentary on the Gospel of Matthew*. Translated by Jeremy Holmes and Beth Mortensen. Latin/English Edition of the Works of St. Thomas Aquinas 33–34. Lander, WY: Aquinas Institute, 2013.

———. *Commentary on the Letters of Saint Paul to the Corinthians*. Edited by John Mortensen and Enrique Alarcón. Translated by Fabian Richard Larcher, Beth Mortensen, and Daniel Keating. Latin/English Edition of the Works of St. Thomas Aquinas 38. Lander, WY: Aquinas Institute, 2012.

———. *Commentary on the Letters of Saint Paul to the Galatians and Ephesians*. Edited by John Mortensen and Enrique Alarcón. Translated by Fabian Richard Larcher and Matthew Lamb. Latin/English Edition of the Works of St. Thomas Aquinas 39. Lander, WY: Aquinas Institute, 2012.

———. *Commentary on the Letters of Saint Paul to the Philippians, Colossians, Thessalonians, Timothy, Titus, and Philemon*. Edited by John Mortensen and Enrique Alarcón. Translated by Fabian Richard Larcher. Latin/English Edition of the Works of St. Thomas Aquinas 40. Lander, WY: Aquinas Institute, 2012.

———. *Commentary on the Letter of Saint Paul to the Hebrews*. Edited by John Mortensen and Enrique Alarcón. Translated by Fabian Richard Larcher. Latin/English Edition of the Works of St. Thomas Aquinas 41. Lander, WY: Aquinas Institute, 2012.

———. *Commentary on the Letter of Saint Paul to the Romans*. Edited by John Mortensen and Enrique Alarcón. Translated by Fabian Richard Larcher. Latin/English Edition of the Works of St. Thomas Aquinas 37. Lander, WY: Aquinas Institute, 2012.

———. *Commentary on the Gospel of John*. Translated by Fabian Richard Larcher. Latin/English Edition of the Works of St. Thomas Aquinas 35–36. Lander, WY: Aquinas Institute, 2013.

———. *Comentum in Quartum Librum Sententiarum Magistri Petri Lombardi*. Opera Omnia 7/2:872–1259. Parma: Typis Petri Fiaccadori, 1858.

———. *De Principis Naturae ad Fratrem Sylvestrum*. Vol. 43 of *Opera Omnia Iussu Leonis XIII P. M. Edita*. Rome: Editori di San Tommaso, 1976.

———. *De Veritate: On Truth*. Translated by Robert W. Schmidt. Chicago: Regnery, 1954.

———. *Disputed Questions on Virtue*. Translated by Jeffrey Hause. Indianapolis: Hackett, 2010.

———. *In Duo Praecepta Caritatis et in Decem Legis Praecepta Exposition*. In *Opuscula Theologica*, 1:245–71. Turin: Marietti, 1975.

———. *On Evil*. Edited by Brian Davies. Translated by Richard Regan. New York: Oxford University Press, 2003.

———. *On the Power of God*. Translated by English Dominican Province. Westminster, MD: Newman, 1952.

———. *Scriptum super Libros Sententiarum Magistri Petri Lombardi Episcopi Parisiensis*. Vol 3. Edited by Maria Fabianus Moos. Paris: Lethielleux, 1956.

———. *Summa contra Gentiles: Liber de Veritatae Catholicae Fidei Contra Errores Infidelium*. Edited by P. Marc, C. Pera, and P. Caramello. Taurini-Rome: Marietti, 1961.

———. *Summa Theologiae*. Edited by John Mortensen and Enrique Alarcón. Latin/English Edition of the Works of St. Thomas Aquinas 13–20. Lander, WY: Aquinas Institute, 2012.

———. *Super Boetium De Trinitate*. Vol 50 of *Opera Omnia Iussu Leonis XIII. P. M. Edita*. Rome: Editori di San Tommaso, 1992.

Aristotle. *The Basic Works of Aristotle*. Edited by Richard McKeon. New York: Random, 1941.

Asci, Donald. *The Conjugal Act as a Personal Act: A Study of the Catholic Concept of the Conjugal Act in the Light of Christian Anthropology*. San Francisco: Ignatius, 2002.

Augustine of Hippo. *On the Holy Trinity, Doctrinal Treatises, Moral Treatises*. Edited by Philip Schaff. Translated by Arthur West Haddan. Buffalo: Christian Literature, 1887.

———. *The City of God*. Translated by Marcus Dods. In *St. Augustine's City of God and Christian Doctrine*, edited by Philip Schaff, 2:16–511. Buffalo, NY: Christian Literature, 1887.

———. *Sermons 151–183*. Edited by John E. Rotelle. Translated by Edmund Hill. Works of St. Augustine III/5. New York: New City, 1992.

———. *On the Morals of the Catholic Church*. Translated by Richard Stohert. In *St. Augustine: The Writings against the Manichaeans and against the Donatists*, edited by Philip Schaff, 4:37–63. Buffalo, NY: Christian Literature, 1887.

———. *Reply to Faustus the Manichean*. Translated by Richard Stohert. In *St. Augustine: The Writings against the Manichaeans and against the Donatists*, edited by Philip Schaff, 4:151–345. Buffalo, NY: Christian Literature, 1887.

SELECTED BIBLIOGRAPHY

Bergamino, Federica. *La razionalità della libertà della scelta in Tommaso d'Aquino.* Rome: EDUSC, 2002.

Blankenhorn, Berhard. "The Instrumental Causality of the Sacraments: Thomas Aquinas and Louis-Marie Chauvet." *Nova et Vetera* 4, no. 2 (2006) 255–94.

———. "The Place of Romans 6 in Aquinas' Doctrine of Sacramental Causality." In *Ressourcement Thomism. Sacred Doctrine, the Sacraments, and the Moral Life: Essays in Honor of Romanus Cessario,* edited by Reinhard Hütter & Matthew Levering, 136–49. Washington, DC: Catholic University of America Press, 2010.

Brock, Stephen. "Quanti atti di essere ha una sostanza? Un approccio alla distinzione reale." In *Sapienza e libertà: Studi in onore del Prof. Lluís Clavell,* edited by Miguel Pérez de Laborda, 57–70. Rome: EDUSC, 2012.

———. "The Legal Character of Natural Law according to St. Thomas Aquinas." PhD diss., Toronto: University of Toronto, 1988.

Butera, Giuseppe. "On Reason's Control of the Passions in Aquinas's Theory of Temperance." *Medieval Studies* 68 (2006) 133–60.

Carney, Francis, W. *The Purposes of Christian Marriage.* Washington, DC: Catholic University of America Press, 1950.

Carpin, Attilo. *Il sacramento del matrimonio nella teologia medievale: Da Isidoro di Siviglia a Tommaso D'Aquino.* Bologna: ESD, 1991.

Cessario, Romano. "The Image of God and the Sacraments." *Dominican Torch* 5 (2007) 11–17.

———. *The Moral Virtues and Theological Ethics.* Notre Dame: University of Notre Dame Press, 1991.

Dauphinais, Michael. "Loving the Lord your God: The 'Imago Dei' in Saint Thomas Aquinas." *Thomist* 63 (1999) 241–67.

De Broglie, Guy. "La conception Thomiste des Duex Finalités du Marriage." *Doctor Communis* 30 (1974) 3–41.

De Finance, Joseph. *Persona e valore.* Rome: Editrice Pontificia Università Gregoriana, 2003.

Dewan, Lawrence. *Form and Being: Studies in Thomistic Metaphysics.* Washington, DC: Catholic University of America Press, 2006.

Doolan, Gregory. *Aquinas on the Divine Ideas as Exemplar Causes.* Washington, DC: Catholic University of America Press, 2008.

Doms, Herbert. *The Meaning of Marriage.* Translated by George Sayer. New York: Sheed & Ward 1939.

Elders, Leo. "La teología de Santo Tomás de la imagen de Dios en el hombre." In *Dar razón de la Esperanza. Homenaje al Prof. Dr. José Luis Illanes,* edited by Tomas Trigo, 299–316. Pamplona: Ediciones de la Universidad de Navarra, 2004.

Erhueh, Anthony. *Vatican II: Image of God in Man: An Inquiry into the Theological Foundations and Significance of Human Dignity in the Pastoral Constitution on the Church in the Mordern World "Gaudium et Spes."* Rome: Urbaniana University Press, 1987.

Espa Feced, Fulgencio. *El Papel de la Humanidad de Cristo en la Causalidad de la Gracia: Influencia de San Agustín en Santo Tomás.* Madrid: Ediciones Universidad de San Dámaso, 2015.

Fuchs, Joseph. "Theology of the Meaning of Marriage Today." In *Marriage in Light of Vatican II,* edited by James T. McHugh, 13–30. Washington: Family Life Bureau, 1968.

Galot, Jean. *Who is Christ? A Theology of the Incarnation.* Translated by Angeline Bouchard. Chicago: Franciscan Herald, 1989.

García de Haro, Ramón. *Marriage and the Family in the Documents of the Magisterium: A Course in the Theology of Marriage*. Translated by William E. May. San Francisco: Ignatius, 1993.

García Jaramillo, Miguel. *La Cogitativa en Santo Tomás de Aquino y sus Fuentes*. Pamplona: Ediciones de la Universidad de Navarra, 1997.

García López, Jesús. *Escritos de Antropología Filosófica*. Pamplona: Ediciones de la Universidad de Navarra, 2006.

———. *Individuo, Familia y Sociedad. Los Derechos Humanos en Tomás de Aquino*. Pamplona: Ediciones de la Universidad de Navarra, 1990.

———. *Metafísica tomista: Ontología, Gnoseología, y Teología Natural*. Pamplona: Ediciones de la Universidad de Navarra, 2001.

———. *Tomás de Aquino. Maestro del Orden*. Madrid: Pedagógicas, 1996.

Garrigou-Lagrange, Reginald. *De Beatitudine: De Actibus Humanis et Habitibus. Comentarius in Summan Theologicam S. Thomae Ia–IIa qq. 1–54*. Torino: Marietti, 1951.

Gil Hellín, Francisco. *El matrimonio y la vida conyugal*. Valencia: Edicep 1995.

Gondreau, Paul. *The Passions of Christ's Soul in the Theology of St. Thomas Aquinas*. Chicago: University of Scranton Press, 2009.

———. "The Redemption and Divinization of Human Sexuality through the Sacrament of Marriage: A Thomistic Approach." *Nova et Vetera* 10, no. 2 (2012) 383–413.

González Moralejo, Rafael. *El Vaticano II en Taquigrafía: La historia de la "Gaudium et Spes."* Madrid: BAC, 2000.

Gredt, Iosephus. *Elementa Philosophiae Aristotelico-Thomisticae*. Vol. 2. Barcelona: Herder, 1946.

Hall, Pamela, H. *Narrative and the Natural Law: An Interpretation of Thomistic Ethics*. Notre Dame: University of Notre Dame Press, 1994.

Häring, Bernard. *Married Love: A Modern Christian View of Marriage and Family Life*. Chicago: Peacock, 1970.

———. *Road To Renewal: Perspectives of Vatican II*. New York: Alba, 1966.

Hildebrand, Alice von. "Dietrich von Hilderbrand, Catholic Philosopher, and Christopher West, Modern Enthusiast: Two Different Approaches to Love, Marriage and Sex." http://www.catholicnewsagency.com/document/dietrich-von-hildebrand-catholic-philosopher-and-christopher-west-modern-enthusiasttwo-very-different-approaches-to-love-marriage-and-sex-999/. Accessed January 23, 2017.

Hildebrand, Dietrich von. *The Encyclical "Humanae Vitae": A Sign of Contradiction*. Translated by Damian Fedoryka and John Crosby. Chicago: Franciscan Herald, 1969.

Hoeck, Andreas. "Holy Communion: Sharing in the Threefold Munus of the Divine Gladiator." *Homeletic and Pastoral Review* (2013). http://www.hprweb.com/2013/06/holy-communion-sharing-in-the-threefold-munus-of-the-divine-gladiator/. Accessed January 17, 2017.

Hübscher, Ignatius. *De Imagine Dei in Homine Viatore Secundum Doctrinam S. Thomae Aquinatis*. Louvain: Ceuterick, 1932.

Jensen, Steven, J. *Knowing the Natural Law: From Precepts and Inclinations to Deriving Oughts*. Washington, DC: Catholic University of America Press, 2015.

Kant, Immanuel. *Foundations of the Metaphysics of Morals*. Edited by Robert Wolf. Translated by Lewis White Beck. New York: Bobbs-Merrill, 1969.

———. "What is Enlightment?" In *On History*, edited and translated by Lewis White Beck. 3–10. New York: Bobbs-Merrill, 1963.

Kauth, Matthew. "Charity as Divine and Human Friendship: A Metaphysical and Scriptural Explanation according to the Thought of St. Thomas Aquinas." PhD diss., Pontifical University of the Holy Cross, 2012.

Koterski, Joseph. "Aquinas on the Sacrament of Marriage." In *Rediscovering Aquinas and the Sacraments: Studies in Sacramental Theology*, edited by Matthew Levering and Michael Dauphanais, 102–13. Chicago: Hillenbrand, 2009.

Lambrecht, Jan. *The Sermon on the Mount. Proclamation and Exhortation*. Wilmington, DE: Glazier, 1985.

Lombo, José Ángel. *La persona en Tomás. Un estudio histórico y sistemático*. Rome: EDUSC, 2000.

MacIntyre, Alasdair. *Dependent Rational Animals: Why Human Beings Need the Virtues*. Chicago: Open Court, 2001.

———. *Three Rival Versions of Moral Inquiry: Encyclopaedia, Genealogy, and Tradition*. Indiana: University of Notre Dam Press, 1990.

Malo, Antonio. *Cartesio e la Postmodernità*. Rome: Armando, 2011.

Mateo Seco, Lucas. "Muerte y pecado original en la doctrina de Santo Tomás de Aquino." In *Veritas et Sapientia. En el VII Centenario de Santo Tomás de Aquino*, edited by Juan José Rodríguez Rosado, 279–315. Pamplona: Ediciones de la Universidad de Navarra, 1975.

Melina, Livio. *Sharing in Christ's Virtues: For a Renewal of Moral Theology in Ligt of Veritatis Splendor*. Translated by William May. Washington, DC: Catholic University of America Press, 2001.

Millán-Puelles, Antonio. *Fundamentos de filosofía*. Madrid: Rialp, 2001.

———. *La formación de la personalidad humana*. Madrid: Rialp, 1963.

———. *La libre afirmación de nuestro ser*. Madrid: Rialp, 1994.

———. *La lógica de los conceptos metafísicos*. Vol. 2, *La articulación de los conceptos extracategoriales*. Madrid: Rialp, 2003.

———. *El valor de la libertad*. Madrid: Rialp, 1995.

Mortensen, Beth. "The Relation of the Juridical and the Sacramental in Matrimony according to Thomas Aquinas." PhD diss., Universität Freiburg, 2012.

Noonan, John, T. *Contraception: A History of Its Treatment by the Catholic Theologians and Canonists*. Cambridge, MA: Harvard University Press, 1986.

Parmisano, Stan. "Spousal Love in the Medieval Rite of Marriage" *Nova et Vetera* 3, no. 4 (2005) 785–806.

Pinckaers, Servais. *The Sources of Christian Ethics*. Translated by Mary Thomas Noble. Edinburgh: T. & T. Clark, 1995.

Ramírez, Santiago. *De Caritate: In II-II Summae Theologiae Divi Thomae Expositio (QQ. XXIII–XLIV)*. Salamanca: Editorial San Esteban, 1998.

———. *De Hominis Beatitudine: In I-II Summae Theologiae Divi Thomae Commentaria (QQ. I–V)*. Vol. 4. Edited by Victorino Rodríguez. Madrid: Instituto de Filosofia Luis Vives, 1972.

Ratzinger, Joseph. *Called to Communion: Understanding the Church Today*. Translated by Adrian Walker, San Francisco: Ignatius, 1996.

———. "Il rinnovamento della teologia morale: prospettive del Vaticano II e di Veritatis Splendor." In *Camminare nella luce. Prospettive della teologia morale a partire da "Veritatis Splendor,"* edited by Livio Melina and José Noriega, 35–45. Rome: Lateran University Press, 2004.

———. "The Church and Man's Calling." Translated by W. J. O'Hara. In *Commentary on the Documents of Vatican II*, edited by Herbert Vorgrimler, 5:159–163. New York: Herder and Herder, 1969.

Reinhardt, Elisabeth. "La perspectiva creacional de la imagen de Dios en el hombre." *Aquinate* 2 (2006) 19–43.

Rhonheimer, Martin. *Natural Law and Practical Reason: A Thomist View of Moral Autonomy*. Translated by Gerarld Malsbary. New York: Fordham University Press, 2000.

———. *Ethics of Procreation and the Defense of Human Life: Contraception, Artificial Fertilization, and Abortion*. Edited by William Murphy. Washington, DC: Catholic University of America Press, 2010.

Rossetti Valdalbero, Carlo Lorenzo. *Novissimus Adam: Saggi di antropologia ed escatologia biblica*. Vatican City: Lateran University Press, 2010.

Sarmiento, Augusto. *El Matrimonio Cristiano*. Pamplona: Ediciones de la Universidad de Navarra, 2001.

Scheeben, Matthias Joseph. *The Mysteries of Christianity*. Translated by Cyril Vollert. London: Herder, 1946.

Scheler, Max. *Formalism in Ethics and Non-Formal Ethics of Values: A New Attempt toward the Foundation of an Ethical Personalism*. Translated by Manfred S. Frings. Evanston: Northwestern University Press, 1973.

———. "On the Rehabilitation of Virtue." *American Catholic Philosophical Quarterly* 79 (2005) 21–37.

———. "Shame and Feelings of Modesty." In *Person and Value*, 1–86. Translated by Manfred S. Frings. Dordrecht: Martinus Nijhoff, 1987.

———. "The Idols of Self-Knowledge." Translated by David R. Lachterman. In *Selected Philosophical Essays*, edited by Davird R. Lachterman, 3–97. Evanston, IL: Northwestern University Press, 1973.

———. *The Nature of Sympathy*. Translated by Peter Heath. New Brunswick, NJ: Transaction, 2008.

Schnackenburg, Rudolf. *The Moral Teaching of the New Testament*. Translated by J. Holland-Smith. New York: Seabury, 1962.

Sheen, Fulton J. *Three to Get Married*. New York: Scepter, 1996.

Selin, Gary. *Priestly Celibacy. Theological Foundations*. Washington, DC: Catholic University of America Press, 2016.

Senovilla García, José Antoio. *La virtud de la piedad en Santo Tomás de Aquino. Fuentes y análisis textual*. Pamplona: Ediciones de la Universidad de Navarra, 2004.

Sommers, Mary Catherine. "Marriage Vows and 'Taking Up a New State.'" *Nova et Vetera* 7, no. 3 (2009) 679–95.

Tanquerey, Adolph. *Synopsis theologiae dogmaticae: ad mentem s. Thomae Aquinatis hodiernis moribus accomodata*. Vol. 2. Paris: Desclée et Soccii, 1935.

Torrel, Jean-Pierre. *Christ and Spirituality in St. Thomas Aquinas*. Translated by B. Blankenhorn. Washington, DC: Catholic University of America Press, 2011.

———. *Saint Thomas Aquinas: The Person and His Work*. Translated by Robert Royal. Washington, DC: Catholic University of America Press, 2005.

Van Roo, William. *Grace and Original Justice according to St. Thomas*. Rome: Apud Aedes Universitatis Gregorianae, 1955.

Waldstein, Michael. "Dietrich von Hildebrand and St. Thomas Aquinas on Goodness and Happiness." *Nova et Vetera* 2, no. 1 (2003) 403–64.

Weinandy, Thomas. "The Human Acts of Christ and the Acts of the Sacraments." In *Ressourcement Thomism: Sacred Doctrine, the Sacraments, and the Moral Life: Essays in Honor of Romanus Cessario*, edited by Reinhard Hütter & Matthew Levering, 150–68. Washintong: The Catholic University of America Press, 2010.

Westberg, Daniel. *Right Practical Reason: Aristotle, Action, and Prudence in Aquinas*. Oxford: Clarendon, 1994.

White, Thomas Joseph. *The Incarnate Lord: A Thomistic Study in Christology*. Washington, DC: Catholic University of America Press, 2015.

Wippel, John. "Thomas Aquinas on Our Knowledge of God and the Axiom That Every Agent Produces Something Like Itself." *Philosophical Theology: Proceedings of the American Catholic Philosophical Association* 74 (2001) 81–101.

www.ingramcontent.com/pod-product-compliance
Lightning Source LLC
Chambersburg PA
CBHW080728300426
44114CB00019B/2505